FAMOUS
CHINESE PLAYS

HANDFORTH

FAMOUS
CHINESE PLAYS

TRANSLATED AND EDITED

BY

L. C. ARLINGTON

AND

HAROLD ACTON

ILLUSTRATED

NEW YORK
RUSSELL & RUSSELL · INC
1963

FIRST PUBLISHED IN 1937
REISSUED, 1963, BY RUSSELL & RUSSELL, INC.
BY ARRANGEMENT WITH HAROLD ACTON
L. C. CATALOG CARD NO: 63—15147
EDITION LIMITED TO 500 COPIES

CONTENTS

* Denotes military and † semi-military plays

ILLUSTRATIONS

MUSIC

Transcribed by J. Hope-Johnstone

INTRODUCTION

Art is art because it is not nature.—GOETHE.

Naturalism, that is to say, to use a particular fact, trivial and accidental details, is really the exact opposite to the true sense of the theatre. Every dramatic work is, above all, a synthesis. . . It is enough that the settings do not disturb the illusion, and for that they must be very simple.—PIERRE QUILLARD, *Revue d'Art Dramatique, 1891.*

How often have we heard foreign friends exclaim : I wish there were some sort of guide to Chinese plays, so that one could follow them more or less intelligently ! Bearing this in mind, we set about filling the gap, with these versions, translations and synopses of thirty-three plays as witnessed on the stage itself. Our aim is to offer a selection eminently popular as well as representative : all these plays are frequently given in the theatres of Peking, and the humblest Chinese are familiar with them. Since it is estimated that fifty plays cover eighty per cent of those usually performed, thirty-three go far towards fulfilling our plan, which is to offer the remainder in a future volume.*

Since the Chinese editions are very unreliable—the language and dialogue of a single play varying in each to such an extent that only a practised eye can recognize it—we have in most cases ignored the chap-books and given the versions as witnessed on the stage. Even so discrepancies abound. They are mainly due to the players themselves, who capriciously substitute words of similar meaning to suit their own tastes ; these are altered again in deference to some other person's whim, and so the process continues until hardly a skeleton of the original text survives. We have many acting editions of famous plays in our possession : but in each case,

---

* The synopses of thirty other plays are given in *The Chinese Drama,* by L. C. ARLINGTON, published by Kelly & Walsh, Shanghai.

except for the identity of certain characters, the diversity of the texts can be very misleading. A translator is thus open to censure from those who are only acquainted with one edition.

We have pruned certain redundancies, and have always aimed at spiritual rather than a too literal accuracy in passages where the latter would have resulted in flatness or worse. But we have avoided all temptations to rewrite. In certain cases, where the play is all plot and the dialogue scrappy and uninspiring, a synopsis has seemed sufficient. Apart from their stage potentialities, like our own operatic libretti, few of these plays are great as literature. Why should they be? The Theatre, as Mr. Komisarjevsky has pointed out, "did not have its origins in dramatic *belles-lettres*, but was conceived in action, dancing and singing. The desire of human beings to express their ideas and the rhythms of their souls in co-rhythmical action, in movement and sounds, and to communicate these rhythms to other human beings, gave birth to theatrical performances."*

The Chinese Theatre remains true to such origins. At the same time it has become an art, and one which, like the *Commedia dell'Arte* is essentially an art of actors and *régisseurs*, though the latter are mostly anonymous. Chinese dramatic literature is a mere facet of the diamond: the scenarios merely constitute the raw material, the canvas for the actors to embroider on. It is for the splendid synthesis of gestures, movements, facial expressions, as well as the singing and dancing and ensembles of the actors (call it team-work if you will) that the Chinese theatre is unique. In our opinion, and in the opinion of anyone who sincerely appreciates the productions of Diaghileff, Copeau, Meyerhold, Craig, Podrecca, Dalcroze, and the spirit of the *Commedia dell' Arte*, these beauties are self-evident and need no

---

* *The Theatre*, by THEODORE KOMISARJEVSKY, London 1935.

explanation. Long before the Russian Revolution Meyerhold was influenced by the conventional methods of production and acting of the Chinese theatre; and Meyerhold is, by common consent, one of the finest living *régisseurs*.

But for those who come to the Chinese Theatre warm from some western drawing-room comedy, or fresh from the latest Hollywood talkie, we must explain a thing or two. Their first remark is bound to refer to its lack of realism, by which they mean its lack of heavily built-up naturalistic illusion. All they can see is a large embroidered curtain hanging at the back of the stage, one or two tables and two or three chairs, plain and often rickety. Oh, Shades of Irving and Beerbohm Tree! Where are we now?

The actor resolves this question as is right and proper : whether it be a tent or a forest depends entirely on him. Actor is too narrow a term : he is scenery, singer, dancer, acrobat, mime, at once. By holding a whip he can indicate that he is riding a horse ; by standing on a chair he can conjure a mountain. Everything is simplified, yes, but also intensified. Because the constituents of the Chinese drama are entirely subordinated to a single artistic intention the result is a higher standard of finish than anything to be seen in western theatres. Our division of theatrical art into the forms of legitimate drama, ballet and opera is an artificial one. To quote Mr. Komisarjevsky again : " All these forms of theatrical art taken separately belong to a very limited theatre, whereas a real, complete theatre unites them one and all rhythmically and idealistically in one and the same production."

Owing to the absence of canvas and cardboard settings, and of the detailed paraphernalia which our producer-dictators have foisted upon us in the magic name of realism, the Chinese drama is infinitely flexible.

It can adapt itself to all phases of atmosphere and life instead of being confined to a few cumbersome *décors*, propped up by an army of stage-hands while the audience is kept waiting.   If M. Jules Supervielle were to give in China, his play about Bolivar he would not have to bother about the arranging of scenes so complicated that one of them represents a passage in the Andes, and another an earthquake in Caracas ; the actors would solve his problem with a few simple movements.   The obvious comparison that springs to mind is with the theatres of Elizabethan England, except that the whole structure is more highly organized and subtle.   You are translated into the Kingdom of Imagination ; if you slough your western prejudices you will attain that happy state of visual dreaming which it is the theatre's highest function to induce.

An ordinary play may contain as many as thirty scenes : it is not limited by time and space.   Without intervals we may watch the whole career of Mr. So and So : nay more, whole armies, cavalry and infantry, in the full clatter of conflict.   Ten soldiers can represent as many thousand men, and their whips do duty for as many horses.*   And with what consummate art the actor can conjure a complete visual impression out of the air !   Nothing so material as a needle and thread is introduced for sewing : the actor's movements suffice, and we can count the stitches under his nimble fingers. To watch a good female impersonator sewing an imaginary pair of shoes is to marvel at a vividness of creation which might aptly be called *surréaliste*.†

Because of its symbolic character, the Chinese drama is a harder taskmaster than ours and requires a greater skill of its actors.   Every symbol must bear such a

---

* In *Chan Wan-ch'êng* (see p. 1) Ts'ao Ts'ao has 830,000 soldiers : these are handsomely represented by thirty men.
† Hsiao Ts'ui-hua, for instance, in *Shih Yü Cho* (see pp. 211, 216).

precise relation to life that it leaves the audience satisfied, and a Chinese audience is highly critical. The actor must follow definite rules and conventions or be taunted and jeered at : his genius, however, as in every art, will be gauged from the delicacy and poise with which he swerves from them without breaking them. It is by the quality of his light and shade under an almost Prussian discipline that the fine actor can be distinguished ; not by the mere excellence of his drill.*

As in fine calligraphy, the brush-strokes must have style as well as correctness. The late T'an Hsin-p'ei, so highly esteemed in bearded civil rôles (*lao-shêng*), always showed that accurate observation must be wedded to theatrical convention. After a performance of *Cho Fang Ts'ao* (see p. 132) when an actor impersonating Ts'ao Ts'ao, in the scene where he slaughters Lü Po-shê (the latter on a donkey, the former on a horse), had drawn his sword sideways from its scabbard, he created a storm in the green-room by pointing out that a rider should draw his sword upwards : if he drew it sideways he would wound the horse's neck. It took some time for others to see the justice of this criticism. This instance shows that Chinese theatrical conventions, however rigid, are not allowed to fossilize : sharp-sighted actors like T'an Hsin-p'ei will see that they are kept alive. Nor are the conventions illogical. Note the movements of the hands. By these, apart from costume, the distinction between the sexes is highly emphasized. Every finger of the female impersonator must contribute to the effect of fragile femininity. A hand with all the digits outstretched is apt to look big and clumsy : they must be bent, and each in a different manner. If a woman points at any person or object, she must do so in a way that will distinguish her from a man,—either by moving

---

* Ma Lien-liang singing *êrh-huang man-pan* is therefore considered superior to T'an Fu-ying.

the arm until the palm is thrust in an upward position
with the index finger pointing at the object, or, if she
is angry, by quickening her action and pointing with the
palm down.   On the stage a woman should never expose
her thumb, but keep it concealed by the middle finger.
In male parts an actor points by sticking his fingers
straight out in front of him.   A *hsiao-shêng*, or " juvenile
lead," keeps his thumb out of sight as much as possible,
but a *lao-shêng*, and more especially a " big painted face "
(*ta-hua-lien*), sticks his thumb up, and thrusts his index
and middle-finger in front of him.   There are some
fifty of these hand-movements, all symbolical ; and this
is none too many when we remember the part played by
the hand since prehistoric times in the communication of
thought, and see how even to-day many eminent conduc-
tors still prefer to sway their orchestras without a baton.

Unless they personate amazons, women do not ride
on the stage : it is presumed that they are too delicate for
that exercise.   A lady must travel in a closed carriage or
sedan-chair, never exposing herself to public gaze on the
journey.   In the case of men, equestrian deportment
varies with their rôles.   In mounting and dismounting,
a gentleman assumes grave dignity, while a warrior or
groom exhibits his muscularity.   In fact the rider's is
almost a double rôle, for the movements of the horse
must be revealed by facial expression as well as by physical
action : the actor must know how to become a centaur
at will.

An oar represents a boat ; a flag, an army ; a chair,
a bridge or a mountain.   A fan may be exchanged for
an umbrella to signify a rainstorm.   A chariot is represented by two yellow flags held horizontally, each
blazoned with a wheel ; the occupant walks between
them.   Deliberately lifting a foot indicates stepping
over a threshold.   Bringing the hands close together in
front indicates closing a door.   To open it, each hand

mimes pulling the upper and lower bolt aside simultaneously ; then bending forward, the actor peeps from side to side. The whole fabric of the door is conjured before our eyes.

By standing stiffly against a pillar an actor conveys that he is hiding or spying. While circulating the stage he is, of course, going from one place to another ; if he paces cautiously with hands extended, feeling his way to right and left, he is groping in the dark. Lifting the skirt, bending down at the waist and treading with measured steps, represents crossing a plank into a boat, going up a ladder, etc. When about to climb stairs or a ladder, a gentleman gives a rapid twirl to one of his long sleeves so that his hand will be free to clutch the railing ; a lady twirls her sleeve round the right wrist and picks up her skirt with the left hand. To descend the stairs the movement is accelerated. Perambulating the stage without extending the arms represents a passage through the courtyards of spacious premises. But if the house is small, the feet are only lifted at the outer entrance and there is no circumambulation of the stage, thus showing that the courtyard is narrow. Whenever the feet are raised with emphasis, progress into the next courtyard or chamber is indicated. A woman takes short steps with body erect but shoulders pressed down to simulate limpness; if young, she trips mincingly, heel and toe fashion (both kept rather high) : her hands are crossed demurely in front of her, and when she turns round, she must turn her whole body. The imitation of compressed feet, by incasing the toes in diminutive shoes, is unfortunately dying out, though a few actors, such as Hsiao Ts'ui-hua and the gifted young Sung Tê-chu, uphold the tradition and act the better for it. The conventions that accompany " golden lilies " remain, however, and to pick anything off the ground the female impersonator must bend swayingly sideways, balancing

himself with the left arm out : Ch'êng Yen-ch'iu does
this with memorable grace in *Mu Yang Chüan* (see p. 316).

An elderly lady advances with faltering and slipshod
steps, her back is bent and she generally has a staff like
a bishop's crozier to support herself. An adult man
struts leisurely with feet wide apart, while a youth takes
rapid strides. A warrior lifts his feet high and wide
apart as if under water, each step in a slow-motion semi-
curve, to indicate steadfastness and courage ; during a
battle he twists and turns with the velocity of an acrobat.
To magnify his physique, instead of sitting, a warrior
leans against the cushions piled high on the seat of his
chair, with legs outspread and elbows pushed out
sideways.

Animals are simulated by painting the face with a
semi-realistic convention for the tiger, pig, or monkey
in question, or by wearing a mask with a costume whose
colour and design resemble the animal's hide. Characters condemned to death are clad in red, and a female
prisoner's head is usually wrapped in a blue silk cloth, to
indicate that her hair is not attired.

Jewels convey a woman's social status. The
coiffure of an official's wife is trimmed with elaborate
enamelled ornaments. Respectable matrons (*ch'ing-i*)
wear clusters of silver spangles, of daedal design.
Ladies of lighter disposition (*hua-tan*) sport spangles of
coloured glass. The female impersonator is a past-
master in all the artifices of facial disguise. If his face is
too chubby, the cheeks are ingeniously plastered with
locks of false hair, and a subtle display of jewellery is
often an effective substitute for reducing-exercises. If
his face is too narrow, the hair is brushed back from the
ears and little jewellery is worn. Since rouge acts as a
shadow, high cheek-bones are richly bedaubed with red
and sunken cheeks neutralized by rouging round them.
An actor with a snub-nose counterfeits the necessary

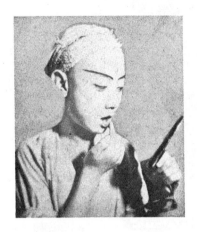
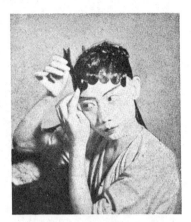

FACIAL PAINTING : TAN, OR FEMALE ROLE

Li Shih-fang, "the little Mei Lan-fang," making up.

(Male impersonation of feminine roles)

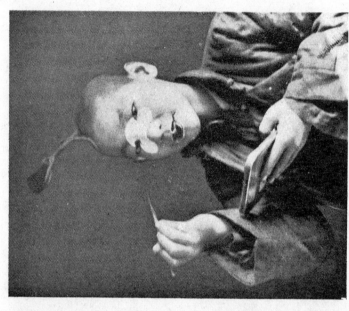

Facial Painting : Ta-hua-lien or "Big Painted Face" (left) ; Ch'ou or Comedian (right)

bridge with paint between the eyes. A burnt match is applied to the corners of the eyes to widen the orbs, and smeared round the eyelids to extend the lashes. A " big painted face " (*ta-hua-lien*) shaves the top of his forehead to lengthen and broaden his features, and paints it in harmony with the rest of his make-up. Altogether there are some two hundred and fifty styles of face-painting.

A face painted red indicates a sacred, loyal personage, or an Emperor ; black, an honest but uncouth personality ; white, a treacherous, cunning and at the same time dignified individual ; and a white patch on the nose, a villain or comedian (the rôles are interchangeable). Mixed colours express a variety of characteristics.* Devils are given green faces; gods and goddesses, yellow ones.

Of costumes the warrior's is the most elaborate. His head-dress bristles with balls and silver ornaments, and is often surmounted by two quivering pheasant-plumes (see frontispiece); four pennants may be attached to his back. Costumes in general have been adapted from the styles of various dynasties ; they are seldom historically accurate. Pheasant-plumes, for instance, originally denoted barbarians ; later they came to be worn in the rôles of Chinese commanders, simply because of their consummate æsthetic rightness, their daring decorative effect. A beggar wears a green silk robe with patches reminiscent of Harlequin. A flighty woman is gaily bedizened ; a demure one is clad in sober black. A ghost appears with a black cloth flung over its head, or with a long strip of white paper either stuck on the cheeks or suspended from above the ear. Death is denoted by a red flag or a red cloth thrown over the face ; a strong wind, by a few black

---

* See L. C. ARLINGTON, *op. cit.*, for a fuller description of these face-paintings.

flags held in the hands of spirits. Jumping *over* a chair means committing suicide by diving into a well; jumping *off* a chair, leaping from a height.

In forming an opinion of a character near by, the actor speaks loud enough to take the audience into his confidence, but secrecy is symbolized by raising his arm between the person he is discussing and himself. Thus, no matter how loud his tone or how low his opinion, his immediate neighbour is not supposed to hear it. Meditation in a quandary is mimed by flickering fingers about the forehead. These are but a few particulars of Chinese theatrical technique. It is to be noted, however, that they are the general principles from which deviations and exceptions are made to suit special circumstances.

The Chinese drama is essentially operatic. The spoken dialogue serves to break the tension and give the singer a rest. Unless he sings extremely well, a Chinese actor will never gain renown. As will be seen from the thirty-three examples in our repertoire, more than two-thirds of each consist of singing; and the orchestra is accommodated on the stage. Hence any production of a Chinese play in a foreign language without the traditional music and technique is apt to be, as Swinburne said of a rhymeless lyric, a maimed thing. It is only by seeing a Chinese play as it is performed on the Chinese stage that one can appreciate the richest and most ancient theatrical tradition in the world.

Chinese music hath charms which too often, alas, do not succeed in soothing our savage breasts. Even a connoisseur like Mr. John Hazedel Levis confesses that the Chinese music of the theatre, " which is almost exclusively heard by foreigners as well as most Chinese, is far from the best of China's music, which is as soft, gentle and subtle as most theatre music is loud, raucous, rough and cacophonous."

The orchestra gives out the time : however shrill or discordant it may sound to our ears, its rhythm is hypnotic. After a sojourn in China one often acquires a taste for it. None will deny that it is a powerful stimulus, especially in military plays ; the swift and complicated dances which are conventions for combat on the stage would be impossible without the time-regulation of the orchestra, and however wild, brutal, bizarre the instruments may sound, they are exquisitely precise. They seem to heighten the colour-scheme ; certainly they quicken the pulse. The various types of musical accompaniment may be classified as :

1. *Hsi-p'i*, " Western Skins " : probably because the instruments were originally covered with skin or leather. They are said to have been developed from the Ch'in airs invented by Hu Hai, the son of the First Emperor (Ch'in Shih Huang) ; the composition and rhymes of which were lost.

The instruments used in civil *hsi-p'i* plays are :

Yüeh-ch'in, " Moon Guitar," so-called from its circular shape. It has four strings, between five or six inches in length, and generally supports the *hu-ch'in* on the stage.

Nan-hsien-tzŭ, also called *san-hsien-tzŭ*, or " three-stringed guitar," an instrument popular throughout China.

Ti-tzŭ, a bamboo flute pierced with eight holes and held parallel to the mouth ; and *so-na*, the Chinese clarionet, which always go in pairs—but the latter is rarely played for vocal accompaniment.

P'i-pa, " Balloon-guitar," with four strings, used in solos.

Hu-ch'in, the sharp and raucous two-stringed fiddle of northern barbarian origin, is the leading instrument of vocal accompaniment in *p'i-huang* drama. (*P'i-huang* is the abbreviation for *hsi-p'i erh-huang*.)

Wêng-tzŭ, also called *hêng-hêng* and *êrh-hu*, a two-stringed fiddle recently introduced into Peking from the South. It is a modification of the *hu-ch'in*, with lower tones.

In the military *hsi-p'i* plays :

Tan-p'i-ku, or single-skin drum, the leading instrument in all plays.

T'ang-ku, or barrel-shaped drum.

Ta-lo, a large gong ; *hsiao-lo*, a small hand-gong : generally beaten at entrances and exits, or to punctuate a particular posture.

Shui-ch'a, also called *ch'i-po* : brass cymbals.

Chia-pan, or castanets : these beat time throughout and are an efficient substitute for our conductor's baton.

P'êng-chung, also called *k'o-po*, clanging bells : a pair of cup-shaped brass instruments which are struck against each other, recently introduced by Mei Lan-fang but only used in *fan-tiao* airs as auxiliary timebeaters.

2. The now equally popular *êrh-huang*, or twin flute airs ; derived from the names of two counties in Hupeh, Huang-p'i and Huang-kang, where they were invented. Originally players were accompanied by two flutes, but it is seldom that a flute is introduced in contemporary *êrh-huang* plays. The same instruments are used in *êrh-huang* as in *hsi-p'i* plays ; the sole difference is that the airs of the former are softer and more melodious, while the latter are sharp and shrill.

3. The cruder and more colloquial *pang-tzŭ*, so-called from an instrument consisting of two pieces of wood, one of which is flat below and rounded above. This is held over the palm of the left hand and struck with the second piece, which is round. The *pang-tzŭ* keeps excellent time for ballads : like

the *hsi-p'i* it originated in Shensi. The same instruments are used in *pang-tzŭ* plays as in *êrh-huang* and *hsi-p'i*, except that the *hu-hu*, a barbarous two-stringed fiddle said to have been invented in Shansi, is substituted for the *hu-ch'in*.

4. The ancient *k'un-ch'ü*, analogous to, and contemporaneous with, our erudite theatre of the Renaissance as " a pastime and a recreation for gentlemen and ladies of select breeding." It was also a means of propaganda for classical culture. Otherwise known as *k'un-ch'iang*, this type originated in K'un-shan, Kiangsu, during the reign of the Ming Emperor Chia Ching (A.D. 1522-1560), and was perfected, if not invented, by Liang Po-lung and Wei Liang-fu, who collected folk-songs called *I-yang* (Bird-hunter songs) and *Hai-yen* (Boat-songs) which they converted into *k'un-ch'ü* airs. These are generally in somewhat slow measure, elegant and dreamy, plaintive rather than gay. Since the *ti*, or flute, predominates, *k'un-ch'ü* music is infinitely more agreeable than *êrh-huang* to western ears ; there is no *hu-ch'in* or any string instrument played with a bow, apart from which the same instruments are used as in *êrh-huang* and *hsi-p'i* plays with the addition of the *chiu-yin-lo*, " nine chiming bells," the *shêng*, a delicate reed-organ, and *huai-ku* or kettledrum. The *k'un-ch'ü* drama flourished for three centuries until the Tai-p'ing Rebellion (1851-1865), and now its star is on the wane. But the plays of its voluminous repertoire are the most poetical that were ever given on the Chinese stage and will live as long as Chinese literature lives.

Actors are classified under four types : *Shêng*, Male ; *Tan*, Female ; *Ching*, Characters with painted faces ; and *Ch'ou*, Comedians or Clowns.

1. *Shêng* are divided into *Wên*, Civil, and *Wu*, Military. These are the leading actors. In Civil

plays *lao-shêng* (old shêng) take the parts of emperors, ministers, and conventional scholars in the prime of life. They are further subdivided into *mo*, with grey beards, and *wai*, with white beards. The majority wear black beards ; are dignified rather than pompous and under-, rather than over-, act. *Hsiao-shêng* correspond to our " juvenile leads," and their make-up is limited to heightening the eyebrows and rouging the cheeks. They play the part of refined young scholars, etc., and are also dubbed *shan-tzŭ hsiao-shêng*, from their tendency to flirt a fan. Among Military *shêng*, there are *wu-lao-shêng*, who enact elderly warriors, also known as *k'ao-pa lao-shêng*, " wearers of back flags," and *hsiao-wu-shêng*, young warriors, beardless and without paint, who specialize in stage-battles and acrobatic feats.

2. *Tan*, subdivided into *lao-tan*, elderly dames with orange bandeau but no make-up ; *ch'ing-i*, virtuous maidens and dutiful matrons ; and *hua-tan*, vivacious and temperamental—often a courtesan or a piquante little maidservant. There are even more precise classifications, *kuei-mên-tan*, virginal and demure ; *hua-shan-tzŭ* and *t'ieh-tan*, who take minor feminine rôles, such as ladies in waiting, and *tao-ma-tan*, " sword-horse-women," or amazons.

3. *Ching*, robust in voice and physique, may either be good or bad characters and are commonly called *ta-hua-lien*, or " big painted face," since they are painted with striking designs resembling masks. The colours generally represent their characters. For a description of these see L. C. Arlington, *op. cit.*

4. *Ch'ou*, also called *san-hua-lien*. These are the comedians so like our western clowns in manner and medium—i.e. slips on banana skins, kicks in the pants, etc. They have a dab of white on the nose and, when they are very villainous, white circles

round the eyes. In military plays they are called *k'ai-k'ou-t'iao* : " Open mouth jumpers." Their female counterparts are called *ch'ou-p'o*. All have the greatest latitude in gagging.

Although men and boys still take female parts, there is a gradual tendency for women to supplant them. That Peking nursery of China's histrionic hopes the *Hsi Ch'ü Hsüeh Hsiao*, or " Juvenile Training Dramatic College," is training a number of young girls as well as some two hundred boys. Young girls are also being privately trained by famous actors who have retired from the stage. Some of them have made their début with notable success.

Hitherto modifications and reforms have been incongruous and insignificant ; even so, we cannot but deplore them. The sole gain (as evidenced in *Hsin Yü T'ang-ch'un* and *Chin So Chi*), has been in a general diffusion of bathos. As for the sporadic efforts of Dr. Hu Shih and his fellow-iconoclasts to eliminate the traditional drama in favour of the modern drama as played on western stages,—happily, they are doomed to failure. For the Chinese drama makes a combined appeal to more senses than our impoverished western drama ; it has a richer variety of resource at its disposal ; moreover, in Dr. Lin Yutang's words,* " through its immense popularity, the theatre has achieved a place in the national Chinese life very nearly corresponding to its logical place in an ideal republic."

Henry James has recorded his conviction that the *Théâtre Français* was such a school of taste as was not elsewhere to be found in the world. Had he visited China he would have been forced to qualify that statement. In view of China's multitudes the influence of the Chinese theatre has been, and will continue to be,

---

* *My Country and My People*, p. 265, New York, 1935.

incalculable.   And for those who wish to gain insight into Chinese character and society its value is incalculable also.

ADDITIONAL TERMS

Ch'i-pa—Refers to the various evolutions of arms and legs of those who don back-flags (*k'ao-pei-ch'i* : also called *pei-hu-ch'i*—see below), in such plays as *Ch'ang-pan P'o* and *Chan Wan-ch'êng* (*q.v.*).   Also applied to those who enact the rôle of *wu-tan*, or amazon, who likewise wear back-flags, as in the play *Chan Huang P'ao*, where T'ao San-ch'un takes the part of *tao-ma-tan* (similar to *wu-tan*).   Generally they carry their favourite weapon, spear or trident or halberd, etc.   To watch these dynamic, sumptuously bedecked warriors and amazons proudly strut up to the footlights, showing, as they advance, the white soles of their buskin-like boots : twirling about, whirling a supple leg and hurling their weapons aloft in perfect time, is to glow with rhythmic vitality oneself.   Such visions of statuesque art are rare in the twentieth century.

Chiao-t'ou—When   parents   or   brothers   and   sisters suddenly meet each other after a long separation, their salutations are accompanied by a few beats of the drum and gong.   (See *San-chiao-t'ou*).

Chiu-lung-k'ou—" Nine dragons mouth."   A spot about three feet away from the man who beats the *tan-p'i-ku* (single-skin drum) who is the leader of the orchestra.   (See *hsi-p'i tao-pan*).

Erh-liu pan—literally a two-six tempo.   The drum beats twice to every six beats of the *pang-tzŭ*.

*Fan-êrh-huang man-pan—A sort of *con dolore* or slow, pathetic style.   Used in the *Mu Yang Chüan*, and *Yü T'ang Ch'un*, etc. (*q.v.*).

---

* The main difference between *êrh-huang* and *hsi-p'i* airs is that the latter are more strident and pitched in a higher key.

Fan-êrh-huang yao-pan—A low, soft, and sweet tune, introduced in tragical plays.

Fan-êrh-huang yüan-pan—Somewhat faster than the *fan-êrh-huang man-pan* (*q.v.*). It generally follows the *man-pan* in eight or ten lines, from one to three sentences.

* *Hsi-p'i man-pan*—Similar to the *êrh-huang man-pan*, only somewhat harsher and pitched in a higher key.

* *Hsi-p'i tao-pan*—Allegro con spirito. Frequent in plays where the actor meets with distress, alarm or excitement. In both the *hsi-p'i* and *êrh-huang* pieces a stanza is played and sung before the actor appears on the stage : either behind the curtain or just as he steps on to the stage. When he arrives within about three feet of the drummer (see *Chiu-lung-k'ou*) he sings a few lines in *hui-lung-ch'iang* (*q.v.*), walks slowly along until he reaches the centre of the stage, and waits till the *hu-ch'in* (two-stringed fiddle) finishes the first bar, whereupon he proceeds to sing in *yüan-pan* (andante con moto).

* *Hsi-p'i yao-pan*—Andante mosso.

* *Hsi-p'i yüan-pan*—Andante con moto.

Hui-lung-ch'iang—" Dragon turning head-tune." This style is soft and long drawn-out, hence the Chinese liken it to the slow swaying motion of a dragon's head. There is no interlude : the song begins with the first note of a bar.

K'u-t'ou—When a person (actor) is in distress he sings several long drawn-out sentences bewailing his misfortune, accompanied by the usual musical instruments. As soon as he stops singing, the gongs and drums strike up. (See *Sao-t'ou*).

---

* The main difference between *êrh-huang* and *hsi-p'i* airs is that the latter are more strident and pitched in a higher key.

K'uai-pan—Allegro.

Li-tzŭ—Inner lining of clothes. This peculiar term is used of actors who take secondary but nevertheless significant parts, on the principle that a robe without lining is incomplete. There is also a *ying-li-tzŭ* (hard or stiff lining) who outranks the ordinary *li-tzŭ*. For example, in the play *Yü T'ang-ch'un* (*q.v.*) the blue-gowned Liu Ping-i is the *ying-li-tzŭ*, and the red-robed Chou Liang-chieh is the *li-tzŭ*. Liu Ping-i does nearly all the questioning. The actor who takes the part of Wang Chin-lung is also termed a *ying-li-tzŭ*. And Ch'ung Kung-tao, the aged turn-key, who escorts Su-san in the act *Nü Ch'i Chieh* (See *Yü T'ang-ch'un*) is a *li-tzŭ*, because he is represented as " soft-hearted " in his treatment of the fair prisoner while *en route*. In all the plays we have seen, the *li-tzŭ*—like Chou Liang-chieh and Ch'ung Kung-tao—represent men who are easily imposed upon, or inclined to play the Good Samaritan. The *ying-li-tzŭ* is rather the reverse : watch the rascally Liu Ping-i during the trial of poor Su-san. How he delights in badgering her, simply to provoke Wang Chin-lung. How smugly he laughs as he tries to make her incriminate her lover. He is the typical *ying-li-tzŭ* of the Chinese stage !

Liu-shui-pan—" Flowing water." Similar to the *hsi-p'i yao-pan* (*q.v.*), but a quicker tempo. Mostly sung by actors in minor rôles, who are allotted a couple of stanzas in this style.

Lung-t'ao—Flag-bearers in the suite of a Commander-in-Chief. They are ranged in groups of four, eight, or sixteen. The great Ts'ao Ts'ao in the play *Chan Wan-ch'êng* has sixteen *lung-t'ao* in his suite. Their flags and clothing are painted or embroidered with the design of a dragon. Hence the term, which means " dragon-covered." The colours generally correspond with those worn by the commander they accompany.

Man-pan—Andante cantabile.

Pei-hu-ch'i—"Back protecting flags." These are triangular flags of embroidered silk worn by actors representing generals and commanders-in-chief. Their colours always match the costume, and they are strapped over the back of the shoulders outside the coat of mail. Originally they signified Imperial tokens of authority, but now they are used to enhance the warrior's martial aspect. Hence six and even eight may be worn, though four is the usual number.

P'u-têng-o—A moth, from the way it rushes into a lighted lamp. The instruments used are the gong and drum, which strike up a combined attack upon the tympanum, indicating the great alarm the player is supposed to experience. Only used in dialogue. The actor speaks a few words, and when he stops, the gongs and drums start banging and bombilating. When he begins to recite the next lines, the gongs and drums are muffled with the musicians' sleeves. All this resonance is metaphorically compared to the strains of a moth's wings as it flutters helplessly against the light. Only used in military plays.

San-chiao-t'ou—When mother and son suddenly meet after a long separation, the mother cries out *êrh-ah !* *êrh-ah !* *êrh-ah !* three times : the son responding thrice with " Mother ! Mother ! Mother ! " Hence this is called *san-chiao-t'ou*. (See *Chiao-t'ou*).

Sao-t'ou—In the *fan-êrh-huang yao-pan* (*q.v.*) style, the third line of the fourth sentence is sung in the *k'u-t'ou* air (*q.v.*), and the last line of the fourth sentence is not sung ; the gongs and drums filling the gap. *Sao-t'ou* refers to the instruments played, indicating a " sweeping " away of all trials and tribulations.

Note

Since we completed our translations of *Ch'i Shuang Hui* and *Ch'ing Ting Chu*, the *T'ien Hsia Monthly* (Shanghai) has published sensitive and scholarly renderings by Mr. Yao Hsin-nung 姚 莘 農 of these perennially popular plays, which he has entitled respectively *Madam Cassia* and *The Right to Kill*. After some hesitation we have concluded that our texts differ sufficiently to warrant their inclusion in this volume, for with the foreign playgoer in mind, we have pruned many of those tautologies which are due to the operatic requirements of the original libretti.

We feel much indebted to Mr. John Hope-Johnstone for supplying us with the musical transcriptions of nine precious arias, and to M. Henri Vetch for his spirited co-operation in reading the proofs and for many valuable suggestions. We also wish to record our appreciation of the generous hospitality which Mr. Li Yung-fu 李 永 福 (字 伯 言) of the *Hsi Ch'ü Hsueh Hsiao*, has so frequently extended to us.

CHAN WAN-CH'ENG 戰宛城

THE BATTLE OF WAN-CH'ÊNG

(IN HONAN)

PERIOD: Beginning of San Kuo, ca. A.D. 199. A *hsi-p'i êrh-huang* play.

DRAMATIS PERSONÆ

Ts'AO Ts'AO, Prime Minister and Generalissimo of Han	*Ching*
CHANG HSIU, Governor of Wan-ch'êng	*Shêng*
CHIA Hsü, his counsellor	*Shêng*
TSOU SHIH, Chang Hsiu's aunt	*Hua-tan*
CH'UN MEI, her maid	
HU CH'Ê-ÊRH, an officer in groom disguise ...	*Ch'ou-êrh*
TIEN WEI, General and body-guard of Ts'ao's tent	*Ching*
HSIA-HO TUN	
HSÜ CH'U	
YÜEH CHIN Generals under Ts'ao	*Ching*
HSIA-HO YÜAN	
Ts'AO AN-MING, Ts'ao's nephew	*Ch'ou-êrh*
Ts'AO AN, Ts'ao's eldest son...	*Hsiao-shêng*
CHANG HSIEN, General under Chang Hsiu... ...	*Ching*
HIS WIFE	*Tan*
LEI HSÜ, General under Chang Hsiu	*Ching*
HIS WIFE	*Tan*
CHANG HSIU'S SERVANT	*Lao-shêng*
SOLDIERS, ATTENDANTS, ETC.	

SCENE I

Enter Ts'ao Ts'ao's eight generals, singing out their respective names : Hsia-ho Tun, Hsü Ch'u, Tien Wei, Yü Chin, Yüeh Chin, Li Tien, Hsia-ho Yüan and Hsü Huang.

HSIAO-HO TUN (*speaks*). Generals all! We are to accompany the Prime Minister to Wan-ch'êng and attack Chang Hsiu. After leaving Hsü-ch'ang, when the army has reached half-way, we shall await the Minister's arrival.

TS'AO (*on appearing*). I have established merit by my diligent labours in the service of the State. I have not enjoyed a single day of peace or leisure. Chang Hsiu, who now commands Wan-ch'êng, must be got rid of, else he'll rebel. I have therefore led my army to attack him. (*Recites in verse*) When the Emperor Hsien Ti left for Hsü-tu, he gave me full authority to punish traitors and reward the loyal. Since Chang Hsiu has not submitted, I am leading my troops to exterminate him.

GENERALS. Our respects to you, Prime Minister.

TS'AO. I am lacking in courtesy, Generals.

GENERALS. Thank you, Prime Minister.

TS'AO. I, Ts'ao Ts'ao, whose distinguishing name is Mêng-tê, am a native of Hsia-p'ei [in modern Kiangsu] in the prefecture of Ch'iao.* I entered public life as a petty military officer. Having quelled insurrections in the North and South, I reaped honour upon high honour. When Li Ts'ui and Kuo Ssŭ rebelled, it was I that rescued the Emperor ; wherefore His Majesty created me Marquis of Wu-p'ing.† All the court-officials, civil and military, were instructed to submit their reports to me first, while I was to memorialize the Throne direct. As Prime Minister I control all state-affairs. My power is unlimited. At present Chang Hsiu holds Wan-ch'êng, and wishes to attack Hsü-tu.‡ Before he stirs, I have seized the opportunity of mustering an army of a hundred and fifty thousand to take him by surprise. Yesterday we reached the middle of our march ; here we are now encamped. (*A canopy is erected and Ts'ao sits underneath*). Generals, please stand in double rows and pay heed to my commands.

GENERALS. We obey, Prime Minister.

---

* This is inaccurate. He was a native of Ch'iao-po-hsien, Anhwei.

† " Tranquillizing by Battle."   ‡ The puppet Emperor's Capital.

TS'AO. Before we launch our attack we must cross the Ssŭ River, whence it is about four hundred li* to Wan-ch'êng. If we take a short cut by mountain paths, we can curtail the journey by a hundred li. Have you any opinions to give me?

GENERALS. We shall abide by your orders, Prime Minister.

TS'AO. Hsia-ho Tun, pay heed to my commands.

HSIA-HO TUN. I am all attention, Sir.

TS'AO. Take the bells off the horses and furl all the flags; let no drum sound. When the army marches through the fields and byways, see that nobody pulls up a blade of the people's corn and that no horse tramples it down. Whoever infringes this order will be promptly executed.

HSIA-HO TUN (*repeats the order so that there can be no mistake*). Your order, Prime Minister, will be obeyed: the army will advance.

The army advances accordingly.

TS'AO (*sings in hsi-p'i tao-pan*). Chiang Shang† attacked the Capital and his rule was dignified and strict. (*Changes to yao-pan*) To-day I am setting forth to attack Wan-ch'êng and who will dare obstruct me? Government in time of peace has its merits and defects, but a Commander-in-Chief sways an army of valiant soldiers vast and solid as mountains.

GENERALS. Prime Minister, a wheatfield lies ahead.

TS'AO. I have issued orders that no horse is to trample the corn; the drums are to cease and the flags are to be furled. A detour must be made around the crops.

GENERALS. We hear and obey.

---

* A *li* is roughly one-third of a mile.

† Chiang Tzŭ-ya, 12th century B.C. Wên Wang's chief counsellor, famous for fishing effectively with a straight piece of iron instead of a hook. See note p. 46.

TS'AO (*sings*). At the word of my command
  Silent soldiers, one by one,
  Furl their flags ; my will is done ;
  Marching through the harvest land.
(*Speaks*) See how cautiously my generals advance ! I am very gratified by such ready obedience.

GENERALS (*seeing a bird fly over Ts'ao's horse, exclaim*). Prime Minister, what sort of bird is that ?

TS'AO. It is only a dove. (*But his horse, frightened by the dove, sheers off into the wheatfields and Ts'ao exclaims*) Ah me, this is most unfortunate ! (*Sings*) My horse has taken fright : I cannot curb him as he canters into the midst of the crops. Through negligence I have broken my own rule, and I am the only one to do so. (*Speaks*) I'll commit suicide.

GENERALS. Prime Minister, stay your hand ! Don't destroy yourself ! In the time of the "Spring and Autumn Annals," the laws were not applied to the persons of the most honourable. It was the horse that took fright and trampled down the grain : it was not intentional. Therefore no rule was broken. Ponder the matter thrice, Prime Minister.

TS'AO. Well, one demerit must be recorded against me. Now cut my horse's head off ! (*Hsia-ho Tun proceeds to do so, and holds the head before Ts'ao for inspection*). Hang it on the yamen gate. I'll cut the hair off my head and hang that on the gate as well. (*Then, to the surrounding generals, in a thundering voice*) Having broken my own rule, I cut off my hair as touching the head. Should anyone break this rule henceforth, no mercy will be shown !

GENERALS. We shall see that it is strictly observed, Sir.

TS'AO. Bring me another horse and we'll proceed. (*Sings*) I lead my troops through hardships untold. This is but a slight instance of my patriotism. I am willing

HOU HSI-JUI AS TS'AO TS'AO

Whose horse (symbolized by the tasselled whip)
sheers off into the wheatfields

Chan Wan-ch'êng

to suffer in the cause of exterminating every single traitor; when this is accomplished we may return to Court and enjoy the fruits of peace.

GENERALS. We beg to report that we are approaching the banks of the Ssŭ River.

TS'AO. Hsia-ho Tun, I appoint you to command the vanguard. Lead a regiment of cavalry and encamp on the banks of the river. I shall command the main forces and follow in the rear. See that there's no mistake.

HSIAO-HO TUN. Generals of the vanguard, follow me to the banks of the Ssŭ River. (*Exit*).

TS'AO. Generals, urge your horses on with speed. (*Sings*) I have received the Emperor's authority to attack Chang Hsiu at Wan-ch'êng. When will the implements of war be laid aside, and peace once more reign over the harassed land? How many worthy lives will then be saved! (*Exeunt omnes*).

SCENE II

CHIA HSÜ (*enters and prologizes*). A single year of war brings three of trouble. (*Speaks*) The Han Empire has now come to its period of decay. It is encompassed by foes on every side. They seize and hold all prefectures and districts, and nobody dares say nay. The people have been reduced to misery and ruin. My surname is Chia, my name is Hsü, and I am Chang Hsiu's counsellor at Wan-ch'êng. I have just received a report that Ts'ao Ts'ao is advancing at the head of five hundred thousand strong to attack the city. His vanguard is already encamped on the banks of the Ssŭ River. It seems to me—his soldiers being many and ours few—that he is in a much stronger position, and that we shall be unable to resist him. It would be more politic to submit. Chang Hsiu has gone to review his troops at the parade-ground. I'll wait till he returns and consult with him as to what measures we had better take.

CHANG HSIU (*is heard behind the stage, saying*). Generals, having reviewed the troops, we'll return to the city.   (*Enters with two generals and a few soldiers*).

CHIA. My respects to you, Master.

CHANG HSIU. Pray be seated without ceremony, Sir. (*To generals*) Pray be seated.

CHIA. How went the manœuvres to-day, my Lord? Did you find themen well disciplined?

CHANG HSIU. Yes, officers and men were all in perfect training.   I hear that Ts'ao Ts'ao has arrived with abundant forces to attack us.   May I enquire from you, Sir, if there is any way to counteract his schemes?

CHIA. Since Ts'ao Ts'ao's army is vastly superior to ours in numbers, my opinion is that we should submit without fighting.

CHANG HSIU. Give me a moment's reflection.

CHIA. Ts'ao has no less than five hundred thousand men and a thousand generals.   If we don't surrender, I fear that this city will be difficult to hold.

CHANG HSIU. I have Generals Chang and Lei and ten thousand invincible warriors.   Besides I have a large force of shield-bearers and broadswordsmen, who could resist ten thousand men with ease.   How can you infer that I shall not gain the victory?

CHIA. Whether we fight or surrender, Master, entirely rests with you.

CHANG HSIU. I have decided to entrust the defence of the city to you, while I go and attack Ts'ao.

CHIA. If you neglect my advice and lose the battle, Sir, it will be too late to repent.   (*Exit*).

CHANG HSIU. All the troops must advance to the fray. (*Generals Chang and Lei, shield-bearers and broadswordsmen enter and announce their arrival*). Let the rank and file fall in and prepare to leave the city for the assault.   (*All quit the stage in marching order*).

Scene III

The fight begins: first come Hsia-ho Tun and his men, followed by Yü Chin, Hsü Ch'u and Chang Hsiu's troops. Hsia-ho Tun is defeated. A great battle ensues between the rival generals. Chang Hsiu's troops are defeated and return to Wan-ch'êng, closing the city-gates behind them.

TIEN WEI (*laughs triumphantly and exclaims*). Aha, their troops have all slunk back into their camp. (*Exit*).

Scene IV

CHIA. I just heard the drums beating outside the city-walls. I await the dispatch-bearer's tidings. (*Chang Hsiu appears*). Already returned, my Lord?

CHANG HSIU. I regret that I did not take your advice, Sir. I have been defeated.

CHIA. You need not distress yourself unduly, Master. We still have time for discussion.

CHANG HSIU. If Ts'ao attacks the city, what can be done?

CHIA. Why not hand over the city-seal to Ts'ao as a sign of submission. At least that will save the city.

CHANG HSIU. But what if Ts'ao refuses it?

CHIA. If our submission is unconditional I can see no reason why Ts'ao should not accept it.

GENERALS CHANG HSIEN AND LEI (*enter, declaring*). We are willing to fight till we drop down dead. Our names will then live on through history.

CHANG HSIU. I command you two generals to defend the city.

GENERALS. We shall obey.   (*Exeunt*).

CHANG HSIU (*to Chia Hsü*). Bring the city-seal and accompany me to Ts'ao's camp. I'll tender my submission.   (*Exeunt*).

SCENE V

TSOU SHIH (*the widow of Chang Hsiu's uncle enters, singing in hsi-p'i man-pan*).

In Spring the days draw long and heavy loom,
While amorous thoughts decline to be subdued.
Alas, my mate is mouldering in his tomb—
And must I waste a life in solitude?

(*Speaks*) My family name is Tsou and I was the second wife of Chang Chi. Unhappily my husband has been dead these three years : I have no son at my knees, only my nephew Chang Hsiu, who is my sole support. Although I have plenty to eat and drink, rich and elegant apparel, and so forth, it is springtime now and I have to sleep all alone, which is terribly trying to the nerves.

(*Sings*) 'Tis pitiful indeed when night is nigh
And woman lonely in her youth must lie !
I'll seek some strapping swain for company.

CH'UN MEI (*her maid, entering with the tea-tray, says*). Here is your tea, Madam. (*Tsou Shih, on lifting a tea-cup, drops and smashes it*). Oh, see what you have done, Madam !

TSOU SHIH. Hearing that Ts'ao Ts'ao had come to occupy the city, I was startled and dropped the cup.

SERVANT (*enters, saying*). I have to report to you, Madam, that things have taken a bad turn.

TSOU SHIH. What's the alarm about ?

SERVANT. Ts'ao Ts'ao's troops have attacked the city. The Master went out to repel them and got defeated.

TSOU SHIH. How are things now ? I heard that Chang Hsiu and Chia Hsü delivered the city-seal to Ts'ao in sign of submission. Well, well, you may go.

CH'UN MEI (*to servant*). Is the fighting still going on ?

SERVANT. No, it has stopped.

CH'UN MEI (*to servant*). Was anyone killed ?

SERVANT. None that I know of.

CH'UN MEI (*with relief*). Amida Buddha ! (*Exit servant*). Madam, do you think that Ts'ao Ts'ao will grant our young gentleman's request and accept his submission ?

TSOU SHIH. With such a noble character as Ts'ao Ts'ao's, why shouldn't he ?

CH'UN MEI. How do you know that, Madam ?

TSOU SHIH (*sings*). My little maid's question is not an easy one to answer. I fancy it is because the bright spring weather induces tender reveries and rapturous emotions. And I am thinking of a handsome man to share my pillow, and the pair of us like inseparable love-birds. (*Exeunt*).

SCENE VI

Two of Ts'ao Ts'ao's adjutants enter and say: We have received orders from the Prime Minister to guard the yamen gate. *Chang Hsiu and Chia Hsü appear.*

CHANG HSIU (*speaks*). Adjutants, we would trouble you to inform the Prime Minister that Chang Hsiu and Chia Hsü, of Wan-ch'êng City, have come to tender their submission. (*Adjutants announce them to Ts'ao*).

TS'AO. Prepare my canopy and ask Hsia-ho Tun to search them before admitting them to my presence. They are to announce their names at the door.

HSIA-HO TUN. Chang Hsiu, so you have come to tender your submission. Have you anything concealed about your person ? (*Chang answers in the negative ; Hsia-ho Tun declares he has to search him ; Chang goes politely through the ceremony and is told he must announce himself*).

CHANG HSIU. I am Chang Hsiu of Wan-ch'êng, and I have brought Chia Hsü my counsellor with me. Though guilty, I beg you to pardon me, Prime Minister.

TS'AO. What is that you are holding ?

CHANG HSIU. The city-seal and a map of Wan-ch'êng.

TS'AO. Hand them to me. (*Laughs triumphantly on examining them*). Be seated.

CHANG AND CHIA. Thank you, Sir.

TS'AO. General Chang, I'll memorialize the Emperor to appoint you Governor of Wan-ch'êng.

CHANG HSIU. Thank you, Prime Minister. Deign to enter the city and examine all our equipment, our treasury and revenues.

TS'AO. You may return. I'll follow at my leisure.

CHANG AND CHIA. We beg to take our leave.

TS'AO AN (*to his father*). You had better be careful. This Chang is full of guile.

TS'AO. Have no fear of that ! Generals Hsü and Tien Wei will escort me into the city ; the others will camp just outside it. Here, fetch the horses. (*Exeunt*).

SCENE VII

Chang Hsiu and Chia Hsü welcome Ts'ao and his generals at the city-gate and invite them to Chang's Palace.

TS'AO. General Chang, what do you chiefly depend on for the city's defence ?

CHANG HSIU. We rely mainly on our shield-bearers and broadswordsmen.

TS'AO. To-morrow I wish to go to the drill-ground and review your troops. I shall require your assistance during the exercises. (*Exit*).

Chang Hsiu's chief generals, Chang Hsien and Lei, followed by shield-bearers and broadswordsmen, appear on the stage and leave city-gates. Ts'ao Ts'ao, his son and nephew, Hsü Ch'u and Tien Wei appear, and also leave the city.

Scene VIII

TS'AO (*taking the principal seat in centre, says to Chang*). Put your swordsmen through their exercises. (*When these are over*) Now put your shield-bearers through their manœuvres. (*These finished, he asks*) Who drilled these men so skilfully?

CHANG HSIU. My late uncle, Chang Chi.

TS'AO. Let them all be transferred to my camp till further orders.

CHANG HSIU. The matter will receive my prompt attention, Sir. (*Exeunt omnes*).

Scene IX

The wives of Generals Chang Hsien and Lei enter, singing : Our chariots stand before the palace-gate. We have come to visit Madam Chang and hear the latest news.

TSOU SHIH (*enters, saying*). I was not aware of your arrival ; excuse me, pray, for not receiving you at a polite distance.

LADIES. Since the fighting has ceased we came to see if you were safe.

TSOU SHIH. All is quiet in the city now. Let us climb the garden-tower and enjoy the air.

LADIES. We shall be enchanted to accompany you, Madam.

TSOU SHIH (*sings*). Ch'un Mei, you lead the way into the garden. We can drink some wine in the tower and cheer ourselves up a bit. (*Exit*).

Scene X

Enter Ts'ao Ts'ao with his son and nephew.

TS'AO (*sings*). Since I took Wan-ch'êng I have not had a moment's peace of mind.

SON AND NEPHEW. Why, what's the matter, Sir?

TS'AO. I cannot tell, but I have been feeling restless and dejected.

NEPHEW. You must not give way to melancholy, Uncle. Let us saunter through the streets and see the sights ; we may also learn what's happening among Chang Hsiu's troops.

TS'AO. That's a bright idea. You go ahead and lead the way. (*Sings*) We'll all take a stroll and enjoy ourselves.   (*Exeunt*).

Enter Tsou Shih, the generals' wives, and Ch'un Mei.

TSOU SHIH (*sings*). Let us first climb the tower and watch the people passing to and fro.

Ts'ao appears with his son and nephew.

TS'AO (*sings*). Through the streets as I saunter along,
          I glance at the bustling throng.
          I raise my head, and peer as I tread,
          In every direction before me outspread.

Tsou Shih is seen in the tower playing on a t'an-ch'in or table-lute.

TS'AO (*sings*). Do I not hear the delicate strains of a lute ?

SON (*to nephew*). The hour is late : you and I had better return to camp.

TS'AO. Yes, you had better retire. I'll linger a while and listen, ha, ha !   (*Exeunt*).

TSOU SHIH (*sings*). Why did that man stand gazing so intently ? Such fine, expressive eyes ! They seemed to peer right through me. All the same, it was rather odd behaviour . . .

LADIES (*to Tsou Shih*). We'll have to be saying good-bye.

MADAM CHANG (*sings*). Farewell, I must be turning homewards.

MADAM LEI (*sings*). Soon let us spend another quiet holiday together.   (*Exeunt matrons*).

TSOU SHIH (*sings*). I would be glad of an assignation with that man, but I do not even know his name or where he lives. (*Looks in every direction, heaves a deep sigh and descends from the tower. The pert maidservant follows, pointing a playful finger at her back. Exeunt*).

SCENE XI

Enter Ts'ao Ts'ao, with his son and nephew.

TS'AO. Just now as I was strolling down the street I saw a pretty woman peep at me. (*Sighs ; his nephew asks why*). Nobody can tell what's on my mind.

NEPHEW. At least I can try to guess, Uncle. You're thinking of that lutanist we saw in the tower to-day, are you not ?

TS'AO. Right you are, but I fear you cannot help me. The affair is doomed to failure.

NEPHEW. If you will put a cart and five hundred soldiers at my disposal, I am sure I can manage it for you.

TS'AO. Very well, do your best.

SON. For one who holds the post of Prime Minister to abduct a citizen's wife, what should the penalty be ?

TS'AO. Humph ! What do you know about such matters ? Leave me at once. (*Exit Ts'ao's son*). (*To nephew*) Make haste and arrange this affair. I'll be waiting here for you. (*Exit Ts'ao*).

NEPHEW. Come on, soldiers, you are to follow me. (*They all make a few rounds of the stage*). We have arrived. Go, seize the woman and take her to the cart. (*Tsou Shih enters*). There she is ; catch hold of her and be brisk about it. (*Tsou Shih and her maid are kidnapped. Exeunt*).

SERVANT (*enters and says*). The soldiers have seized my mistress and her maid. I'll have to break the news to my young master. (*Exit*).

Scene XII

Ts'ao's nephew comes to report.

TS'AO. Back at last! Has the mighty business prospered?

NEPHEW. It has.

TS'AO. Where is the lady?

NEPHEW. She is in the camp, Sir.

TS'AO. Make haste; bring her straight in. (*Tsou Shih and Ch'un Mei enter*). Ah, what a beauty! Please come in. (*Ts'ao beams all over her*). Exquisite! She is indeed a beauty. (*To servants, etc.*) All of you retire. (*To Tsou Shih*) To whose family do you belong, my pretty maid?

TSOU SHIH. I was Chang Chi's wife and am therefore Chang Hsiu's aunt; I was born of the Tsou family.

TS'AO. So you are married! I must apologize for my bad manners.

TSOU SHIH. I am unworthy of such honour.

TS'AO. I fear I may have given you offence.

TSOU SHIH. You are too kind to suggest such a thing.

CH'UN MEI (*pertly*). Why all this idle talk?

TS'AO (*to Tsou Shih*). I have long heard of your fragrant name. I have just accepted your nephew Chang Hsiu's submission! (*Chuckles*) It was entirely for your sweet sake!

TSOU SHIH. You are in truth my benefactor, Prime Minister.

CH'UN MEI (*teasing*). It is getting late, Madam, we had better return.

TSOU SHIH (*without conviction*). I fear it is; we will have to go home.

TS'AO (*ardently*). Stay! This meeting proves our affinity through the three stages of re-incarnation. I trust you will share my bed-chamber. And when I return to Court, I'll raise you to a lady of the very first rank.

TSOU SHIH (*melting*). Oh, thank you, Prime Minister.

CH'UN MEI (*roguishly*). You two ought to feel ashamed of yourselves !

TS'AO (*to maid*). Fetch the lamp.

CH'UN MEI. Where are you going ?

TS'AO. To relax and repose in the ante-room. (*Laughing, he clutches Tsou Shih's hand and says*) Let us retire like man and wife ; let us enjoy ourselves like love-birds never to be parted. (*Speaks*) What is the name of this little minx ?

TSOU SHIH. Ch'un Mei [*i.e.*, Spring Plum-blossom].

TS'AO. Well, Plum-blossom, if you serve us nicely, we'll reward you handsomely. (*Pushes her out of the room*). Lady, pray doff your outer garments.

TSOU SHIH. Most eagerly ! (*Sings*) Your handmaid will share your couch and do your bidding. But don't let Chang Hsiu come to hear of it !

TS'AO (*sings*). Nestling to-night in each other's arms we shall fulfil our blissful destiny. How could an outsider know of our love-affairs ? (*Exeunt*).

CH'UN MEI (*appears, saying*). It is midnight now, and dark as a cave. Where shall I seek repose ? My mistress and Ts'ao Ts'ao are snug inside the chamber. I wonder what they are up to at this moment !

TS'AO'S NEPHEW (*sneaks in, saying*). I see that the lady has an attractive maid. I'll run after her and have a good time. (*He gropes about in the darkness and finally collides with her*).

CH'UN MEI. Oh ! Who is that ?

NEPHEW. Don't make such a hullabaloo ! The Prime Minister is my uncle, and I am a young gentleman. If you share my couch I'll present you with a pair of gold bangles, and some lovely new dresses, and silver galore besides.

CH'UN MEI. I am too afraid.

NEPHEW. What on earth are you afraid of ?

CH'UN MEI. I am afraid your whiskers will tickle my mouth.

NEPHEW. Feel me. I haven't a single whisker!

Exeunt ensemble.

SCENE XIII

CHANG HSIU (*entering, says*). I have only submitted to Ts'ao for the time being. When my opportunity comes, I am all prepared.

SERVANT (*entering*). I have to report, Sir, that things have taken a bad turn.

CHANG HSIU. What is there to be alarmed about?

SERVANT. Last night at dusk a number of soldiers burst into the Palace and forcibly abducted Madam Chang and her maid Ch'un Mei.

CHANG HSIU. Whose troops were they?

SERVANT. They did not look like ours, Sir.

CHANG HSIU. Did they steal any money or plunder any effects?

SERVANT. No, Sir, they left everything intact.

CHANG HSIU. You may go. I'll investigate this instantly. (*Exit servant. Chang soliloquizes*) Whose soldiers could they have been, to kidnap the women and touch nothing else? They must have been Ts'ao Ts'ao's. I'll make inquiries. (*To groom*) Saddle my horse. (*He mounts and rides straight off to Ts'ao's camp. On arrival he dismounts. At sight of Ts'ao's nephew, asks*) Who are you?

NEPHEW. It is now near midday and I haven't yet had a wink of sleep. Ah, you are General Chang, I presume?

CHANG HSIU. May I trouble you to inform the Prime Minister that Chang Hsiu has come to see him.

NEPHEW. Dear me! The Prime Minister is still sound asleep in bed.

CHANG HSIU. I have urgent business with him.

NEPHEW (*calls out*). Uncle, there's some one to see you, Sir.   (*Ts'ao and Tsou Shih come out*).

TS'AO. Who is it?

NEPHEW. Chang Hsiu.

TS'AO (*in great alarm*). How now! What is to be done? (*To Tsou Shih*) You had better run and hide yourself at once. (*Exit Tsou Shih*). Nephew, invite Chang to come in.

CHANG HSIU (*on entering*). Your Excellency is above and I am below. I have come to pay my respects, Sir.

TS'AO. Be seated.

CHANG HSIU. Thank you, Sir. You have doubtless had a strenuous time of it these last few days.

TS'AO. Yes, mighty strenuous! I am thinking of staying a few days longer for a little recreation and enjoyment before proceeding to the Capital.

CHANG HSIU. Why not prolong your sojourn, Sir?

TS'AO. You, Sir, are a man of lofty principles: unless you consider it beneath your dignity, why not address each other as uncle and nephew?

CHANG HSIU. I am under great obligation to your extreme kindness, Sir.

TS'AO. My dear nephew, all men say that I am proud and ambitious. They do not realize how much I esteem nobility of character and revere fine scholarship. I am never a dissembler in my relations with such men.

CHANG HSIU. I have long desired to know you, Sir.

TS'AO (*to servants*). Serve the tea. (*Ch'un Mei comes in with the tea-tray; at sight of Chang she flutters off in alarm*).

CHANG HSIU (*equally surprised, exclaims*). Ah, who was that?

TS'AO. You need not be surprised, my dear nephew. You are a man of consummate ability. Tact and discretion in every circumstance, eh? (*Chuckles roguishly*).

CHANG HSIU. I'll be taking my leave.

TS'AO. At your own convenience.

CHANG HSIU (*turning his back on Ts'ao, mutters to himself*). It must have been this treacherous Ts'ao who forcibly abducted my aunt. Ts'ao, you rebel, if I fail to kill you, I swear I am unworthy to be called a man! (*Turns round and sits down again*).

TS'AO. What are you muttering about? Are you vexed about something?

CHANG HSIU. Why should I be vexed, Prime Minister?

TS'AO. Do call me uncle!

CHANG HSIU. Yes, Uncle.

TS'AO. My dear nephew, your future destiny and honours are all in my safe keeping.

CHANG HSIU. Thank you, Prime Minister. I shall now be taking my leave.

TS'AO. You must excuse me for not seeing you off.

CHANG HSIU. I am unworthy of such a compliment. (*To groom*) Fetch my horse. (*To himself*) I must not let a word or look betray me. I'll strike as soon as I see my opportunity. (*Exit Chang*).

TS'AO (*gleefully*). I have discovered another confidential friend in this Chang Hsiu.

TSOU SHIH (*entering in négligé, exclaims*). Prime Minister!

TS'AO. Your nephew has just paid me a visit, dear lady. While he was here Ch'un Mei stepped in with the tea. He seemed surprised, but made no remark. Judging from appearances, I feel sure that he harbours no evil intentions.

TSOU SHIH. I was behind the screen and heard everything distinctly. That nephew of mine is a deep schemer, Sir. You had better beware of treachery.

TS'AO. You are right. Let us move from here to Tien Wei's camp. There we'll be perfectly safe.

TSOU SHIH. As matters stand, we had better start at once.

TS'AO. Quickly, fetch your clothes and get dressed. (*Sings*) It is not safe to remain in the city. Tien Wei's camp will provide us with better lodging.

TSOU SHIH. I'll wear a disguise and slowly ride beyond the city-walls. (*Exeunt Ts'ao and Tsou Shih on horseback*).

SCENE XIV

CHANG HSIU (*arriving, says*). May Heaven assist me in killing that rebel Ts'ao and achieving my ambitions! (*To adjutant*) Bid Chia Hsü and my generals come hither to conference.

Enter Chia Hsü with Generals Chang Hsien and Lei.

CHANG HSIU. Please be seated. You find me much perturbed.

CHIA AND GENERALS. How is that, Sir?

CHANG HSIU. My servant reported that some soldiers —he knew not whence they came—abducted my aunt and her handmaid by force.

CHIA. You should make inquiries at Ts'ao Ts'ao's camp, my Lord.

CHANG HSIU. Precisely what I did! And while I was engaged in conversation with Ts'ao Ts'ao, Ch'un Mei the handmaid entered with the tea.

CHIA. Then Her Ladyship must also be there. Are you going to avenge this insult?

CHANG HSIU. Who ever heard of not avenging such an insult? But I fear that Tien Wei's halberds and lances will prove a formidable hindrance.

CHIA. If you could send a man of tried ability to Tien Wei's camp to remove those weapons of his, all obstacles would vanish.

HU CH'Ê (*an officer of enormous strength, speaks up*). I can steal Tien Wei's halberds, my Lord.

CHANG HSIU. Have you truly the courage and skill to succeed?

HU. Positively, my Lord.

CHANG HSIU. Please be seated then, and I'll do you obeisance.

CHIA. Hu Ch'ê, your orders are to equip yourself as a groom and exercise your horses just outside Ts'ao's camp. I have a plan in mind; its success depends upon your strict obedience.

HU. Your orders shall be obeyed, Sir. (*Exit Hu*).

CHIA (*to adjutant*). Here, you go with the Master's card and invite General Tien Wei to join us at a banquet. (*Exit adjutant. Chia to attendants*) Lay the table with meats and wine. Generals Chang and Lei, as soon as our guest arrives, you are to conceal yourselves in the southern wing.

GENERALS. Your commands shall be obeyed, Sir. *Adjutant comes to announce Tien Wei's arrival. Exeunt generals.*

CHANG HSIU. Invite him in.

TIEN WEI (*on entering*). My respects to you, Sir.

CHANG HSIU. General Tien, I must apologize for not going out to meet you.

TIEN. I am unworthy of the compliment. I received your card of invitation but am ignorant of the occasion to which I owe it.

CHANG HSIU. I merely prepared a coarse meal so that we could enjoy a drink together.

TIEN. I fear I am putting you to a lot of inconvenience.

CHANG HSIU (*to servants*). Let the wine and savouries be served. (*Hu Ch'ê leads a neighing horse across the stage*).

TIEN. What is that noise outside?

CHANG HSIU. The groom is leading his horse up and down.

TIEN. Call him in. I should like to see it. (*Groom leads horse in. Tien scrutinizes it*) How many li can it travel in a day?

CHANG HSIU. Through a single day and night this horse can cover a thousand li; it can gallop over the highest mountains as if on level ground.

TIEN. I must mount such a splendid creature and see how he goes. (*Mounts and dismounts several times, exclaiming*) A noble steed, a truly magnificent steed!

CHANG HSIU. It seems you have taken quite a fancy to him, General.

TIEN. Every good soldier likes a good horse.

CHANG HSIU. In that case, General, I'll make you a present of him.

TIEN. Then I'll thank you most cordially on the spot.

CHIA. As it is an unruly beast, we'll give you the groom as well.

TIEN. That's very generous of you; I thank you again. See that he has plenty of fodder, groom; I'll shortly be riding him back to camp.

HU. Your orders will be obeyed, General.

CHANG HSIU. Have some wine, General.

TIEN. Delighted! Let's drink together, Sir.

CHANG HSIU. It has come to my ears, General, that you surpass all others in military prowess. Now that I meet you face to face, I can perceive that this is not empty hearsay.

TIEN. You flatter me, Sir.

CHIA. Your capacity for potations is said to be equally great. Let us drain a big bumper together.

CHANG HSIU. Come on, General, I'll have a full goblet with you.

CHIA. Let me have one with him too!

Tien swallows a capacious wine-bowl to the dregs.

CHANG HSIU. Drain another! (*Tien empties this*).

CHIA. I'll fill you another, General.

TIEN. I have had plenty for the time being.

Shows symptoms of intoxication.

CHANG HSIU. It's getting late, General, you had better return to your camp.

TIEN (*to groom*). Here, bring me the horse. (*Tries to mount but tumbles off*).

CHANG HSIU. Get the cart ready : he's far too drunk to ride.

Groom hitches the horse to cart and Tien climbs in. The generals who have been concealed sneak out to bind him but Tien's strength defeats their purpose.

TIEN. What are you two trying to do with me ?

GENERALS. We are escorting you, Sir.

TIEN. Quite unnecessary. Much obliged all the same. (*Is trundled off in the cart, followed by groom*).

CHANG HSIU (*to Chia Hsü*). What are your orders, Sir ?

CHIA. Take a company of horses and men and attack Ts'ao's camp at nightfall.

CHANG HSIU. We must make our plan succeed.

Exeunt omnes.

SCENE XV

Tien Wei and groom (Hu Ch'ê) appear. Tien undresses and goes to bed ; the groom leaves him.

HU (*entering stealthily, says*). Since boyhood I have always been the boldest of the bold. I have gone through dragons' pools and braved the tiger's lair. Yesterday I received orders from my master to steal Tien Wei's double-headed halberds. (*Repeats this*). How brightly all the stars are glittering ! 'Tis proof that even Heaven will assist me. The hour is late : the time is ripe for action. (*Slips into Tien Wei's tent, steals the weapons and says*) Now that the halberds are in my possession, I'll sound the signal for Chang's attack. (*Blows a trumpet. Chang Hsiu rushes into Tien Wei's tent, slaying to right and left. Exeunt Chang and soldiers*).

TIEN (*wakes up in great alarm, looks for his weapons, finds them gone and says*). I cannot find my double-headed halberds ; my life is at an end !

Chang Hsiu enters leading some soldiers to attack Tien Wei who, deprived of his trusty halberds, picks up two dead soldiers and makes a rush at Chang. They fight a few rounds. Seeing that even so Tien is getting the best of it, Chang takes out his bow and arrow and shoots Tien dead.

TS'AO'S NEPHEW (*enters, saying*). Ai ya! What's all the hubbub about? I'll go at once and tell my uncle.

TS'AO TS'AO (*appears dressed in woman's clothes, followed by Tsou Shih, and exclaims*). What is the matter?

TS'AO'S SON. The camp is in utter confusion; the armies are making a terrible clamour and the drums beating to quarters.

TS'AO. Go instantly and see what it is all about.

His son goes off and returns to say that the tents where the horses are have caught fire.

TS'AO. That's only a trifle: why all this fuss about nothing? Take yourself off. (*Exit son*).

TSOU SHIH (*appears half-dressed, i.e., in trousers, and says*). Prime Minister, come quickly!

TS'AO. I am coming, I am coming!

SON (*rushing in*). Father, Father!

TS'AO. What now?

SON. Chang Hsiu has attacked the camp.

TS'AO. Where is Tien Wei?

SON. Tien Wei is dead.

TS'AO. Ai ya!

His nephew comes in and seizes Ch'un Mei's hand, Ts'ao likewise grasps Tsou Shih's, and all flee together. Chang Hsiu chases Ts'ao across the stage. Ts'ao's nephew comes in, meets Chang Hsiu, who kills him. Exeunt omnes.

SCENE XVI

Ts'ao Ts'ao, his son, Tsou Shih and Ch'un Mei appear. Ts'ao laughs aloud.

SON. What are you laughing about?

TS'AO. I laugh because Chang Hsiu is a fool in military tactics. Had he posted a few men here I would never have been able to escape.

TS'AO'S GENERALS (*entering*). Our respects to you, Prime Minister.

TS'AO. Since you have all arrived, you may escort this lovely lady to my camp.

GENERALS. Women are not allowed to stay in the camp, Sir.

TS'AO. Dear me, I forgot it was against the rules. Well, well! I suppose I can do without this beauty. Tsou Shih, you may go your own way now.

TSOU SHIH. Ts'ao Ts'ao, you have done me great wrong. It is entirely due to you that I am in this plight. And now you cast me off! Too late I find you are without a conscience.

Exeunt Ts'ao and suite. Chang Hsiu arrives with soldiers, sees Ch'un Mei and kills her.

TSOU SHIH. Chang Hsiu, have you gone mad, to murder people like this?

CHANG HSIU. Not another word, Tsou Shih! Lewd woman, you have ruined our family's reputation. Why should I spare your life? (*Thrusts his spear through her body*).

A violent battle ensues between Ts'ao's generals and Chang Hsiu. The former are defeated and Chang gives orders to cease fighting. All retire.

Finis

* * *

An ideal cast for this lively play would be: Yang Hsiao-lou as *Chang Hsiu*, Hao Shou-ch'ên as *Ts'ao Ts'ao*, Hsiao Ts'ui-hua as *Tsou Shih*, Hou Hsi-jui as *Tien Wei*, and Yeh Shêng-chang as *Hu Ch'ê*. Any of these actors taken singly would make the play worth seeing. The scenes are so rich in variety that there is not a boring moment. Ts'ao Ts'ao's appearance in female garb is unforgettably comic, but the great scene is where Tien Wei finds his halberds missing. Chang Hsiu wears mourning for the occasion of murdering his aunt: it is quite a sophisticated business. The sword-play, and the mimic fighting of the various generals, are swift and subtle in the extreme; their technical resources seem infinite and one lives at a higher pitch while witnessing them.

The incidents will be found in Mr. C. H. Brewitt-Taylor's translation of *San Kuo Chih Yen-i* or *Romance of the Three Kingdoms*, Vol. I. Chap. XVI, pp. 169 onwards.

CHANG HSIU ABOUT TO KILL HIS AUNT TSOU SHIH

Chan Wan-ch'êng

CH'ANG-PAN P'O 長 板 坡

THE BATTLE OF CH'ANG-PAN P'O*

PERIOD : End of Han, A.D. 207.   A military play in *p'i-huang* style.

CHIEF CHARACTERS

CHAO YÜN, or CHAO TZŬ-LUNG, General under Liu Pei, hero of the play.	*Wu-shêng*
CHANG FEI, General and sworn-brother of Liu Pei	*Chin-tzŭ hua-lien*
LIU PEI, Generalissimo (eventually Emperor of Shu)	*Shêng*
MI FU JÊN, his first wife ... ...⎞	*Ch'ing-i*
KAN FU JÊN, his second wife ... ...⎠	
TS'AO TS'AO, Prime Minister of Han	*Ching*
HSÜ SHU, ex-Counsellor of Liu Pei	*Lao-shêng*
HSIA HOU-ÊN, sword-bearer to Ts'ao	*Ch'ou-êrh*

SCENE I

If the play is performed in its entirety, the formidable Ts'ao Ts'ao and his eight generals appear by way of prologue, all " dressed up to the nines " in gorgeous coats of mail, parading in the ch'i-pa style (see page xxvi). These eight generals are : Chang Ho, Hsü Huang, Hsü Ch'u, Li Tien, Ts'ao Hung, Chang Liao, Ts'ao Hsiu, and Yüeh Chin. They form ranks and Ts'ao Ts'ao swaggers into their midst. The generals thunderingly proclaim that they are wolves, tigers and leopards, eager for the fray. Ts'ao Ts'ao boasts that he controls an army of heroes who will sweep the wolves (not his own, of course, but Sun Ch'üan and Liu Pei) off the face of the earth ; and that he will cut off all the heads of his enemies without reporting to the Emperor.† He informs the audience that he is a native of the Ch'iao district in the State of P'ei, and

---

*Name of a place in the district of Hsin-yeh, Honan, where a great battle was fought in A.D. 207 between the forces of Ts'ao Ts'ao and Liu Pei.

† The puppet Emperor Hsien Ti.

that Hsien Ti had appointed him Prime Minister of Han.
"How I abominate," *says he,* "those three brothers of
the Peach Garden!* During the battle at Hsin-yeh
they all but decimated my army, and then escaped to
Chiang-ling [in Hupeh]." *He commands Chang Ho and
Ts'ao Hung to take a company and capture Liu Pei alive, and
the other generals to reinforce them.*

SCENE II

LIU PEI *(from behind the curtain sings in hsi-p'i tao-pan
style).* The Prince [*i.e., himself*] shall govern by the Rule
of Right and restore the fortunes of our glorious Han!

*He then appears on the stage, accompanied by his two wives,
the Ladies Kan and Mi, Chao Yün, Chang Fei, Chien Yung,
Mi Chu and Mi Fang (Lady Mi's brothers), two carters, two
men leading horses, some flag- and standard-bearers, and
four men, women and children, representing the refugees Liu
Pei has saved from carnage.*

LIU *(sings).* Who could have dreamt that we
should thus be scattered! Make haste, send men and
cavalry to search for the missing heroes. We have
escaped the tiger's lair only to fall into the dragon's pool.
(Speaks) Alas, I grieve for my poor land and people.
When shall we ever be blessed with peace again?

CHAO YÜN. Sire, our armies are scattered like stars
and are utterly demoralized.

CHANG FEI. We have certainly had a rough time
of it, my Lord.

LIU. Why are you sighing, brother?

CHANG FEI. Since you and I took the oath in the
peach-orchard we have fought many a victorious battle,
but with all these refugees to defend we have lost a
battle we could have easily won. Why shouldn't I sigh?
My heart is very sore.

---

*Liu Pei, Kuan Yü and Chang Fei, who swore a solemn oath of loyalty
in the latter's peach-orchard. A.D. 184.

LIU. From oldest times it has ever been thus, victory or defeat ; so why lament ?

CHAO (*to Chang Fei*). My third brother, even though Ts'ao's army were awe-inspiring as Mount T'ai, I'll wager that the two of us, lances in hand, could force our way into Ts'ao's camp and kill him.

CHANG FEI (*to Chao*). But who is to protect the ladies if we go ?

CHAO. I shall protect them.

LIU (*mounts his horse and sings in hsi-p'i*). Since the day of our oath in the peach-orchard, though we have succeeded in destroying over a million Yellow Turban Rebels, we have not enjoyed a single day's repose. Compelled to leave Hsin-yeh now, I am full of dread. Alas, it is too late to indulge in vain regret !

CHAO (*sings*). Rest at ease, my Lord, and dispel your alarms : your brothers are with you.

Chang Fei exhorts him likewise. A hubbub is heard behind the curtain.

LIU (*sings*). Ah me ! Ts'ao's men are advancing in swarms. (*In the distance Ts'ao's eight generals pass them in review*). (*Sings*) They are like a forest of spears, like a mountain bristling with lances. (*Addressing Chao Yün*) Alas, my fourth brother ! (*Sings*) Make haste and put the fear of Heaven into them !

Exeunt Liu Pei and followers.

CHANG FEI (*sings*). I'll wait for you at the Tang-yang bridge. (*Exit*).

CHAO (*sings*). Let the chariots of Their Highnesses follow close behind me. Alone on my horse I'll break through the ranks of that rebel Ts'ao.

Ts'ao's eight generals appear and fight several rounds with Chao Yün, who disables seven of them. Chang Ho is left to finish the contest with Chao Yün; neither of them loses and both leave the stage. They reappear and fight more rounds : Chang Ho is defeated and Chao Yün chases him off the stage.

SCENE III

Enter Ladies Kan and Mi.

LADY KAN (*sings in hsi-p'i*). On every side we are hemmed in by the foe.

LADY MI (*sings*). It is inconceivable that we shall ever escape.

LADY KAN (*sings*). Chao Yün, Chao Yün, where are you?

While she is singing, Chang Ho and Ts'ao Hung come charging in with their horde, killing and maiming. The ladies escape, pursued by Chang Ho and Ts'ao Hung. Exeunt.

SCENE IV

Liu Pei appears surrounded by six of Ts'ao's generals.

LIU (*sings in hsi-p'i*). I am entirely surrounded by Ts'ao's generals and troops.

TS'AO'S GENERALS (*shouting in unison*). Liu Pei, do you still refuse to surrender?

LIU (*sings*). I surrender with every breath of my body. The heroes have fallen into Heaven's snare!

Chang Fei enters, fights a few rounds with Ts'ao's men and rescues Liu Pei. While they are leaving the stage Ts'ao Hung attacks and wounds Mi Fang and makes his exit.

SCENE V

CHAO (*enters, singing in hsi-p'i tao-pan*). I have driven my charger to his utmost strength, searching everywhere. Yet nowhere can I find the Ladies Mi and Kan. (*He draws up to Mi Fang, prostrate on the grass, and asks if he has seen them with Prince A-tou*).

MI FANG (*speaks*). The ladies have made their escape with the little Prince. Ts'ao Hung pursued them. When I impeded him he attacked and wounded me; then stole my horse and left me lying here for dead. I know not what has become of Their Highnesses.

One of Ts'ao's generals appears, is promptly attacked and killed by Chao Yün, who appropriates the dead man's horse and tells Mi Fang to mount it and go in search of Liu Pei. Mi Fang thanks Chao for saving his life and departs.

CHAO (*speaks*). I must uphold my reputation for bravery; I'll hack my way through the enemy's ranks and seek out the ladies and the little Prince.

SCENE VI

Ts'ao's generals Li Tien and Yüeh Chin are about to capture Mi Chu when Chao Yün dashes in and rescues him, defeating the generals. Exeunt. Chao Yün reappears, encounters Chang Ho and overcomes him.

CHAO (*sings in hsi-p'i tao-pan*). Rank after rank, I've hacked my way; I wax in strength, the more I slay. (*Reining in his horse and looking round, he says*) Ah! that looks like a company fleeing in this direction. (*Sings*) Maybe the ladies are in their midst. (*Enter Lady Kan, accompanied by Mi Chu and four refugees. They hail Chao Yün, who says*) Alas, my mistress, I have come too late! I fear you have suffered much alarm and distress, entirely through my fault. But I did not know where to search for you all.

LADY KAN (*speaks*). When we were attacked by Ts'ao's troops we abandoned our chariots. Lady Mi escaped with A-tou in her arms, I know not whither. I happened to meet Mi Chu, who brought me here.

CHAO (*to Mi Chu*). You protect Her Highness on her journey forward. (*Exeunt. Chao speaks*) I'll fight my way again through Ts'ao's camp and try to discover Lady Mi and the little Prince. (*Exit*).

SCENE VII

Enter Liu Pei, Chien Yung and Chang Fei. The latter starts building a bridge for them to cross the river.

CHANG FEI. Where has Chao Yün disappeared to, I wonder !

LIU. He has gone to attack Ts'ao's camp.

CHANG FEI. He must have thought that you were captured, my Lord, with nobody to protect you, and slipped over to the enemy's camp dissembling allegiance to Ts'ao Ts'ao.

CHIEN. Don't be so suspicious, General. He has gone there to try and find Her Highness and the little Prince.   (*Liu Pei echoes this opinion*).

CHANG FEI. I beg you to forgive my rudeness, elder brother. (*Exeunt Liu and Chien*). Just wait till I meet him ! I'll scare the life out of him.

Enter Chao Yün, accompanied by Lady Kan, Mi Chu and four refugees.

CHANG FEI. Ho ! Chao Yün, why did you betray my brother ?

CHAO. Don't be so suspicious ! As I could not find the ladies and A-tou, I broke through Ts'ao Ts'ao's ranks again and fell in the rear. What do you mean by talking of betrayal ?

CHANG FEI. If my elder brother and Chien Yung had not told me the true facts, I would certainly have nothing more to do with you.

CHAO. Have you not caught sight of Lady Mi and the Prince ?

CHANG FEI. I know they cannot be very far away.

CHAO. Mi Chu, you escort Her Highness across the bridge.

CHANG FEI (*after this is done*). Ha, ha ! my fourth brother, you are a mighty clever general !

CHAO. You guard the bridge while I pursue my quest. (*Exit. Chang mounts the bridge, in this case a chair, looks round and laughing makes his exit*).

SCENE VIII

Enter Ts'ao Hung chasing Lady Mi ; he shoots her with an arrow ; she falls and he leaves the stage.

LADY MI (*sings in hsi-p'i tao-pan*). I have been struck by a rebel's arrow ; how can I move, disabled by this wound ? Chao Yün, Chao Yün, where are you ? *Chao rushes in.*

CHAO. Here, my Lady ! I am Chao Tzǔ-lung of Ch'ang-shan. To test my courage and ability I have broken single-handed through Ts'ao Ts'ao's ranks. Hearing my Lady's voice, I hurried hither.

LADY MI (*sings*). Do I indeed behold Chao Yün before me ?

CHAO. Your Highness has been alarmed. I trust the Prince is well ? This is entirely through my fault and I, a general without competence, should therefore die ten thousand deaths. (*He kneels and makes obeisance*).

LADY MI. Your arrival is exceedingly fortunate, General ; now A-tou's life is saved. But as for me, I am badly wounded and quite unable to walk. Take pity on the House of Han ! Your Prince, this precious burden, I now confide to your care. His melancholy fate—his life or death, his safety or his ruin,—are in your hands. Not only will Hsüan-tê (Liu Pei) be grateful to you for this noble act : his ancestors now lying in their graves will be deeply grateful too. All that is left to them is this little A-tou, a scrap of bones and blood ; protect him, General, break through the rebel ranks, then I may die content on the desert-plain. (*Weeps*).

CHAO. I beseech you, Lady, mount into my saddle and clasp the Prince to your bosom. I will set forth on foot ; with my single spear I can fight through the rebel forces.

LADY MI. You are mistaken, General. How could a feeble woman suffering from a grievous wound keep pace with you ? Besides, I am unable to ride : it is for you to mount the horse. How can you expect to succeed if you fight your way through the rebel host on foot with your single spear ? Pray seize it and go your way ; far better save one A-tou than thousands like myself ! (*Weeps. Hubbub of Ts'ao's soldiers behind the stage*).

CHAO. Quickly, my Lady ! Mount into my saddle and make your escape. If Ts'ao's men come this way, what will we do ?

LADY MI. Give me a moment's reflection. (*Turning her back on Chao*). The loyal hero ! But if the foe appear, we shall all be caught in a trap. What is the best course ? Ah, I have it ! There is a dried-up well near by : why not jump into it and end my life ? (*Sings in hsi-p'i*) General, you are brave and true. Take this child and flee before it is too late ! Here is A-tou : I entrust him to you.

CHAO (*on receiving A-tou, loosens his armour, places the child in his tunic and sings*). I must preserve the life of Liu Pei's heir. (*To Lady Mi*) Mount my horse and escape, Lady. I'll carry the child and fight through the rebel forces.

LADY MI (*sings in hsi-p'i tao-pan*). General, I implore you not to stay a moment longer. Save the Prince ; I can die and be buried anywhere. (*She stands on the brink of the well*). Oh, General, look ! the rebel troops are coming.

CHAO. Where ? (*As he turns, the lady leaps into the well. Discovering which, he proceeds to sing in hsi-p'i*) Alas, she has destroyed herself. How terrible ! (*Speaks*) Now that Her Ladyship has perished, I can only shield the little Prince by concealing him in my tunic. (*He breaks down the wall surrounding the well and covers Lady Mi with the bricks*).

Scene IX

Enter Ts'ao Ts'ao's captain and sword-bearer, Hsia Hou-ên, with Ts'ao's Green Blade Sword slung across his back. Chao kills him and appropriates the weapon.

CHAO (*speaks*). I have long heard that Ts'ao Ts'ao possessed two precious swords, the " Green Blade" and the " Trust in Heaven." The latter he always carries himself. I have heard that this " Green Blade " can cut through iron as if it were mud. I'll test it ! (*He hacks at a stone so that sparks fly out, represented on the stage by three flashes of light*). This blade unquestionably has no peer ; I'll apply it to Ts'ao Ts'ao's men and slice them to slivers.

Ts'ao's generals arrive and fight several rounds with Chao ; the " Green Blade " proves as good as his word and cuts them all down. The musical accompaniment, k'uai-pan, is fast and furious during the conflict. Exeunt omnes.

Scene X

Enter Ts'ao Ts'ao and Hsü Shu.

TS'AO (*sings in hsi-p'i tao-pan*). I command an army of a million heroes. (*Music changes to k'uai-pan*). We shall chase Liu Pei's troops and slay them as tigers slay sheep. I'll take the road to Ching-shan. (*Ts'ao and Hsü stand on chairs indicating mountains ; Ts'ao sings*) We'll soon see who is weak and who is strong !

Enter Ts'ao Ts'ao's generals and Chao Yün. A contest ensues in which the former are defeated. Ts'ao Hung then asks Chao Yün his name. " I am Chao Tzŭ-lung of Ch'ang-shan!" he retorts. They fight : Ts'ao Hung loses and runs away with Chao Yün in hot pursuit.

TS'AO (*sings in hsi-p'i tao-pan*). Who is that general in a white helmet and coat of mail with the flashing sword ? He is as awe-inspiring as one of the heavenly immortals.

HSÜ SHU. He seems to have hit your fancy, Prime Minister.

TS'AO. I cannot imagine who he is.

HSÜ. That man has a remarkable reputation; he is Chao Yün of Ch'ang-shan, better known as Chao Tzŭ-lung. In courage he equals ten thousand men; nobody can resist him.

TS'AO. A fine general! a fine general!

HSÜ. If the Prime Minister wishes to acquire this general, where's the hitch?

TS'AO. What clever scheme have you in mind, Sir?

HSÜ. Let the Prime Minister issue commands that he is to be captured alive without being injured in any way soever, and that any disobedience is to be severely punished. When he is captured and brought to camp I'll contrive that he submits and joins us. What is your opinion, Sir?

TS'AO. An excellent plan. Make your arrangements, Sir. (*Hsü Shu issues instructions accordingly, then laughs*). In less time than the swallowing of a meal I have done more to assist Liu Pei than if I had given him a million soldiers, ha, ha! *　　　　　　　　　　　　　　　(*Exit*).

SCENE XI

CHAO YÜN. The rebel Ts'ao has issued a mandate that I am not to be killed, but it says nought about my killing him! Wait till I put forth my strength, I'll flay him alive! (*Challenging Ts'ao's generals*) Listen! which of you is willing to come out and fight to the death?

Ts'ao's generals surround him : he falls into a pit and changes into a dragon. Successive flashes of light indicate the appearance of a supernatural being.†　At sight of the dragon Ts'ao's generals recoil in panic.

---

* Hsü Shu had been Liu Pei's chief adviser before Chu-ko Liang. Ts'ao Ts'ao tricked him away by means of a forged letter, purporting to come from his mother, whom he held as hostage. Though Ts'ao Ts'ao treated him well, he never won him over to his service. See *San Kuo*, Ch. XXXVI.

† Such a metamorphosis is explained by the fact that an Emperor's offspring can be dragons as well as the Emperor himself. Chao Yün's Imperial charge enveloped him in the process.

CHAO (*as he emerges from the pit exclaims*). Wondrous! the Son of Heaven performs a hundred miracles to assist me! (*To Ts'ao's generals, standing in the distance*) Which of you will engage in a contest with me? Come on, come and give battle! (*They attack and are defeated, pursued by Chao, who says*) I, Chao Yün, have slain seventenths of the enemy. I feel as if I were entering No Man's Land. Let me see how the young Prince is faring. Ah, he is still fast asleep! To think that I, Chao Tzŭ-lung, should have fought and won such a battle! it kindled me to put forth all my vigour; it made me an object of dread. With my long spear and short sword I have proved my virtue. At Ch'ang-pan P'o I saved the little Prince. Who will not hear of the valiant Chao Tzŭ-lung? (*Again he is attacked by four of Ts'ao's generals whom he puts to rout; and the stage is cleared for the next scene*).

Scene XII

Enter Chang Fei bristling, his eyes popping in every direction.

CHANG FEI. I wonder why Chao Yün has not returned? (*Enter Chao*).

CHAO. How are you, brother?

CHANG FEI. Make haste and cross the bridge; the enemy is close on your heels. I'll hold the bridge until you cross it. (*Chao does so. Exit*).

CHANG FEI. Ai ya! Just see them come up, like a torrent flooding heaven and earth, and only me, single-handed, to resist them. What shall I do? Aha, I've a sudden inspiration. (*To soldiers*) Lop the branches off those trees, tie them to the horses' tails and gallop to and fro. The clouds of dust you raise will gull the enemy! They'll think I've an army behind me. (*Takes up his station on the bridge,—i.e., a chair—with spear poised ready for action and lusty guffaws*).

Enter Ts'ao Ts'ao, leading his generals.

TS'AO (*to generals*). The road lies straight ahead : why don't they advance ?

A GENERAL. There's a man on the bridge. He is blocking the way. Our captains fear an ambush.

TS'AO. Go and find out who it is.

GENERAL. Hi ! You on the bridge there, what name do you go by ?

CHANG FEI. I am the great general Chang I-tê of Yen. *So formidable is the mere sound of his voice that Ts'ao's general falls off his horse in panic groaning :* " Alack-a-day ! "

TS'AO. Ai ya ! I had long heard that Kuan Yü and Chao Yün had a third sworn-brother named Chang I-tê, a hero of heroes, a man in a million ! On seeing him to-day for the first time I am almost stricken dumb !

CHANG FEI (*bellowing like a bull*). What's the meaning of this, you cowards ? If you will not fight, why don't you run away ?

TS'AO. All of you retreat at once !

Exeunt, except Chang Fei.

CHANG FEI (*roars with laughter and says*). Tear down this bridge without delay ! (*His soldiers do so and retire*).

Re-enter Ts'ao and his generals. A messenger reports that Chang Fei had only twenty men, and tells of the branches tied to horses' tails, and of the bridge's destruction.

TS'AO (*to messenger*). Run and make further investigations, then report to me. (*To generals*) Muster the cavalry and gallop in pursuit before it is too late.

SCENE XIII

After escaping, Chang Fei meets Liu Pei, and boasts about his trick and the destruction of the bridge. Liu Pei condemns this action, foreseeing that Ts'ao Ts'ao will be sure to realize how matters stand and hasten in pursuit. In the meantime Chao Yün reaches Liu Pei's camp with A-tou, whom he delivers safe and sound. Liu Pei angrily pushes the child aside, saying : " To preserve that suckling I nearly lost my

most loyal champion, a general whose whole body is
one mass of courage ! " †

Finis

*   *   *

The sequels to this play are *Shê Chan Ch'ün Ju*, " The Debate
with the League of Scholars" ; *Chieh Chien*, " Borrowing Arrows" ;
Chieh Tung Fêng, " Borrowing an East Wind " ; *Huo Shao Chan
Ch'uan*, " The Burning of the Boats " ; and *Hua Jung Tao*, " The
Road to Hua Jung," where Kuan Yü captures Ts'ao Ts'ao only to
release him (Ts'ao's second capture and release), for which K'ung-
ming threatens to behead Kuan Yü.

Ch'ang-pan P'o requires a tremendous cast : our printed version
is the mere framework of colossal technical feats, prodigies of
precise and supple movement. Such is the rhythmic beauty of the
scenes that the mind need hardly follow : the eye becomes intoxicated
by the human kaleidoscope shifted in continual harmony on the
retina. The substance of the play will be found in the *San Kuo Chih
Yen-i* (see Mr. C. H. Brewitt-Taylor's version, Vol. I, Chapters
XLI, XLII). Chinese theatrical technique imposes a form on this
diffuse and straggling material. Chao Yün, alias Chao Tzŭ-lung,
gains the proportions of a full-fledged hero, whereas Liu Pei, or Liu
Hsüan-tê, later to become Emperor of Shu (modern Szech'uan)
is relegated to a comparatively subordinate rôle. Kan Fu Jên was
A-tou's mother, but Mi Fu Jên, who sacrificed her life for the
child, has been singled out for special praise by poets. One bard
wrote : " Her comely form was hidden in the cold, lonely waters
of a well, while winds blew overhead. Her spotless life, her
words, her acts, were wholly admirable. Bright as a crimson
sun in an azure sky were her noble spirit and her loyalty . . . . .
I've writ, that ages hence men may feel abashed and emulate a
woman."

The gleaming, vermilion-faced Kuan Yü appears once or twice
during the play, accompanied by four men who carry large square-
shaped blue, red, green and black flags inscribed with the emblem
T'ai-chi, (the " grand origin, extreme, or terminus " of Chinese
cosmogony). Since he merely passes on his way to borrow troops
from Liu Ch'i of Chiang-hsia, a relative of Liu Pei's, we have not
considered it necessary to include him in the cast.

No actor has yet excelled Yang Hsiao-lou in the rôle of Chao
Yün.

---

† Literally : gall.

Mɪ Hᴇɴɢ (*sings*). In spite of my vaulting ambition, luck has been against me. I am like a dragon in shallow water: suddenly there is a thunder-clap, and he sails through wind and cloud to the skies.

CHI KU MA TS'AO 擊 鼓 罵 曹

BEATING THE DRUM AND CURSING TS'AO

Also called *Ch'ün Ch'ên Yen* : " Official Banquet." A *hsi-p'i* play.

PERIOD : End of Han and beginning of the Three Kingdoms.

DRAMATIS PERSONÆ

MI HÊNG, a young scholar	*Chêng-shêng*
TS'AO TS'AO, Prime Minister of Han	*Ching*
K'UNG JUNG, one of his advisers	*Shêng*
CHANG LIAO, one of his generals	*Shêng*

SCENE I

MI HÊNG (*by way of prologue*). Great is my ambition. I possess ingenuity, knowledge and experience. Furthermore, I possess ability. (*Recites a line of verse*) Words gush from my lips like a torrent : on artifice I rely. If a man makes most of his inborn strength, a king or a marquis he'll die. (*Speaks*) My surname is Mi, my name is Hêng, and I am also styled Chêng-p'ing. I am a native of the P'ing-yüan district in Shansi and was born in the village of Hsiao-i. From earliest youth I have read many books and my scholarship is considerable. K'ung Jung, Governor of Pei-hai, being a close friend of mine, has recommended me to Ts'ao Ts'ao. Though all men know that Ts'ao Ts'ao is Prime Minister, he is really a traitor to the Han dynasty. No thoroughly decent and educated man can respect him. But I am about to enter his palace to-day, and shall have to adapt myself to circumstances as they arise. I shall see how he treats me. Never having encountered the mighty and the powerful, I am apprehensive of blundering in etiquette and injuring my prospects. (*Sings*) In spite of my vaulting ambition, luck has been against me. I am like a dragon in shallow water : suddenly there is a thunder-clap, and he sails away through wind and cloud to the skies.   (*Exit*).

TS'AO TS'AO (*enters singing in hsi-p'i yao-pan*). For years the Three Kingdoms have been ravaged by war. Daily I ponder and scheme to annihilate the States of Wu and Shu, so that the Empire may be blessed with peace and prosperity.

CHANG LIAO (*enters singing in hsi-p'i yao-pan*). The Prime Minister has requested me to draft a letter for him.* (*Speaks*) My respects to you, Prime Minister.

Ts'ao bids him take a seat, Chang thanks him.

TS'AO. Have you written the letter according to my instructions ?

CHANG. It is written. But who will you send to deliver it ?

TS'AO. Yesterday K'ung Jung recommended a man named Mi Hêng. I shall send him.

K'UNG JUNG (*enters singing in hsi-p'i yao-pan*). I have already told Mi Hêng to call on the Prime Minister. (*Speaks*) My respects to you, Prime Minister.

TS'AO. Is Mi Hêng coming too ?

K'UNG. He is outside, awaiting your summons.

TS'AO. Bid him enter.

K'UNG. I obey your commands. (*To Mi*) Mi Hêng, please come in.

MI HÊNG. Here I am. (*Sings in k'uai êrh-liu-pan*) Ts'ao's palace inspires me with awe. It is protected by guards on every side : it is like the Court of the Emperor himself ! (*To Ts'ao*) Prime Minister, you are above : I, Mi Hêng, salute you, Sir.

TS'AO. On coming to visit me you should follow the usual ceremony. You do not even kneel. This is really most reprehensible !

---

* Inviting the support of Liu Piao, a distant kinsman of the House of Han, Governor of Ching-chou (Hupeh), and adversary of Ts'ao Ts'ao.

MI. Ah me! I was as courteous as it was within my power to be. Yet there he sits tight without a single move, neither acknowledging nor returning my salutation. Instead, he reproaches me for not prostrating myself before him. I had heard that no gentleman could respect him. Now that my eyes behold him in the flesh, this rumour turns out to be true. K'ung Jung, you made a sad mistake in recommending me to such a boor! (*Sings*) Men say that Ts'ao Ts'ao's crafty. He is on a par with Chao Kao of Ch'in,* a deceiver of his sovereign, an interloper in affairs of state, and an arrogant, overbearing blackguard. He can rely on his troops to terrorize and oppress the Emperor. While I stand in his presence, I have not the slightest fear of his soldiers or of his weapons displayed with such ostentation. (*Proceeds to laugh contemptuously*).

TS'AO. What are you laughing about?

MI. I laugh because you have not a single man of ability in your service, in spite of all your panoply and power.

TS'AO. Every one of my subordinates is a man of outstanding genius. My civil officers are more than competent to govern the Empire, and my generals to pacify the land. What do you mean by saying that I have no capable men?

MI. Tell me which of your civil officers are honest, or which of your generals brave?

TS'AO. Among my civil officials I can count Hsün Yü, Hsün Yu, Kuo Chia and Ch'êng Yü. Liu Pang † had Chang Liang and Ch'ên P'ing, but even they are thrown into the shade by mine. As to military leaders, I have Li Tien, Yüeh Chin, Hsü Ch'u and Chang Liao, whereas Liu Pang had Tsên P'êng and Ma Wu, neither of whom

---

* A eunuch in the service of the First Emperor and a byword for duplicity.

† First Emperor of the Han dynasty 202 B.C.

can bear comparison with my generals. My brother Ts'ao Jên is the most brilliant genius in the Empire, and Hsia-ho Tun is the bravest general in the world. Can you still maintain that I have no capable men ?

MI. You say these subordinates of yours are men of ability ; I declare they are nothing of the kind.

TS'AO. What is your opinion of them ?

MI. Let me enlighten you. As for your civil officials, you might allow Hsün Yü and Hsün Yu to condole with the dead ; perhaps Kuo Chia and Ch'êng Yü are fit to sweep graves. Li Tien and Yüeh Chin at a pinch could herd cattle and horses. Chang Liao and Hsü Ch'u might be employed to beat drums and clang gongs. Ts'ao Tzŭ-hsiao might be allotted the post of some money-grubbing prefect. The rest of them are mere jackanapes and gluttons, riffraff not worth mentioning.

TS'AO. And what special talents have you, that you dare to brag like this ?

MI. Since childhood I have studied all the classics, astronomy, geography, the three doctrines* and the nine systems of philosophy. I am thoroughly versed in these. I am qualified to serve emperors such as Yao and Shun as minister, and stand beside Confucius and Yen Tzŭ in virtue. I am the most illustrious scholar in the Empire. How could I join a gang of traitors and corrupt scoundrels like yourself ! K'ung Jung ! You were mistaken in recommending me to him. (*Sings*) Apart from my ambition, my learning and talents are as high as the heavens. I care not for pelf, but heroes I revere. My dignity and fame are universal. How could I stoop to serve a traitor like Ts'ao ?

CHANG LIAO. Mi Hêng, your remarks are outrageous. Such an insult to the Prime Minister deserves the drawing of my sword. (*Draws to strike*).

---

* Confucianism Taoism and Buddhism.

MI HÊNG. Why draw your sword, Chang Liao? (*Offering his neck*) Come on, then: kill me if you wish! K'UNG JUNG (*sings*). General, calm your anger, pray excuse him.

TS'AO. Don't soil your precious weapon, General. Let him alone for the nonce. I have a way to deal with him.

CHANG LIAO. I'll let him off this time.

MI. Ahem. I dare say you will!

TS'AO. Mi Hêng, to-morrow being the festival of New Year, I shall give a great banquet in the Palace to all my officials. I happen to be short of a drummer-boy and can confer this post on you. Are you disposed to accept it?

K'UNG JUNG (*aside*). You can endure it for a while, Mi Hêng. Do say that you are willing.

MI. Hm, yes. I'll play the drummer.

TS'AO. You will have to be here to-morrow morning early : if you come late you will be punished according to martial law. (*To Chang Liao*) Now put him out of the tent.

CHANG LIAO (*to Mi*). Get out of here : away with you!

MI (*laughs ironically and proceeds to sing in êrh-liu-pan*). No doubt the rebel prides himself on his cunning. To mortify a hero he appoints me his drummer. The more I ponder it, the more I smart. But when I beat the drum to-morrow I'll put that brigand out of countenance. Though I'll tolerate it for to-day, I have a capital plan to subvert his. (*Exit*).

K'UNG JUNG (*sings*). Mi Hêng has talent but his nature is too proud : I fear he is likely to lose his head by the knife. (*Exit*).

CHANG LIAO (*sings*). Mi Hêng is far too arrogant. The Prime Minister should have him executed. (*Exit*).

TS'AO. Mi Hêng is ignorant of the projects I have in mind : there would be no point in killing him just now. (*Exit*).

Scene II

MI HÊNG (*behind the stage is heard saying in chiao-pan*). I am all prepared. (*He then appears, singing*) My parley with Ts'ao has so infuriated me that my mind is like tangled hemp. In quaffing wine with a good friend a thousand cups are too few ; if speech is inapt for the occasion half a sentence is too much. I have just wasted precious words on Ts'ao Ts'ao. To-morrow being New Year's day, he is to banquet all his officials and I am appointed chief drummer : it is clear that he intends to hold me up to ridicule. I'll take advantage of this opportunity to insult him before the entire assembly, for which he will probably kill me. But at any rate I shall leave a reputation behind me for denouncing a traitor. My name will be handed down in history throughout the ages. And though I am aware of the fierce tiger at large on the mountains I'll beard him in his den. I am like Han Hsin,* who was insulted for "crawling under the fork," and then became a general and saved the House of Han. To-morrow I will betake myself to Ts'ao's camp and insult him while beating the drum. Though I may lose my life, my name will travel to the uttermost ends of the earth. (*Exit*).

Scene III

FOUR HIGH OFFICIALS (*approach, saying*). To-day is the first of the New Year and the Prime Minister Ts'ao has invited us to his banquet. This is the door of his palace : there are captains on guard. Please announce our arrival.

Chang Liao appears and invites them in ; he then goes to inform Ts'ao that his guests have arrived and returns to

---

* D. 196 B.C. While a youth he was dared by one of the bullies in the market-place of Huai-yin (Kiangsu) either to fight or " pass under my fork " —i.e. crawl between his legs. He preferred the latter and was called a coward, but subsequently had a brilliant though chequered career and was ranked as one of the Three Heroes.

*bid them be seated. Ts'ao enters pompously to the strains of
martial music.*

OFFICIALS. We have come, Your Excellency, to pay
our respects.

TS'AO. I return the compliment. To-day being
New Year's festival I have a banquet specially prepared.
Pray drink a few bumpers of wine to honour the
occasion.

OFFICIALS. We fear we are putting Your Excellency
to a deal of inconvenience.

TS'AO. General Chang Liao, let wine be poured and
the cups be filled. (*All sit and drink to each other's health*).

TS'AO. I have a new drummer, gentlemen, whom I
have ordered to play for us so that we may relish our
wine the better.

OFFICIALS. We look forward to hearing him.

TS'AO (*to servants*). Bid the drummer come in.
They obey, and Mi Hêng is heard behind the stage:
" I'm coming".

MI HÊNG (*enters singing in hsi-p'i tao-pan*). The treacherous ministers are plotting against the House of Han.
As in the time when the Ch'u and Han generals* were
struggling for supremacy, here is the traitor Ts'ao Ts'ao
deceiving the Emperor†, and subjecting all the officials
to his will. For my country's sake I'll extirpate the
traitors. But I bear no murderer's knife. In the centre
sits Ts'ao the usurper, and his colleagues beside him.
New Year's day is an unlucky day for him ! Feigning
madness I'll strip myself stark naked and curse the tyrant.
(*Slipping off his outer blue gown, he sings*) As I swagger
along in my old blue gown I am ready to burst with
rage. Without even pausing for breath I'll rush into
his camp.

---

* Hsiang Chi and Liu Pang.

† Hsien Ti, who was a mere puppet in his hands.

TWO ADJUTANTS (*stop him, saying*). Here, drummer, the Prime Minister is holding a banquet for all his officials. How dare you exhibit yourself in such tattered old clothes ? It's positively indecent.

MI (*sings*). You pair of petty officers are making a noise about nothing.

ADJUTANTS. To say that we are making a noise is laughable, ha, ha !

MI (*sings*). You need not laugh. Hearken to me : I have precedents set by the ancients. There was Chiang * who fished with a barbless hook, and Chang Liang † also ; remember that these both suffered dire poverty and distress. In divesting myself of my frayed blue gown I'll exchange it for one of purple.

ADJUTANTS. How can an impoverished, supercilious creature like you presume to compare yourself with the venerable statesmen of yore ?

MI HÊNG (*sings*). You fellows despise me, but mind you don't mistake a tiger for a rabbit. Some day good luck will come to me : I'll don the robes of ceremony with the belt of jade and hold high rank at Court.

ADJUTANTS. What dreamy babble is this in broad daylight ?

MI HÊNG (*sings*). Don't say that I am indulging in day-dreams. Before you know it I'll ascend to the skies. I'll remove my remaining rags and rush like a hero into the midst of the camp.

ADJUTANTS. Wo there ! You can't go in stark naked like that. The Minister will have you punished.

---

* Chiang Tzǔ-ya, or Lü Shang, 11th and 12th century B.C. Wên Wang discovered him fishing with a straight piece of iron instead of a hook (upon which the fishes willingly impaled themselves), and appointed him his chief counsellor. Chiang was eighty years old at the time.

† Chang Liang, died 187 B.C. After his plot to kill the First Emperor of Ch'in failed he met an old man who had dropped his shoe over a bridge. As he went to fetch it the old man presented him with a book on military tactics, saying : " Read this and you will become the teacher of princes." He subsequently became counsellor to the first emperor of the Han dynasty ; one of the Three Heroes.

MA LIEN-LIANG AS MI HÊNG BEATING THE DRUM

Chi Ku Ma Ts'ao

MI. I am willing to suffer all the punishment your Minister can mete out. Lead me outside his hall and watch what he does to me.

ADJUTANTS (*to Ts'ao*). The drummer, Your Excellency.

TS'AO. Tell him to beat the drum thrice.

Mi does accordingly.

OFFICIALS. Hark! what beautiful tones of drumming! Let us enjoy a few more bumpers of wine.

TS'AO (*sings*). The roll of the drum resounds like thunder. We'll empty three more cups of wine.

Chang Liao serves it with a wrathful countenance and K'ung Jung, suffused with shame, goes out to interview Mi Hêng, who stops drumming and struts in full view of the assembled guests.

TS'AO. Ah me! (*Sings*) Mi Hêng is naked as he was born. I'll keep my temper for the moment and question him. Mi Hêng!

MI HÊNG. Ts'ao Ts'ao!

TS'AO. Why do you call me by name?

MI HÊNG. You addressed me as Mi Hêng, therefore I address you as Ts'ao Ts'ao.

TS'AO. I have not offended you in any way: here I am entertaining my guests and you appear naked before us. What sort of behaviour is this?

MI. I have stripped to show my own white body. I wish to prove that I am a gentleman immaculate and pure.

TS'AO. If you are a pure and immaculate gentleman, who is a foul blackguard I would like to know?

MI. You are.

TS'AO. I am the ruling Prime Minister: how dare you apply such an epithet to me?

MI. Listen, and I will tell you.

TS'AO. Proceed.

MI. You cannot distinguish between the great and the low, hence your vision is turbid. You are deaf to the advice of loyal ministers ; hence your ears are turbid. You have never studied the classics ; hence your speech is foul. You are always scheming to usurp the throne ; hence your heart is foul. I am the most distinguished scholar in the Empire, yet you appoint me your drummer to insult me. Ts'ao Ts'ao ! You are a traitor, the mean, befuddled spawn of an abject generation. (*Sings in k'uai-pan*) In the days of yore Wên Wang sought out Chiang Tzŭ-ya, who became his chief counsellor : Sovereign and Minister rode together in the same chariot. It was right and proper that the Prince should seek a loyal Minister to assist him in governing the Empire. I am a man of dignity and talent, yet me you compel to be your paltry drummer ! Being a Minister of State will avail you naught : your treacherous name will go down through the ages.

TS'AO (*sings in hsi-p'i yao-pan*). I have a great army under valiant generals. Who would dare to spurn my glory and prevent it from being blazed throughout the Empire ? I am a brilliant strategist, and my plans are laid long in advance. I am no paltry insignificant drummer.

MI. Rubbish ! (*Sings*) This Ts'ao Ts'ao vastly over-rates himself : he is only a pretentious humbug. Your position at Court as Prime Minister will avail you naught. The beat of my drum is like thunder. It is to warn you that a treacherous cur will have no decent place of burial.

OFFICIALS. Prime Minister, why do you sit in such dejection ?

TS'AO. That drummer prates absurdly. My argument with him has put me out of temper. That is why I am sitting here in gloom.

OFFICIALS. Let us go and inquire what induced him to talk in such a manner.

TS'AO. Thank you, gentlemen, for venturing to trouble yourselves on my account.

OFFICIALS. Here, drummer. What is your name and surname, and where is your home? Let us hear everything distinctly.

MI (*sings*). I can hardly express or subdue the hatred in my heart. If you will hear me, gentlemen, I shall try to tell you all. I am a native of P'ing-yüan in Shansi. My surname is Mi, my name is Hêng, and I am also styled Chêng-p'ing. My personal friend K'ung Jung recommended me to the traitor Ts'ao. But Ts'ao is unaware of my special gifts : I would rather be a loyal man's drudge than a prince among traitors.

TS'AO. Mi Hêng, your talents are confined to the fluency of your tongue.

MI (*sings*). The traitor says that I am a mere quibbler. The same might be observed of Chang I and Su Ch'in*. When I reach the summit of my career, I'll obliterate Ts'ao with a single stroke of my pen.

TS'AO. Gentlemen !

OFFICIALS. We hear you, Prime Minister.

TS'AO. Mi Hêng declares that I'm a traitor. How have I shown myself to deserve this appellation ?

OFFICIALS. Your Excellency is a great and loyal Minister. (*Ts'ao laughs triumphantly*).

MI. In your youth you were an insignificant official, an adopted son of the eunuch Ts'ao. Since you have attained high rank you have chosen to forget your ancestry. Your treacherous name will abide throughout the ages.†

---

* Both clever political adventurers of 4th cent. B.C. who relied on their tongues and rose from plebeian rank to high positions (MAYERS' *Chinese Reader's Manual*, Nos. 17 and 626). See p. 136.

† Prophetic words !

CHANG LIAO. It exasperates me to have to listen to such ranting. How dare he curse and slander the Prime Minister like this ! I'll draw my precious blade.

MI. At it again !

OFFICIALS (*singing in unison*). General, curb your fury ; be slow to draw your sword.

TS'AO. General, spare him yet awhile. Don't soil your precious blade on such a creature.

CHANG LIAO. Humph ! I'll let the scoundrel off then.

MI. Don't thwart him, gentlemen ! Chang Liao, you imagine that I am unaware of your identity. You were formerly an officer under Lü Pu. When your leader was captured and put to death by Ts'ao, you grovelled to your master's murderer. A man that turns his back on his master for material advantage ; a soldier terrified of death, who would rather endure life as a slave ; how dare you stand there blustering and drawing your sword against me ? You are really a fox posing as a majestic tiger, a dog snarling because it's egged on by its master, in short, a shameless coward.

TS'AO. Mi Hêng, I have a letter which I wish you to take to Ching-chou ; if Liu Piao will pay allegiance to me I will give you an official post.

MI. Stuff ! Nothing would induce me to comply with such a request. Who wants to be a hack or cow of yours ?

OFFICIALS. Prime Minister ! (*Sing*) Pray calm your indignation for the present, and we'll persuade Mi Hêng to go to Ching-chou. (*Speak*) Mi Hêng, the Prime Minister wishes you to go to Ching-chou and deliver a letter to Liu Piao demanding his allegiance. He will secure an official post for you. But if you decline he'll be vexed and take your head off. Haven't you an old mother, or a wife and children relying on you for support ? Mr. Mi, you had better give this matter your careful consideration.

MI (*sings*). Since all of you gentlemen combine to advise me, I feel like one who is startled out of a dream. From ancient times it has been said : Before reproving others, amend your own defects. I'll rub my chest and soothe my rage awhile. (*Puts on his clothes and sings in k'uai-pan*). Under the circumstances I have no alternative but to hasten and acknowledge my error. I am willing to proceed to Ching-chou as your delegate.

TS'AO. Mi Hêng ! (*Sings*) You yourself are entirely to blame for such errors as have been committed. If the speech is inapt, half a sentence is excessive. Persuade Liu Piào to submit, and I shall guarantee that you'll wear the black gauze cap and purple gown.

MI (*sings*). Make haste and give me the letter. I'll set forth at once and take the ferry across the river. If my subtlety fails I'll willingly perish on strange soil and become a wandering demon. (*Exit*).

TS'AO. A deplorably arrogant creature, that Mi Hêng ! I can foresee that when he reaches Ching-chou his life will, very probably, be curtailed ! (*Exeunt omnes*).

Finis

* * *

The incidents in this curious play "with a head but no tail" as the Chinese express it, will be found in Vol. I, Chapter XXIII of the *San Kuo*. It throws an interesting light on Ts'ao Ts'ao's methods of getting rid of people indirectly. Mi Hêng reminds one of Apemantus in *Timon of Athens ;* but his is the star-rôle in the conflict between two arrogant personalities. The high-flown bookworm's contact with realities unhinged him ; his tactless manner put Ts'ao Ts'ao's back up from the start, and he courted his own downfall.

It is a historical fact that his manipulation of the drum moved the audience to tears, and being the cynosure of every eye, he "slipped off his frayed robe and stood in full view, naked as he was born. The assembled guests covered their faces." (On the stage he merely doffs his outer robe, but the actor must be a proficient drummer : Yen Chü-p'êng excels in this arduous rôle).

Ts'ao Ts'ao sent him to Liu Piao, whom he lampooned ; even so his life was spared yet awhile. When asked why he did not put Mi Hêng to death Liu Piao retorted : " He shamed Ts'ao Ts'ao, but Ts'ao did not kill him as he feared to lose popular favour. So he sent him to me, thinking to borrow my hand to slay him and so suffer the loss of my good name. I have sent him on to Huang Tsu to show Ts'ao that I understood." It was reserved for Huang Tsu, the crazy governor of Chiang-hsia (Hupeh) to kill him when both were the worse for liquor, because Mi Hêng had told him : " You are like a god in a temple ; you sit still and receive sacrifice, but the lack of intelligence is pitiful "... Ts'ao Ts'ao heard of his death with pleasure. " The putrid bookworm has just cut himself up with his own sharp tongue," he observed.

CH'I SHUANG HUI 奇雙會

An Extraordinary Twin Meeting

Also called *Fan Ma Chi* : " A Horse-dealer's Record " ; and *San La* : " The Three Hand-pulls."   A *k'un-ch'ü (k'un-ch'iang)* play.

Period : Uncertain, probably Ming.

Dramatis Personæ

Li Ch'i, an old prisoner.	*Lao-shêng*
Li Kuei-chih, his daughter	*Ch'ing-i*
Chao Ch'ung, Magistrate of Pao-ch'êng ...	*Hsiao-shêng*
Li Pao-t'ung, Li Ch'i's son, alias Li-t'ai	*Hsiao-shêng*
Hu Ching, Retired Magistrate of Pao-ch'êng ...	*Ch'ou*
Chin Tzǔ or Warder of Pao-ch'êng Gaol ...	*Ch'ou*
Soldiers, servants, etc.	

Synopsis

In the Hsi-an district of Shensi there lived a horse-dealer named Li Ch'i, whose wife died after giving birth to a son and daughter, named Pao-t'ung and Kuei-chih respectively. Subsequently he married a woman of the Yang family named San Ch'un. While he was in Szech'uan buying horses, his second wife was enjoying a liaison with one T'ien Wang, the beadle of the place. Fearing that the children would " tell father," she drove them out of the house. The desperate little boy jumped into the river, but he was rescued by a fisherman called Li, who took him home and reared him as a son, giving him the name of Li-t'ai. He eventually distinguished himself in the examinations and obtained the appointment of Judge on Circuit. The little girl was adopted by a family named Liu and married, in due course, to a scholar named Chao Ch'ung whom she accompanied to Pao-ch'êng in Shensi upon his appointment as magistrate of that place.

Li Ch'i returned from Szech'uan in the meantime to find both children missing. His wife tells him that they had suddenly died of a fever. He proceeds to question the slave-girl Ch'un Hua, who dares not tell him the truth : alarmed for her own safety she goes and hangs herself. The adulterers now proceed to accuse Li Ch'i of having caused her suicide by an assault upon her virtue. They bribe Hu Ching, the local magistrate, who has Li Ch'i tortured and cast into prison. There he remains till Hu Ching hands over his magistracy to Chao Ch'ung (Kuei-chih's husband).

On taking up his post Chao Ch'ung sets forth on a tour of inspection, leaving his wife at the yamen. One night she hears such pitiful sounds of lamentation from the adjoining gaol that she sends her maid to make inquiries. When she hears that one Li Ch'i, who has been a captive for many years, is responsible, Kuei-chih is at once reminded of her own father, and orders him to be admitted to her chamber. After questioning him she discovers that he really is her father, but being the magistrate's wife she decides not to make herself known to him yet. So she gives him money for necessities and warns the gaolers to treat him kindly. Her husband returns : instead of greeting him joyfully she bursts into tears and tells him about her discovery. " But your name is Liu," he says ; " how can this Li Ch'i be your father ? " She then recounts how she and her brother were driven out by their stepmother, and her subsequent adoption by the Liu family. " I too was driven from home by my stepmother," says Chao Ch'ung ; " I must think of a plan to obtain Li Ch'i's release."

Li Pao-t'ung, the Judge on Circuit, is about to arrive at Pao-ch'êng, so Chao Ch'ung prepares a report on Li Ch'i's case. Since women were not allowed to petition in person, he tells Kuei-chih to dress in male attire and accompany him to the Judge's yamen, crying that she has a grievance to redress. The former magistrate Hu Ching has also come to welcome the Judge, who is Kuei-chih's brother. On reading the petition Li is amazed to find that it concerns his own family and that the suppliant is closely related to him, but he is considerably baffled by Kuei-chih's disguise. Feigning anger he threatens to inflict torture if there be any infraction of the truth. Kuei-chih prostrates herself in terror, and her hat falls off exposing " a woman's crowning glory." Whereupon the Judge discreetly conducts her to his private apartment, and soon ascertains her identity. They remain closeted together for so long that her jealous husband suspects the worst and creates an uproar. The Judge goes out and asks the reason for this unseemly conduct ; then drags him to his apartment without any further explanation. Chao Ch'ung is too alarmed to utter a word. The Judge then summons Li Ch'i. After confirming that he is his long-lost father, he pulls him in turn to his apartment—whence the title of the play, San La : " The Three Hand-pulls." Li Ch'i is thunderstruck at the scene that ensues, for the magistrate Chao Ch'ung, his wife Kuei-chih and last the Judge Li all filially fall on their knees before him. Enlightened at last, the old man's joy is boundless. The corrupt magistrate, Hu Ching, commits suicide by jumping down a well. Pao-t'ung then orders his stepmother and her paramour to be brought before him and executed.

THE PLAY

By way of prologue an actor representing the spirit of the planet Venus appears on the stage, saying: Li Ch'i lies in prison suffering great agony of mind. Since he cannot communicate with his daughter, I have deputed the spirit of an owl to transmit his plaint to her, so that she may be aware of his plight and take steps to redress his wrongs.*

ACT I. SCENE I

WARDER (*enters muttering to himself*). I am the warder of the city gaol and nine out of ten are my foes. If they are in funds, they are my friends, if not, they are my foes, and there's no end to my beating and cursing, for what have *I* to fear? Pay up, say I, or grin and bear it. (*Speaks*) They all say that I am a tyrant, more cruel than the King of Hell himself. Those who fall into my clutches have two of their three souls frightened to death.† I am the warder of Pao-ch'êng district gaol. The former magistrate Hu Ching entrusted old Li Ch'i to my tender mercies. It is an age since he came here, yet he has never yielded me a single cash. I'll call him out and ask for money. If he refuses I'll take the skin off his back. (*Shouts*) Here you, Li Ch'i!

LI CH'I (*quavers from the back of the stage*). I am coming. (*Enters and sings*) Great is my mental anguish, but to whom can I relate my grievances? I had only my son and daughter, and where are they now? Oh, Heaven above, why inflict all this pain and punishment

---

* The Chinese believe that when a person is innocent, some beneficent spirit above will intercede for him. In this case it was the Spirit of Venus, and since the owl can see by night, it was used as a medium.

† An expression derived from the Chinese animistic belief that man has three souls and seven *p'o*. " The souls come from the *Yang*, or Heaven. The *p'o* come from the *Yin*, or Earth. In life these act in unison." See Clifford H. PLOPPER : *Chinese Religion seen through the Proverb*, Chapter IV, and *The Religious System of China*, by J. J. M. DE GROOT, Book II, Part I.

on miserable me? If I be guilty of any wrong, let the King of Hades take me.

WARDER. Make haste, old bones, be brisk! What are you loitering for?

LI CH'I. Alas, the worst has come to the worst! (*Sings*) Hearing your dread summons, elder brother, I am palsied with fright. Here in the presence of the Prison-God I kneel to you, entreating that you will be merciful and spare my life. (*Kneels*) Elder brother! * I have never been wanting in politeness or respect towards you . . .

WARDER. That'll do. Stand up!

LI CH'I (*speaks*). Why have you summoned me, Sir?

WARDER. There's no oil for the lamps. Money is needed ; if you have any it is high time to hand it over.

LI CH'I. In such dire straits how can I produce money?

WARDER. Just listen to this : those who dwell on mountains depend on timber for a living ; those who dwell by a river depend upon the waters.† Never mind how much it is, you have got to pay up; otherwise, look out for yourself! I'll give you a taste of the ankle-squeezers, and even worse.

LI CH'I. In truth, elder brother, I haven't a cash in the world. Please, Sir, be merciful to an unfortunate destitute.

WARDER. If every one of you wanted my mercy I would have to starve. Pay up or I'll put you to the torture, and that's flat.

LI CH'I. From ancient times it has been said : " Pity the orphans and the friendless, cherish the aged and assist the poor " ;—spare an old man what's left to him of life ! Better save one life than build a pagoda of

---

* Merely a term of respect.

† e.g. Il faut que le prêtre vive de l'autel—S. Paul.

seven tiers. Brother, in your official capacity I beg
you to perform an act of kindness.

WARDER (*sings*). Hearken to him! I am seething
with rage, my teeth grind so that I can hardly open my
mouth to speak. With one kick I'll send you sprawling
in the dust—a cursed old convict to prate like that! Why,
ever since you came here I haven't seen the colour of a
brass cash. I'll strap you on the rack ; I'll shackle your
hands and feet ; I'll bind your hair to the general's
pillar and flog you within an inch of your life. I'll drive
nails into the soles of your feet ; I'll be the King of
Hell and you'll be a puking devil. You are doomed
as well as damned !   (*Exit Warder*).

LI CH'I (*sings*). I weep for my daughter Kuei-chih :
I weep for my son Pao-t'ung. I know not whether
you be dead or alive, or if you know of my anguish in
this prison. My children, oh, my children !

The owl sent by the planet Venus arrives in the shape of
a man with a horse-hair duster and transmits Li Ch'i's
plaint—by repeating the words from a chair—to the inner
apartments of the yamen.

SCENE II

KUEI-CHIH (*enters, singing*). I hear the drum in the
watch-tower beating the third watch. It is midnight,
yet I hear a sound of wailing.

KUEI-CHIH (*calls maid*). Bid the house-steward go behind the yamen and inquire who is grieving so piteously. (*Speaks*) My husband Chao Ch'ung has gone into the country to inspect the cultivation of crops : he has not yet returned. Suddenly I hear a sound as of terrible weeping. Who can it be, so late at night ? . . .

House-steward returns to say that the gaolers maintain they have heard nothing.

KUEI-CHIH. Tell them they must go to the men's quarters and find out. They must go from cell to cell.

Steward goes again and questions Warder.

WARDER (*reluctantly*). Yes, there is an old convict here called Li Ch'i. He was imprisoned by the former lord magistrate Hu Ching. As a result of torture, he is covered with boils and sores. That's why he is making such a din.

Steward reports to the maid, who tells her mistress.

KUEI-CHIH. Ai-ya ! It seems to me that he bears my Father's name. Perchance it is he, but what crime could he have committed ? As I am separated from him by so many buildings, how shall I be able to see him and ascertain the true facts ? Though many names in this world are identical, I feel I should send for him and find out. (*To maid*) Go tell the yamen clerks and assistants on my behalf to get the keys and open Li Ch'i's cell and bring him to me for inquiry.

Yamen runners obey.

LI CH'I. I tremble to hear that Her Ladyship has summoned me. I wonder what she can require !

The maid announces him, and he is admitted to Kuei-chih's apartments.

KUEI-CHIH. Take a quilt off the couch and put it on the floor so that the old convict can tell me his story in greater comfort. (*Maid obeys*).

LI CH'I (*kneels*). You are above, my Lady ; I, Li Ch'i, am below.

KUEI-CHIH. Alas, I feel dizzy at the sight of this aged prisoner kneeling before me ; I know not why. (*Gazes at him kindly*) Where is your home, old prisoner ? What is your name and surname ? And what were you convicted for ? Tell me the whole story.

LI CH'I. Please hear me patiently, Your Ladyship ! (*Sings*) I could not tell all that is on my mind, nor all that I have suffered. If I should tell you the sum of my grief, Lady, you would scarce believe me. I've been nearly done to death.

KUEI-CHIH. Where is your home ?

LI CH'I. I come from Pao-ch'êng district in the prefecture of Han-chung, Shensi, and am a native of Ma-t'ou village. Li Ch'i is my name.

KUEI-CHIH. In sooth this old prisoner bears my father's name. The particulars of his birthplace are also identical. He must be my own father. I wonder what crime he committed. But stay ! there are many in the world who share a name. I must not be rash. I shall have to inquire more closely into his connections. (*To Li Ch'i*) Who was your wife and what was her maiden-name ?

LI CH'I. I married a girl of the Wang family, but she died long ago.

KUEI-CHIH. Have you a daughter ?

LI CH'I (*sings*). My wife left me a son and a daughter.

KUEI-CHIH. What are their names ?

LI CH'I. My son's name is Pao-t'ung, my daughter's is Kuei-chih. As there was nobody to look after them, my second wife Yang Shih, San-ch'un. . . .

KUEI-CHIH. What sort of trade were you engaged in ?

LI CH'I. I traded in horses, buying them at Hsi-ling and selling them in Szech'uan. It was when I returned home from Szech'uan that I found my son and daughter missing.

KUEI-CHIH. You should have asked your wife what had become of them.

LI CH'I (*sings*). When I asked her she said they had died of disease. When I asked the maid Ch'un Hua she said they had gone astray and could not be found.

KUEI-CHIH. Since both of them told you different tales, your inquiries should have been more minute.

LI CH'I. Your Ladyship! (*Sings*) I beat Ch'un Hua and she hanged herself on a room-beam. When my wife asked me why she had killed herself I said I did not know; and it was T'ien Wang the beadle who cut the body down.

KUEI-CHIH. It was a great mistake to drive Ch'un Hua to suicide and let an outsider deal with the corpse instead of attending to it yourself.

LI CH'I. Yes, I made a serious blunder there. (*Sings*) That blackguard T'ien Wang also wanted some hush-money.

KUEI-CHIH. Did you give it to him?

LI CH'I. Oh no, dear Lady. Even if I had had any I would never have given it to him. (*Sings*) How could I pay to turn truth into falsehood! T'ien Wang falsely accused me and bribed the magistrate Hu Ching, who did not trouble even to inquire into the case but promptly sentenced me to forty blows of the bamboo. Your Ladyship cannot imagine what I suffered; I could not help but sign a confession acknowledging my guilt. I hope that when your husband returns you'll ask him to investigate my case thoroughly. Woe is me, Lady, for I have been treated worse than a dog. If you succour me, your kindness will never be forgotten.

KUEI-CHIH (*aside, sings to flute accompaniment*). To hear all this grieves my heart to the core. Oh Father, my Father, that your daughter should have been enjoying a life of ease while you were enduring such anguish! He does not know who I am: how can I rescue him and save his life? (*Maid brings in the tea*).

MAID. Please take your tea, Madam. (*She rejects it*).

Why are you weeping, Madam?

KUEI-CHIH. I have been cut to the heart by this old convict's tale: I needs must weep. Go fetch me fifty ounces of silver. (*Maid goes out and returns with the money*). Give it to Li Ch'i and tell him it is all for his own expenses. And bid the yamen people take good care of him: he is not to be starved or maltreated or fleeced of his money. Whoever ill-uses him will be severely dealt with. (*When the sum is handed to them, the gaolers sing out*: "We dare not!"). Now lead the old prisoner back to his cell, but the gaolers are to treat him kindly, remember.

LI CH'I. Thank you, my Lady. (*Sings*) I'll wait until the lord magistrate returns to his yamen: I'll tell him all about my persecutions. And if I am released from this hell of a prison and restored to my old life, I shall never forget his benevolence.

KUEI-CHIH (*sings*). As soon as my husband returns, I'll tell him all about my father's wrongs. (*Exit*).

ACT II

Chao Ch'ung appears and sends the steward to invite his wife to come in. Enter Kuei-chih and her maid.

KUEI-CHIH (*to herself*). Because of my father's plight I cannot check my tears.

CHAO CH'UNG (*rising to greet her, says*). Please be seated, my Lady.

KUEI-CHIH. You have returned, Sir; pray be seated.
Both sit, and suddenly Kuei-chih bursts into tears.

CHAO CH'UNG. Why are you weeping, wife?

KUEI-CHIH. During your absence I committed an offence against the law.

CHAO CH'UNG. What have you done that was contrary to the law?

KUEI CHIH. I had the door of the prison opened.

CHAO CH'UNG (*much alarmed*). Oh, you did, did you? If any of the convicts escaped, my career is in danger, my very life is in danger—and all on your account. How could you do such a thing?'

KUEI-CHIH (*sings*). You come back and at once begin to rail at me, instead of treating me with common kindness. (*Weeps*) Ah me!

CHAO CH'UNG. What do you mean by accusing me of harshness? A lady should not lift her skirt when walking or show her teeth when laughing, nor should she leave the inner apartments unless there be a cogent reason : such is the correct decorum.

KUEI-CHIH (*sings*). If your father happened to be in gaol, could you even enjoy the post of a seventh-grade magistrate?

CHAO CH'UNG. Your strange words give me cause for meditation. They seem to bear no relation to actuality : I cannot understand. (*Speaks*) What is the meaning behind your speech? (*Sings*) Our marriage has always been blissfully happy. If there is anything on your mind, please tell me all about it.

KUEI-CHIH. I feel entirely bowed under with sorrow : if I tell you all and you cannot take the requisite responsibility, I shall have spoken in vain.

CHAO CH'UNG. My dear wife, if you harbour any grievance, let me hear it, and I'll certainly do my utmost to redress it.

KUEI-CHIH. But if I tell you, you must not be cross.

CHAO CH'UNG. I only want you to stop crying, then I'll not be cross. Please be frank.

KUEI-CHIH (*sings*). The load of sorrow on my heart cannot be compressed into a few lone words. If I told you all, it would be the death of me.

CHAO CH'UNG. Where was your home?

KUEI-CHIH. My home was in Pao-ch'êng district, in the prefecture of Han-chung and in the village of Ma-t'ou.

CHAO CH'UNG. What was your worthy father's name?

KUEI-CHIH (*sings*). My father's name is Li Ch'i.

CHAO CH'UNG. You must be mistaken.

KUEI-CHIH. How mistaken?

CHAO CH'UNG. I thought your surname was Liu. How can you say that your father's name is Li?

KUEI-CHIH. My original surname was Li. As a child I was driven from home by my father's second wife. The Liu family found and adopted me, and when I grew up I took their surname. (*Sings*) My mother's family-name was Wang, and she died long ago. She left a boy and a girl : the son was called Pao-t'ung and I was the daughter. As there was nobody to look after us, my father married again ; his second wife was a woman of the Yang family named San-ch'un. He then went off to Szech'uan to trade in horses, and we were already scattered on his return.

CHAO CH'UNG. When your father found you both missing, he should have closely examined Yang Shih as to your whereabouts.

KUEI-CHIH (*speaks*). How can you understand the long and the short of it, my Lord? (*Sings*) He did ask Yang Shih what had become of us, and she told him that we had died of disease. When he questioned the maid Ch'un Hua, she denied all knowledge of where we were, so that he beat her and she hanged herself. When Yang Shih asked my father where the maid was, he said he did not know. On finding her corpse she ran and told one T'ien Wang, who cut the body down. Between them they concocted a tale that my father had caused her death, and filed their statement with the magistrate Hu Ching, whom they bribed. My father was arrested sentenced to forty blows, and thrown into gaol.

CHAO CH'UNG. Your father blundered in letting an outsider take the body down instead of doing it him-

self. Who was this T'ien Wang, and what did he do
for a living ?

KUEI-CHIH. He was the local beadle.

CHAO CH'UNG. My father also fell into his snare once
and suffered torture. But I doubt if he would admit it now.

KUEI-CHIH. Oh, my Lord ! If he was innocent how
could he have suffered torture ? It was because my
father was tortured that he signed a confession of guilt.

CHAO CH'UNG. Alas ! He should never have done
so. That was a fatal error.

KUEI-CHIH. My Lord, I beseech you to redress my
father's wrongs. For this single favour I'll bestow nine
in return.

CHAO CH'UNG (*sings*). My heart is wrung by this
discovery. We were both in the same predicament.
She was driven out by her stepmother, and I was driven
out by mine.

KUEI-CHIH. You too ?

CHAO CH'UNG. Yes, we were both in the same plight.
(*Both weep*). Do not grieve. Let me see your father's
confession and sentence and I'll find a way to save him.

KUEI-CHIH . All depends on you, my Lord.

CHAO CH'UNG (*sends for the document, then dismisses
the servants and says*). Let me read it to you, dear.
(*Reading*) " The accused Li Ch'i, now in Pao-ch'êng gaol,
having been found guilty of assaulting his slave-girl
Ch'un Hua, so that she went and hanged herself, the
punishment to be inflicted on him shall accordingly be
referred to the Board of Punishment of the Mid-Autumn
Assizes."

KUEI-CHIH (*weeps*). Alas for my poor dear father !

CHAO CH'UNG. Don't weep, my Lady : the Judge on
Circuit will be arriving here to-morrow. Why don't
you prepare a petition stating your father's wrongs ?

KUEI-CHIH. Excellent ! But who is to draw it up for
me ?

HAN SHIH-CH'ANG
as Li Kuei-chih

PAI YÜN-SHÊNG
as Chao Ch'ung

(Bashfulness denoted by the lady's sleeve)

Ch'i Shuang Hui

CHAO CH'UNG. That's easy enough : I am at your service. Do you fancy that I, a magistrate presiding over a district, could not even write a petition ? You belittle me too much !

KUEI-CHIH. Then I beg you, Sir, to write one for me now.

CHAO CH'UNG. But there is no one to grind the ink for me !

KUEI-CHIH. Let me grind it for you, my Lord.

CHAO CH'UNG (*sings*). In penning a petition one should state the full particulars of the case, especially concerning the petitioner, name and surname.

KUEI-CHIH. State that the petitioner's name is Li. . . .

Here there is much by-play of teasing and hesitation, as a young woman was most unwilling to divulge her given name even to her own husband. It was only known to her paternal, and in this case her adopted, parents, who had arranged the marriage and respected the daughter's reserve in this matter. Chao Ch'ung insists ; and eventually, with great coyness and reluctance, hiding her face in her sleeve, Kuei-chih reveals her name.

CHAO CH'UNG (*playfully*). Aha, Kuei-chih ! (*Sings as he writes*) The petitioner Li Kuei-chih, aged twenty-one, is a native of the Lin Yu hamlet, Ma T'ou village, Pao-ch'êng district, Shensi. Her mother, *née* Wang, died long ago ; her father then married a woman of the Yang family named San-ch'un, who drove his little son Pao-t'ung with Kuei-chih out of the house. (*The circumstances as we know them are related in full, winding up with*) I beg Your Excellency to investigate the case and release my father, whereupon our entire family will burn incense to reward Your Excellency's favour in our behalf. (*Turning to his wife*) Here is the document all written out.

KUEI-CHIH. But since the Judge on Circuit has such a big retinue, how shall I, a woman, be able to present it ?

CHAO CH'UNG. When I go to seek audience with the Judge to-morrow you can accompany me disguised as a man-servant : on arriving at the yamen you call attention to your wrongs and hand in the petition.

KUEI-CHIH. But I still have no notion how to conduct myself.

CHAO CH'UNG. Let me enlighten you. When you accompany me to-morrow to the Judge's yamen, place the petition on the top of your head, crying, " Your Excellency, I have a grievance." Then kneel down and the paper will be taken from you ; after glancing at it, the Judge will tell you to lift your head. You will reply : " I am guilty and dare not ! " He will say : " I forgive you for the present. Your case will come up for trial to-morrow morning. " That is merely the correct procedure.   (*Exeunt*).

ACT III.   SCENE I

LI PAO-T'UNG (*the Judge on Circuit comes on the stage soliloquizing*). The fragrance of pen and ink brings fame throughout the Empire. But loyalty to the Emperor and one's parents is best of all. (*Speaks*) I have received the Imperial Command to visit Pao-ch'êng and investigate how the laws are being administered. (*He proceeds to tell the story of his life*) . . . The Emperor entrusted me with the precious sword of Imperial Authority with instructions that if I discovered any acts of violence, robbery or other infractions of the law, I was first to give sentence of execution even before reporting to the Throne. To-day a court-trial is to be held : I shall order the list of cases to be brought in and see what is on the register.   (*Exit*).

SCENE II

CHAO CH'UNG (*entering*). Where is Kuei-chih ? (*She enters in man's disguise*). Be quick and call attention to your wrongs.

KUEI-CHIH. Your Excellency, I have a grievance.

HU CHING. Why don't you come to my yamen and make your appeal? It will cost you exactly the same. * (*To Judge*) Your Honour, there's a young man outside appealing for redress.

LI PAO-T'UNG. Let him be admitted for examination. (*Kuei-chih comes in and kneels*). If you have a written statement, hand it in. (*He takes the petition, reads it and manifests considerable alarm. Then, speaking*) The petitioner may lift his head! (*Kuei-chih in fear and trembling keeps her head lowered*). Aha! According to the plaint the petitioner is a woman by name of Li Kuei-chih. How is it that a man appears in this court claiming to be the petitioner? There must be some local bully mixed up in the case. (*To lictors*) Get the ankle-squeezers ready.

KUEI-CHIH (*knocks her head on the floor in fright and her hat falls off ; she screams*). Your Excellency, please don't be angry. I am . . . I am indeed a woman.

LI PAO-T'UNG (*aside*). Then you must be my sister. (*To lictors*) Leave the court and close the doors.

Exeunt lictors. Li Pao-t'ung rises from the bench, catches hold of Kuei-chih's sleeve and leads her to his private apartments, i.e. both make a few rounds of the stage, representing transit from one room to another.

SCENE III

LI PAO-T'UNG. Please be seated, sister. (*He kneels*) Oh sister, my dear sister!

KUEI-CHIH (*evincing surprise*). Who are you?

LI PAO-T'UNG. Don't be dismayed, I am your brother Li Pao-t'ung.

KUEI-CHIH. Oh! are you indeed Pao-t'ung, my long-lost brother?

---

* We must remember that Hu Ching has the rôle of a *ch'ou*.

Both break down, and after many loving exclamations, sing : As brother and sister meet again to-day, we cannot restrain our tears from flowing like strings of pearls.

SCENE IV

CHAO CH'UNG (*entering excitedly*). Alas, what can have happened to my wife? She came here to present her petition and His Excellency took her into his apartment and has detained her there an unconscionable time. What is the best course of action? Ah, I have it. What do I care about keeping my position? I'll break in and see what they are up to.

HU CHING. I wonder what is the matter with my friend Chao : he seems unusually agitated.

CHAO CH'UNG. A young man came in just now with a petition. Did you see him?

HU CHING. Yes, I noticed the youth you're referring to. His Excellency pulled him out and he has not yet returned. I wonder what's at the back of it.

CHAO CH'UNG. Indeed! Do you know whether His Excellency has a wife?

HU CHING. He has neither wife nor family to my knowledge.

CHAO CH'UNG (*showing alarm*). That looks bad!

HU CHING. What do you mean?

CHAO CH'UNG. None of your business! I am going to break in and see. (*He pulls up his robe and rushes forward : Hu Ching tugs him back. Exeunt*).

SCENE V

Li Pao-t'ung overhears the scuffle and sends servants to inquire what the noise is about. They return saying that it is the magistrate Chao Ch'ung.

LI PAO-T'UNG. What impudence to come and raise a disturbance at my yamen gate! He thinks he can flout me because of my youth. I'll go out and see him.

KUEI-CHIH. Stay! The Pao-ch'êng magistrate is your own brother-in-law Chao Ch'ung. I beg you not to make trouble with him.

LI PAO-T'UNG. Oh! so Chao Ch'ung is my brother-in-law. I desire to make his acquaintance.

KUEI-CHIH. Don't frighten him!

LI PAO-T'UNG. Yes, now I understand. Please retire, sister, for the time being. (*Kuei-chih withdraws. Li to lictors*) Tell the Pao-ch'êng magistrate Chao Ch'ung to come into Court.

SCENE VI

CHAO CH'UNG (*kneeling on his arrival*). I make my salutation to Your Excellency.

LI PAO-T'UNG (*banging on the table*). Rubbish, you bold unmannerly specimen of a Pao-ch'êng petty magistrate. How dare you thrust yourself into my yamen and make such an uproar? Do you imagine because I am young that you need not conform to the rules of propriety?

CHAO CH'UNG. I assure Your Excellency that it is on account of the youth who came in recently to offer a petition. I saw him go through to your inner apartments. Since he did not come out again, I lost control of myself.

LI PAO-T'UNG. May I ask what relation he bears to you?

CHAO CH'UNG (*stammering*). He is my . . . my . . .

LI PAO-T'UNG (*interrupting*). He is your what? Be quick and tell me.

CHAO CH'UNG. Oh, Your Excellency, I, I cannot tell you!

LI PAO-T'UNG (*loudly, showing anger*). Speak out. How is he related to you?

CHAO CH'UNG (*weakly*). He, she . . . is my . . . my . . . my wife!

LI PAO-T'UNG (*to runners*). Shut the door.
*The runners all retire. Li Pao-t'ung seizes Chao Ch'ung's
hands, leads him into the antechamber and makes him sit down.*

SCENE VII

KUEI-CHIH (*comes in smiling and draws Chao Ch'ung
by the sleeve, saying*). My husband. (*Then, pointing at Pao-
t'ung*) Who do you think he is?
CHAO CH'UNG. I don't know.
KUEI-CHIH. He is your brother-in-law.
CHAO CH'UNG. Oh, he's your brother! I'll go and
speak to him.
KUEI-CHIH. Yes, do.
CHAO CH'UNG (*trembling*). Oh, ah! Then you are
my big . . . big . . . .
LI PAO-T'UNG (*who has been sitting impassive and non-
committal throughout this little pantomime*). Big, big . . .
what?
CHAO CH'UNG (*is so nervous that he can only just
utter*). Your Excellency!
LI PAO-T'UNG. Brother-in-law, pray be seated . . .
And now please tell me, brother-in-law, how my father
came to be sentenced. You know the full particulars.
What course had we better pursue?
CHAO CH'UNG. Your Excellency is vested with full
powers, so where's the difficulty?
LI PAO-T'UNG. My mind is resolved. You may
withdraw to the antechamber. (*Exit Chao. Li calls
to runners and handing them an arrow with a small triangular
flag attached, says*) Here is your warrant. The ex-
magistrate Hu Ching is to go to Pao-ch'êng gaol and
bring the convict Li Ch'i to this court for investigation.

SCENE VIII

HU CHING (*coming out with the arrow, says to himself*).
This is a bad business, a very bad business! For His

Excellency to send me on this mission may spell my ruin. It was I who tried the case, accepted a bribe, forced a confession out of Li Ch'i and recommended capital punishment. If Li Ch'i reveals the truth, I fear that I, Hu Ching, will be the sufferer. Well! life and death are all a matter of fate. Riches and honour depend on Heaven. I'll go to the gaol and put the wind up Li Ch'i so that he will not dare go back on his former evidence. (*On arrival at the yamen he sends for Li Ch'i and says to him*) His Excellency the Judge on Circuit has instructed me to summon you to his Court for re-trial. When you appear before him, stick to your original confession. If you retract a word of it, His Excellency will certainly aggravate your punishment. That would be gruesome! So mind you're very careful what you say.

LI CH'I. Alas, Your Honour, I wonder what the outcome of it will be.

HU CHING. How can I tell? Make haste and come with me.

SCENE IX

On arrival at the Judge's yamen their presence is announced, and Li Pao-t'ung summons them before him.

LI CH'I (*sings*). It is with a heart full of dread that I enter this Court. I feel as if I were entering the depths of hell.

LI PAO-T'UNG (*to runners*). Remove the prisoner's shackles. (*Turning to Li Ch'i*) Now then, Li Ch'i, tell me your troubles from beginning to end. I may be able to save your life.

LI CH'I (*handing in his petition, relates his long narrative, winding up with*). Hu Ching, the late magistrate, accepted bribes and forced me to confess that I was guilty. Alas, Your Excellency! I, the innocent petitioner, have been most barbarously persecuted. (*Sings*) I hope Your

Excellency will deal with me justly as this is a matter of life or death. For one act of mercy I shall render nine in return.

LI PAO-T'UNG. For a master to drive his slave to suicide is no crime against the law, hence there can be no sentence of death in this case. This only shows the stupidity of the examining magistrate. I shall have to investigate this case thoroughly, and all those responsible for a wrong verdict will be punished.

HU CHING (*soliloquizing*) This will be the end of me! His Excellency intends to punish the examining magistrate and I am the very one who tried the case and recommended the death-sentence. Li Ch'i has now retracted his confession. If His Excellency reverses my sentence, my life is in danger. Why should a man of my age expose his neck to the executioner's knife? I know what I'll do! There's a well just outside. I'll jump into it and drown myself, and at least preserve my body intact. (*He acts accordingly, whereupon yamen-runners appear and inform the Judge of his fatal immersion*).

LI PAO-T'UNG. Have him hauled out at once.

LI CH'I. Your Excellency, hear me. This proves that Hu Ching was guilty of preferring a false charge against me and that I am innocent. (*Sings*) My injuries are chiefly due to Hu Ching, who took bribes and recommended the death sentence. I hope that Your Excellency will repeal the sentence and release me, for which gracious act I'll burn a brazier full of incense in thanksgiving.

A gong is struck thrice and all the yamen staff withdraw.

ACT IV

LI PAO-T'UNG. Father, please rise.

Li Ch'i, who has been kneeling throughout, shows surprise and consternation, while his son helps him to his feet.

LI CH'I. Your Excellency, what may this portend?

LI PAO-T'UNG. Don't be alarmed, Father. I am your son, Pao-t'ung.

LI CH'I. Is this true? I can scarcely believe it.

LI PAO-T'UNG. Father, it is absolutely true.

LI CH'I (*wipes his eyes with his coat-sleeves to have a clearer view, weeps and sings*). I never thought that my son and I would ever meet again! Who could have imagined that we should meet to-day! My son, though you have risen to the enjoyment of wealth and honour, I know not whether your sister be dead or alive.

LI PAO-T'UNG. Father, it was my sister who presented the petition.

LI CH'I. What? Your sister has come too? Where is she?

LI PAO-T'UNG. She is within the yamen. I'll send for her at once. (*He sings for her to make haste. Enter Kuei-chih*). Our father is here.

KUEI-CHIH (*kneels and weeps*). Oh, my poor Father!

LI CH'I (*weeps likewise and utters tender exclamations, then sings*). For father and daughter thus to meet again brings the tears to my eyes, as if I had just drunk some heady wine. (*Here Chao Ch'ung slips in stealthily*).

LI CH'I (*alarmed, pointing towards him*). Who is he?

LI PAO-T'UNG. He is your son-in-law, the Magistrate of Pao-ch'êng.

CHAO CH'UNG (*salutes Li Ch'i, saying*). Pray, venerable Sir, permit me, your son-in-law Chao-ch'ung, to make my bow to you.

LI CH'I (*speaks*). So you are His Honour the Magistrate of Pao-ch'êng, the " father and the mother of the people ! " (*Sings*) But oh, I am still consumed with loathing for T'ien Wang: the villain should be slain. And that vile strumpet Yang Shih, the cause of all my torment, how I abhor the fiend! Yea, she was to blame for this long separation from my own flesh and blood. (*To Chao Ch'ung*) Are you aware of the facts of my family's misfortune?

CHAO CH'UNG. Yes, your son-in-law knows all.

LI CH'I (*sings*). Our family, long dispersed in exile, is now united again. It is the will of Heaven and the will of the spirits that we should be avenged. Dry wood encounters spring once more. A proof that Almighty Heaven has taken pity on us ; a proof that Heaven does not err and that good and evil are clearly distinguished. (*Speaks*) That infamous pair Yang Shih and T'ien Wang must be seized and punished.

CHAO CH'UNG. Your son-in-law has already issued a warrant for their arrest and punishment.

LI CH'I. That is good : and a further proof that an official knows how to fulfil his duty.

LI PAO-T'UNG. Father, please take the seat of honour and we will all pay our respects to you.

LI CH'I. What is the use of kneeling ! We are all assembled again : again we are united. What happiness !

KUEI-CHIH AND CHAO CH'UNG (*together*). It is our duty to kneel to you. Please change your coat and headgear.

LI CH'I (*exchanges his prison-clothes for a gentleman's apparel. The young trio kowtow to him. He smiles and speaks*). Let us all greet one another !

THE TRIO (*sing alternatively*). We have received the Imperial bounty and enjoy a thousand measures of grain. The whole family rejoices at this happy meeting. Who can deny that Heaven bestows an equable reward ? To-day we know for certain that Heaven is always just.

LI CH'I (*sings*). T'ien Wang is like a bird caught in a snare : Yang Shih is like a fish caught in a net. Their flesh will be sliced into a thousand slivers. My heart feels satisfied. (*Speaks*) You may deceive Man, but Heaven you cannot deceive.

KUEI-CHIH. Good and evil depend on the turning of the wheel.

CHAO CH'UNG. He who injures others is bound to receive retribution.
LI PAO-T'UNG. Who shall Heaven spare ? Assuredly not the wicked ! (*Exeunt omnes, chuckling joyfully*). *Finis.*

*   *   *

The main onus of the performance and responsibility for delighting or boring the audience are thrown on the actor impersonating Li Ch'i, for the *lao-shêng* is often boring, as old men can be in actual life ; and Li Ch'i's sufferings are apt to seem endless. (Job, dramatized, must maintain his patience, while the audience may not be able to preserve theirs). Those who have enjoyed Han Shih-ch'ang's *k'un-ch'ü* company will always identify Wei Ch'ing-lin, so reminiscent of Chaliapine, with the leading character. The gaoler's rôle is treated comically, not as one might imagine from the dialogue, realistically. In the company we refer to it is played by an extremely vivacious youngster, hence our feelings are not subjected to needless torture. To see Han Shih-ch'ang and Pai Yün-shêng as Kuei-chih and Chao Ch'ung respectively is to enjoy the perfection of Chinese comedy. Kuei-chih is all gossamer lightness and amorous coyness even in the midst of her tears ; she manipulates the rather callow official who is her devoted husband with feline tact, until his tremors for the safety of his own position subside in a kittenish tête-à-tête. It is an enchanting picture of a young Chinese married couple, the sort of couple you may read about in Shên Fu's *Six Chapters of a Floating Life*, translated by Lin Yutang. Most amusing is Chao Ch'ung's scene in the yamen when he imagines the judge seducing his wife ; as when he teases Kuei-chih about her name, the maximum fun is extracted from the situation.

For condensed imaginative acting and a disciplined *ensemble* we have seen none to better the performances of Han Shih-ch'ang's company in this play ; and it is matter for the profoundest regret that *k'un-ch'ü* is losing favour ; its rhythms are too subtle and intricate, too full of delicate shades, for the rapidly modernized city mob. But a Westerner who is fortunate enough to hear it will acquire a totally different conception of the resources of the Chinese stage. This is one of the few living favourites in Han Shih-ch'ang's repertoire and is even given by companies that have not been specifically trained to sing *k'un-ch'ü*.

CH'I TANG T'UNG O PAO 妻黨同惡報

A WIFE AND HER WICKED RELATIONS
REAP THEIR REWARD

PERIOD : Ming.   A *pang-tzŭ* play.

DRAMATIS PERSONÆ

CHI SHAN-HSIANG, a wealthy merchant ...	...	*Lao-shêng*
CHI KUANG-JÊN, his son by first wife ...	...	*Hu-tzŭ-shêng*
LIU SHIH (Mrs. Chi Kuang-jên)	...	*Chêng-tan*
TSOU SHIH, the merchant's second wife ...	...	*Ch'ou-p'o*
		(*or Ts'ai-tan*)
HUAI CHUNG, Tsou Shih's elder brother ...	...	*Ch'ou*
TA PAO, Tsou Shih's son	...	*Ch'ou*
HUI YÜEH, Abbess of the Lotus-flower Convent		*Lao-tan*
LIU SHÊNG, Liu Shih's younger brother ...	...	*Hsiao-shêng*
HSIAO-T'UNG, Liu Shih's son	...	*Wa Wa-shêng*

SCENE I

Enter the merchant Chi Shan-hsiang. Ta Pao, his son by Tsou Shih, follows. Huai Chung appears and asks Chi for money. Chi refuses and turns him out. Ta Pao secretly tells him to go to a neighbouring wine-shop and promises to procure the funds from his mother.

CHI SHAN-HSIANG (*speaks*). Righteous conduct is an everlasting heirloom, which increases from generation to generation. My wealth of untold millions is comparable to that of T'ao Chu. * My name is Chi Shan-hsiang and I am a native of Shang-yüan district in Kiangsu. My first wife left me a son called Chi Kuang-jên, who married a girl of the Liu family : she is virtuous and filial in the highest degree. My estate comprises a thousand acres of fertile fields of grain. I have shops in nearly every corner of the district. It is now the

---

* Fan Li, a Minister of Yüeh, who withdrew from official life in 472 B.C. and amassed a fabulous fortune ; hence known as T'ao Chu Kung, used in the sense of millionaire.

season for settling my accounts and collecting my loans.
Yesterday I dispatched my son Kuang-jên with this
purpose to all the shops in the western area. I myself
will see to the shops in the east. I intend to entrust my
son's wife, Liu Shih, with all my affairs in the meantime.
(*Sings out*) Ta Pao !

TA PAO. Yes, Sir.

CHI SHAN-HSIANG. Ask your elder brother's wife
to come here. I have something to tell her.

Exit Ta Pao.

LIU SHIH (*entering, speaks*). " Cool showers falling ere
the Spring, do fragrant early flowers bring. No frost
till autumn ends its days, the yellow leaf its fall delays. "
Every blessing on you, Father !

CHI SHAN-HSIANG. No ceremony, daughter-in-law.
Be seated.

LIU SHIH. What are your instructions, Father ?

CHI SHAN-HSIANG. It is now three years since I
checked the accounts of my various establishments.
Yesterday I sent your husband to see to those in the
west : I shall attend to those in the east myself. All my
family affairs, the money and keys to my treasury, I
shall confide to you.

LIU SHIH. I shall obey your orders, Father.

*Chi Shan-hsiang hands over account-books, keys, etc. Ta
Pao stands by, denoting by gestures that he does not approve
of this proceeding.*

LIU SHIH. When do you intend to start on your
journey, Father ?

CHI SHAN-HSIANG. Immediately.

LIU SHIH. Then I shall not prepare anything special
for you now, but wait to welcome you on your return.

Exit Liu Shih.

CHI SHAN-HSIANG (*to Ta Pao*). Ask your mother to
come in : I have something to say to her.

Ta Pao does accordingly.

TSOU SHIH (*entering*). So you are off to collect your loans? Who will look after the house, I'd like to know?

CHI SHAN-HSIANG. You can look after it while I'm away.

TSOU SHIH. There is no great responsibility about that, so don't go fretting yourself.

CHI SHAN-HSIANG. Don't indulge in too much gossip : just help to keep an eye on things. (*To servant*) Order my horse.

TSOU SHIH. Why such haste? I have warmed some wine to speed the parting guest.

CHI SHAN-HSIANG. Good! I'll drink a few cups in deference to your consideration. (*After drinking, sings in hsi-p'i yao-pan*) Chi Shan-hsiang leaves home to settle his affairs : he advises Tsou Shih to pay attention to details and keep a good eye on the house. I must now set forth on my eastward journey. (*Exit*).

SCENE II

TSOU SHIH (*to Ta Pao*). Look here, my son, the old man has decamped and left me in charge of everything. This will suit us down to the ground.

TA PAO. Don't be too sure, Mother mine. He only left you in charge of the domestic side of it, not the business. Your joy is all in vain.

TSOU SHIH. On his departure, your father appointed me to manage the household ; surely he meant that the property and business were inclusive?

TA PAO. You are sadly deluded, Mother. I saw him with my own eyes hand over all the account-books and keys of the money-lockers to sister-in-law Liu Shih.

TSOU SHIH. Can this possibly be true?

TA PAO. How could I deceive you?

TSOU SHIH. Ha, ha, you bald-headed old rascal! When you left you promised to hand everything over to me, and instead you only put me in charge of the larder: it's to your son's wife that you entrust the property and business. What sort of principle is this? I know: it's because she is young and winsome, eh? If things are to continue like this, how will they end?

TA PAO. I am much afraid that when the time comes we'll not get any of the inheritance. You had better think out some precautionary measure without delay.

TSOU SHIH. You speak to the point. I'll have to think of a scheme. (*Scratches her head*). I've found it! You go and call your uncle in.   (*Ta Pao obeys*).

TSOU SHIH (*soliloquizing sotto voce*). I'll have to ponder some artful plan to cut the grass and pull out the roots. The family inheritance must revert to me and mine.

HUAI CHUNG (*entering*). What is the matter, Sister?

TSOU SHIH. Sit down and let us have a chat. When your brother-in-law went off, he handed over all the account-books and keys to Liu Shih instead of to me. I am almost speechless with rage. I sent for you to find a way to rid us of Liu Shih, so that the property will revert to me. If you discover one, your trouble will not be wasted or your services forgotten.

HUAI CHUNG. Where's the difficulty? Let me enlighten you. Get hold of a monk's cap, and one night steal with it into Liu Shih's bedroom pretending to be a thief, and drop it on the floor. As soon as she rushes out you pick it up and accuse her of gross misconduct with a monk. On her husband's return, just show him the cap as proof of her guilt. He may beat her to death out of jealousy. That'll make an end of her.

TSOU SHIH. But they are so fond of each other that he may not believe me. Even if I told him to beat her I fear he wouldn't do it.

HUAI CHUNG. But you'll have the cap as a proof. When he sets eyes on that he is bound to fly into a terrible rage and either kill or divorce her. Won't that wind up this little business of ours ? What do you think of my plan, Sister ?

TSOU SHIH. Capital ! But how am I to go about it ?

HUAI CHUNG. When you have chosen your night to turn the trick and everybody is fast asleep—you and Ta Pao pretending to sleep like the rest of them—you both get up, stealthily open Liu Shih's door and throw the cap on the floor. Then scuttle into the yard and shout : Thieves ! That will alarm the servants, who will dash out to see what is up. Finding the door of Liu Shih's bedroom open, you go in with the excuse of seeing if anything has been stolen. Then, in the presence of the whole assembly, pick up the cap which you carefully retain to show her husband, proof positive that she had a monk in her room.

TSOU SHIH. An excellent scheme. Now let us begin to carry it out. Ta Pao ! here is an ounce of silver. Go down to the nearest hat-shop and buy a monk's cap. Hide it up your sleeve and don't let any one catch sight of it.   (*Ta Pao takes the money and runs on his errand*).

HUAI CHUNG. Well, Sister, I'll be taking my leave.

TSOU SHIH. If anything transpires, I'll let you know. (*Exit Huai. Ta Pao comes in with the cap, and she slips it up her sleeve, saying*) This very night we will carry out our arrangement.   (*Exeunt*).

SCENE III

LIU SHIH (*appears and says*). My husband has now been absent many days. I am beginning to grow anxious about him.

HSIAO-T'UNG (*Liu's little son, enters lisping*). I've just come back from school. How are you, Mamma ? I make my bow to you.

LIU SHIH. You had better run and eat your evening rice, and then we'll go to bye-bye.

Both retire to bed. Ta Pao comes in, drops the cap on

the floor and slips away. Tsou Shih appears and shouts,
" Thieves ! " *at the top of her voice. Liu Shih and her son
wake up, the former crying* : " Where ? "

TSOU SHIH (*picking up the cap, says*). Well I never !
A monk's cap in here ! Aha, I understand. There's
rather more than thieves concerned in this, that's plain.
Well, it's no use wasting words ; we'll all go back to bed.
If there is anything to discuss, we can leave it till to-
morrow. (*All go out except Liu Shih and her son*).

LIU SHIH. How did such a cap appear in my room,
I wonder. It's very bewildering. Well, we can only
go back to bed again. (*Exit*).

SCENE IV

CHI KUANG-JÊN (*appears, soliloquizing*). I'm home
from my tour, but why should my eyelids quiver so and
my heart be all in a flutter ?

*Dismounts from his horse and enters the front courtyard.
Ta Pao and Tsou Shih come out to exchange greetings.*

TSOU SHIH. Did you find the business flourishing on
your trip ?

CHI KUANG-JÊN. Yes, thriving, Mother.

TSOU SHIH. Your father has not yet returned.

CHI KUANG-JÊN. Is all in order at home ?

TSOU SHIH. In fine order except for that wife of yours.
She is a loose lot : you really should keep her under better
control.

CHI KUANG-JÊN. Why, what tricks has the baggage
been up to ?

TSOU SHIH. There was a hubbub in her quarters one
night. Thinking it must be a thief, Ta Pao and I got
up and rushed to her bedroom. And what should we
find but a monk's cap lying on the floor ! (*She takes it
from her sleeve and shows it to him*). It looks like a monk's,
doesn't it ?

CHI KUANG-JÊN (*seizes the cap with fire in his eyes, then speaks*). Could that abject creature behave so brazenly ? (*Sings*) To hear this makes my anger blaze within me. What scandalous impudence, what odious lack of shame ! My rage is enough to toss the cap off my head ! (*Advances towards his wife's room ; the music stops and the drums beat frantically*).

TSOU SHIH. Ta Pao, you follow him in and see what they have to say to each other. And mind you come back at once and tell me what happens.

Exeunt Ta Pao and Tsou Shih.

SCENE V

LIU SHIH (*appears and sings*). It is a long time now since father and son went away. Their absence fills me with anxiety. I'll take a book and sit by the window and watch for their return.

CHI KUANG-JÊN (*enters with a knife in his hand, singing*). Mother has just informed me of Liu Shih's disgraceful conduct. Now with my lusty knife I enter her bedchamber.

Knife raised, he darts at his spouse : both vociferate.

LIU SHIH (*sings*). Why do you want to murder me ? (*Speaks*) Why do you rush into my room speechless and clutching a knife ? Do you want to kill me ? I cannot understand.

CHI KUANG-JÊN. A fine creature you are to ask me such a question !

LIU SHIH. I haven't done anything wrong that I am aware of.

CHI KUANG-JÊN. You foul trollop, dare you deny it ? When I am away from home you should wait on your mother-in-law and behave with all the respect that is due to family ties. Instead you seek to ruin our reputation. What excuse is there for such conduct ?

LIU SHIH. Who told you that ?

CHI KUANG-JÊN. My mother told me. Now do you dare deny it?

LIU SHIH. My husband, listen to me. She is my stepmother. She harboured resentment and tried to injure me because I was put in charge of the business. You had better inquire into this, not blindly believe all you're told. You should make allowances for our relation as man and wife.

CHI KUANG-JÊN. How do you account for the monk's cap that was found in your bedchamber?

LIU SHIH (*speaks*). There is something sinister about this! (*Sings*) At sight of the monk's cap I am filled with alarm. I fear I shall not escape with my life. I shall go forward and implore him on my knees: Husband, consider the love between man and wife!

CHI KUANG-JÊN (*speaks*). Ungrateful jade! You have brought disgrace upon my house. Our predicament is like the " Yellow Millet Dream and Awakening."* Who are you, and who am I? (*Speaks*) Here is my sharp blade and a hempen rope. Either cut your throat or hang yourself on a beam—you can choose between them. The sooner you are dead the better. (*He is about to leave when Liu Shih catches hold of him. He pushes her down, exclaiming*) You shameless strumpet!

Exit Chi.

LIU SHIH. Stay! My husband believes my stepmother's lies, fabricated to bring about my death. First I shall render thanks to my parents for rearing me, then I'll hang myself on a beam. (*Bows in the direction of her parents' home, then weeping, sings*) It is all on account of Tsou Shih's malice against me; she seeks to blast my life. Heaven has brought me this calamity. I fear

---

* Alluding to the famous dream of Lü Tung-pin, who fell asleep while a pot of millet was put on the fire, dreamt that he became Emperor, lived out his life as such and awoke to find that the millet was still uncooked,—here used in the sense of living in a fool's paradise.

there is no escape. Evidently fate has decreed that I am to destroy myself and go to the Underworld. Why not seize the rope and hang myself? (*She is about to do so when she pauses and reflects, singing*) And I shall die, leaving a sullied name. (*Speaks*) If I kill myself to-day my father-in-law will not know the truth when he returns. My evil fame will never be effaced. I have often heard of the Lotus-blossom Convent. Thither I'll go, cut off my hair and take monastic vows. First I'll write a letter to my father-in-law explaining how things came to such a pass. Yes, that is what I'll do! (*Sings in êrh-huang tao-pan*) As I lift my pen I cannot check my tears. (*Her little son comes in from school and bows to her. She tells him to eat his rice, and he leaves the room. Liu Shih proceeds to sing in êrh-huang yüan-pan*) I take up my pen and try to express myself clearly : " My respects to my venerable Father-in-law. This is all because of ill luck in our household. Wishing to destroy my reputation, my stepmother spread false and evil rumours about me, to the effect that I had dishonoured the family. Unable to suffer such fabrications, I am going to the Lotus-blossom Convent to take the monastic vow. This letter is written to explain my reasons."

HSIAO-T'UNG (*toddling in*). Mother, I have finished my meal.

LIU SHIH (*sings*). My son, I have something to say to you. Here is a letter. Keep it carefully concealed on your person, and don't let anyone see it whatever happens. When your grandfather comes back, you must give it to him. Now run away to school.

HSIAO-T'UNG. Where are you going, Mamma?

LIU SHIH. I am going to your uncle's house. (*Exit child. Liu sings*) It fills me with anguish to part from my child like this. Brushing my raiment, I slowly wend my way towards my brother's dwelling to tell him all that has happened. (*Exit*).

SCENE VI

Liu Shih first goes to her mother-in-law's grave and recites her doleful tale with many a tear.

LIU SHÊNG (*her younger brother, appears and says*). After ten griping years of endless study, I have not yet attained my heart's desire! I wonder when a better day will dawn.

LIU SHIH (*rushes in, singing*). Hither I hied me in such frantic haste that ere I know it I stand at my brother's threshold. (*Speaks*) Quickly, open the door!

LIU SHÊNG. Who is it?

LIU SHIH. Your sister.

LIU SHÊNG (*opening the door*). Oh, it is you! Come in, Sister. But why? What's amiss? Your face is wet with tears.

LIU SHIH (*weeping, says*). Oh, brother mine, there are things you could not guess. (*She proceeds to relate them, winding up with*) I have seen through her plot to destroy me, and there is nothing left for me but to enter a nunnery .... I have heard that there is a Lotus-blossom Convent near by. Brother, I beg you to escort me thither.

LIU SHÊNG. Sister, there's a common saying that it is easy to leave one's family, but hard to return. You had better go back and make the best of things.

LIU SHIH. My mind is already resolved. If you will not accompany me, I'll go alone.

LIU SHÊNG. Don't be vexed; I'll go with you, Sister.

LIU SHIH. Let us start at once. (*Sings*) Sadly I leave for the Lotus-blossom Convent. (*Exeunt*).

SCENE VII

ABBESS OF THE CONVENT (*appears, saying*). I, Hui Yüeh, have been in this nunnery for more than twenty years, receiving many converts. As the weather to-day is fine and clear, I'll call them out and expound our Holy Laws.

FOUR YOUNG NUNS (*appear*, *saying*). We have come at your bidding, Lady Abbess.

ABBESS. Good. Now stand aside and hear the words of the Law.

LIU SHIH (*enters with her brother and sings*). Arriving at the Lotus-blossom Convent, my tears gush like a stream of lucent pearls. I abandon the world and enter Buddha's portals.

LIU SHÊNG. Lady Abbess, we salute you.

ABBESS. What brings you hither? Enter and be seated. Have you come to burn incense?

LIU SHIH. Nay, but I yearn to be admitted to your convent as a nun.

ABBESS. Those who leave home to take monastic vows generally do so on account of poverty or sickness. It seems to me that this young woman is neither poor nor ailing. What prompts you then to cut off your hair and join our sisterhood? There is a common saying that it is easy to leave home, but hard to return to lay life. If you take my advice, you will not do it.

LIU SHIH. I am firmly resolved : do not try to dissuade me.

ABBESS. Since you are so determined, you will have to provide a sponsor.

LIU SHÊNG. I'll be her sponsor.

ABBESS. How are you related to each other?

LIU SHÊNG. I am her brother.

ABBESS. That will do! (*To Liu Shih*) You may enter our sisterhood. (*To Liu Shêng*) And you may go home.

LIU SHÊNG (*sings*). Parting from my sister at the convent gate, I cannot check my grief.   (*Exit*).

ABBESS. First let me ask if you have a father or mother-in-law, a husband, or any children.

LIU SHIH. Nay, I have none of these.

ABBESS. Then there is no impediment. I shall cut off your hair to-morrow, after which you will come with me and worship Buddha. (*Exeunt*).

SCENE VIII

Tsou Shih and Ta Pao appear on the stage.

TA PAO. Mother, I saw my elder brother's wife run out alone.

TSOU SHIH. Make haste and call your elder brother.

CHI KUANG-JÊN (*entering*). What is the matter, Mother?

TSOU SHIH. Your wife has bolted. Why don't you go and give chase?

CHI KUANG-JÊN (*sings*). This is very alarming! I must set forth in search of her at once.

He rushes out with Tsou Shih and Ta Pao in pursuit.

SCENE IX

Enter Liu Shih, the Abbess and four young nuns.

LIU SHIH. Is this the day I am to lose my hair?

ABBESS. This is the day. (*To nuns*) Bring me the instruments, then go and offer incense in the Hall of the Buddhas. While you are reciting the liturgies I shall cut off your hair. (*Nuns hand Abbess the shears*).

ABBESS. It is pitiful to cut such beautiful hair.

LIU SHIH (*seeing her severed tresses on the floor, weeps and sings*). My heart aches to see my silken tresses shorn. I cannot check my tears. But it is my fate to leave the world and enter the cloister.

ABBESS. Here is a *kuan**, where you must stay to solicit alms.

LIU SHIH. Lady Abbess, should my father-in-law or my husband attempt to visit me, please deny them admittance. But if my son arrives, pray let him in.

———————

* A small brick cage for nuns to sit in.

ABBESS (*aghast*).   So you really have relations after all !   (*Exeunt Abbess and Liu Shih*).

SCENE X

Chi Kuang-jên encounters Liu Shêng.

CHI KUANG-JÊN. Oh, it is you, Brother !

LIU SHÊNG. Where are you going in such haste ?

CHI KUANG-JÊN. Do you know where your sister is ?

LIU SHÊNG. She has taken vows in the Lotus-blossom Convent.

CHI (*rushes off without more ado, arrives at the Convent and says*).   I shall go straightway and ask for the Abbess.

ABBESS (*appears and says*).   Who am I addressing ?

CHI. Have you a woman here by name of Liu, who has recently taken her vows ?   (*The Abbess answers in the affirmative and permits him to visit her.   Exeunt*).

SCENE XI

Liu Shih is sitting in a chair.

CHI KUANG-JÊN (*approaching*).   Oh, my beloved wife !   (*Sings*)   It shocks me to see her so changed.   In truth she has abandoned all worldly cares !   Your husband has come to take you hence.   You should not have been so rash.

LIU SHIH. You speak at random.   As for me, I have not done this without careful forethought and considera-tion.   I am not preparing myself for this life, but for the life to come.   You must speak to me no more of husband and wife.

CHI KUANG-JÊN. All I can do is to go down on my knees and beseech you.   Let me explain everything. (*Speaks*)   Alas, dear wife, I admit that I am to blame. I should not have heeded your stepmother's slanders. She wished to compass your death.   But who could have dreamt that you would fly here and resort to such desperate means ? At home there is nobody to look after Father or rear our only child. How could you bear to desert us thus ? I urge you to turn home with me at once.

LIU SHIH (*sings*). To-day I am like a stone cast into the sea, like a broken mirror that can never be repaired. I am deaf to your entreaties.

CHI KUANG-JÊN. Alas, this is terrible ! (*Sings*) She will not listen to me : her heart is like a stone. But there is no help for it ; I leave the Convent gate in lasting sorrow, and maybe we shall never meet again.

Exeunt Chi, Liu Shih and Abbess.

SCENE XII

CHI SHAN-HSIANG (*enters singing in hsi-p'i yao-pan*). I have passed the many stages of my journey. Clutching my reins I reach my humble home.

Enters room ; Tsou Shih and Ta Pao come in.

TSOU SHIH. Well, at last you've returned ! The minute you turned your back, Liu Shih eloped with somebody.

CHI SHAN-HSIANG. Nonsense ! My daughter-in-law is a model of virtue. Is it likely that she would ever do anything of the kind ? (*Sings*) To listen to such stupid scandal is enough to make one's blood curdle. I'll send for Liu Shih's son and carefully inquire into the matter.

HSIAO-T'UNG. Oh Grandfather, I am so glad you've come home ! I have a letter from Mother which she asked me to give you.

CHI (*takes it, singing in tao-pan*). Before I even read this letter, my tears gush forth in showers. (*Changes to yüan-pan time*) I'll open it and see what it contains. (*Reads*) " My respects to you, venerable Father-in-law. On account of an unfortunate affair in the household, my stepmother schemed to ruin my reputation and even to take my life. She procured a monk's cap, and accused me of indulging in illicit intrigue with a monk. Unable to suffer such gross calumny, I am going to the Lotus-blossom Convent, henceforth to be a nun."

Chi Kuang-jên enters at this point, and all he gets in answer to his salutation is a slap in the face. His father sings : You dolt! (*Speaks*) When your wife left home, why didn't you go and fetch her back?

CHI KUANG-JÊN. I went, but she refused to listen to me. She told me she had made up her mind never to return.

CHI SHAN-HSIANG. You're a worthless lout. Here, come along with me and bring your son. We'll all go straight to the nunnery and use every power of persuasion. (*Sings*) Grandfather and son set forth to lead Liu Shih home from the Lotus-blossom Convent.

TSOU SHIH (*entering*). Where are you off to, husband?

CHI SHAN-HSIANG. Just wait till I have brought back my virtuous daughter-in-law and see how you'll be dealt with, you venomous thing. I'll settle your vile existence!   (*Exeunt Chi, son and grandson*).

SCENE XIII

TSOU SHIH (*having summoned Ta Pao*). Go at once and call your uncle Huai Chung. (*Ta Pao goes*). If I don't think of a plan, my very life is in danger.

HUAI CHUNG (*arriving with Ta Pao*). Why have you sent for me, Sister?

TSOU SHIH. My husband has gone to fetch his absconding daughter-in-law. Her return will be my perdition. You had better think of a scheme as soon as possible.

HUAI CHUNG. Where's the hitch? Get hold of a knife and stand at some convenient street-corner. When your old man comes along, stab him in the liver and finish him off.

TSOU SHIH. Excellent! If at first you don't succeed, try again! Ta Pao can take the knife and keep me company. We'll make a nice clean sweep of them, and no more nonsense.

HUAI CHUNG. Admirable! We three can waylay them in some appropriate nook and massacre them all.

Exeunt.

SCENE XIV

CHI SHAN-HSIANG (*enters with son and grandson and says*). We have reached our destination.

ABBESS (*entering*). Who are you, Sir?

CHI SHAN-HSIANG. Is there one Liu Shih, a member of the Chi family, among your inmates here?

ABBESS. There is indeed, Sir.

CHI SHAN-HSIANG. Will you take us in to see her?

ABBESS. Follow me.

They make a few rounds of the stage, indicating that they are passing from one room to another. Liu Shih is visible in the distance.

CHI SHAN-HSIANG. Alas, dear daughter-in-law! (*Sings*) I cannot check my tears to see you in such guise. I am overcome with grief. (*Speaks*) Daughter-in-law, while I was absent my son committed the folly of listening to my wife, whose foul tongue slandered your fair fame so that you fled to this nunnery for refuge. To-day you had better come back home with me.

LIU SHIH. Did you receive the letter I wrote you?

CHI SHAN-SHIANG. I did. I grant that your step-mother is evil: it was monstrous of her to try and injure you like that. But a thousand times, ten thousand times, I implore you to return, if only for my sake, to save your old father-in-law from mortification.

LIU SHIH. My tresses are severed, my vows are made: how can I now return to a worldly life?

CHI SHAN-HSIANG (*to Abbess*). You should have prevented her. Why did you allow this to happen?

ABBESS. I urged her many a time to think the better of it, but she would not hear me. What else could I do ?

CHI SHAN-HSIANG (*to his grandson*). Kneel down before your mother and beseech her to return with us.

HSIAO-T'UNG (*kneeling, says*). Oh Mother, dear Mother ! When you were at home we used to eat together, sleep together and were never parted for a single day. How can you abandon me like this ! There is no one to look after me now, no one to help me dress. I am left like a lonely orphan. Ten thousand times I implore you to come back. Mother, have you no love for your only son ? (*Sings*) I hope my mother will not forget her only boy. Surely she has not forgotten a mother's love ?

LIU SHIH (*sings*). His voice moves me to anguish. Listen, my son, and I'll try to answer you clearly. It is not that your mother's heart is indifferent to you. But having gone so far, I cannot retrace my footsteps . . .

CHI SHAN-HSIANG (*interrupting*). Such stubbornness is enough to goad an aged man like me to frenzy. I'll beg the Abbess to intercede on my behalf. (*To Abbess*) This daughter-in-law of mine is very perverse : she declines to go back to the world. Please exert your influence and gently persuade her to return. Come to my house to-morrow, and I'll give you a thousand ounces of silver to cover Liu Shih's expenses and repair your convent as well. Now we must be taking our leave. Farewell ! (*Sings*) Parting from the Abbess at the Convent door, three generations return to their modest home.

*   *   *

The play either ends at this point or with the wicked trio meeting their just deserts. In the latter case we see Tsou Shih, Huai Chung and Ta Pao arrested on their murderous mission by the God of the Soil, who points accusing fingers at them. They fall on their knees and cut their own throats with the knives they had intended for quite a different purpose.

Like most *pang-tzŭ* plays, this has a melancholy effect on the audience. Chi Shan-hsiang is blamed for putting his daughter-in-law (instead of his wife) in charge of the property. Tsou Shih's villainy is therefore somewhat mitigated, for she was smarting under a severe loss of face. Liu Shih's determination to give up the world is highly applauded. The crude plot was evidently founded on fact ; the dramatist merely superimposed the conventions of his stock-in-trade with the minimum of artistry. There are no highlights : every reaction is simple and straightforward. It is chiefly interesting as a characteristic specimen of the average, rather humdrum, Chinese domestic drama.

CHIN SO CHI 金鎖記

THE GOLDEN LOCKET PLOT

Also entitled *Liu Yüeh Hsüeh*: "Snow on the Sixth Moon";
Chan Tou O: "The Decapitation of Tou O"; and *Yang Tu Chi*:
"The Mutton-broth Plot."

This play has gone through many transformations since the
Yüan playwright Kuan Han-ch'ing wrote *Kan T'ien Tung Ti Tou
O Yuan*: "The Resentment of Tou O which moves Heaven and
Earth," of which Bazin aîné has left an admirable translation.
Originally a Yüan *k'un-ch'ü* play called *Chui Po Ch'iu*: "Close
White Fur," with reference to the summer snow-fall when the
heroine was to be executed, it was plagiarized by an unknown Ming
playwright, who changed its name to "The Golden Locket,"
setting it to the musical time called *êrh-huang* (*chêng-pan*).

DRAMATIS PERSONÆ

Tou O, a young matron ...	...	...	...	*Ch'ing-i*
Tou Shih, her mother-in-law	...	...	...	*Lao-tan*
Ch'ien Wei-ming, a magistrate	...	...	...	*Ch'ou-êrh*
Wardress of the Gaol ...	...	...	...	*Ch'ou-p'o,*
				or *Ts'ai-tan*

SCENE: SHAN-YANG IN KIANGSU

Tou O is a young grass widow: her husband, like Ulysses, has
disappeared and she, like Penelope, remains faithful and chaste.
She lives with her mother-in-law whom she serves devotedly.
Their next-door neighbours are an old peasant woman and her son
Chang, nicknamed the Donkey, who conceives a lustful passion
for the pretty matron.

Tou O's mother-in-law falls ill and in her feeble condition she
fancies a little mutton broth. Mrs. Chang tells her son to procure
some from the market. This gives him an opportunity to dispose
of his chief obstacle and fulfil his designs on Tou O: he poisons
the broth before bringing it in to the old lady. After a sniff Mrs.
Tou wisely rejects it, on the plea of insufficient appetite. The
Donkey's mother, however, whose pet proverb was probably
"waste not, want not," swallows it down and dies. Chang accuses
Tou O of murder but tells her that if she marries him he will not
take the case to Court. When she indignantly spurns this proposal,

he rushes off to charge her before the Shan-yang Magistrate. Instead of examining the case thoroughly, the magistrate summons Tou O and has her cruelly beaten. She refuses to confess, and is sent to prison. Most performances open at this point.

SCENE I

WARDRESS (*appears on the stage, saying*). I am in charge of the female prisoners, and nine out of every ten of them I hate. Those with money are welcome enough, but those without are thrashed and cursed unmercifully. I don't care how many enemies I have : for I am the wardress of Shan-yang gaol. Tou O has long been an inmate here and I haven't extracted a copper from her yet . . . If she gives me something to-day, well and good. If not, little she knows what a walloping's in store for her ! My rage must find an outlet. Hie, Tou O ! Get out of there quick, will you ?

TOU O (*is heard behind the stage crying*: " Oh Bitterness ! " *She then appears, weeping—actually singing in êrh-huang yao-pan*). Suddenly I hear my name. I'm all of a tremble, and there's no hiding-place. Madam Wardress, your anger terrifies me. What did you call me for ?

WARDRESS. Keep calm. It's only to say that those who live in the mountains need fuel and those who live near the river need water. Just fork out some cash and reward me for all my troubles.

TOU O. What can you be thinking of ? Here I am quite innocent, locked up in prison, and at home we haven't a farthing. How am I to procure the wherewithal to pay you ? I hope you'll think of some way to relieve me instead of tormenting me for money.

WARDRESS. Here's another one asking me to accommodate her ! If I am always to be performing charitable actions, what am *I* to live on, will you tell me ? Come up a little closer. (*She smacks her face and continues in êrh-huang yao-pan*). Just hark at her ! Such cackle makes me angrier than ever. It's enough to make me grind my teeth with rage. I'll lash you with my whip ! (*The girl weeps and the Wardress sings*) You worthless thing, you ! I'll flog you to death. (*Gradually the Wardress is mollified by the girl's despair*).

SCENE II

Tou O's mother-in-law comes to visit her with a few meagre provisions and the Wardress only admits her after an abortive attempt to squeeze money from her.

TOU SHIH (*at sight of Tou O sings in érh-huang yao-pan*). She looks so changed I can hardly recognize her. It cuts me to the heart and tears my bowels and liver from my body.

TOU O. Oh, Mother, what brings you here ?

TOU SHIH. I came to offer you some food and drink.

TOU O. I couldn't taste a mouthful of anything.

TOU SHIH. But you must try to eat a little.

WARDRESS. Wait a minute, just let me see what you've brought.

TOU SHIH. Pray look.

WARDRESS (*inspecting food*). Why there's nothing but plain rice and water : you can scarcely call that nourishment !

Tou O faints away, and her mother-in-law revives her.

TOU O (*sings in yao-pan*). A single bite would choke me to death. (*In san chiao-t'ou time*) Please bear with me patiently, dear Mother-in-law. Since we were parted I have been on the verge of death.

TOU SHIH (*to Wardress*). My daughter cannot eat a thing : how would a cup of cold water do ?

WARDRESS. I'll fetch her some. (*Exit*).

TOU SHIH. Your hair is all dishevelled ; let me comb it for you.

While the old lady is dressing her hair, the Wardress comes in and crudely announces that a dispatch has arrived

*from the Capital, condemning Tou O to be executed at noon
to-morrow.*

SCENE III

CH'IEN WEI-MING (*Magistrate of Shan-yang appears,
saying*). I am superintendent of all the executions. Those
who want to save their lives must pay dearly for them.
The power is entirely in my hands : everything depends
on me . . . This morning I received a dispatch from my
superior, the Lord Prosecutor, to execute Tou O. (*To
executioners*) Remove Tou O to the execution ground
and when the hour has struck report to me.

The doors of the gaol are closed and he departs.

SCENE IV

*Enter Executioners with Tou O, who advances with her
head in a cangue.*

TOU O. Alas, for me there is no way to Heaven,
nor a road to the realms below. How should I not be
affrighted ; even the prison guards must tremble in
dismay ! (*Sings in fan-êrh-huang man-pan*) And all this
trouble and sorrow for no fault of mine ! Almighty
Heaven, be merciful and lighten my burden ! I am
innocent of any wrong. How shall I ever be able to
endure it ! My husband is abroad, and cannot return.
(*Weeps*) Oh, my husband ! (*Proceeds to sing in fan-êrh-
huang yüan-pan*) My mother-in-law is far too old to accompany me along the crowded thoroughfares. How can I
expose myself all alone to the public gaze ? Those who
know of my case will say that my innocence has not
been proven, while those who are ignorant will say I am
a murderess. I feel as if I were going before the King
of Hell after my burial.

EXECUTIONERS (*to Tou O*). Why don't you come
along ?

TOU O. Pray, Sirs, conceal my body at once after my execution.

EXECUTIONERS. Why should we do that?

TOU O. I fear that if my aged mother-in-law catches sight of my dead body, her own life will be in peril. Let me make my obeisance to you. (*Sings in fan-êrh-huang yao-pan*) Pray, Sirs, allow me to prostrate myself before you, and conceal my corpse as soon as I am dead.

TOU SHIH (*enters singing in chêng-êrh-huang yao-pan*). The noise of guns reverberates to Heaven. Oh pitiful! that little Tou O should meet with such a death!

EXECUTIONERS. Who are you?

TOU SHIH. I am her mother-in-law and have come to offer her some wine.

EXECUTIONERS. Very well, you may give her some.

TOU SHIH. Thank you. (*Sings*) I see my poor girl bound with cruel ropes. (*Speaks*) Alas, my child, since things have come to this pass, have you any words to say to me before we part?

TOU O. What is there left for me to say at such a time, dear Mother?

TOU SHIH. If your father returns, what am I to tell him when he asks after you?

TOU O. Oh, if Father returns, don't tell him I was executed; you may say that I died of illness . . . Oh Mother, do not cry so!

TOU SHIH. This is no time to worry about me. A white-haired crone must see a black-haired maiden to the grave. Our order is reversed. (*Weeps*) The Little Dipper is the Star of Life.

TOU O. The Pole Star is the Harbinger of Death.

BOTH (*singing*). And so our lease of life is predetermined. *Exit Tou Shih.*

SCENE V

MAGISTRATE (*enters and says to executioners*). Come, her time is up!

EXECUTIONERS. Aye, my Lord, her time is up.

MAGISTRATE. Bring Tou O hither bound. (*Executioners bind and bring her in*). Tou O! How could a woman so tender in years commit such a dastardly crime! To-day, you are going to be beheaded. You need not repine: your death is well deserved. (*To executioners*) Away with her!

TOU O (*in chiao-t'ou*). Oh Heaven, that I in my innocence should suffer all this sorrow! With all the laws and penalties, surely there must be some spark of kindness left in the world! (*Sings in yao-pan*) I gaze into the sky above and my heart is wrung with despair.

Suddenly it begins to snow, i.e. two young immortals throw strips of white paper into the air to simulate a snowstorm. The Grand Secretary Tou happens to be passing through Shan-yang. Snow in midsummer! Something must surely be amiss, some gross miscarriage of justice . . . When he finds that the Magistrate has given orders for Tou O's execution, he sends a special messenger to stop the proceedings, and orders another trial. Tou O is unbound, and her mother-in-law comes on the stage.

TOU SHIH (*sings in yao-pan*). In the sixth moon a fall of snow restores my dear daughter to me. (*To Tou O, who has swooned*) Arouse yourself!

TOU O (*sings in tao-pan*). I was led fettered to the execution ground and my three souls had fled. How can a corpse return again to life? (*Speaks*) Tell me truly, Mother-in-law, am I not dead?

TOU SHIH. There are certain things we cannot know, my child. Because there was a sudden snowfall during the sixth moon, the Grand Secretary Tou, who happened to pass through this district, suspected that some cruel injustice was being perpetrated, and stayed the execution pending a re-trial by himself. This is the cause of your salvation.

TOU O. I have been protected by the gods. Let us both make our obeisance to Heaven!

Subsequently Donkey Chang is found guilty and sentenced to be hacked to pieces.

* * *

There are several versions of this poignant play. In Ch'êng Yen-ch'iu's, the most frequently performed, Ts'ai Chang-tsung, the son of a censor, is engaged to Tou O, the daughter of a high official, in token of which he presents her with a golden locket. Shortly after the wedding Ts'ai leaves for the Capital to compete in the Imperial Examination; his servant, Chang the Donkey, pushes him into the river and returns with a tale of death by misadventure. Ts'ai's mother falls ill from grief, and the plot continues as above except that old Mrs. Ts'ai is accused of the murder and Tou O, to save her mother-in-law, declares that she herself administered the poison. The dénouement is happier, for Ulysses is restored to his Penelope; Ts'ai Chang-tsung, who had escaped drowning, returns triumphantly from the Imperial Examination to the embraces of his virtuous and self-sacrificing spouse. Dr. A. E. Zucker's version in *The Chinese Theatre*, pp. 39-40 (Boston, 1925), is a crude summary of Kuan Han-ch'ing's play translated by Bazin aîné, which, with *Chao's Orphan*, was considered by the great scholar Wang Kuo-wei as the most tragic of all Yüan dramas*. Unfortunately this is never acted nowadays, for it is superior to its progeny in every respect. The chief points in common are the poisoning (except that Chang Lü-êrh's father swallows the broth intended for the old lady), and the colloquy between Tou O and the executioner on the way to the scaffold. There is also a magnificent summer snow-storm, but Tou O invokes it. "You may be sure," she tells her mother-in-law, "that snow will fall continuously for six months, and that a drought will then afflict the land for three years." She is beheaded, and her outraged ghost sees to it that her father, now Lord Chief Justice, will avenge her in Act. IV. Chang Lü-êrh is picturesquely nailed to a wooden donkey and cut into a hundred and twenty pieces, while the provincial governor and those responsible for her execution are banished to the frontiers and deprived for life of further exployment.

It is worthy of note that the later the variations the more insipid, stilted and conventional the speech and action. The wardress is just a type of female clown : her speeches are almost identical with those of the warder in *Ch'i Shuang Hui* (p.p. 55 foll.)

---

*For a better summary see Ch'ien Chung-shu : " Tragedy in Old Chinese Drama," *T'ien Hsia Monthly*, Vol. 1, No. 1, p. 41.

CH'ING TING CHU* 慶 頂 珠

THE LUCKY PEARL

Also entitled *Ta Yü Sha Chia*: "A Fisherman kills a family."
PERIOD: Northern Sung (A.D. 960-1127).   A *hsi-p'i* play.

DRAMATIS PERSONÆ

HSIAO ÊN, a fisherman	*Lao-shêng*	
KUEI-YING, his daughter	*Ch'ing-i*	
LI CHÜN, a swashbuckler	⎱ *Erh-hua-lien*	
NI JUNG, another	⎰	
TING LANG, a servant of the Ting household ...	*Ch'ou-êrh*	
TING YÜAN WAI, a retired official	*Pai-ching*	
TA CHIAO SHIH, a champion boxer	⎫	
FOUR HSIAO CHIAO SHIH, assistant boxers ...	⎬ *Ch'ou-êrh*	
KUO HSIEN SHÊNG, secretary to Ting Yüan Wai	⎭	

This play is partly a burlesque, holding rapacious officials up to scorn. The victims of oppression are a poor old fisherman and his attractive daughter who, taxed to the limits of endurance, bring retribution on the local bully and his satellites.

The prologue consists of the fisherman and his daughter singing as they cross the stage in a boat. As soon as they row out of sight two swashbucklers appear.

SCENE I

LI CHÜN. I've fought fierce tigers on the southern mountains.

NI JUNG. And I've kicked the scaly dragon that swims the northern seas.

LI CHÜN. My name's Li Chün. I'm known as "the Dragon that confuses the river-currents."

NI JUNG. My name is Ni Jung, alias "the Curly-haired Tiger."

---

*The full meaning is : "A lucky pearl to be worn on the crown of the head." It was generally a pearl of peculiar shape which the bridegroom presented to his *fiancée*, equivalent to our wedding-ring. But instead of being worn on the finger, it was fixed on the apex of the bridal head-dress.

LI CHÜN. Since we have leisure to-day, let us take a stroll along the river-bank. (*Sings in hsi-p'i yao-pan*) I can remember when I exterminated the notorious rebel-brigand Fang La in years gone by.

NI JUNG (*also in hsi-p'i yao-pan*). You are truly a hero, Brother!

LI CHÜN (*sings*). I declined to wear the ceremonial robes and belt of jade (i.e. enter official life).

NI JUNG. I would rather join the braves of rivers and lakes (i.e. go about redressing wrongs, in Robin Hood style).   *Exeunt.*

SCENE II

KUEI-YING (*sings behind the curtain in hsi-p'i tao-pan*). Onward the river rolls, and waves break high. (*Comes on stage and sings in k'uai-pan*) My father and I make our living on the turbulent waters. No painter's brush could depict the beauty of these verdant hills and waves. The home of every fisherman is his bark.

HSIAO ÊN (*enters and sings in hsi-p'i yao-pan*). Father and daughter catch fish in the river: we may be poor, but what do we care if people laugh at us? (*To Kuei-ying*) Hold fast the rudder! I am ready to cast the net. Alas, age is beginning to tell on me: my strength is failing.

KUEI-YING. If you are beginning to feel your age, Father, why not give up fishing?

HSIAO ÊN (*speaks*). If I did that, how could we live?

KUEI-YING (*weeps and sighs*). Alas!

HSIAO ÊN. Don't weep, my dear. The weather is too hot! Let us seek a cool nook under the trees to rest. I have already caught a few fish. Go and put them in the hold ready for sale so that I may procure some wine to cheer me.

Li Chün and Ni Jung appear, singing in hsi-p'i yao-pan.

LI. Idly we saunter by the riverside.

NI. Mightily ever eastwards roll the billows.

LI. I pause to view the prospect far and wide.

NI. I spy a bark beneath a fringe of willows.

LI (*speaking*). Now that I'm nearer I can discern a figure on board that looks remarkably like my old comrade, Brother Hsiao. I'll call out and make sure . . .

KUEI-YING. Father, somebody's calling you from the bank.

HSIAO ÊN. I'll see who it is. (*Stands up and gazes towards the newcomers*). Why yes, it's Brother Li! Are you coming on board, Brother?

LI AND NI (*in unison*). We were just on our way to see you.

HSIAO ÊN. Wait while your clumsy brother wipes and hands you the oar (*gestures accordingly*) . . . Who is this other gentleman? I have not yet had the pleasure of his acquaintance.

LI. This is Mr. Ni Jung, the Curly-haired Tiger. Let me introduce you two brethren.

NI JUNG. You are too punctilious, Sir. (*He grasps Hsiao's hand and gives it a tight squeeze*).

HSIAO ÊN. Why do you grip me so hard, Brother?

NI JUNG. I was only testing your strength.

HSIAO ÊN. I am old and useless. (*Both laugh; Hsiao sings to Kuei-ying*) Come out of the hold and greet your two uncles. (*She obeys. Follows a characteristic specimen of Chinese polite conversation which we print as such rather than for any inherent interest*).

NI JUNG. Who is this maiden?

HSIAO ÊN. It's my little daughter, Kuei-ying.

LI CHÜN. How old is she?

HSIAO ÊN. Sixteen.

LI CHÜN. Is she engaged to anyone yet?

HSIAO ÊN. Yes, she's already betrothed.

LI CHÜN. To whom, may I ask?

HSIAO ÊN. To Hua P'êng-ch'un, the son of Mr. Hua Jung.

LI CHÜN. I hope the two families are well matched. *Li and Ni turn to take leave.*

HSIAO. Don't go yet! I've caught a few fish to-day ; stay and help me to digest them with some wine.

LI AND NI. We fear our visit has put you to a deal of trouble.

HSIAO ÊN. What sort of talk is this among brethren ? (*To Kuei-ying*) Bring us the wine, dear. (*They sit down to drink*). Now, as I live on the produce of the waters, I dread the mention of two words : *kan* and *han* (i.e. to dry up, either through heavy frost or lack of rain). Whoever uses them is to drink three cups as forfeit.

LI CHÜN (*lifts his cup and says*). "*Kan pei !*" (*Chinese for " no heeltaps." He is promptly fined three cups*).

KUO (*enters while the party is thus engaged, and sings in hsi-p'i yao-pan*). While idly strolling by the shore, I spy a little boat. (*Speaks*) Hallo ! I see there's a pretty wench on board. I'll take a few steps forward and snatch a furtive glance.

LI AND NI. Brother Hsiao, there's a fellow spying on us from the bank.

Hsiao steps on shore and asks him who he is.

KUO. I've only come to ask my way.

HSIAO ÊN. Whither ?

KUO. To Mr. Ting's house.

HSIAO ÊN. Do you see that white wall like a figure eight just ahead of you there, with the big black varnished door and the two flag-poles ? That's the Ting Mansion. (*Kuo pays no attention : his eyes are riveted on Kuei-ying*). How now ! You are not even listening.

Exit Kuo in consternation.

HSIAO ÊN (*shouting after him*). Dog's head and brains !* I am sure you're up to no good ! (*Returns to boat. Li and Ni inquire who it was and he tells them. Enter Ting*

---

*Epithet for one whose eyes are continually roving in all directions.

Lang, Yüan Wai's servant, calling out for Hsiao En: Li Chün draws Hsiao's attention to the fact. Hsiao urges them to drink a little more, but they say they have tippled enough. He then steps on shore again). Well, well, if it isn't Ting Lang-êrh! And what has brought you hither?

TING LANG. I've come to collect the fishing-tax.

HSIAO ÊN. The river's almost dry for lack of rain and the nets have long been empty. Some other day when I am in funds I'll go along and pay the tax to the Ting family.

TING LANG. Although you offer fair words, I've worn out a pair of shoes on this errand. Who'll give me the money to buy new ones?

Hsiao En returns to his boat and tells his friends what Ting had come for.

LI CHÜN. I'll call him back and exchange a few words with him.

HSIAO ÊN. But don't cause a rumpus, whatever you do!

LI CHÜN. I quite understand! *(To Ting Lang)* Ho you, come here!

TING LANG. Oh, there's another of them. Well, I'll turn back.

LI CHÜN. What's your business?

TING LANG. To collect the tax on fishing.

LI CHÜN. Have you the Emperor's permission?

TING LANG. No.

LI CHÜN. Well, where did you get your authority from?

TING LANG. From His Honour the Magistrate.

LI CHÜN. It must be that Lü Tzǔ-ch'iu you refer to?

TING LANG. I refer to His Honour the Magistrate*.

LI CHÜN. Be off with you and tell him to abolish the fishing-tax. If he doesn't, there's a chance that

---

*Li Chün purposely pronounces the magistrate's name, while Ting refers to him as "His Honour," as it is not complimentary to use an official's cognomen.

something inconvenient may happen if we meet in the road.

TING LANG. You talk pretty big ; what is your name anyway ?

LI CHÜN. I'm the Dragon that confuses the Rivers.

TING LANG. You mean you're the stink-bug in a ball of dung.

LI CHÜN. Just wait till I give you a walloping, you eight days' spawn of a turtle ! (*Here Hsiao En begs them to desist. But Ni Jung joins in the vituperation*).

NI (*to Ting Lang*). Roll back, and I'll gouge out your eyes and boil them in liquor ! I'll flay your hide and mix it with dog-skin to make a plaster for carbuncles.

TING LANG. Stop bragging ! What's your name I'd like to know ?

NI JUNG. I'm Ni Jung, the Curly-haired Tiger.

TING LANG. What sort of louse in a mongrel's hair are you ?

NI JUNG. Look out for a thrashing, you mouldy spawn of a turtle !

TING LANG. Just wait, don't be in such a hurry. I'll first take off my hat and gown. . .

Hsiao En attempts to dissuade them from fighting.

TING LANG (*to Hsiao*). You hold him while I run away.　　　　　　　　　　　　　　　　　　(*Exit*).

LI AND NI. Why are you so feeble, Brother Hsiao ?

HSIAO ÊN. The power and influence of the Ting family are very considerable.

LI AND NI. But they are not princes !

HSIAO ÊN. They have a quantity of retainers.

LI AND NI. But our brethren also are many.

HSIAO ÊN. They have abundance of riches.

LI AND NI. They cannot buy us over, though.

HSIAO ÊN. It's a very ticklish problem.

LI AND NI. You had better retire from this water business.

HSIAO. It's time I did, but then I'd have nothing to live on, I fear. I'd just become a beggar.

LI CHÜN. I'll present you with a hundred ounces of silver.

HSIAO. I'd be too ashamed to accept such a gift.

NI JUNG. And I'll present you with a thousand pounds of rice.

HSIAO. I could not accept, I would really feel ashamed!

LI AND NI. Never mind shame! We'll go and fetch the money and the rice.

Both depart. Hsiao sees them off with expressions of gratitude. Afterwards they discuss the appropriateness of Kuei-ying's engagement " as they are of equal status," *and decide to send the wedding presents to her new home. Parallelwise the old fisherman and his daughter admiringly discuss the recent guests and their knight-errantry.*

HSIAO ÊN (*sings*). Look yonder, the evening shades are falling fast. (*Speaks*) It is getting late; we had better steer for home. . . . (*Exeunt, after a refrain reminiscent of* The Miller of Dee : " *I care for nobody, no, not I*," *etc.*).

SCENE III

Enter Ting Yüan Wai and his secretary Kuo.

YÜAN WAI. I have stored a thousand piculs of grain.

KUO. Yes, all our granaries are full.

TING LANG (*enters and says*). I've just arrived from the river to report to you, Sir.

YÜAN WAI. Come to the point then. What about the fishing-tax I sent you to collect this morning?

Ting Lang reports his conversation with Hsiao En and trouble with the swashbucklers, after which he is told he may go.

KUO. This is a trifling affair : let me settle it.

Yüan Wai tells him to proceed with great circumspection.

Exit Ting Yüan Wai.

KUO (*to himself*). It seems to me that we had better send the boxers along. (*He shouts, and four boxers appear*). Where is your chief? (*They reply that he is practicing at the back*). Tell him to come here.

CHIEF BOXER (*appears saying*). It's good to gorge and good to booze but sleep is better fun. And when there is a fight, I am the very first to run. What's up, my lads?

THE FOUR BOXERS. Mr. Kuo wishes to see you.

Kuo tells them about the fracas with Hsiao En, etc., and that they are required to go and enforce payment of the tax and avenge their master's insult.

CHIEF BOXER. We are here to guard the mansion, not to collect taxes.

KUO (*persuasively*). But it's only for this once!

CHIEF BOXER. Well, we'll help you out this time, but mind there's to be no second time. Get the carts ready!

KUO. Are the carts to be used for transporting the money collected?

CHIEF BOXER. No, they're to carry our men, not the silver.

KUO. How ludicrous! (*Exit laughing*).

CHIEF BOXER. Are any of you fistical fellows acquainted with this Hsiao En?

FOUR BOXERS. Oh yes, we all know him by sight.

CHIEF BOXER. Capital! We'll pick up chicken's feathers as we go along.

FOUR BOXERS. What do you mean by that?

CHIEF BOXER. I mean we'll have more courage if we stick together. (*Exeunt omnes*).

SCENE IV

昨夜　晚　　　　　吃酒　醉
tso yeh　wan .... ch'ih chiu　tsui

合　衣　　　　而　　臥
ho　i .... êrh　wo ....

鵑　驚　醒　了　　　夢　裡　南　柯
chi　ching hsing liao　.mêng　li　nan　k'o

架　上
chia shang

HSIAO ÊN (*enters rather muzzily, singing in hsi-p'i man-pan*). Last night I got tippled and slept in my clothes. Already the cocks are crowing on the rafters. While I was dreaming they woke me up.

My two comrades advised me to have done with fishing. It's high time I did retire, to stay at home and rest. But I'm too poor and can think of no other means of supporting myself in old age. I have woken up early this morning. Is it not crows that I hear?* Hither

---

*Unlucky omens.

and thither they fly calling to each other . . . I think
I'll go into my grass hut and quench my thirst with tea.

Kuei-ying appears with a tea-tray.

KUEI-YING (*singing in hsi-p'i yao-pan*). How ill-fated
am I to have lost my mother in early youth: only poor
Father and I are left to fish by the river! (*Speaks*) Here's
your tea, Father.

HSIAO ÊN (*takes the cup and drinks, then looking at
Kuei-ying's clothes, says*). Didn't I tell you not to wear
your fishing-clothes at home?

KUEI-YING. I was born and brought up in a fisherman's family. If you don't want me to dress like this,
how am I to dress?

HSIAO ÊN. Not listening to your father's advice
shows that you are unfilial.

KUEI-YING. There's no need to be angry, Father.
I'll go and change.

HSIAO ÊN. Very well, see that you do so in future.

*Here the boxers all strut in and a deal of irrelevant
verbiage follows as to whether Hsiao is at home or not,
and much dawdling for fear of being attacked by the fisherman's
friends. Finally Hsiao opens his cottage door: the chief boxer,
true to the universal conventions of farce, slips and stumbles.
"Oh, I've slipped on a water-melon peel!" he observes.
Pretending not to see Hsiao, one of his myrmidons then inquires:
"Has Mr. Hsiao come out?"*

CHIEF BOXER. So you are at home, Mr. Hsiao. I
wish to see you about something. (*Examining him
closely*). Why he's nothing but a feeble old man!

HSIAO ÊN. Where do you folks come from?

CHIEF BOXER. We're Mr. Ting's fine fistical fellows.

*They tell him their mission; he makes the same excuses and
says he will pay the tax on some future date at the Ting Mansion.*

CHIEF BOXER. Others have come and heard the same
tale. I, the chief boxer, have come to-day to see that
you pay up.

HSIAO ÊN. I had nothing for the others, and I have less for you. (*Inflates his chest and strikes a threatening attitude*).

CHIEF BOXER. He's showing fight! Help me to get out of this quick before I lose any blood. We mustn't show any signs of weakness : we must resist him strength for strength. Have you brought the chains? Shackle him, and drag him away. (*To Hsiao*) Do you know what these things are?

HSIAO ÊN. Yes, they are instruments of Imperial law but what are you applying them to me for?

BOXER CHIEF. These chains are something that will shorten your wretched old life, let me tell you.

HSIAO ÊN. Quite useless! (*He throws them off and tramples on them. The chief boxer, too cowardly to go nearer and pick up the chains, orders his myrmidons to do so*).

BOXERS (*nervously*). You haven't taught us how to play this sort of trick.

CHIEF BOXER. What a pack of nincompoops! Just look at me! (*To Hsiao*) What ho, Hsiao Ên, have you ever seen a sight so strange as that?

HSIAO ÊN. Strange as what?

CHIEF BOXER. A bird with two polls.

HSIAO (*looking round*). Where?

CHIEF BOXER. Right here, in my hands : I picked it up while you were looking the other way. (*He begins to fasten the chain round Hsiao's neck*).

HSIAO ÊN. You sneak-thief, you worthless worm!

CHIEF BOXER. Remove him. If he has the money, well and good : if not, away with him!

An argument ensues as to whether he is to be shackled. Hsiao bursts the chains, throws them over the chief's head and shouts : " Haul him away! " The myrmidons start off with their chief in shackles instead of the fisherman.

CHIEF BOXER. Stop it. Where are you tugging me off to?

ASSISTANTS. Why, we've been heaving the wrong fellow!

CHIEF BOXER. There's not a single eye between the lot of you! This old codger's a wily one. We can't take him by force, better try persuasion. (*To Hsiao*) Your Honour, never mind if you have no cash. Come over the river with us and visit Ting Yüan Wai. Whether you pay or not is up to you ; and whether he defers the tax is up to him. It has really nothing to do with us boxers anyway.

HSIAO ÊN. I catch your drift. You want me to cross the river with you to visit Ting Yüan Wai : whether he accepts the money or not rests with him, and not with you. Gentlemen, I have no leisure!

CHIEF BOXER. So you cold-shoulder my advances. You'll neither pay up nor come along with us. If you don't, we are many against you . . .

HSIAO ÊN. A set of sucklings. You want a fight, do you? When I was young, I was as keen to fight as a child is to slip on a pair of new shoes on the first of the year : I rejoiced at the very idea. But now I am old and useless in a struggle.

CHIEF BOXER. I'd like to test you.

HSIAO ÊN. In what way?

CHIEF BOXER. Test *you*, you antiquated rat, licking a cat's whiskers right over its nose and waiting for death!

HSIAO ÊN. Are you really so anxious to fight me, baby? (*The dialogue continues in the same strain until the fisherman says*) All right then. Wait until I take off my coat and I'll show you something. (*Sings in hsi-p'i yao-pan*) May I expose the seven apertures of my body to fiery flames if I don't . . .

CH'EF BOXER. I'll go one better and riddle your carcass with eight holes until it smokes!

HSIAO ÊN. Old as I am, I'm in such a boiling rage that I could grind my teeth to powder! (*Starts fighting with the boxers and sings*) I'm the stalwart Hsiao Ên who roams the lakes and rivers.

HSIAO ÊN CHALLENGES THE CHIEF BOXER

Ch'ing Ting Chu

MEI LAN-FANG   WANG SHAO-LOU
AS KUEI-YING   AS HSIAO ÊN

Kuei-ying tries to restrain her father
from going to the Ting Mansion

Ch'ing Ting Chu

CHIEF BOXER. And I'm the famous Tso T'ung-chui (Chief Brass-hammer).

HSIAO ÊN. How many battles have you fought, great and small? As for me, I'm the fierce lonely tiger of the mountains.

CHIEF BOXER. We'll see! I'll have a round with you. If you are the tiger, I am the hunter to kill it.

HSIAO (*sings*). Who's afraid of a mere domestic watchdog?

After further braggadocio, they butt into each other; the four boxers are beaten and quit the stage. The chief begs Hsiao on his knees to let him off.

HSIAO. It's easy enough to let you off, but first I'll give you three punches to remember me by.

CHIEF BOXER. Three punches! why I'll take three hundred if you let me off and consider myself in luck.

Hsiao continues to belabour him and Kuei-ying joins in with a stick. The chief boxer bolts.

KUEI-YING. I can fight too!

HSIAO. You can! But this will only bring trouble on us. He is bound to tell the Ting family. Fetch my clothes quick; I'll go to the yamen before him and lodge a complaint.

KUEI-YING. He belongs to an official's household, better not go!

HSIAO ÊN. You are a child: what do you know of such things? You look after the home while I am away.

Exit Kuei-ying.

HSIAO ÊN (*solo*). Just as I am sitting quietly at home with the door closed, sudden calamity descends from Heaven upon me! (*Exit*).

SCENE V

Enter the Boxers and Secretary Kuo.

KUO. So you have returned. Have you brought the money with you?

CHIEF BOXER. No. We were all routed by that old blackguard, Hsiao Ên.

KUO. To-morrow I'll have him taken to the yamen for punishment. That should appease your wrath.

CHIEF BOXER (*to his myrmidons*). Let's go and have our wounds dressed. (*Exeunt omnes*).

SCENE VI

Kuei-ying appears singing in hsi-p'i yao-pan to express her anxiety about her absent father : Father has been gone a long time, and still no tidings.

The hubbub of a magistrate's yamen is heard from behind the stage. Then voices counting ten, twenty, thirty, forty : Hsiao En is getting forty strokes of the bamboo. After which he totters on to the stage.

HSIAO ÊN. Curses on that Lü Tzŭ-ch'iu ! He is not an honest and upright official. He had no right to punish me like that. A quiet and peaceful subject like me goes to complain at the yamen and the vicious curs, without a single word, set on me with forty strokes of the heavy bamboo and want me to apologize into the bargain ! But there's no help for it. I can only gnash my teeth and hurry home. (*On arriving he sings out*) Kuei-ying, open the door !

KUEI-YING (*opening*). At last you've returned, Father ! But why are you in such a dreadful state ? (*Hsiao tells her. She bursts into tears*). You have been most barbarously treated !

HSIAO ÊN. I don't mind the pain so much as I resent being ordered to apologize to the Ting family.

KUEI-YING. Are you going to, Father ?

HSIAO ÊN. I wish I could grow a pair of wings to fly across and kill the lot of them.

KUEI-YING. Father, you had better not go.

HSIAO ÊN. A mere child like you knows nothing of such matters. Make haste ! fetch my coat and cap and the steel sword. (*She fetches them*). Stay here and look after the place in the meantime.

KUEI-YING. I'll accompany you, Father.

HSIAO ÊN. You are a girl and had better stay at home.

KUEI-YING. But isn't this a fine chance to show my courage?

HSIAO ÊN. All right. Get ready to come along with me.

KUEI-YING. What about our things here?

HSIAO ÊN. We don't need any of them. (*Kuei-ying fears they will be stolen during their absence and bursts into tears*). Don't cry so. Have you brought that lucky pearl (*Ch'ing Ting Chu*) with you? (*Kuei-ying says yes*). If anything untoward happens, you had better run off to your mother-in-law's, where you'll be safe.

KUEI-YING. What about you, Father?

HSIAO ÊN. Don't worry about me. (*They board the boat*). My child, sailing by night is not the same as by day : steady the rudder, you must be more cautious than usual. (*Sings in hsi-p'i k'uai-pan*) This affair is none of my seeking. I feel as if I were going through fire. I am crossing the river to-night to slay the whole family. If only I had wings to cross more swiftly ! Why have you slackened the ropes, child?

KUEI-YING. Do you really mean to murder them, Father?

HSIAO ÊN. Of course, I am in earnest !

KUEI-YING. In that case I'll not go : I dare not.

HSIAO ÊN. Pah ! When I didn't want you to, you insisted on coming : now that we're half-way, you want to turn back ! Very well, I'll take you back.

KUEI-YING. I'll go with you, Father. I don't want to return. I could not possibly part with you so !

HSIAO Ên (*sings and weeps*). Alas, my poor, dear daughter !

Scene VII

They reach their destination, moor the boat and disembark.
HSIAO ÊN. My child, bear this in mind. Henceforth
no matter where we are, if I upbraid, you too upbraid.
If I say strike, you strike! We have now arrived at the
Ting Mansion. Hey there! Anybody at home? (*The
Chief Boxer appears and opens the door*). I've come to tender
my apologies to Ting Yüan Wai. (*The Chief Boxer, after
some conventional fooling, goes off to announce him*).

Scene VIII

Enter Ting Yüan Wai and his secretary Kuo.
TING. Last night I had a very curious dream.
KUO. So had I! I dreamt that Yen Lo, King of the
Underworld, had invited me to drink with him.
CHIEF BOXER. Hsiao Ên has come to offer his
apologies.
TING. Show him in. (*Enter Hsiao, whom he addresses*)
You impudent old wretch, what made you attack my
employees as if they were wild beasts? And what have
you to say in defence of such conduct?
HSIAO ÊN. With respect to this fishing-tax, have
you the Imperial sanction?
TING. No.
HSIAO ÊN. Have you authority from the Six Boards?
TING. No.
HSIAO ÊN. By whose authority do you levy it, then?
TING. By His Honour the District Magistrate's.
HSIAO ÊN. Can you mean that Lü Tzǔ-ch'iu? (*Sings
in hsi-p'i yao-pan*) Lü Tzǔ-ch'iu, you are far too avari-
cious! By what right did you sentence me to forty
strokes of the bamboo? (*To Kuei-ying*) Curse him,
denounce him, my dear!
KUEI-YING (*sings in hsi-p'i yao-pan*). The thieving cur
and rebel! May Heaven utterly destroy him! He

takes advantage of his official status to oppress the innocent. May he die without a clod of earth to cover his wretched carcass! ‡

TING (*to his servants*). Bring her here!

HSIAO ÊN. Ho, slowly there! We have, in the goodness of our hearts, brought you an offering.

TING. What is it?

HSIAO ÊN. We have come to present you with a pearl which we fished up out of the river.

TING. Let me see it.

HSIAO ÊN. There are too many eyes about.

TING (*to attendants*). Leave the room, all of you. (*Exeunt servants*). Where is it?

HSIAO ÊN. Here! (*Promptly draws his sword and kills Ting Yüan Wai and Kuo. He then says to Kuei-ying*) Daughter, help me to dispose of the rest.

The four assistant boxers come in and are slain. The Chief Boxer follows, and is likewise put to the sword.

Exeunt the fisherman and his daughter. Finis.

*   *   *

This is an unusually fresh and animated play. Although the audience's sympathy is focused on the aged fisherman and his daughter, the dramatist does not sentimentalize unduly about their plight; the action consequently moves with comparative speed. The desperate *dénouement* is un-Confucian; the social satire is tactfully neutralized by a deal of pure knockabout farce, but pity and anger are there despite the grotesque antics and fantastic jargon of the comedians. It need hardly be said that Hsiao Ên was prevaricating when he told the rich landlord he had fished the pearl out of the river; it was just a ruse to excite his covetousness and get rid of his underlings. The theme is by no means antiquated. Brawls between fishermen and tax-collectors are as frequent nowadays as during the Northern Sung dynasty. In Peking one often hears of similar cases outside the Tung Pien Mên, not to speak of the vicinity of Peitaiho Beach.

---

‡ The last is one of the worst maledictions that could blight a Chinese ear.

CHIU KÊNG (or CHING) T'IEN 九更天

THE DAY OF NINE WATCHES

Also called *Ma I Chiu Chu* : "Ma I rescues his Master"; and *Kun Ting Pan*: "Rolling on a Spiked Board."

PERIOD : Uncertain. It has been assigned to the Shang dynasty (1766-1122 B.C.) somewhat fancifully, as there were no Triennial Examinations in those remote days. The plot probably originated in the Sung dynasty, when the civil service examinations were already instituted. Moreover, a *T'ai Shih* Scholar by name of Wên T'ien-hsiang (A.D. 1236-1282) was one of the most distinguished and loyal ministers of the Sung dynasty : he refused to submit to Kublai Khan, and was executed in consequence. An *êrh-huang hsi-p'i* play.

DRAMATIS PERSONÆ

MA I, a heroic servant	*Lao-shêng*
MI CHIN-T'U, Ma I's master	*Hsiao-shêng*
YAO SHIH, Mi Chün-hsing's young widow ...	*Hua-tan*
HOU HUA-TSUI, Yao Shih's paramour	*Ch'ou-êrh*
WÊN T'AI SHIH, Minister of Justice	*Ching*
MAGISTRATE OF MO-LI HSIEN	*Shêng*
MA YÜEH-HSIANG, Ma I's daughter	*Ch'ing-i*
MA SHIH, Ma I's wife	*Lao-tan*
LI SHIH, Hou Hua-tsui's wife	*Ts'ai-tan*

SCENE I

A young scholar named Mi Chin-t'u is on his way to the Capital to compete in the Examination, accompanied by Ma I, a trusty old family retainer. Spending the night at an inn, both are haunted by the same ghastly dream: Mi's brother Chün-hsing appears to them all dabbled in blood and beseeches them to avenge his murder. Instead of pursuing their journey they saddle their horses and turn home.

SCENE II

YAO SHIH (*enters and sings in hsi-p'i yao-pan*). Ever since I murdered my husband, my heart has been all of a flutter. My very flesh creeps at the memory. If my husband's younger brother returns and this affair leaks out my own life will be in serious danger!

Chin-t'u and Ma I return and, after the usual courtesies, Yao Shih sends Ma I away to take a rest. Chin-t'u asks Yao Shih why she is in mourning; she tells him of his brother's sudden death. He breaks into lamentation and, on hearing that the corpse is in an ante-room, goes to burn incense at the foot of the coffin.

MI CHIN-T'U *(after paying respects to the coffin, sings in hsi-p'i tao-pan).* Before your coffin I weep tears of blood, my brother, oh my brother! *(Sings in hsi-p'i yao-pan)* I feel as if a blade of steel had pierced me·through the heart.

YAO SHIH. Do not weep, Brother: once dead, man cannot come back to life again!

CHIN-T'U. I must keep wake beside the coffin.

YAO SHIH. You will feel too lonely all by yourself. . . . Let me keep you company.

CHIN-T'U. You are a widow now: it would be inconvenient if the neighbours saw us keeping wake together.

YAO SHIH. No matter; let me stay with you.

CHIN-T'U. Humph! what sort of decorum would that be? Leave me alone, I say.   (*Exit*).

YAO SHIH *(sola)*. Ha! So you spurn me and ignore my request! What is the best course for me now? (*Reflecting*) Ah, I have it! I'll go and see Hou Ta Yeh (her paramour) and discuss the matter with him. (*Walks about the stage, indicating that she is on her way. Sings out*) Hou Ta Yeh, open the door!

HOU *(appearing)*. What are you coming here for at this time of night?

YAO SHIH. Mi Chin-t'u has returned. The matter is urgent. You had better decide at once what is to be done about it.

HOU (*after a moment's reflection*).   Ah! I've an idea!
I'll make my wife drunk, cut off her head and hide it
under my couch.   I'll dump the body on Chin-t'u's
threshold.   Then I'll report to the magistrate that he
tried to ravish his sister-in-law and killed her when she
rejected his advances.   Isn't this a brilliant solution?

*Yao Shih agrees and the plan is fulfilled accordingly.   An
officer goes to Mi's house, drags him away from the coffin and
puts him under arrest.*

SCENE III

THE MAGISTRATE (*enters with his horde of lictors and
takes his seat on the bench; then addresses the prisoner*).   Mi
Chin-t'u, you are a scholar.   Why did you murder your
sister-in-law, Yao Shih?   Tell me the entire truth without evasion.

MI.   This is the first I hear of it.

MAGISTRATE (*to lictors*).   Put him in confinement
until I have investigated the case.

Exit Chin-t'u with yamen-runners.

SCENE IV

HOU (*entering*).   Well, that was very nicely settled.
Now I think I'll go home. (*Knocks at his door.   It is
opened by Yao Shih, who has been hiding in his house.   She
asks him how the affair came off and he tells her*).

YAO SHIH.   Then I had better go home.

HOU.   How now! Wait a moment : don't forget you're
supposed to be dead!

YAO SHIH.   But where am I to live in the meantime?

HOU.   Why, here with me, of course.   Come along
to the ante-room.   We'll have some wine, and so to
bed.   I'm feeling quite exhausted.   (*Exeunt*).

SCENE V

*Enter Magistrate and attendants.   Chin-t'u is summoned
to appear, in shackles.   The Magistrate proceeds to question*

him about the murder. Mi protests his innocence. The Magistrate sends lictors with his card to interview Mi's teacher and ask if he will stand bond for him. They report that the teacher refuses to undertake this responsibility.

MAGISTRATE (*to lictors*). Remove his cap and robe. (*Since Mi holds official rank, he cannot be punished before this ceremony is performed. When he is disrobed the Magistrate says*) I can see that unless I inflict corporal punishment you will refuse to confess. (*To lictors*) Prepare the heavy instruments of torture.

Chin-t'u is forced to kneel and the chia-kun, a wooden instrument for squeezing the ankles, is clapped on. Unable to stand such exquisite pain, he faints away. He is revived by a douche of cold water in the face.

MI (*singing in hsi-p'i yao-pan*). Your Honour, I cannot endure this punishment. My heart brims over with such a sense of wrong that I am tongueless.

MAGISTRATE. Make haste and confess!

LICTORS. He refuses to confess, Your Honour.

MAGISTRATE. Clap the ankle-squeezers on again if he insists on being stubborn.

MI. I'll confess, Your Honour, I confess!

MAGISTRATE. See that he signs his confession, then off with him to gaol! (*Mi is shackled and taken out, weeping. Ma I, on seeing that his master's life is in danger, comes crying out that he has a grievance to redress. He is led before the Magistrate, who asks*) What manner of old dog are you, to come howling in here?

MA I. I have come to lodge a complaint on behalf of my master, Your Honour.

MAGISTRATE. Well, out with it! (*When Ma I has related the story from beginning to end the Magistrate exclaims*) But your master has already confessed to the crime!

MA I. Already confessed? There must be some terrible mistake! Please, my Lord, be merciful!

MAGISTRATE. Very well. Since you are such a loyal and devoted servant, I'll grant you three days to bring me your mistress's head; whereupon your master shall be released. (*Exeunt*).

MA I. I don't know where to look for the head, but if I fail to find it I must go home and consult my wife. Perhaps I'll have to kill my daughter and bring her head as a substitute. Yes, that's what I had better do! (*Exit*).

SCENE VI

Enter Ma I's wife and daughter Yüeh-hsiang, separately.

MA SHIH (*sings in êrh-huang yao-pan*). My husband has been away a long time now. I am really getting very worried about him. Day and night he never leaves my thoughts.

YÜEH-HSIANG (*sings in êrh-huang*). Last night I dreamt a fearful dream. When mother comes, I must tell her about it.

MA I (*from behind the curtain*). Well, well! Home at last. (*He appears with a large knife in his hand*). But when I think of this ghastly business, my heart is dull and heavy. I feel as if ten thousand knives were piercing my vitals. It is in sorrow that I enter my humble abode; even so, I must adapt myself to circumstances.

After the usual bows, he tells the cause of his delay and his master's misfortune, all spun out at unconscionable length from beginning to end; Ma I's wife suggests they devise a plan to save the master.

MA I. When I explained the case to the Magistrate, a man of clear perception, he promised he would release my master on condition I brought him the head.

MA SHIH. Well then, you had better try and look for it.

MA I. Alas, I know it is all a trumped-up charge. Where am I to find the head; what am I to do? I came here purposely to consult you. I can only think of killing our own dear daughter; then I could take her head to the Magistrate and tell him it belongs to my mistress.

MA SHIH. We have been married over fifty years without a son at our knees, only this slip of a girl. Nothing on earth will induce me to listen to such a proposal!

YÜEH-HSIANG. Never mind, Father. It will not matter much if you kill me. My sole concern is, who will look after you in your old age? Who will mourn at your grave?

Mother and daughter weep and repeat this important question. Mother Ma tries to console Yüeh-hsiang by saying: "I'll persuade your father to invent some other plan." *But Ma I argues that he owes this sacrifice to so kind and considerate a master.*

MA I (*finally sings*). Oh, it breaks an old man's heart to witness so sad a scene. (*Speaks*) I must be resolved to make an end of it! (*Sings*) To cut off a head with a steel blade is unbearably cruel. Suit yourself, my daughter, as to how you will die!

He throws the knife on the ground.

YÜEH-HSIANG. I see a sharp knife glittering on the floor. Far better that I bear this painful burden! I'll take the weapon and end my life with a single blow.

Seizes it and cuts her throat.

MA SHIH. Oh, husband! Our little daughter has destroyed herself!

MA I (*groans, cries* "Alas!" *and sings in êrh-huang yao-pan*). At the sight of my poor child's blood-smeared corpse my heart is almost broken. I'll now remove her head. (*Suits action to words. Exeunt Ma I and wife*).

SCENE VII

MAGISTRATE (*enters saying*). Owing to this confounded head affair, day or night I haven't been able to snatch a moment's rest. (*Sits on the bench and orders Mi Chin-t'u to be brought forward. He asks him where the head is. Mi is about to be tortured, after further protestations of innocence, when Ma I appears with his daughter's head. After examining it the Magistrate exclaims*) But this is false !

MA I.   What do you mean by false, Your Honour ?

MAGISTRATE.   This belongs to a young girl, as can be seen from the way the hair is dressed ; it never belonged to a matron.   Where did you procure it ?

MA I.   Alas, Your Honour, I don't know who murdered my mistress or where to find her head.   To save my master's life I urged my daughter to commit suicide and cut off hers.   Here it is, Your Honour !

MAGISTRATE.   You are certainly a very loyal and devoted servant.   Go home and get your master's coffin ready.   Away with you !

The Magistrate leaves the bench while Ma I kneels and cries for mercy, knocking his head on the floor.   The lictors drive him away.

MA I (*dazed*).   What did His Honour signify ?

LICTORS.   He meant that you have not saved your master's life—on the contrary, you have endangered it, by bringing a spurious head in here.   (*Ma I swoons away*).

LICTORS.   There goes another !   (*Exeunt lictors*).

MA I (*comes to and sings in êrh-huang tao-pan*).   Alas, a single word has severed my three souls !   One soars to heaven, one sinks into the earth, and one abides with the corpse.   I've sent my master to the hill of cruel knives.*
(*Speaks*) Stay !   I had only thought of rescuing my master, not of jeopardizing him.   What is the best course now ?
(*After brief reflection*).   Ah !   I have heard that the T'ai Shih Wên can unravel knotty cases like a god.   I had better go off and submit matters to him.   (*Exit*).

SCENE VIII

WÊN T'AI SHIH (*enters, takes his seat on the bench and says*).   To-day is the third.   Bring in the notice-board of Proclamations and let us see what cases are to be tried.

---

* Execution ground.

MA I AND THE SPIKED
BOARD

WÊN T'AI SHIH

Chiu Kêng T'ien

Ma I beats a drum behind the curtain, announcing that he has a wrong to redress, and the Minister orders him to be admitted.

MA I (*sings to the accompaniment of the p'u-têng-o*).* I appeal to Your Excellency against the decision of the Mo-li Magistrate. (*He repeats this several times and hands over his petition*).

MINISTER (*reading it*). You audacious fellow! Is there a vestige of truth in the facts as stated herein? Do you know the laws of the land?

MA I. I know them well, Your Excellency, and that is why I am here.

MINISTER. There's the tiger-head lever-knife awaiting you: do you think you'll be able to endure that?

MA I. I could endure walking on a hill of knives, let alone the knife you speak of.

MINISTER (*to lictors*). Put him on the rack!

MA I (*sings in êrh-huang yao-pan*). To-day I am to suffer terrible chastisement on my master's account, but my life is in the hands of the gods.

MINISTER (*singing in êrh-huang yao-pan*). So, so. Little Ma I can stand his punishment without wincing, even without a delicate change of hue! There may be something in this version of his! (*To lictors*) Let him down! (*To Ma I*) My tiger-head punishment is nothing— a mere bagatelle!—you still have the board of thirty-six spikes in store for you.† Do you think you'll be able to bear that?

MA I. I could go through fire and flood, and suffer ten thousand deaths without a flinch.

MINISTER (*to lictors*). Put him on the rack!

MA I (*upon being stripped, cries out*). Mighty Heaven! I only demand redress, to save my unhappy master. Protect me, Heaven, from this stern ordeal!

---

* *See* Introduction, p. xxix.
† The prisoner was rolled naked over this ingenious harpsichord.

Once on the spiked board he is rolled over and over until the flesh hangs in shreds from his limp and macerated body. The orchestra strikes up some thrilling music in the meantime. The Minister, persuaded at last that Ma I is telling the truth, orders him to be removed, more dead than alive. He prepares a dispatch and orders his men to saddle their horses. Exeunt omnes.

Scene IX

Enter the Three Shades of Mi Chün-hsing, Yüeh-hsiang and Li Shih (Hou Hua-tsui's wife).

MI'S SHADE (*sings in êrh-huang yao-pan*). My curse on Yao Shih for intriguing against me ! I'll go and report her to the City God. (*The first watch of night is struck while the Shade addresses the God*) I, the ghost of Mi Chün-hsing, have a matter to report.

Yüeh-hsiang and Li Shih echo his words.

MI'S SHADE. I hear that to-day the T'ai Shih Wên is coming here to worship : let us betake ourselves to him and plead our cause. (*Sings in êrh-huang yao-pan*) Within the temple of the City God we'll plainly state our trials and tribulations. . . . (*Exeunt the Three Shades*).

Scene X

It is now the second watch. The Minister's runners arrive on horseback with the dispatches. The Minister then descends at the Ch'êng Huang Temple, kneels and burns incense.

MINISTER (*to runners*). You may leave me. But don't go too far away ! (*Soliloquizing*) I think I'll take a nap. (*Lies down and falls asleep. The third watch of the night is struck. The Three Shades approach the slumbering Minister, bow to him and retire. A monkey with a flower in its mouth then springs across the stage, frightening the Minister out of his doze*).

MINISTER (*rises and says*). It is precisely the third watch. It seems to me I saw three ghosts who came

and implored me to redress their wrongs. Suddenly
they vanished. And surely I saw a monkey too : it had a
flower in its mouth and jumped as if it were afraid of me.
Let's see ! *Hou* (monkey) has the same sound as *Hou*
of Hou Hua-tsui : *Hua* (flower) is the same as the
second character in his name, and *Tsui* (mouth) coincides
with the last. Hou Hua-tsui is undoubtedly connected
with this murder. I must go with all speed to Mo-li
Hsien before it is too late. (*To lictors*) Light the lanterns
and torches : we must proceed at once to Mo-li Hsien.

SCENE XI

*It is now the fourth watch. Two executioners, four soldiers
and two lictors appear with Mi, bound and shackled.*
MAGISTRATE (*enters and takes his seat on the bench. Addressing executioners*). When the fifth watch strikes at
daylight remove Chin-t'u and cut off his head without
delay. (*Exeunt omnes*).
*At the fifth watch—the usual time of daybreak—two
messengers appear with the Minister's dispatches : the Minister
follows with his runners. The night-watchmen enter, wondering
why it is still so dark : they decide to make six watches of it.
While they are striking, the Minister is seen approaching in the
distance. At the end of the sixth watch, the night being as
dense as ever, the seventh is struck. Two messengers arrive
and beat the yamen-drum. The dispatch is handed to the
lictors, who take it in to the Magistrate.*
MAGISTRATE (*opening and reading the dispatch*). Why, this
is from the T'ai Shih. He is on his way to investigate the
head murder-case. How many watches have been struck ?
NIGHT-WATCHMEN. We have already struck seven,
Your Honour, and it is not daylight yet.
*The Magistrate exclaims that it is all very strange and
orders another watch to be struck. Two more riders appear and
beat the yamen-drum. Another dispatch ! The Magistrate tears
it open with increasing agitation, exclaiming that there must be*

some very serious grievance to be redressed. His attendants announce the Minister's imminent arrival. During the preparations for his reception, the night-watchmen, very perplexed because the darkness has not yet lifted, beat the ninth watch. The Minister and his staff arrive upon the scene.

MAGISTRATE (*to Minister*). My best respects to Your Excellency.

MINISTER. Are you the Magistrate of Mo-li ?

MAGISTRATE. Yes, Your Excellency.

MINISTER. Why don't you hold up your head ?

MAGISTRATE. I crave Your Excellency's pardon : I dare not.

MINISTER. You are pardoned.

MAGISTRATE. I thank Your Excellency.

MINISTER. Bah ! You bold and presumptuous specimen of a magistrate, you. So you forced Mi Chin-t'u to confess under torture. His servant Ma I has reported you.

MAGISTRATE. My mean ability is to blame, Your Excellency. Please have mercy on my unworthiness.

MINISTER. Bring Chin-t'u here ! (*When the prisoner is brought in, shackled and bound, he addresses him*) Chin-t'u, let me hear the full particulars of your case, without the slightest evasion.

The prisoner proceeds to relate them at length.

MINISTER. You may go ! (*To Magistrate*) Who first reported the case ?

MAGISTRATE. Hou Hua-tsui, Your Excellency.

MINISTER. Aha ! Hou Hua-tsui ! Let him be brought before me.

Hou is led in, and again the Minister asks for full particulars.

HOU. I know nothing whatever about it.

MINISTER. Scoundrel ! I can see that unless torture is applied you'll not confess. (*To lictors*) Prepare the instruments. . . .

HOU. Wait ! Slowly, Your Excellency : I confess.

MINISTER. You deceiving, murderous blackguard! You bestial slave and vile adulterer! (*To lictors*) Bring Yao Shih here.

Seeing her lover, Yao Shih asks him why he is there. He tells her that he has been arrested. She kneels before the bench.

MINISTER. How and why did you murder your husband? Make a clean breast of it, or severe punishment will be meted out to you.

YAO SHIH. This affair was entirely instigated by Hou Hua-tsui. As for me, I had nothing to do with it.

MINISTER. I can see that you will not confess until you are tortured. (*To lictors*) Prepare the instruments. . . .

YAO SHIH. I confess, Your Excellency. I share the guilt with Hou Hua-tsui.

MINISTER (*to scribes*). Take down their depositions.

The result of the trial is that Hou is condemned to be sawed in half, and Yao Shih to be disembowelled and sliced. Before leaving Court, Hou says to Yao Shih: " If we are to die, we may as well die together! " *The Minister orders the Magistrate to return to his office and await further instructions. The latter superfluously observes :* " I understand this case quite clearly now. I was duped. But now it is too late! " *Exit. The Minister summons Ma I and Chin-t'u, who come in blubbering.*

MINISTER (*to Ma I*). You have proved yourself an exceptionally faithful and devoted servant. You command my admiration and esteem. How many sons have you?

MA I. I have no sons, Your Excellency, only a slip of a daughter. And she is dead, as Your Excellency knows . . . (*He breaks down, choking with sobs*).

MINISTER (*to Chin-t'u*). That this case has been cleared up is entirely due to Ma I's unswerving loyalty. He even risked death to prevent a miscarriage of justice. I therefore propose that you become his adopted son, to support and protect him in old age, until he passes from this earthly life. What do you think of my proposal?

CHIN-T'U. I welcome it, Your Excellency.

MINISTER. Then make your bows to each other as father and son, with myself as witness, in token of your promise.

After doing so, both thank the T'ai Shih for his kindness and clemency and wend their way home ; Chin-t'u to pursue his studies and support his çi-devant servant and newly-adopted pater. Hou Hua-tsui and Yao Shih meet their just deserts under the executioner's axe.

Finis

*   *   *

Here again the happy dénouement depends on supernatural intervention. Buddha, in his infinite mercy, prolongs the darkness of the night from five—the usual number—to nine watches. Hence the title of the play. But for his dream it is doubtful whether Wên T'ai Shih would have solved the murder so promptly : his methods bear a striking resemblance to those of the bungling magistrate he rebukes.

Portia's :   " Ah ! but I fear you speak upon the rack,
          Where men enforced do speak anything,"

would have struck such ears as gibberish, and as for the quality of mercy, it was certainly strained with a vengeance. How the Divine Marquis would have relished the board of thirty-six spikes, not to speak of the tiger-head lever-knife ! We highly recommend the scene of Ma I's ordeal to all sadist friends.

Ma I's is an exceedingly arduous rôle, and the only contemporary Peking actors who do it full justice are Ma Lien-liang and T'an Fu-ying. The severest test of his sensibility and mimetic power occurs in the scene with his wife and daughter, when he appeals to them for a head to show the magistrate.*   The way he manipulates the knife, all trembling with emotion ; his wavering as he alternately advances and recedes, not knowing whether to kill the girl himself or let her perform the deed ; the cold blade slipping from his hand ; his anxiety mingled with fear, longing and at the same time dreading to see what his daughter will do with it, until his wife, after an

---

*We suggest " The Significance of the Severed Head in Drama " as a fruitful theme for transatlantic theses.

eternity, cries frantically that the fatal deed is done—all " compose "
into a highly dramatic spectacle. Even the most sophisticated
audience sits spellbound while Ma I is put through his drastic
paces. The other rôles are apt to fade into insignificance. As for
the unfortunate Yüeh-hsiang, she is just another of filial duty's
victims, and in her enforced suicide a Chinese audience sees nothing
very strange, since filial duty is a duty to society in general. Western
barbarians may be excused for begging to differ, in extending their
sympathy to the daughter rather than to her parent, whose "sacrifice"
seems callous, and more than tinged with egotism : we have a
horrible suspicion that he is attitudinizing, playing to the gallery,
and that " face " is his ruling religion. Ma I and Yüeh-hsiang
are the nearest equivalents to Agamemnon and Iphigenia in Chinese
drama. For a Clytemnestra (insomuch as she is a mother defending
her child), see *Pao Lien Têng* (p. 324). Like Iphigenia, Yüeh-hsiang
is all maidenly reserve, calm dignity and resolute courage, which
only serves to make the sacrifice more difficult to condone.

CHO FANG TS'AO 捉 放 曹

THE CAPTURE AND RELEASE OF TS'AO TS'AO

PERIOD : End of Han, circa A.D. 190.   A *hsi-p'i êrh-huang* play.

DRAMATIS PERSONÆ

CH'ÊN KUNG, Magistrate of Chung-mou ...   ...   *Lao-shêng*
TS'AO TS'AO, then a rising official ...   .   *Ching*
LÜ PO-SHÊ, a sworn brother of Ts'ao Ts'ao's father   *Mo*
WANG SHÊN, a yamen-runner   ...   .   *Ch'ou*
INNKEEPER ...   .   *Ch'ou*

While Wang Yün and other officials loyal to the Han dynasty burst into tears during a banquet because of Tung Cho's subjugation of the State, Ts'ao Ts'ao, who is among the guests, claps his hands and laughs aloud : " If all the officers of the Government blubber till dawn, and then from dawn till dusk, will that dispose of Tung Cho ? " He borrows a " seven precious " sword* from Wang Yün and swears to slay the usurper. The attempt is facilitated by strategy, in Ts'ao Ts'ao's words : " I have bowed my head to Tung Cho with the sole desire of finding a chance to destroy him. Now that he begins to trust me I have opportunities to approach him."

He finds Tung Cho in the guest-room, sitting with Lü Pu on a couch. The latter is sent out to select a good horse as a gift for Ts'ao Ts'ao. In the meantime Tung Cho, whose corpulence is such that he cannot long remain in a sitting posture, rolls over face downwards on the couch. Ts'ao Ts'ao is about to strike when Tung Cho catches sight of his action in a mirror and asks : " What are you doing, Mêng-tê † ? " Lü Pu returns leading the horse, so Ts'ao astutely falls on his knees and says : " I have a fine sword here which I wish to present to Your Excellency." Tung Cho accepts it ; and they go to look at the horse which Ts'ao, profuse in gratitude, says he would like to try. As soon as he is in the saddle he gallops off at breakneck speed. When Tung Cho's son-in-law, Li Ju, hears about it, he confirms their suspicions : " His conscience pricked him, so he fled ; there is no doubt that he intended assassination." Tung Cho orders Ts'ao Ts'ao's arrest, offering a large reward and a patent of nobility to his captor, " while

---

*A sword engraved with the Seven Stars of the *Pei Tou* or Ursa Major Constellation.

† Ts'ao Ts'ao's literary name.

those who sheltered him would be held to share his guilt." On the way to Ch'iao-chün Ts'ao is recognized and captured by the guards at Chung-mou. The play begins at this juncture; and it is graphic enough in speech and action not to require further introduction. Some performances begin with Scene II.

SCENE I

CH'ÊN (*Magistrate of Chung-mou, enters reciting that since he has received the Imperial bounty, it is his duty to deal justly with the people under his jurisdiction. He then hums a few verses to the following purport*). He who wears the black gauze cap should first practise loyalty to the Throne and filial piety. If an official is upright, the people will rejoice. All the classics have been handed down in my household from generation to generation : their virtue is as vast and deep as the sea. (*Speaks*) I, the magistrate of this district, am surnamed Ch'ên and named Kung; my distinguishing name is Kung-t'ai. In youth I took my second degree : by Imperial grace I have been appointed magistrate of Chung-mou. A few days ago I received a letter from Minister Tung Cho to apprehend the murderous Ts'ao Ts'ao; also a picture, for purposes of identification. Whoever captures him will be rewarded with a thousand ounces of gold as well as a patent of nobility. I have already ordered Wang Shên and other messengers to comb the city, but none of them have yet returned.
Enter Wang Shên.
WANG. Your Honour, you are above and I am below! I salute you and come to report respecting Ts'ao Ts'ao.
CH'ÊN. Let your communication be brief.
WANG. Permit me to congratulate you, Sir. You are fortunate indeed, Sir !
CH'ÊN. How so ?
WANG. We have caught Ts'ao Ts'ao, Your Honour.
CH'ÊN. Where's your proof ?
WANG. This precious sword, Sir.

CH'ÊN. Hand it to me. (*Wang Shên does so*). You have done exceeding well, and you will be rewarded for this with a thousand ounces of gold.   Let the prisoner be admitted.   (*Ts'ao Ts'ao is led in*).

TS'AO (*singing in hsi-p'i liu-shui-pan*).   I have leapt over the dragon's pool, escaped from the tiger's lair, and even from the perils of fire and flood.   Who could have dreamt that I would fall into a trap laid for me by the magistrate of Chung-mou ?   My anger pierces the very heavens.   Let us see what this Ch'ên Kung intends to do with me.

CH'ÊN (*sings in hsi-p'i yao-pan*).   When Ts'ao Mêng-tê appears in my yamen, loudly the lictors and runners proclaim his approach : in two rows stand the clerks, like tigers alert on the hill-sides.   Behold the assassin's face ; how cruel and evil it is ! Confronting me, the Magistrate, why don't you fall on your knees ?   What is the reason for this unseemly conduct ?   (*To runners*) Can this truly be Ts'ao Ts'ao ?

TS'AO. Since you are acquainted with my name, why take the trouble to ask ?

CH'ÊN. Why don't you kneel in my presence ?

TS'AO. Above, I kneel to the Son of Heaven : below, I kneel to my parents.   Why should I kneel to a petty magistrate like you ?

CH'EN. Even a prince when he breaks the law is reduced to an equal footing with commoners.

TS'AO. What crime have I committed ?

CH'ÊN. You attempted to assassinate Grand Secretary Tung Cho ; dare you suggest you are innocent?

TS'AO. Did you witness this attempt ?

CH'ÊN. Although I did not witness it in person, I have the Grand Secretary's dispatch in front of me. How dare you bandy words with me like this ?

TS'AO (*aside, sings in hsi-p'i liu-shui-pan*). Hearken to him ! I am as full of dread as if a knife were cutting through my heart. Pondering the matter I feel sure that a few specious phrases will bring him over. I'll urge him to abandon his post and follow me. (*Speaks*) Ch'ên Kung-t'ai, among the court-officials of to-day can you distinguish the loyal from the traitors ?

CH'ÊN. Holding a provincial post, how can I know anything of Court affairs ?

TS'AO. As a provincial magistrate, of course you cannot be expected to know what songs are sung at Court. But are you not aware that Tung Cho is a villainous traitor, guilty of countless detestable crimes ? His cruelty and arrogance exceed all bounds. All men are stricken dumb at the mere sound of his name. Now that he has allied himself with Lü Pu his ambition is to usurp the Throne. You are a scholar of extensive views and lofty education. Give the matter your consideration, and tell me who could be more pernicious than that traitor Tung Cho ?

CH'ÊN (*in êrh-liu-pan*). Cease railing at Tung Cho, Ts'ao Mêng-tê ! His ability is great and he has ruled the country with a firm hand. He destroyed the Yellow Turbans : even if he be denied vast merit, he is certainly free of defects. He drove forth and exterminated the meddlesome eunuchs of the Palace. Thanks to the awe his name inspires, he enlisted the services of Lü Pu. When he gives a command, it is like a tumbling mountain; a single call of his voice, and a hundred respond. Having captured you, I shall see that you are conveyed to the Capital and handed over to Tung Cho. The reward will be a thousand ounces of gold and a patent of nobility. You may be likened to the moth that blindly flies into the flame, to the fish caught in the net, and to the tiger that leaves its mountain-fastness and is caught upon the roadway. Having seized the tiger, why should I let him return to his lair ? If I released you, you would only injure me. To capture a tiger is difficult ; to let him go is easy. Consider this !

TS'AO (*sings in hsi-p'i k'uai-pan*). If you hand me
over to Tung Cho I'll tell him that Ch'ên Kung is
the real assassin. I can produce your letter to prove it,
ha, ha! How you will manage to extricate yourself is
hard for me to say.

CH'ÊN (*sings in k'uai-pan*). This discourse fills me
with trepidation! Whatever am I to do? If I let
him go, the blame will fall on me; and if I don't, I
fear some great calamity will be the result. I rack my
brains without being able to discover any clear solution.
Shall I imitate Su Ch'in, who released Chang I*? The
cases are similar. Since he is in my power, it remains
for me to decide whether I release him or not. But if
I am to set him free we will have to come to some clear
understanding.

TS'AO (*sings in k'uai-pan, ironically*). Ch'ên Kung-
t'ai, your words betray that you are a ninny! How
could you, a petty magistrate, aspire to have your
name blazoned among the great of the earth? If you
take my advice you will desert your post and follow me,
to enlist in the service of the loyal vassals, muster men
and horses, attack the Palace traitors and annihilate them
utterly. Only then can you don the robes of State and
become an authentic noble. Ch'ên Kung-t'ai, all men
say that you possess exceptional ability and voluminous
learning. Consider my words; can any doubt still
linger?

CHÊN (*sings in k'uai-pan*). While I listen to him
I feel as one just wakening out of a dream. The
post of a petty seventh-rank magistrate conforms but
ill with my consummate talents. It would be better for
me to throw up my post and follow him among men of
high degree; even to run to the ends of the earth, join

---

*Two adventurous and subtle politicians of the fourth century B.C. who were
fellow-students early in life but later became rivals (MAYERS' *Chinese Reader's
Manual*, Nos. 626 and 17). See note on p. 49.

the feudal lords, reorganize the Court, and then with Ts'ao Ts'ao reap the benefits. Myself I'll loosen his shackles. (*To yamen-runners*) Leave the room : I have a way to deal with him. (*Exeunt runners ; he continues in yao-pan, pointing to Ts'ao Ts'ao*) Hand in hand we'll go into the antechamber so that I may thank you for your visit and pay you my respects. I hope you'll forgive my seeming lack of deference. (*Speaks*) I must apologize to Your Honour for being so rudely detained by my underlings. I hope you will excuse them and mè.

TS'AO (*graciously*). Don't mention it ! I am much obliged to you for letting me off. In the days to come I shall certainly repay your kindness.

CH'ÊN. I have often heard of your plot to present the precious sword. Through Heaven's fault it was not successful. What does Your Honour intend to do now ?

TS'AO. My intention is to wander to the ends of the earth if necessary, enlist the support of all the feudal lords, assassinate Tung Cho, and set up the House of Han.

CH'ÊN. I am anxious to join you, but do not know if this would meet with your approval.

TS'AO. Most certainly ! My only fear is for your family. Won't they suffer for it ?

CH'ÊN. My mother, wife and sons are all in their native home, so there's no obstacle as far as they are concerned.

TS'AO. In that case we need not delay. Let us leave the city at once ; the local spies will be less apt to spot us by night.

CH'ÊN. Wait till I issue my orders. (*To runners*) Here ! Take my official seal and hand it over to my deputy : I am leaving on a tour of inspection. I shall be gone ten days at the utmost, but may possibly return sooner. Get my horse ready.

Ch'ên and Ts'ao mount and ride off.

[Performances often begin with the next scene.]

SCENE II

LÜ PO-SHÊ (*enters soliloquizing*). I had a bad dream last night : whether it was lucky or unlucky is hard to say. (*Speaks*) I am a native of Ch'ên-liu : on the death of my father and brother I reaped a fine inheritance. My whole life has been spent in a large community of good companions. Last night—it was during the third watch—I had a dream, but whether it portended good or evil I really cannot tell. Morning is already past and gone, and it is now near midday. Nothing has happened yet. As I have leisure I think I'll take a stroll through the village. (*Sings in hsi-p'i yüan-pan*) I had a bad dream last night. I saw a tiger chasing sheep and goats : they could find no safe retreat, and the tiger devoured them all. Somehow I cannot stop wondering about its import.

Ts'ao Ts'ao's voice is heard behind the stage, saying : " Horsemen coming ! " *Enter Ch'ên and Ts'ao.*

TS'AO (*sings in hsi-p'i yao-pan*). The cassia in the eighth moon burgeons, scent on every spray.

CH'ÊN. The hoofs beneath us galloping, our chargers seem to fly.

TS'AO. The universe I view aloft, upon my saddle high.

CH'ÊN. Methinks I see an aged man : he's ambling on our way.

LÜ. Bless me if this isn't young Ts'ao Ts'ao !

TS'AO (*showing alarm*). You are mistaken. I'm not Ts'ao Ts'ao.

LÜ. Don't be dismayed. I am Lü Po-shê, friend and sworn brother of your father's : don't you recognize me ?

TS'AO. So that's who you are ! I'll dismount and make my salute. I hope you'll forgive me for failing to recognize you.

LÜ. I am unworthy of such a compliment. It's no fault of yours if at first you did not make me out.

CH'ÊN. Come on, Your Honour. We have no time to waste.

TS'AO (*to Lü*). Give my regards to your wife when you return. I should like to call on you, but being pressed for time I shall have to bid you farewell. . . .

LÜ. Stay ! You are a distinguished official ; besides, your father is a sworn brother of mine. As it is getting late, why not come to my cottage and spend the night ? There is no such principle as passing a friend's door without entering. Let me lead your horse.

TS'AO. No : that I cannot allow.

LÜ. I'll lead the way then.

CH'ÊN (*aside*). Is it safe to go ?

TS'AO. Quite safe : he is a friend of my father's.

LÜ. Come on ! (*Sings in hsi-p'i liu-shui-pan*) No wonder the wick of my lantern cracked last night, and this morning all the magpies set up a din. I feared my dream must be a bad omen from heaven, and now this honourable man arrives at my door !

A PAGE (*enters, announcing*). The Master has returned.

LÜ. Here, take the horses to the backyard and give them an extra share of fodder.

TS'AO. But don't remove the saddles !

They all enter the cottage.

LÜ (*pointing to Ch'ên*). Who is this gentleman ?

TS'AO. The Magistrate of Chung-mou, His Honour Ch'ên Kung, whose literary name is Kung-t'ai.

LÜ. Well, well, so His Honour is the Father and Mother of our district ! I was not aware of it. Please excuse me.

CH'ÊN. How dare I accept the compliment ! Pray forgive me for entering your abode with such scant ceremony.

LÜ (*to Ts'ao*). How do you happen to find yourself in this condition, Sir ?

TS'AO (*in chiao-pan*). That's a long story. (*Sings in hsi-p'i yüan-pan*) Tung Cho is a tyrant : he flouts his Prince and oppresses the people, who gnash their teeth with impotent rage ; he is a tiger in human shape ; and he insults all the feudal lords. Therefore I tried to assassinate him, and after failing, had to flee for my life. I travelled day and night until I was caught and shackled at Chung-mou. But for His Honour here, who kindly released me, by now we would have all been like frost on the roof.

LÜ (*sings in liu-shui-pan, to Ch'ên*). Hearing these tidings, I kneel before Your Honour to thank you for your kindness. Had you not released our friend Ts'ao Ts'ao, all of us would certainly be, as he expresses it, like frost on the tiles !

CH'ÊN (*speaks in chiao-pan*). Old friend ! (*Proceeds to sing in hsi-p'i k'uai-pan*) Thank you for your words, Sir. To release the loyal, as I have done, is merely right and proper. I am willing to join his righteous faction, to destroy the traitors and restore the House of Han.

LÜ. Now I understand why His Honour's father came here last night and left this morning early, to flee to the uttermost ends of the earth.

TS'AO (*interrupting*). This is sad news ! (*Sings*) It is enough to make my tears fall down in torrents. It involves my whole family, none of whom can escape their cruel fate. Children cannot even meet their parents or assist each other in any way. I myself must flee to the uttermost ends of the earth.

LÜ. Don't grieve so, Sir ! In the future you and your father are bound to meet again. Let me order my servants to prepare a pig and a sheep and serve some wine to welcome you two gentlemen.

TS'AO AND CH'ÊN. Don't let us upset your usual domestic arrangements : take no particular trouble on our account !

LÜ. With such distinguished guests how could I do less ? Furthermore, if I do not entertain in my own home, who will entertain me when I go abroad ?

Exit Lü.

CH'ÊN (*to Ts'ao*). Since your father has effected his escape, why should you weep like this ? In truth you are a very filial and loyal man !

TS'AO. Why should not the love of a son for his parent give vent to tears ?

CH'ÊN (*in chiao-pan*). Oh, Your Honour ! (*In k'uai-pan*) Restrain your grief, Sir : pull yourself together ! But ever bear in mind the twin words Filial and Loyal. Keep up your strength and mettle : exterminate the traitors, reform the administration and blazon a brilliant name for yourself.

LÜ (*enters with a wine-pot, singing in hsi-p'i yao-pan*).
In time of cheer one's spirits seem to fly.
The harvest moon is radiant in the sky.

TS'AO. Where are you off to, Uncle, at this time of night ?

LÜ. I have plenty of food in the larder, but am short of good wine. I am going to the Western village to buy some of the best I can procure to treat you two gentlemen.

CH'ÊN. But you need not put yourself to all that trouble on our account, Sir !

LÜ. Pray be seated awhile. I'll soon be back to entertain you. (*Sings in yao-pan*) My heart is rejoiced when worthy guests descend at my door. To express my gratitude I'll fetch the wine myself. (*Exit*).

CH'ÊN (*sings in yao-pan*). That he should take the trouble to go and purchase the wine himself shows that in courtesy he is worthy to compare with Mêng Ch'ang-chün.*

TS'AO (*sings in yao-pan*). My father and he were boon companions : they both swore brotherhood under one stick of incense.

---

*A minister of the Ch'i State, *d.* 279 B.C., proverbial for his hospitality, which attracted so many " friends and adherents " that his abode received the designation of " the little Empire."

Voices are heard behind the stage : Lü's servants are telling each other to make haste and sharpen the knives.

TS'AO (*sings*).   Kung-t'ai, do you hear that ?

CH'ÊN. Hear what ?

TS'AO. The noise of knife-grinding at the back : it looks as if they intended to murder us.

CH'ÊN. Our old friend, in his goodness of heart, is merely having a pig killed for us.   Dispel your doubts !

TS'AO. What do you say to going round and taking a look ?

CH'ÊN. No harm in that.

TS'AO (*sings in yao-pan*).   Let us go to the back and reconnoitre.

Lü's servants are heard behind the stage saying : "We'll bind him first before the slaughtering."

CH'ÊN (*sings in yao-pan*).   I can't make it out : we'd better be cautious.

TS'AO. "First bind and then slaughter ! "   That must refer to us.   Who else could it refer to ?

CH'ÊN. Their voices are hard to distinguish.

TS'AO. I understand !

CH'ÊN. What do you mean ?

TS'AO. Under the pretence of buying wine that old dog Lü Po-shê has reported our presence here to the officials, hoping to reap the reward himself.

CH'ÊN. I cannot think so.   The old man has a kindly countenance ; besides, he is a sworn brother and friend of your father's.   You ought to give him the benefit of the doubt.

TS'AO. One cannot judge by appearances these days. He may look innocent outwardly but be a traitor at heart.   We should strike first.

CH'ÊN. Forbear, Your Honour ; don't be so hasty ! Wait until he returns and watch his movements : we can decide what course to follow then.   It will not be too late.

TS'AO. If we wait, he will have a gang of ruffians with him. They'll bind us, then what can we do? From days of yore it has been aptly said: "He that strikes first has all the advantage : he that bides his time only reaps the calamity." (*Sings in yao-pan*) How I detest the old ruffian ! He is utterly devoid of a conscience.

CH'ÊN. It is highly improbable that he has such an evil nature.

TS'AO (*sings*). I am sure he has run for the reward.

CH'ÊN (*sings*). If he was thinking of a reward, why should he have set about it in such a way ?

TS'AO (*sings*). I'll take my sword and rush to the back.

CH'ÊN (*clutching his sleeve*). Don't, Your Honour !

TS'AO. Leave hold of me !

(*Takes his sword and leaves*).

CH'ÊN (*sings*). Alas ! The whole family, old and young, are now in mortal danger. (*Exit Ch'ên*).

TS'AO (*re-enters flourishing his sword and singing in hsi-p'i yao-pan*). They have brought this trouble on themselves. How can a petty devil withstand the King of Hell ? With my precious sword I have massacred the lot.

In some performances an old woman, a maidservant and two page-boys appear in this scene and Ts'ao goes through the ceremony of murdering them.

CH'ÊN (*reappears sighing* " Alas ! " ; *then sings*). I am so aghast that my three souls and their affinities are all struck dumb.

TS'AO. My anger is not yet appeased : I am going to the outer kitchen.

CH'ÊN (*again clutching his sleeve, speaks*). Whither now ?

TS'AO. I am off to fetch some fuel and set the whole place on fire.

CH'ÊN. Mercy on us ! After murdering the family are you still not satisfied ? Now you are wanting to burn the house down. This sort of thing will never do !

TS'AO. The old dog has no sentiment, so why should you take umbrage and think that I am lacking in public spirit? If at first you don't succeed, try again. I'll sweep them all off the face of the earth. (*Sings in yao-pan*) I'll take a torch and set the place alight.

CH'ÊN (*in yao-pan*). Having slain them all, do you really wish to burn the house?

TS'AO. I draw my sword and go to the kitchen.
Gestures accordingly.

CH'ÊN (*sings*). I see a fine fat pig already bound. (*Speaks*) Your Honour has murdered an innocent family.

TS'AO. On what grounds can you maintain such an assertion?

CH'ÊN. With the best of intentions Lü kills a pig to feast us with, and you murder his whole family as a reward for such generosity. Is this not killing under misapprehension?

TS'AO. Where's the proof?

CH'ÊN. Go and see for yourself.
Ts'ao does so and discovers the pork.

TS'AO. Ah, I have made an awful blunder!

CH'ÊN. I can't think what you'll say to the old man when he returns.

TS'AO. Our best plan is to escape: we'll mount our horses and gallop away.

CH'ÊN. Since things have come to this pass, that's the only course left open to us.

TS'AO. Make haste!
Both mount and make several turns of the stage.

TS'AO. Away we gallop and leave the village behind us! (*Exit*).

CH'ÊN (*sings in k'uai-pan*). I had always imagined that Ts'ao Ts'ao was a pillar of the State: now I discover he's a brute, although he happens to wear the face of a man. (*Exit*).

Scene III

lü po-shê (*enters singing in yao-pan*). Having bought some wine I return with a merry face and a joyful heart. Slowly I wend my way homewards.

Ts'ao and Ch'ên appear on horseback.

ts'ao. Since you have returned, let us dismount.

lü. Where are you two gentlemen going?

ts'ao. My escape from danger is a trifle; but if I prolonged my stay you might be compromised, so I'll be off!

lü. I have already told my servants to kill a pig for you. I had no evil intention in going to buy the wine myself.* It is getting late : you had better stay the night, and start your journey in the morning.

ts'ao. Quite so. But I have no time to lose: I really must be going.

lü. If you don't come back with me I'll be obliged to use entreaties.

ch'ên. Pray do not trouble to detain us, Sir. Return by yourself and we shall meet again.

ts'ao. Come, let us be going. Farewell! (*In yao-pan*) I bid uncle good-bye and straddle my horse.

Exit Ts'ao.

ch'ên (*sings in hsi-p'i yao-pan*). I feel as if a knife had pierced my heart. I thank you for your kind intentions, Sir; they will be turned to loathing when you discover your family's fate. In Ts'ao's presence I could not tell you all : do not bear hatred against me, but against him.   (*Exit Ch'ên*).

lü (*sings in yao-pan*). Mêng-tê says good-bye and gallops away. Why do Ch'ên Kung's tears roll down like tangled hemp? Can it be that some member of my household offended him? I cannot imagine what went amiss, that he should behave in such fashion. When

---

* *i.e.*, he could have sent a messenger instead.

I'm home I'll inquire and get to the root of it. (*Exit Lü*).
Re-enter Ts'ao and Ch'ên.

TS'AO (*sings in yao-pan*). I pull in my reins and check my steed.

CH'ÊN (*sings in yao-pan*). Ts'ao Ts'ao is reining in his horse : what can the matter be now ? (*Speaks*) Why don't you go forward ?

TS'AO. In the haste of my flight I forgot an urgent matter.

CH'ÊN. What are you referring to ?

TS'AO. I have forgotten to advise my uncle about two particulars.

CH'ÊN. For pity's sake, pray spare the old man's life !

TS'AO. Mind your own business. Here, Lü Po-shê, come back !   (*Ch'ên and Ts'ao dismount*).

LÜ (*sings in yao-pan*). Although we met, we have not yet enjoyed a confidential chat. Now Mêng-tê is calling me back. (*Speaks*) Have you two gentlemen decided to return with me ?

TS'AO. Yes, we have changed our minds. Just look behind you and see who's coming ! (*Lü turns round, asking :* "Where ? " *Ts'ao cuts him down, examines his weapon and observes*) Well, I've finished with Lü Po-shê !

CH'ÊN (*sings in yao-pan*). Alas, to watch the butchering of that harmless unsuspecting old man was a ghastly experience. His dark blood mingled with the yellow earth. A whole family massacred by this Ts'ao Ts'ao ! I shall have to remonstrate with him. (*To Ts'ao*) You have slain his entire household without a word of regret : and now you have put Lü Po-shê to the sword as well. By what sort of principle do you justify all this bloodshed ?

TS'AO. I killed the old dog to avoid any trouble in future : this is what I call cutting off the grass and pulling out the roots.

CH'ÊN. Are you not afraid that Heaven and man will curse you for such conduct ?

TS'AO. I would rather betray the world than let the world betray me.

CH'ÊN (*showing alarm*). Oh!

TS'AO. Quite so!

CH'ÊN (*sings in hsi-p'i man-pan*). Hearken to him! He frightens the life out of me. He is a terrible monster. (*Turns his back*). He is an ungrateful brute. How I loathe myself for being led into this! At first I thought him a man of sterling qualities, but now I see he is a rebel of the worst type. I am on a narrow path and there is no turning back and escaping him. Well! the flower must float with the tide, and not the tide with the flower. I'll have to put up with him for the present and go where he goes. When the state reform is accomplished I may be able to persuade him to heed my advice.

TS'AO. What is all this muttering about?

CH'ÊN (*sings in êrh-liu-pan*). What do you mean by saying that I mutter? You are a man of correct principles, but you have made a desperate mistake in killing Lü Po-shê, a sworn brother of your father's, who bore him no ill will, and slaughtering his whole family into the bargain. I can see no justification for such an act.

TS'AO (*sings in yao-pan*). Don't bear me a grudge for this, Ch'ên Kung-t'ai. Let us mount and away. (*Both mount their horses*). (*Sings in k'uai-pan*) Let me tell you the story in detail as we ride along. When Lü Po-shê went to buy the wine himself, I grew alarmed and suspicious. I killed him under the delusion that he was an enemy. You say I should not have done so, but surely you must realize that mowing down the grass and pulling up the roots prevents it from sprouting again?

CH'ÊN (*sings aside in yao-pan*). Even good advice fails to move him : he is more stolid than horses and cattle, a veritable frog in a well.*

---

* *i.e.*, can only discern the " little tent of blue " above him.

TS'AO (*sings in yao-pan*). Come on, whip up your horse : it is getting late. We'll have to seek shelter at an inn. (*Both arrive at inn*). Kung-t'ai, let's put up here. It's too late to proceed any farther. (*Both dismount*). Where is the innkeeper ?

INNKEEPER (*comes in*). Do you two gentlemen desire to spend the night ?

TS'AO. We do. Provide for the horses.

INNKEEPER. Very well; let me attend to them. (*Ts'ao and Ch'ên take seats*). What will you have to eat, gentlemen ?

TS'AO. I'm for a pot of warm wine. (*Innkeeper gives orders. Ts'ao to Ch'ên*) Come and join me over a cup of wine !

CH'ÊN. I feel too exhausted to swallow anything after our long ride.

TS'AO. How can you go without food ? It's obvious that you are annoyed because I disposed of Lü's family. Is this not a fact ?

CH'ÊN. Since we are fellow-travellers, how could I harbour any resentment against you ? You are too suspicious by far !

TS'AO. Aye, all my life I have been suspicious of everybody and everything. (*Sings in yao-pan*) I'll swallow three cups of wine, and so to bed to dream of hearth and home. (*Proceeds to doze off*).

CH'ÊN (*in chiao-pan*). He has fallen asleep. Ugh, how I abhor him ! (*Sings in êrh-huang man-pan*) The bright round moon is beaming through the window, and my heart is as tangled as hemp. But it is too late now to repent. I am a wanderer, wavering and unsettled. Too late to repent ! As guests we betook ourselves to Lü's abode ; and our host truly deserved to be called a man of lofty principles. He killed a fatted pig, bought wine, and made ready to entertain us handsomely. Who could have foreseen that Ts'ao would prove so mistrustful, and put

his whole family to death in the twinkling of an eye!
The blood of that poor old man was mixed with the
yellow soil! It was an untimely end. After suffering
such a wrong his spirit will have to be propitiated. But
why should I repine? I was not the culprit. There
are spirits roaming about in the void who can testify
to my innocence. (*It is now the second watch. Ch'ên
continues to sing, but in êrh-huang yüan-pan*) The drum
in the watch-tower strikes the second watch : the more
I ponder, the more acute is my sense of the injury.
Too late to repent! I have abandoned my official post,
and even my robes. Too late to repent! I have absconded from my magistracy, discarded my official robes
and headgear. I fancied that Ts'ao Ts'ao was a person
of broad intellect and consummate ability, that he was
the very man to reform the Dynasty and confound the
traitors. (*The third watch is struck*). Ts'ao Ts'ao sleeps like
a log—nay, like a frog in a well. He is like the water-
dragon, his body covered with scales ; he is like a fierce
tiger, shorn of his claws and fangs. If I don't strike
now that he's asleep, it will be like letting the tiger loose,
to return to his lair and destroy more victims. (*He
draws his sword and is about to strike when Ts'ao turns over.
Ch'ên sings*) I was just about to cut off his head.
(*Ts'ao turns again and continues to sleep. Ch'ên sheathes his
sword*). Ah me! (*Sings*) That was a risk, another foolish
blunder! (*Speaks*) Wo, stay your hand! If I slay him,
when daylight comes, will not the people of the inn be
implicated? What's to be done? Ha, I know my
course! Here are pen and ink on the table : I'll indite a
few lines of verse. But what theme shall I select as a
warning to him? (*He meditates, when the fourth watch is
struck*). Ah, I have it! I'll take the Fourth Watch
as my theme. (*Writes*).

The Fourth Watch strikes : thick night's still overcast.
My office and its robes are of the past.

To slay Lü's innocent family one and all
Is Ts'ao Ts'ao's crime, and he is bound to fall.
(*Calls*) Your Honour, your slumber's very sound. I know
you now for what you are, an execrable traitor ! (*He
peruses his lines*). Well, I had better look for my horse
and make my escape. (*Takes lamp and does so, singing
in yao-pan*) I, Ch'ên Kung, repent me of my folly. Why
should I accompany this rebel to the ends of the earth ?
The flower may float with the current, not I !
                    Exit Ch'ên. The fifth watch is struck.
TS'AO (*wakes up and sings in êrh-huang tao-pan*).
I dreamt I had returned to my old home. (*Looks round*).
Ah ! I don't see Ch'ên Kung here : what's wrong, I
wonder ? Where can he have gone to ?   But there's some
writing on the table ; I'll read what it says. Oh, so Ch'ên
Kung inscribes verses to vilify me, does he, and then
bolts ?   Well, in the near future I'll get even with him :
I'll have my revenge ! (*To innkeeper*) Here is the money
for my board and lodging. I'll be off. (*Sings in yao-pan*)
My curse on Ch'ên Kung for this. How dare he scribble
such slanderous stuff ! When I've enrolled all the feudal
lords I'll muster a troop of cavalry, catch Ch'ên Kung,
and show no mercy on him, none whatever.

                    Finis

                 *   *   *

In the populous world of *San Kuo* plays, some half-dozen figures
cannot fail to stand out in high relief, even to the confused bedazzled
tyro : for they speak a language that is their own and nobody
else's. Foremost of these unforgettable personalities are Ts'ao
Ts'ao, Kuan Yü and K'ung-ming. The latter two are all but
superhuman : Kuan Yü's aura was enriched by centuries of romantic legend until he was deified; and K'ung-ming's magical feats
tend to strain even the most pertinacious " suspension of disbelief."
Remains the all too human (in the worst sense) Ts'ao Ts'ao. Sly,
tough, cruel, wanton, cold-blooded, unscrupulous, ruthless, pompous, sententious and sentimental—even these adjectives fall
short of the mark. He is an unmitigated villain. Yet his rascality

appeals to the imagination : the more one sees of him, the more one submits to his snake-like spell. This is mainly due to the art which Chinese actors have lavished on him for generations, polishing the rôle, from facial make-up to the most trivial tricks of speech, until it attained the acme of perfected villainy.

In *Cho Fang Ts'ao* we may witness Ts'ao Ts'ao's debut, his rise from mediocrity. Ch'ên Kung is the typical stepping-stone : he receives a sympathy he hardly deserves from the Chinese audience. Examined impartially, he is a feeble opportunist who betrayed his Government, a man easily swayed by rhetoric. When he had a magnificent chance to repair his ruin he deliberately threw it aside. Cowardice is the only explanation, since he realized that Ts'ao Ts'ao " differed in nought from his enemy Tung Cho, " and that all was to be gained by ridding the world of such a monster. However tragic the plight of Lü Po-shê, one cannot help wondering why the bad dream that so obsessed him did not put the kindly gaffer on his guard. He was altogether too pressing under the circumstances ; men flying for their lives are apt to be highly strung !

It is worthy of note that Frederick the Great re-echoed Ts'ao Ts'ao's most popular maxim at the beginning of his career, when he wrote : "If one has cut down a tree, it is wise to destroy the roots as well, lest the aftergrowth replace the tree in time." Like all thorough villains, Ts'ao Ts'ao revels in sob-stuff : he is incurably sentimental. He loves parading his filial solicitude : after annihilating his kind old host and family, he can blissfully lie down and slumber like a child, to dream of " home, sweet home." His pique on discovering Ch'ên Kung's pasquinade is a delightful piece of irony.

After the murder of Lü Po-shê, in subsequent plays, there is a subtle change in Ts'ao Ts'ao's make-up, a triangular tilt to his sharp suspicious eyes, to denote the cruelty of his character full-fledged. Needless to say, he is far more real on the stage than in literature, as will be seen from a comparison of this play, crude as it may be, with the same incidents described in the *San Kuo Chih Yen-i*, or " Romance of the Three Kingdoms," Chapter IV, pp. 39-42.

The performances of a Hao Shou-ch'ên show us plainly why the spirit of the *San Kuo* remains perennially fresh ; they truly deserve to be described (we beg indulgence for introducing a term grown threadbare by excessive abuse) as *living history*. During the hours we watch the stage the semi-transparent veil that shrouds these events in the Chronicles is lifted : we behold a romantic vision which will impose itself on our historical studies and increase their fascination.

CHU LIEN CHAI 珠簾寨

PEARLY SCREEN CASTLE

Also known as *Chieh Pao*: "Sending Precious Gifts"; and *Shou Wei*: "Winning over Chou Tê-wei." A *hsi-p'i êrh-liu* play.

PERIOD: T'ang (A.D. 880)

DRAMATIS PERSONÆ

LI K'O-YUNG, King of Sha-t'o in Mongolia	...	*Lao-shêng*
CH'ÊNG CHING-SSŬ, Tutor of the T'ang Emperor	...	*Lao-shêng*
LI SSŬ-YÜAN, Li K'o-yung's eldest son	... ...	*Hsiao-shêng*
CHOU TÊ-WEI, a brigand chieftain ...	... ...	*Wu-shêng*
TA HUANG NIANG, principal Queen (Chinese)	...	*Ch'ing-i*
ERH HUANG NIANG, secondary Queen (Mongolian)		*Hua-tan*
WANG T'IEN-LUNG \\ WANG T'IEN-HU } robber-captains ...	... ...	*Wu-ching*
LAO CHÜN, head-groom	...	*Ch'ou-êrh*
SOLDIERS, SERVANTS, etc.		

SYNOPSIS

When, in A.D. 880, the rebellious robber-chieftain Huang Ch'ao captured Ch'ang-an the Capital, Emperor Hsi Tsung fled to Hsi-ch'i Mei-liang-ch'uan (in Shensi). Thence the Emperor dispatched his tutor Ch'êng Ching-ssŭ with precious gifts to Li K'o-yung at Sha-t'o in Mongolia, soliciting aid, but Li had private reasons for refusal. Fortunately for the T'ang cause, Li's eldest son opposed his father's wishes and persuaded the two Queens to force him to go to the Emperor's assistance. This was made easier by Li K'o-yung's fear of his secondary consort, a famous Amazon (whence his name has become synonymous for a hen-pecked husband). The Amazon appointed Li K'o-yung Leader of the Vanguard, but owing to his absence when the troops were mustered she put him in command of the rearguard—his son commanding the vanguard in his stead. At "Pearly Screen Castle" the army was defeated by a brigand-chieftain, Chou Tê-wei, but the Amazon spurred her husband to further attack. Chou was no match for Li as far as military tactics were concerned, but the latter was old enough to be his father. Fearing he could not conquer Chou, Li exhibited his skill in archery by bringing down two geese with a single arrow. Chou was so deeply impressed that he promptly offered him allegiance. Whereupon Li and Chou advanced together to attack Huang Ch'ao's stronghold.

ACT I. SCENE I

Ch'êng Ching-ssŭ enters with several soldiers bearing the gifts for Li K'o-yung.

CH'ÊNG (*speaks*). How I abominate Huang Ch'ao for fomenting this rebellion ! He had no right to invade the Capital. I have now received His Imperial Majesty's command to proceed to Sha-t'o and apply for troops to come to our assistance. (*Sings*) I, Ch'êng Ching-ssŭ, detest Huang Ch'ao for fostering revolt and forcing our lord to flee to Hsi-ch'i Mei-liang-ch'uan (in Shensi). Our people, too, are suffering terrible privations in consequence. (*Repeats himself*).

The robber-captains Wang T'ien-lung and Wang T'ien-hu enter with a band of followers.

WANG T'IEN-LUNG (*speaks*). We two brothers are kings of the forest and have forcibly seized the Pass of the Tiger Peak.

WANG T'IEN-HU. We do nothing but rob the travellers passing to and fro. Brother, as we have been idle these last few days, what think you of leaving the mountain to-day ?

WANG T'IEN-LING. Let us. Come along, fellows, we'll all go together.

Ch'êng Ching-ssŭ is seen advancing with his train. The robber-captains call out : Deliver up those wares, and we'll allow you to pass.

CH'ÊNG (*showing great alarm*). Impudent robbers, know that I am Ch'êng Ching-ssŭ, former Minister to His Majesty the T'ang Emperor : how dare you plunder treasures of State ! Have you no fear of the laws ?

WANG T'IEN-LUNG. Don't talk so much. Here are the goods, men, grab 'em !

Ch'êng escapes. The robbers order their men to remove the booty to their lair. Exeunt omnes.

SCENE II

LI SSU-YÜAN (*enters, leading a few soldiers, and speaks*). I am Li Ssŭ-yüan, Heir-Apparent of Sha-t'o. I have been ordered by my father the King, to go hunting in the wilds. (*Repeats this in song. Exit Li*).

CH'ÊNG CHING-SSŬ (*enters and speaks*). Woe is me! I had sincerely hoped to escort the treasure to Sha-t'o and obtain military succour. Unexpectedly, half-way towards my destination, I fell in with robbers, who plundered me of my charge. How shall I ever bear to confront my sovereign again? I had better thank His Imperial Majesty for his many favours and then commit suicide. (*Weeps and sings in hsi-p'i yao-pan*) To far off Ch'ang-an I make my bow, thanking His Majesty for his bountiful grace. Pardon your minister for failing to obtain the troops to succour you. Owing to the loss of my precious consignment, I pass to the Nether World.
(*Hangs himself to a tree*).
Li Ssŭ-yün appears and orders his men to cut him down.

LI (*on recognizing him*). Ah me! Is this not Mr. Ch'êng the Minister? Feel him and see if there is any breath left in his body.

SOLDIERS. He is not dead : there is still a flicker of breath.

LI. Are you reviving, Uncle Ch'êng ? *

CH'ÊNG (*sings*). I hear somebody calling me. (*Looks round as in a daze and sings*). Do I behold my worthy nephew ?

LI. What made you try to hang yourself, good uncle ?

CH'ÊNG. Dear nephew, when that rebel Huang Ch'ao revolted there was nobody to withstand him, so I craved

---

*The word " uncle " is merely used as a term of respect to an older man, especially to a father's friend.

His Imperial Majesty's permission to go to Sha-t'o and raise troops for his defence, and he provided me with a convoy of precious gems. Suddenly, just as I was crossing the Tiger Peak, some robbers attacked and plundered me of everything. Not daring to return empty-handed, I decided to hang myself. I entreat you, dear nephew, to think of some way to regain the lost treasure and save my life.

LI. I do not think the robbers can be far away. Come with me, let us chase them and try to recover the booty.

They mount their horses and set forth. The two robber-chiefs are seen together. One of them remarks : Isn't that the young Prince ?

CH'ÊNG. My dear nephew, those are the very robbers that attacked me.

LI. Ho, you bandits ! How dare you carry off the crown-jewels ? What punishment should you receive for this ? Stay here ; don't run away ! Do you see this sword of mine ?

BOTH ROBBERS (*kneeling*). Pardon us, oh Prince. We did not know that these belonged to the State. Had we realized it, we would never have dared to steal them. They remain unopened and intact : we will promptly return them and beg Your Highness to excuse us.

LI. Where are they ?

ROBBERS. Here, Your Highness. Please count them.

LI. Pray examine them, Uncle Ch'êng, and see if all are there.

CH'ÊNG (*doing so*). Yes, they are still intact.

LI (*to robbers*). Mark, Heavenly King and Heavenly Tiger, I happen to be familiar with you and shall let you off for the nonce. But if ever you commit another crime like this I'll certainly take your lives. Now get you gone.

ROBBERS. We thank Your Highness for showing us such mercy. Rest assured that we will never do such a thing again. (*Exeunt*).

LI. You wait outside the city-gates, Uncle Ch'êng, while I go and announce your arrival to my Father the King.

CH'ÊNG. Thank you kindly, Nephew.

Exeunt Li and Ch'êng.

SCENE III

LI K'O-YUNG (*enters and says*). I, Li K'o-yung, who am now a sovereign king, once served the T'ang Emperor as minister. Because of my repeated victories on the field of battle, I was created Prince of Chin. The selfsame year His Majesty gave a great banquet in the Tower of Five Phœnixes, and I was among the guests. Unfortunately the Empress's brother Tuan Wên-ch'u made mock of me on that occasion, criticizing my table-manners and want of politeness, causing such wrath to rise within me that I laid violent hands on him and flung him on the floor in the Imperial presence. He spat blood, and there and then gave up the ghost. The Emperor was so angry that he ordered my removal and instant execution. As luck would have it, the Minister Ch'êng Ching-ssŭ begged me off. Instead of being decapitated I was exiled to Sha-t'o. There I encountered several kings, each of whom challenged me to fight him. I used the same eighty-one pound sword I had fought with when the dynasty was established, and conquered them one by one. They submitted and set me up as High King over them all. I gained two princesses as well, and begat eleven sons. Ever since I mounted the throne as King of Sha-t'o, feasting and wine, music and song, have been my sole engagements. In sooth a well-contented man am I !

LI SSŬ-YÜAN (*entering*). My Father the King is above : your son has returned to report.

LI K'O-YUNG. Back again! What sort of luck did you have? How many birds and animals did you bag?

LI SSŬ-YÜAN. I didn't succeed in shooting anything this time. However, I have brought important news.

LI K'O-YUNG. Pertaining to what?

LI SSŬ-YÜAN. Huang Ch'ao has rebelled, and the Emperor has fled to Mei-liang-ch'uan in Shensi.

LI K'O-YUNG. The impudent rogue! So he dares to rebel when the Emperor has nobody to protect him. Hear my commands! You are to go at once to the two Queens and tell them to prepare for war. You will lead the vanguard yourself, consisting of four hundred and fifty thousand native and Chinese troops, to restore the T'ang dynasty and exterminate the rebel.

LI SSŬ-YÜAN. Your commands shall be obeyed, Father.

LI K'O-YUNG. Stay! Come to think of it, it was the T'ang Emperor who exiled me to Sha-t'o. At that time I swore an oath that I would never help to support his dynasty. I withdraw my first commands.

LI SSŬ-YÜAN. So be it, Father.

LI K'O-YUNG. How did you hear of the Emperor's escape from Ch'ang-an?

LI SSŬ-YÜAN. I heard it from Uncle Ch'êng Ching-ssŭ, who has newly arrived.

LI K'O-YUNG. Oh! has he indeed? Order our men to fall in and receive him.

Li Ssŭ-yüan retires with a number of men to escort Ch'êng into the city.

SCENE IV

Li K'o-yung and Ch'êng meet in the former's yamen, and greet each other joyfully.

CH'ÊNG. I have not seen you since our parting at Ch'ang-an. You have grown old, Prince.

LI K'O-YUNG. You too: your whiskers are quite white.

CH'ÊNG. Yes, I'm an antiquated old fogy, ha, ha!

LI K'O-YUNG. Let us clasp hands and retire to a more private chamber.

Both go out, and return : another room is indicated.

CH'ÊNG. Pray be seated, Prince, and let me prostrate myself before you.

LI K'O-YUNG. Stop! You were my benefactor and saviour. It is for me to prostrate myself to you, Sir.

CH'ÊNG. How dare I accept such an honour! It would surely be the means of curtailing my happiness.

LI K'O-YUNG. Here, Ta T'ai Pao!* Come and kowtow to your Uncle Ch'êng.

LI SSŬ-YÜAN. Pray be seated, Uncle, and let me prostrate myself before you.

CH'ÊNG. Never mind ceremony : let us waive it.

LI K'O-YUNG. Sit down, then, and we'll talk of good old times.

CH'ÊNG. As we have been separated by such a long distance I could not come sooner to inquire after your health. Forgive me, Prince.

LI K'O-YUNG. How dare I accept such an honour! Is His Majesty the Emperor well, and is the Court thriving?

CH'ÊNG. Yes, all are well and have inquired after your welfare, Prince.

LI K'O-YUNG (*to his son*). See that the banquet is prepared.

LI SSŬ-YÜAN. It is already served, Sir.

LI K'O-YUNG. Take the seat of honour, brother, and share my humble diet. Let me pour out a goblet of wine for my benefactor.

CH'ÊNG. Your younger brother dares not accept such an honour, Prince.

LI K'O-YUNG. Drink, I beg you. I was just thinking of our parting at the Tower of Five Phœnixes : how many autumns have passed since then!

---

*Li Ssŭ-yüan, so-called because he is the eldest of Li's numerous progeny.

CH'ÊNG. Now that we meet again we can chat about old times.

LI K'O-YUNG (*sings in hsi-p'i tao-pan*). T'ai Pao, dismiss the servants. (*Changes air to yüan-pan*) I shall relate the particulars of what befell. When the Emperor gave that banquet in the Tower, all his officials came to congratulate him on his birthday. Among them was Tuan Wên-ch'u, the Empress's brother, who taunted me for lack of table-manners and ignorance of etiquette. Whereupon I flew into such a rage that my very breath pierced the Pole Star. So I gripped him and flung him down in the Emperor's presence ; and there he gave out a last gasp with the blood still spurting out of his mouth and nostrils. The Emperor in his fury ordered me out to instant decapitation. Had it not been for you, my dear benefactor, who saved my life at the risk of your own, how could we have met here to-day to exchange confidences ?

CH'ÊNG (*sings*). Ever since you left, the Court has never ceased bewailing your absence.* But the great distance of our separation prevented me from inquiring after your health. I hope you will forgive my lack of courtesy.

LI K'O-YUNG (*sings in hsi-p'i yao-pan*). T'ai Pao, exchange these cups for larger ones. (*Changes air to liu-shui-pan*) As I kneel in your presence I feel mortally ashamed of myself, thinking of the time I killed Tuan Wên-ch'u, when the Emperor was so incensed that he ordered my head to be cut off. Had it not been for your intercession, how could I be alive and well to-day ? Where, within the range of high heaven and wide earth, has there ever been such a paragon of kindness ? I offer you this flowing goblet in token of my gratitude.

Ch'êng takes the goblet. Both rise. Exit T'ai Pao.

---

*Literally : all the officials have wept tears falling in double streams.

CH'ÊNG (*sings in k'uai êrh-liu-pan*). While I receive the plum-flower cup with my two clumsy hands I shall relate my tale from beginning to end. In the *chia-tzŭ* year, during the examination of candidates for the second degree, there came a wandering scholar * from Shantung who wrote his essays in such beautiful script that the examining official marked him off to stand on the leviathan's head.† On the third day after that, he was allowed to ride on horseback in the palace-grounds, the butt of all the ladies, who laughed till the tears rolled down their cheeks. And when the Prince beheld his uncouth appearance, he drove him out and removed his name from the list. The degraded *chuang-yüan* ‡ was so provoked in consequence that he posted a warning outside the palace-gate that he would straightway start a rebellion. He carried out his threat and the Emperor had to flee. Hence I have been deputed to bring you some costly gifts and invoke your military aid.

LI K'O-YUNG (*sings*). What you tell me of Huang Ch'ao's revolt does not perturb me in the least. Having been banished by the T'ang Emperor, why should I send my men to relieve him? Come, brother, you and I had better continue with our feasting : your references to the T'ang Emperor annoy me.

CH'ÊNG (*sings aside in hsi-p'i san-pan*). Li K'o-yung expresses displeasure because I have raised this subject, but I have some knowledge of his character. The old fellow is very partial to precious gems. I'll have them brought in for him to view. (*Orders them to be brought in*).

LI K'O-YUNG (*scrutinizing them, sings in hsi-p'i yao-pan*). When I see such a dazzling display, I cannot conceal my pleasure. A large red robe with a belt of jade, a

---

* Huang Ch'ao.
† First on the list.
‡ Senior Wrangler.

phœnix-cap crowned with precious pearls, and a delicate hairpin of beaten gold. Although I am quite aware of the purport of these gifts, I'll feign my ignorance. I turn round and ask : · You are an upright official ; whence come these rarities ?

CH'ÊNG (*sings*). They were sent to you by the T'ang Emperor as tribute.

LI (*sings*). Being devoid of merit I feel far too abashed to accept them.

CH'ÊNG (*sings*). They were purposely sent to Your Highness, that you might lend us troops.

LI (*sings*). I am now too old and feeble to go forth to battle.

CH'ÊNG (*sings*). You are full of courage, Prince, in spite of your age. At the mere sound of your name, Huang Ch'ao will lay down his arms. But if you demur to sending men and horses he will say that you are senile and exhausted.

LI (*sings*). If he chooses to laugh, let him laugh at the Son of Heaven. Why laugh at me ? Huang Ch'ao would find no burial place if I went forth to battle.

CH'ÊNG (*sings*). After this speech you should verily come to our aid.

LI. Were the T'ang Emperor dead, I should go at once.

CH'ÊNG. May I ask you, Prince, if these gifts appeal to your taste ?

LI. Why shouldn't they ? Since you have come such a long journey it would be both disrespectful and unjust if I refused them. On the other hand I should feel heartily ashamed of myself if I accepted them. Come, come, I might as well take the lot ! (*To servants*) Remove them !

CH'ÊNG. This old fellow is grossly unfair : he grabs the gifts but will not send the troops ! I shall produce the Emperor's Edict commanding me to apply for the troops. (*Pulls it out of his sleeve and speaks*) I kneel before the Imperial Edict. (*Kneels accordingly*).

LI (*sings*). My worthy brother acts unreasonably. How dare you take out the Imperial Edict to try and coerce me ? If anyone so much as mentions borrowing troops, his head will be dislodged without mercy.

Li Ssŭ-yüan enters and stands on one side.

CH'ÊNG (*sings*). The Prince's rage is all too manifest. I turn to Li Ssŭ-yüan and blame him for cutting me down from the tree. You should never have restored me to life. How can I bear to return and confront the Emperor, now that all hope of succour has been denied me ? (*Weeps*).

LI SSŬ-YÜAN (*advancing*). Uncle Ch'êng ! (*Sings*) Do not despair ! I'll go and beg my father to assist you.

CH'ÊNG. Pray lose no time.

LI SSŬ-YÜAN (*entering his father's tent, sings*). I've come to beseech you to listen to me, Father. When you were in trouble Uncle Ch'êng came to your rescue, and you should now send troops to repay his kindness. Never mind the Emperor's predicament ; do this for your benefactor's sake.

LI K'O-YUNG. Silence, you slave ! (*Sings in k'uai-pan*) I wish to converse with my benefactor. (*To servants*) Bid the executioners unsheathe and whet their swords. Away with him ; off with his head !

Executioners bind Li Ssŭ-yüan and prepare for his execution.

CH'ÊNG. Put up your swords ! (*Sings in k'uai-pan*) Though I am a high official of the Emperor, to see T'ai Pao led out to execution makes my blood run cold. Prince, if you wish to kill a man, kill me ! Make haste and set your son at liberty.

LI K'O-YUNG (*sings*). Since you talk reason, brother, I'll forgive him. (*Speaks*) Let him be freed !

LI SSŬ-YÜAN. I thank you, Father and King, for your clemency.

LI K'O-YUNG (*sings*). Prostrate yourself before His Excellency, who interceded for you.

LI SSŬ-YÜAN (*doing so, speaks to him privily*). Come nearer to me, Uncle.

CH'ÊNG. What is it?

LI SSŬ-YÜAN (*turning his back, aside*). Pray ease your mind, Uncle. My father lives in dread of his second Consort. I shall persuade her to insist upon sending the troops.

CH'ÊNG. Well spoken, Nephew. Make haste and talk it over with her. (*Exit Li*).

LI K'O-YUNG (*speaks*). Worthy brother Ch'êng, there are three ancient heroes I would call to mind. (*Sings in tao-pan*) During the Han dynasty there were three great men—(*changes air to yüan-pan*) Liu Pei, Kuan Yü and Chang Fei, who swore the Oath of the Peach Garden. At Hsü-chow they parted, later to meet at the ancient Capital.* You, Sir, may be likened to Liu Pei, and I to Kuan of the Beautiful Beard. I advise you not to return to Ch'ang-an; abide with me and enjoy the fruits of leisure. *Exeunt.*

SCENE V

Enter the two Queens.

FIRST QUEEN (*sings in hsi-p'i yao-pan*). Last night I dreamt I went to Ch'ang-an City.

SECOND QUEEN (*speaks*). I would gladly go and view the pageants there.

LI SSŬ-YÜAN (*enters and says*). My respects to you, ladies. (*Weeps*).

FIRST QUEEN. Why do you weep, my son?

LI. Uncle Ch'êng has come to sue for troops. The King not only refused to send them, but gave orders that I was to be beheaded. I would now be a corpse if Uncle Ch'êng had not interceded for me. I beg you to urge the King to send those troops.

---

*Ch'ang-an.

FIRST QUEEN (*sings*). Since it was His Excellency Ch'êng who came for them, he ought to have them.

SECOND QUEEN. I'll insist upon their dispatch!

Exeunt Queens.

SCENE VI

Enter Li K'o-yung and Ch'êng Ching-ssŭ.

CH'ÊNG (*sings in k'uai-pan*). One day has passed; another is at hand. I feel as if my heart were scalded in boiling oil. Towards Ch'ang-an I gaze but cannot see it. I wonder if the Emperor is safe!

LI K'O-YUNG (*sings in yao-pan*). Do not fret about the Emperor, worthy brother. Remain with us here at Sha-t'o. We have plenty of official robes and headgear to fit you.

CH'ÊNG (*sings*). I do not need your caps of gauze and python robes.

LI (*sings*). I advise you not to vex yourself unduly; just ease your heart with feasting and with wine.

CH'ÊNG (*sings*). Although I sit at the banquet-board I seldom have felt so depressed.

LI (*sings*). Lift your head and look about you : see the myriads of banners fluttering in the breeze, the mountains of grain stacked up in all directions! My sons are all blessed with courage and military genius. The eldest far surpasses Lü Pu in ability; the second is equal to the renowned Ma Ch'ao; the third can capture tigers on the mountains; the fourth is a brilliant strategist; the fifth can flourish a battle-axe big enough to hack his way through a mountain; the sixth excels in archery; the seventh is famous in handling the spear; the eighth is equally famous with the lance; the ninth can wield a pair of double-headed maces; and the tenth is supreme in plying the iron whip. As for the eleventh, he is an expert swordsman. Let Huang Ch'ao approach if he dares : spear-point to spear-point, I'll fight him single-handed. Come, come, I'll fill you a bumper of wine to dispel your gloom.

CH'ÊNG (*sings*). Although I sit at the banquet-board I have seldom felt so depressed.

SCENE VII

Enter the two Queens, followed by Li Ssŭ-yüan.

FIRST QUEEN (*sings*). Approaching the portals of the central hall, we see the great king sitting at the feast. (*Speaks to son*) T'ai Pao, go to His Majesty and announce our arrival.

LI SSŬ-YÜAN (*entering the King's apartment, says*). I come to announce that the two Queens are waiting to see you, Sire.

LI K'O-YUNG. Which Queen?

LI SSŬ-YÜAN. Both Queens desire to visit you, Sire. They have something special to discuss.

LI K'O-YUNG. Tell them I have a guest from Ch'ang-an to look after; and that shortly I shall see them in my camp.   (*Li Ssŭ-yüan obeys*).

FIRST QUEEN (*sings*). The King has given orders not to admit us.

SECOND QUEEN (*sings*). I would like to see what sort of handsome gentleman this Ch'êng, our benefactor, is. (*Speaks*) Stay! I can hear them converse. I am sure he is splendid: I'll go and steal a glance.

Ch'êng and the Second Queen look at each other and laugh.

SECOND QUEEN (*speaks*). Why, he is quite antique!
                                                        Exit.

CH'ÊNG (*sings*). It is plain that Li K'o-yung stands in awe of his wife. My fear that he will not send the troops begins to vanish.

SCENE VIII

Enter the two Queens with swords and banners.

BOTH QUEENS (*singing*). Armed with swords and banners, we order you to listen to us, T'ai Pao. (*Speak*)

You shall announce to your father the King that the two Queens have come a second time to visit him, and that he must see us willynilly. Nothing can shake our resolve.

Exit Li Ssŭ-yüan accordingly.

LI K'O-YUNG. What? My Consorts again!

LI SSŬ-YÜAN. The Queens have come a second time to see you.

LI K'O-YUNG. Did you not tell them that I am busy with a guest, and will see them later on?

LI SSŬ-YÜAN. The Queen Mother says you must see her: you have no choice in the matter.

LI K'O-YUNG. What a nuisance they are!

LI SSŬ-YÜAN. I'll pretend that the King has agreed to admit them.

FIRST QUEEN (*sings in hsi-p'i yao-pan*). We sisters twain enter the King's tent.

SECOND QUEEN (*sings*). We'll inquire about our benefactor's health.

Both enter tent and kneel before Ch'êng Ching-ssŭ.

CH'ÊNG (*kneeling also, sings*). Ch'êng Ching-ssŭ picks up his robe to kneel before the mat,* begging the two Queens to hear his request. His Majesty refuses to send military aid, so that I dare not return to Ch'ang-an.

FIRST QUEEN (*sings*). Rise, Honourable Sir, I hear your words.

SECOND QUEEN (*sings*). As for sending troops, I have authority to send them.

BOTH QUEENS (*addressing Li K'o-yung*). Our respects to Your Majesty.

LI K'O-YUNG. What brings you into my tent?

BOTH QUEENS. What brings His Honour Ch'êng into your tent?

LI K'O-YUNG. He has come to beg for troops.

QUEENS. Then it behoves you to dispatch them.

---

* i.e. at the banquet-table.

LI K'O-YUNG. I have already declared that I would not under any circumstances render assistance to the T'ang Emperor.

QUEENS. But you have already accepted his gifts.

LI K'O-YUNG. Gifts? Ahem! Those were presented to me by my worthy brother Ch'êng.

QUEENS. Where are the phœnix crown and the crimson robes?

LI K'O-YUNG. I have stored them in my treasury.

QUEENS. From times of yore it has been said: A gentleman never forgets old friends. Therefore it behoves you to send the troops for the sake of an old friend.

LI K'O-YUNG. Who will dare send them if I refuse to do so?

SECOND QUEEN. I give you a chance to save your reputation; even if you have ceased to care about it, would you dare to repeat three times in succession: "I won't send troops"?

LI K'O-YUNG. Not thrice, I repeat, but thirty, nay three hundred times, I stick to my refusal.

SECOND QUEEN. Dare you repeat thrice in succession that you will not send the troops?

LI K'O-YUNG. Do you really think I am afraid of saying: "I won't send any troops"? Well, I won't, I won't and I won't!

SECOND QUEEN. You are wondrous bold! Now listen to my orders! (*Sings*) If you won't send them, I will. (*Speaks*) Here, T'ai Pao, this is my authority. (*Hands him an arrow with small triangular flag attached*). Issue commands that all the Mongol and Chinese Banner Corps, consisting of four hundred and fifty thousand men and horses, are to prepare for battle.

The Second Queen appoints herself Commander-in-Chief and tells Li Ssŭ-yüan to inform the King that she has appointed him to command the vanguard. He is to wait punctually in front of the Palace. Herself will muster the troops.

LI SSŬ-YÜAN. What if the King comes late?

SECOND QUEEN. He'll lose his head! (*Exeunt Queens*).

LI SSŬ-YÜAN. Hear me, Oh Father and King. The two Queens have appointed themselves Commanders-in-Chief of the troops. They told me to notify you that you are to lead the vanguard. The whole army of Sha-t'o is to set forth to restore the T'ang Emperor and exterminate Huang Ch'ao. The Queens enjoin you to report at the palace gate while they muster the troops; they add that you must be punctual. If you come late your head shall pay the forfeit. (*Exit*).

LI K'O-YUNG. This is outrageous! Come back, T'ai Pao, and we'll discuss this matter.

CH'ÊNG. He has already gone. You and I had better discuss it.

LI K'O-YUNG. Alas, my worthy brother! (*Sings—aside*) T'ai Pao is a mischief-maker: it was he that egged the women on to make trouble. I'll have to row with the tide against my will. (*Speaks*) For your dear sake I'll move my forces from Sha-t'o.

CH'ÊNG (*sings*). You need not make such a show of kindly sentiment, Oh Prince. Everything is as clear to me as lamplight. It was the two Queens who decided that the army should move. Your humbug does not hoodwink me, ha, ha!

LI K'O-YUNG (*sings*). Worthy brother, pray do not indulge in such immoderate laughter! It is because your stupid brother fears . . . fears . . .

CH'ÊNG. Fears what, may I ask?

LI (*sings*). My womenfolk,—as you will soon discover if you make enquiries at Sha-t'o. Although a hen-pecked husband, I am happy enough as a king. I enjoy old age, and have all the drink I desire. (*Chuckles merrily*).

Exeunt.

Scene IX

Enter Li's ten younger sons and give a display of their various military talents. The eldest follows.

LI SSŬ-YÜAN (*says*). The silver helmet glitters on my head ; my coat of mail wards off the sharpest steel. I ride a famous charger called White Dragon. I am burning to annihilate Huang Ch'ao.

Eight standard-bearers and eight swordsmen enter.

LI SSŬ-YÜAN. My respects to you, brothers.

BROTHERS (*in unison*). The same to you, elder brother.

LI SSŬ-YÜAN. The Queens are mustering the troops at the palace gate. We had better go and assist them.

BROTHERS (*in unison*). Well said. Lead on the horses.

Exeunt.

Scene X

Li K'o-yung enters, performs a series of arm and leg exercises and leaves the stage. The Queens enter with the flag and arrow of authority, followed by eight men with banners and eight with swords, and Ch'êng Ching-ssŭ. The Queens take seats in the centre, and Ch'êng sits on one side. The eleven brothers enter and stand in rows on either side of them.

BROTHERS. Our respects to Your Majesties.

QUEENS. Thank you ! (*To Li Ssŭ-yüan*) Are men and horses ready ?

LI. All ready, Your Majesties.

SECOND QUEEN. Good, prepare for the muster.

LI (*to soldiers*). Beat the drums and respond to the roll-call.

SECOND QUEEN. First division ! (*Eight standard-bearers reply :* " Here ! ") Second division ! Left Wing, right Wing. (*All reply :* " Present ! ") All the T'ai Pao ! (*The eleven sons of Li K'o-yung call :* " Present ! "). Leader of the Vanguard ! (*No reply*).

BROTHERS. He has not yet arrived.

SECOND QUEEN. What! The Leader of the Vanguard is absent from the first roll-call! He ought to . . .

CH'ÊNG CHING-SSŬ. Forgive him please, Your Majesty, for my sake.

SECOND QUEEN. Since you plead for him, I'll hold another roll-call. (*The procedure is repeated. All respond except Li K'o-yung*). The second muster, and still he has not come! He should be dealt with according to martial law.

LI SSŬ-YÜAN. Queen Mother, pray forgive my Royal Father on the score of advanced age. Maybe he has some difficulty in buckling on his armour. Please have the patience to hold another muster.

SECOND QUEEN. Are you pleading for your father the King?

LI SSŬ-YÜAN. I hope you will do me this favour, Royal Mother.

SECOND QUEEN. Beat the drums for the Leader of the Vanguard. (*Drums beat. She sings out*) Leader of the Vanguard! (*No reply*).

BROTHERS. There is no sign of him yet.

SECOND QUEEN. T'ai Pao, take the name of the missing member and hang it on the palace gate.

Li Ssŭ-yüan does so.

Li K'o-yung's voice is heard behind the stage : "The cavalry advance!" *He enters, accompanied by a few generals.*

LI K'O-YUNG (*sings in hsi-p'i k'uai-pan*). I suddenly hear the loud report of guns, and see the troops file forth in grand array. Not one but glows all eager for the fray. I arrive at the palace gate and dismount from my steed. (*Seeing the notice of his absence posted up, he becomes alarmed*).

LI SSŬ-YÜAN. Father, you have missed the roll-call!

LI K'O-YUNG. What do I care about that? Go and tell the Queens to come and receive me.

Exit Li Ssŭ-yüan.

THE QUEENS. For such dereliction of duty it behoves him to come and implore our forgiveness : instead, he orders us to go to him ! Tell him to report to us at the entrance-gate.

LI SSŬ-YÜAN. Leader of the Vanguard, attention to orders ! The Queens require you to report yourself to them at once.

LI K'O-YUNG (*much angered*). Monstrous ! (*Sings*) The Queens have now taken control of the army and appoint me to lead the vanguard. If I disobey, they will keep me out of the bedchamber at night. I'll tell my aide-de-camp to report my arrival. (*On entering, sings*) There they sit, the two ogresses, conspiring against me. If they say nothing, neither shall I.

SECOND QUEEN. Is that the Leader of the Vanguard standing there ?

LI K'O-YUNG. Quite so ; it is he.

SECOND QUEEN. To-day I had to call the roll thrice. Why were you absent ?

LI K'O-YUNG. I had some difficulty in buckling on my armour, and was therefore delayed.

SECOND QUEEN. To miss roll-call is an offence against army discipline. Decapitation is the penalty. Here ! Let him be taken out and beheaded !

CH'ÊNG CHING-SSŬ. Show some consideration for me, I crave, and acquit him.

SECOND QUEEN. Since you, our benefactor, intercede for him, I'll revoke the death-sentence. But he cannot escape corporal punishment. (*To lictors*) Give him eighty strokes of the bamboo.

LI K'O-YUNG. Having absolved me from the death-sentence, you might as well absolve me from the flogging.

LI SSŬ-YÜAN. The King, my father, is advanced in age ; I beg you to forgive him.

SECOND QUEEN. Since you plead for him, my son, I'll let him off this time. Instead of commanding the vanguard he shall command the rearguard with three thousand veteran troops. T'ai Pao shall now lead the vanguard, destroy Huang Ch'ao, and restore the T'ang Emperor to his throne. *Exeunt.*

Act II. Scene I

Enter Chou Tê-wei, accompanied by four soldiers.

CHOU. I have held this pass for years, and my name is known throughout the empire. I am lord of the Pearly Screen Castle and shall yet be lord of the ten thousand li around. (*Speaks*) I, Chou Tê-wei, am lord of the Pearly Screen Castle. I command five hundred stalwart hillsmen. We rob all travellers passing through. My scouts have just reported that a rich convoy is approaching. I must gather my men and plunder it without delay.

Chou and his gang make several rounds of the stage, indicating their descent of the mountain. The eleven brothers, accompanied by eight standard-bearers and eight swordsmen come in contact with the robbers.

LI SSŬ-YÜAN (*speaks*). That rider yonder : is he not Chou Tê-wei ?

CHOU. Precisely.

LI. How dare you block my passage ?

CHOU. Hand over your treasure and I'll let you pass.

LI. Audacious braggart ! (*To Brethren*) To slaughter ! To slaughter !

A fight ensues. Chou is victorious and the brothers escape, pursued by Chou and his men. Exeunt omnes.

Scene II

Enter the Second Queen with Chêng Ching-ssŭ and eight standard-bearers.

SECOND QUEEN (*sings*). Before we advance further we must wait for the scouts' report.

ELEVEN BROTHERS (*enter and report*). Please Your Majesty, when passing the Pearly Screen Castle, the robber-chieftain Chou Tê-wei rushed out with his gang and demanded our treasure. They were seized in the ensuing struggle and we were routed with many casualties. We have just come back to report.

SECOND QUEEN. Alternate victory and defeat are inevitable in warfare. You may all retire to rest and refresh yourselves. Ta T'ai Pao, take this arrow of authority to your father and tell him to come here at once. *Exit Li Ssŭ-yüan.*

CH'ÊNG CHING-SSŬ. When the King arrives, you must spur him on to fight.

SECOND QUEEN. Trust me!

Enter Li K'o-yung, Li Ssŭ-yüan and Aide-de-camp.

LI K'O-YUNG (*sings*). Arriving at the gate, I dismount from my charger. I wonder what is required of me now! (*Enters hall and sits in the centre chair*).

SECOND QUEEN. That is not your chair : it belongs to the Commander-in-Chief.

LI K'O-YUNG. Well, where am I to sit then ?

SECOND QUEEN. There is no seat for you. You are to stand and take my orders.

CH'ÊNG. The Prince is old ; pray let him take a chair.

SECOND QUEEN. In deference to our benefactor, I'll allow you to sit.

LI (*thanking her, sits down and says*) Why have you sent for me ?

SECOND QUEEN. When passing the Pearly Screen Castle the brothers were plundered by the robber-chieftain Chou Tê-wei : they were no match for him.

LI. That Chou! Why, he is a mere suckling. What skill in war has he ?

SECOND QUEEN. Since he was able to defeat our men, he must have some ability ; though young, he is hard to vanquish. I have summoned you to attack him. If you win, I have something nice in store for you.

LI. What can that be, I wonder?

SECOND QUEEN. You follow me, and I'll tell you. *She covers her face with her sleeve and whispers a promise of conjugal bliss in his ear.*

LI. You have fooled me more than once in that respect. I refuse to go!

SECOND QUEEN. You are becoming senile and impotent, I can see.

LI. My heart is young though age has come upon me. There is a time-honoured saying that a tiger is terrible even when it is old: the older the buck, the stiffer the horn. Give me the arrow; I'll go and grapple with Chou Tê-wei at once. (*Takes arrow and sings in hsi-p'i êrh-liu-pan*).

Though I am old, my beard and hair turned white,
In martial skill I am a man of might.
My strength increases in the years' despite.

Let the presumptuous mountain bandit swagger forth: he shall meet the famous eighty-one pound halberd that fought for the T'ang dynasty. And let a banquet be prepared within my tent, so that I may enjoy the fullness of my victory. (*Speaks*) Lead in my panther-tiger charger! (*Mounts it and sings*) Now shall I go to encounter Chou Tê-wei.

SECOND QUEEN. I welcome such glad news.

Exeunt.

SCENE III

Enter Li K'o-yung with eight standard-bearers and eight swordsmen. Chou Tê-wei arrives with four of his men. They start fighting.

LI K'O-YUNG. Is that Chou Tê-wei advancing towards me?

CHOU. It is, and no mistake.

LI. Why do you block my passage?

CHOU. Allow me to keep the treasure, and I'll let you go by.

LI. Stuff and nonsense. Here, officers, protect my flank. (*Sings in hsi-p'i tao-pan*) Beat the battle-drums for the fray. (*Changes to yao-pan*) Chou Tê-wei, you are a mere suckling. Where are your qualifications that you dare to challenge me?

The contest begins. Chou is defeated and escapes, pursued by Li. He then returns with bow and arrow.

CHOU (*sings*). That old fellow is surely a valiant fighter : his swordsmanship is superior to mine

Chou shoots an arrow and runs away : Li catches it in his hand.

LI. You may mock me because I am old, but your shot did not equal my catch. (*Exit*).

CHOU (*entering, sings*). The old fellow caught my arrow very neatly. I'll have another try.

Li catches the arrow again.

LI (*sings*). That's the second arrow I caught. Your marksmanship is verily superb. But why bother to sell the Three Character Classic at Confucius's door? *

Exit.

CHOU (*returns, singing*). I've come to a stand on newly conquered land.

LI (*likewise returns, singing*). Defeated, don't fancy that you will escape my hand!

CHOU (*speaks*). Our skill on horseback is even. Let us dismount and test our skill with bow and arrow.

LI. What are the conditions?

CHOU. We'll set up a post a hundred paces away and hang a cash thereon. The winner must hit the coin and make it ring.

LI. Who shoots first?

---

*i.e. teach your grandmother to suck eggs.

CHOU. I will.

LI. Then go ahead.

CHOU (*sings*). I fit my arrow to the bow. (*Takes aim, shoots and hits the mark, making it ring; laughs triumphantly and sings*) I've got the best of that old man at last! (*Speaks*) I hit the bull's-eye : now it is your turn.

LI. Wait till I shoot! (*Sings*) I take my bow and fix my eyes on the post, but cannot see the mark. The sun has set behind the western hills, and the light grows dim. How could these old eyes have lost their vision like this? I bow my head in meditation. (*A wild goose cries overhead: the orchestra produces an imitative sound*). I have a sudden inspiration.

CHOU. Why don't you shoot?

LI. The coin is a dead thing : I want something live to shoot at, something quite out of the common.

CHOU. What live thing is there to shoot in this barren wilderness?

LI. Lift your head, baby, and use your little eyes.

CHOU. A couple of birds, that's all.

LI. With a single arrow I'll kill the pair of them.

CHOU. What if you don't?

LI. If I miss, I'll let you keep the treasure ; but if I hit, what do you propose to do?

CHOU. If you bring down those birds with a single arrow, I'll willingly salute you as my master.

LI. Good! Watch and see. (*Sings*) I pray to Heaven with all my heart that the gods will beam on me with friendly eyes, so that bringing down this couple of geese to-day I may also bring this warrior into my fold. (*Aims at the geese, which apparently are hanging about overhead waiting to be shot, and transfixes both with a single arrow. The birds are represented by black cloths flung into the air*).

CHOU (*sings*). I hasten forward and fall on my knees : right willingly I acknowledge you as my father.

Li K'o-yung helps him to his feet. Exeunt. Finis.

CHU SHA CHIH 硃砂痣

THE CINNABAR MOLE

The second part is known as *Tai Mai Tzŭ*: "Buying a Son by Proxy." An *êrh-huang* play.

PERIOD : Sung

DRAMATIS PERSONÆ

HAN YÜAN-WAI, a Good Samaritan ... ... *Wai*
CHIANG SHIH, Wu Hui-ch'üan's wife ... ... *Chêng-tan*
WU HUI-CH'ÜAN, a merchant ... ... *Shêng*
YÜ-YÜN (T'ien-tz'ŭ), Han Yüan-wai's long-lost son *Wa Wa Shêng*
CHIN SHIH, an ancient widow ... ... *Lao-tan*
HAN FU, Han's servant ... ... *Shêng*
MEI P'O, a go-between ... ... *Ch'ou-p'o*

"The Humanitarian Rewarded," as we might call this play, concerns Han Yüan-wai, a Good Samaritan who lived during the Southern Sung dynasty. His wife died, leaving him with an only son, Yü-yün. While he was travelling to take up his post as Prefect in Szech'uan, during the war between Sung and Chin, the child was lost. No trace of him could be found despite the fact that Yü-yün had what passports term a special peculiarity : a vermilion mole on the sole of his left foot. In his sad predicament as childless widower, the worthy Han decided to remarry at the age of fifty. So he settled the matter with a professional go-between to whom he advanced one hundred ounces of silver.

The play opens with a bridal scene.

ACT I. SCENE I

Enter Han Yüan-wai (singing in êrh-huang yao-pan).

HAN. Ha, ha ! The lamps in all the rooms burn brilliantly this evening. How strange that I should be a bridegroom at the age of fifty !

A servant announces that the bridal chair has arrived. Soon the bride appears accompanied by her maid.

THE GO-BETWEEN (*to Han*). Congratulations, Sir. And now please pay me my reward.

HAN. The servant will hand it to you.

THE GO-BETWEEN (*aside*). Although I feel much gratified, I am also somewhat grieved at this woman's marriage !

HAN (*to maid*). Light the lamp and let me have a glimpse of the bride. (*Singing in êrh-huang man-san-yen*) In the lantern's glow I can see a beautiful woman. She bears a close resemblance to my former wife.

The bride weeps and sighs : " Alas ! "

HAN (*singing in êrh-huang yüan-pan*). May I ask why the tears are streaming down your cheeks ? Is it because you consider me too old to be your mate ?

CHIANG SHIH. No, no ! It is not that . . .

He asks her more questions of the same kind to which she always replies in the negative.

HAN (*in êrh-huang yüan-pan*). It is not this and it is not that—these negatives are hard for me to fathom. If you have anything on your mind, please tell me. Why be afraid ?

CHIANG SHIH. Honoured Sir, pray hear my supplication. (*Sings in êrh-huang chêng-pan*) I feel abashed about what I wish to say, and cannot check my tears . . . My poor husband is mortally ill : he has been bedridden for so many years that we have not enough money to support us. So he decided to sell me as a concubine. At first I was quite willing : eager for wealth and honour I rashly agreed. Pity a poor man and his wife who must bear such a separation ! Have mercy on us, dear Sir, and release me from this contract. And when I die and go to the regions beyond I shall never forget your kindness.

HAN (*singing in êrh-huang yao-pan*). Ah, listen to her words ! She still has a husband. How could I be responsible for parting them ! I'll never perpetrate such a wrong. I swear to the Heavens above that henceforth I'll remain a lonely widower . . . (*To servant*) Escort this lady to her home. The money I provided for gifts to her and the go-between need not be returned. Give her two hundred ounces of silver besides, so that both husband and wife may enjoy my favour, and a spouse's virtue be well ensured.

Chiang Shih thanks him.

HAN. It's a mere trifle. (*Then he burns the marriage certificate in her presence, observing*) I would have the same done by me.

SCENES II AND III

On seeing his wife return well-provided with cash Wu Hui-ch'üan is so overjoyed that he recovers from his illness. " How could such a kind man exist in this cruel world ! " he exclaims. Straightway he goes with his wife to thank Han personally for his signal generosity. They kneel before him.

HAN (*sings in êrh-huang yao-pan*). We have all been taught since time immemorial to help others in distress. This is a trifling matter. Pray rise and let me bow in acknowledgment of your thanks. All virtue, benevolence and righteousness come from above.

Follows a characteristic exchange of Chinese courtesies.

WU. You, noble Sir, are my benefactor. How could I venture to sit in your presence ?

HAN. Since we wish to have a chat, why stand on ceremony ?

WU. Well, by your leave I'll take a seat.

HAN (*to Chiang Shih*). You take a seat too . . . (*To Wu*) Your wife informed me that you were suffering from a severe disease, and that you would wait until you were fully recovered before coming to visit me.

WU. You can't imagine, Sir : as soon as I received the money I was cured.

HAN. Really ! Cured so suddenly ! From what you say money turns out to be something worth possessing.

WU. It is indeed, Sir !

HAN (*sings in ting-pan*). I rescued you in time of danger and distress : I relieved your poverty and respected the virtue of your consort, because I knew you were a worthy man, through your marriage to such a worthy woman. I have no sons, but this was foreordained. Had I parted you from your wife, I would have sullied my name.

WU. Why don't you remarry? You may still beget a son : there is no telling.

HAN. That has all been fixed by destiny. I had a son and lost him ; if I remarried now that I am past fifty I doubt if I could have another.

WU. Why not purchase one? Then at least you would have some one to lean on in old age.

HAN. Well, yes, that *could* be done. But it would not be feasible to get one from this neighbourhood. And were I to get one from some remote place, one who was poor and unreliable, I should have already reached my dotage by the time he grew to manhood. If he disobeyed me and made my life wretched it would be worse than having no son at all.

WU. I have some bills to collect in Szech'uan and intend to go there as soon as possible for that purpose, thanks to your generosity. If I should find a likely lad I'll buy him and present him to you in return for all your kindness.

HAN. Capital! I'll thank you in anticipation.

Act. II. TAI MAI TZŬ
"Buying a Son by Proxy"
SCENE I

An old widow called Mrs. Chin relates in soliloquy how she found Yü-yün whom she named T'ien-tz'ŭ and reared to support her in old age. But the child is now twelve years old and, in lieu of supporting her, is a drag on her very slender resources. She decides to sell him.

T'IEN-TZ'Ŭ (*appears, saying*).

The Emperor honours the noble heart :
Aim high for literary art.
Of other pursuits the virtue's small,
The study of books excels them all.

MRS. CHIN. " The study of books excels them all ! "
What's the good of books when we have nothing in the
larder ? No rice, no fuel, and if I want a drink of water
I have to fetch it for myself. A fig for your books !

T'IEN-TZ'Ŭ. When your stepson grows to manhood,
his name will appear on the roll of graduates.

MRS. CHIN. And in the meantime we'll both be drift-
ing hither and thither without a roof over our heads.

T'IEN-TZ'Ŭ. Have no fear, Mother. When I grow up
I'll become an official and you'll be a lady of high degree.

MRS. CHIN. You talk big ! Just listen to me. This
is a year of famine : existence won't be easy for either of
us. I have a mind to sell you to some rich family so that
you'll have a home to be happy in and I'll have enough
to live on.

T'IEN-TZ'Ŭ. I'll not be sold !

MRS. CHIN. Here, lad. I've got to tell you the bare
truth : you are not the son of my womb. During the
fighting with the Chins on the eighth day of the fourth
moon, I found you on the road to Ch'ing-chou : you
were still in swaddling-clothes.

T'ien-tz'ŭ weeps and calls for his dear mother.

MRS. CHIN. Ai ya ! I tell him that he is not my own
son and he calls out for his dear mother ! If I don't sell
him now, when he grows up he'll probably sell me ! . . .
Don't cry, child. Sit down and listen to what I have to
tell you. (*Sings in êrh-huang man-pan*) The husbandman
tills the fields and depends upon his toil for food and
clothing. With the study of books, though you may learn
ten million chapters, you'll find it hard to obtain rice and
fuel. I don't think you will ever amount to anything.

T'IEN-TZ'Ŭ. Oh Mother! (*Sings in êrh-huang yüan-pan*)
Please don't take me away from my books : I don't want
to be a farmer. I have great ambitions and a fixed ideal.
Wait until my feathers have grown. Then, like the
Rukh's journey of ten thousand li, I'll soar to high
estate. I'll wear a cap of black gauze and a gorgeous
robe of purple.

MRS. CHIN (*sings in êrh-huang yüan-pan*). What stuff
is this about sprouting wings like a Rukh and flying ten
thousand li ? More likely you'll not be worth a nag or
even a cow. And even if you were my real son, I
couldn't afford to keep you any longer. To-day we'll
have to part. Bolt the door tight and follow me.
Within a few minutes mother and son will part for ever.

SCENE II

*Mrs. Chin with a bunch of grass ready to tie round the
boy's arm as a sign that he is for sale, sings out :* " A son for
sale ! " *At this juncture Wu comes along. After some
equivocation as to whether the child or the grass is for sale,
Wu buys the boy for fifty ounces of silver. While the child is
crying his heart out the hag gives him such disagreeable parting
advice as :* " Late to bed and early to rise ! " " Mind
you're not as sluggish as you were with me ! "

SCENE III

*Wu takes the boy to present to his benefactor ; telling him
to wait outside until he is called for.*

HAN. So you have already returned ! Please be
seated . . . Did you collect all of your debts during your
sojourn at Ch'êng-tu ?

WU. Yes, all.

HAN. You are most fortunate !

WU. Entirely due to your great kindness, Sir. Excuse
me a moment. (*Goes out and fetches T'ien-tz'ŭ, saying*)
Come along with me to see His Honour Han !

The lad makes his bow and asks after His Honour's health, etc.

HAN. Never mind ceremony. Sit down. (*T'ien-tz'ŭ refuses on the score of age and status*). Listen to me! Take a seat . . . Ah, Mr. Wu, this son of yours is well up in ceremony, I see. (*Wu tells him that he has brought him as a present. Han, overjoyed, sings in p'ing-pan*) Elder brother Wu, so you have been true to your word, and planned a descendant for me! I owe you the deepest gratitude. Such kindness of heart, such a brilliant solution, surpasses my fondest expectations. Some day I shall surely make surplus amends. (*Speaking*) Now that I've a son I need fret no more. How much did you spend on this boy, Sir? You must allow me to reimburse you.

WU. I dare not, Sir. Were my wife and I to crush our bodies and grind our bones we could never repay your great bounty to us.

HAN. Then all that is left for me to utter is thank you, Sir.

WU. And now I must bid you farewell, Sir.

HAN. Why such haste?

WU. It's long since I have been away from home and I fear that my wife will be anxious.

HAN. I'll not detain you then.

After further courtesies Wu departs, leaving Han alone with his son.

HAN (*to T'ien-tz'ŭ*). Sit down and let me have a careful look at you. (*Sings in êrh-huang yüan-pan*) My son understands the rules of right conduct; he understands the rules of propriety. He is fair to look upon: he is cast in a different mould from the average child. Watching him closely he seems fit to take up any official position in life. His forehead is wide, his features well-formed, his eyes and brows are beautiful. Now that you have a home you should study diligently. Are you listening to your father, who is explaining all things clearly to you?

T'IEN-TZ'Ŭ. I studied hard at my former home but I lacked a good teacher to instruct me.

HAN (*sings in êrh-huang yüan-pan*). What he says proves that he has a heart : he is bright and intelligent. If he enters official life, there will not be the slightest error in his ways . . . On what day of the moon and in what year were you born ? Tell me quickly, so that I can have your horoscope cast.

T'IEN-TZ'Ŭ. I do not know, Sir.

HAN. Didn't your mother tell you ?

T'IEN-TZ'Ŭ. She does not know either.

HAN (*sings in êrh-huang yüan-pan*). Incredible ! How can he be ignorant of his birthday ? How old are your parents ? Are they still alive ? Who were they ? Who sold you then ?

T'IEN-TZ'Ŭ. My father died five years ago ; my mother is seventy-two years old. I am now thirteen, and was sold on account of her poverty.

HAN (*in êrh-huang yüan-pan*). There is something strange in this, it's worth investigating. How could a woman of sixty give birth to a son ! He cannot be her own : how else could she have borne to part with him ?

T'IEN-TZ'Ŭ. Oh, now I remember. Before Mother sold me she said I wasn't her own son : during the wars with the Chins she found me on the road to Ch'ing-chou on the eighth day of the fourth moon.

HAN (*laughs with joy and sings in yüan-pan*). The closer I question, the closer I come to the loss of my own child. That was the very day . . . on the way to Ch'êng-tu while there was fighting all around us. Your resemblance to your father and mother is quite remarkable. (*Speaks*) My own son had a cinnabar mole on the sole of his left foot. Have you one ?

T'IEN-TZ'Ŭ. Yes, on my left foot.

HAN. Take off your shoes and socks and let me see. *T'ien-tz'ŭ does so.*

HAN. My son! (*Sings in êrh-huang yao-pan*) You are my true-born son Yü-yün! We were sundered in time of distress. Twelve years have passed since then and my pretty boy was never out of my thoughts. Such was my remorse that I could not eat or drink or sleep in peace. It was on your account that I resigned my official post and returned to my old home. Who could have thought that to-day you and I should be re-united!

YÜ-YÜN. Where has Mother gone to?

HAN. Your mother has long since passed away. (*Yü-yün weeps and cries out for his mother*). Don't cry, son. Your mother is peacefully at rest . . .

YÜ-YÜN. Please send for Mrs. Chin so that we may all share happiness and honour together, and repay her for rearing me so long.

HAN. Very well! To-morrow I'll send a man to fetch her. To-day flesh and bones are happily joined again: father and son behold each other once more. Only I fear that it is all a dream!

YÜ-YÜN. How can it be a dream in broad daylight, Father?

BOTH. No, it is not a dream!

HAN (*beaming with parental pride*). Come along with your father, Son.

Finis

*   *   *

Like *Chuang Yüan P'u*, this play depicts the importance attached to progeny and the misery of a childless man in China. Not a play for confirmed bachelors, but instructive to students of Chinese social psychology, hence we have included it in our repertoire.

CHUANG YÜAN P'U 狀元譜

A Chuang Yüan's* Record

Also known as *Ta Chih Shang Fên*: "A Nephew worshipping at his Ancestral Graves after a drubbing."   A *hsi-p'i* play.

PERIOD: Sung

DRAMATIS PERSONÆ

CH'ÊN PO-YÜ, a philanthropist	*Lao-shêng*	
CH'ÊN FU JÊN, his wife...	*Lao-tan*	
CH'ÊN TA-KUAN, his nephew	*Hsiao-shêng*	
CHANG KUNG-TAO, a poor man	} *Ch'ou-êrh*	
CHU TS'ANG, a custodian of the family graves ...		
CH'ÊN CHIH, a family retainer	*Shêng*	

Since himself had not been blessed with offspring, Ch'ên Po-yü, a prosperous native of Ch'ang-an in Shensi, adopted his orphaned nephew Ta-kuan. The boy's foster-parents doted on him and gave him the best education available. At the age of thirteen he took his preliminary degree (*hsiu-ts'ai*) but he soon fell in with low company and turned to a life of dissipation. His uncle tried to curb him. Impatient of control, he insisted on being allotted his share of the family property and behaved so outrageously that his uncle gave way and washed his hands of him. Ta-kuan left home to sow his wild oats, pursuing those paths which Hogarth has immortalized in "The Rake's Progress." After three years he found himself in the gutter without an oat to sow.

The play begins in a year of drought and famine: Ch'ên Po-yü opens his granary and distributes free grain to the needy.

SCENE I

Enter Chang Kung-tao, a ruined merchant with six children to support.

CHANG. I'm out of luck! Nothing in the house, my money spent and not a scrap of food; and now a drought comes on top of all these misfortunes! How shall I ever make both ends meet? I hear that Ch'ên

---

*Senior Wrangler in the Triennial Examinations.

Po-yü is distributing grain gratis. I think I'll take my sons along and see what he can do for me. (*Sings out to his sons*) Here, where are you all?

They arrive and ask what they are called for. He tells them to fetch some empty sacks and follow him to the Ch'ên Mansion. On arrival they knock at the door, and are questioned by the servant Ch'ên Chih, who then goes off to tell his master.

CH'ÊN PO-YÜ (*entering, says*). My house confronts the East, hence it is ever pervaded by the warmth of Spring. Those who accumulate virtue have blessings to spare. (*To servant*) What is it?

CH'ÊN CHIH. Chang Kung-tao has come to call, Sir.

CH'ÊN PO-YÜ. Show him in. (*When Chang and his sons are admitted, he asks*) Whose children are these?

CHANG (*being a clown*). Yüan Wai (you) are my son!

CH'ÊN CHIH. Did you ever hear such nonsense?

CHANG. I mean, excepting yourself, Yüan Wai, they are all my sons.

CH'ÊN PO-YÜ (*to servant*). Take them all to the back and give them something to eat. (*To Chang*) Pray, what is your age?

CHANG. Thirty-five years all told, Sir.

CH'ÊN. Only thirty-five and you have six strapping boys!

CHANG. Sir, paupers are always blessed with progeny.

CH'ÊN. You are extremely fortunate!

CHANG. Alas, I fear I cannot support them all.

CHANG'S SONS (*entering with servant*). Thank you kindly for the hearty meal, Sir.

CH'ÊN PO-YÜ. May I ask what brought you here?

CHANG. Hearing that you were distributing free grain, Sir, we came for some to save us from starvation.

CH'ÊN PO-YÜ (*to servant*). Provide them with enough to fill eight bellies.

CHANG. Hie! wait a minute. If you are going to give us grain, please let us have enough for ten.

CH'ÊN. You, your wife and your six sons add up to a total of eight, why then should you require provisions for ten?

CHANG. I am not deceiving you, Sir. My wife is nearing confinement.

CH'ÊN. But even after her delivery your family would only number nine.

CHANG. The fact is, Sir, my wife has either two at a time or none at all.

CH'ÊN. Two for certain?

CHANG. Two for quite certain, Sir.

CH'ÊN. Let him have enough for ten mouths then, besides two pieces of cotton cloth and ten strings of cash.
            When these are distributed the children retire.
CHANG (*to Ch'ên*). How many sons have you, Sir?

CH'ÊN. What? Me? (*Waves his hand with fingers extended*).

CHANG. Ai ya! Five sons? (*Ch'ên says nothing*). I'll ask Ch'ên Chih. (*To servant*) Ch'ên Chih, how many sons has your master?

CH'ÊN CHIH. None.

CHANG. What? A family of such exalted virtue childless? (*Aside*) I'll try on a bit of flattery. Mr. Ch'ên, since you have accumulated so much virtue, you must have a galaxy of sons to adorn your hearth and home.

CH'ÊN. Reckless fancies!

CHANG. With your permission I'll take my leave, Sir.

CH'ÊN (*to servant*). See them off the premises. (*Exeunt Changs with servant, who returns*). Ch'ên Chih, whose children are those that Chang brought here, pretending they were his to cadge more grain?

CH'ÊN CHIH. They are all his own offspring, Sir.

CH'ÊN. But he has only reached the age of thirty-five. How can such a young man be the parent of six lusty sons?

CH'ÊN CHIH. They are all the fruits of his ancestors' accumulated merit, Sir.

CH'ÊN. So that's it! Alas! What about my ancestors? Had they no merit at all? (*Sings in hsi-p'i slow time*) At the age of thirty-five this Chang is blessed with six brisk boys; I am over fifty now and utterly unblest. Ah, just for the sake of sons and daughters I'll wander far into the hills and worship at distant temples: just for their sake I'll build great roadways and repair high bridges. Only I fear me that the Great Limit is nigh at hand. Who will come to burn incense at my grave? Open the granary! (*Exit*).

Scene II

TA-KUAN (*enters and speaks*). Poor and lonely amid the clamour of the market place, none ever seeks me out. If I had wealth piled up like mountains, remote relations would flock to visit me. Unfortunately both my parents expired while I was young. I have squandered all I had from my foster-parents, who reared me up till manhood. At fifteen I became a *hsiu-ts'ai* scholar. Alas, I should never have listened to the counsel of evil companions who instigated me to make trouble at home. I insisted on grabbing my share of the property, then swallowed it all in reckless revelry. My reputation is gone, and I am now reduced to beggary. I hear that my uncle has opened his granary and is distributing free grain: I think I'll go and apply for some to keep myself from starving. (*Sets forth on journey; speaks*) From youth my fate has been calamitous. I lost my reputation through listening to evil counsel. At the cross-roads I am the butt of all. It is useless grumbling at others: I have only myself to blame. (*On arrival is admitted by the family retainer*).

CH'ÊN CHIH. Oh, my young Master, is it you? How did you ever come to be all in rags like this?

TA-KUAN. Alas, what is the good of talking? Since I left my uncle's home I have indulged in every sort of vice, and am now reduced to beggary.

CH'ÊN CHIH. What business brings you here?

TA-KUAN. I heard that my uncle was giving alms so came in hope of a dole.

CH'ÊN CHIH. Wait while I go and tell Master.

TA-KUAN. If my uncle looks pleased, I'll go in; but I shan't if he looks annoyed.

CH'ÊN CHIH. Well, let's arrange it this way. If your uncle looks glad I'll motion you to step in; if not, I'll wave you away.

TA-KUAN. I'll be strolling outside here in the meantime.

CH'ÊN CHIH (*to Ch'ên Po-yü*). Somebody has come to call, Sir.

CH'ÊN PO-YÜ. In spite of poverty, to have sons is to have somebody to lean on. Wealth without sons is utter vanity. (*To servant*) What is that you are saying?

CH'ÊN CHIH. The young master has returned, Sir.

CH'ÊN PO-YÜ. Which young master?

CH'ÊN CHIH. Master Ta-kuan, Sir.

CH'ÊN PO-YÜ. Ask him to come in.

Ch'en Chih calls to Ta-kuan, who comes running in.

CH'ÊN CHIH. Where were you running off to?

TA-KUAN. I saw you wave your hand, so I thought my uncle must be angry.

CH'ÊN CHIH. No! I was beckoning, not waving you off.

TA-KUAN. Then my uncle showed signs of joy at the prospect of seeing me? Well, I'll go in. (*To uncle*) Ah! you, Sir, are above: your nephew is below. I bow in salutation.

CH'ÊN PO-YÜ. Never mind formalities. How have you been?

TA-KUAN. Well, Sir; and you?

CH'ÊN PO-YÜ. What condition have your affairs been
in recently ? (*Looks up and sees that Ta-kuan is in rags*).
What ? You, you are Ta-kuan ? (*The latter replies in the
affirmative*). You are Ch'ên Min-shêng ? (*his pet name*).

TA-KUAN. I am indeed, Uncle.

CH'ÊN PO-YÜ. How did you fall into such frightful
squalor ?

TA-KUAN. Since I left home, Uncle, I led a life of
sordid dissipation. (*Ch'ên Chih waves his hand and is
ordered out by his master*).

CH'ÊN PO-YÜ (*to Ta-kuan*). Hurry up and tell me all
the particulars. (*Ta-kuan recounts his prodigal existence.
The servant comes back and makes signs to him to stop talking :
he is ordered out again*). Let me hear the fullest particulars,
I say !

TA-KUAN. I have told you all there is to tell, Sir. If
you wish me to, I'll repeat it. (*Proceeds to do so*).

CH'ÊN PO-YÜ (*in a towering rage*). Aha, so that's it.
And now you're reduced to beggary ! Why don't you
beg for food outside ? Why come here ?

TA-KUAN. I heard that you were distributing free
meal, Sir, so I came to stave off the pangs of hunger.

CH'ÊN PO-YÜ. Oh ! So my son has also come a-
begging. Well, since others may have their share, I
don't see why you should be denied yours. Come closer.
(*Servant motions him to approach and is ordered away again.
Ta-kuan comes nearer and his uncle feels his clothing*). So
you are Ta-kuan, our little Min-shêng ! You low blackguard ! (*The old man's wrath explodes : he flies at him and
gives him a beating*).

TA-KUAN (*sings in hsi-p'i yao-pan*). Please don't be
angry with me, Uncle. Believe me, I speak truth, Sir,
I have squandered all my property in dissipation. Have
mercy on me for the sake of my dead parents !

CH'ÊN PO-YÜ (*sings in hsi-p'i yao-pan*). For mentioning your parents I shall slap your face : it only makes

matters worse. Would you goad an old man like me into a frenzy ? (*Striking him, sings*) It would be best to kill you as a bankrupt heir.

Scene III

MRS. CH'ÊN (*enters, singing in hsi-p'i yao-pan*). In the front hall I hear sounds of pitiful weeping. I hasten to inquire what is the matter. (*Speaks*) Oh, husband, who is that you are beating so unmercifully ?

CH'ÊN PO-YÜ. Whose son do you think I should be beating ? Use your own eyes, good wife.

MRS. CH'ÊN. Ah me, if it isn't Ta-kuan ! Why are you striking a boy who has no parents ?

CH'ÊN. I am quite aware that he is an orphan. Do you mean to say that I, his uncle, should not correct him on that account ?

MRS. CH'ÊN. Not that way, I implore you. I cannot bear to see you beat him. It makes me utterly miserable.

CH'ÊN. Stuff and nonsense ! However many sons you had, I'd beat them all if they were like this one. If you say you feel sorry for the brute, regardless of old age I'll slap your face as well.

MRS. CH'ÊN (*weeping*). Oh, please take pity on my Ta-kuan !

CH'ÊN (*threatening*). If you cry, I'll . . . .

MRS. CH'ÊN. I'll try not to then.

CH'ÊN CHIH (*begins to weep too*). Poor Master Ta-kuan !

CH'ÊN. Stop snivelling. I won't allow it.

CH'ÊN CHIH (*sniffing*). I won't cry, Master.

CH'ÊN. We'll see who has the audacity to blubber now. I remember when our foster-son's parents lay on their death-beds, mortally sick, their last words to me were : " Do not mourn for us, only protect our son Ta-kuan and rear him up to manhood." And with these words they passed away. You, Ta-kuan, were then just seven years old, and I brought you up, sent you to

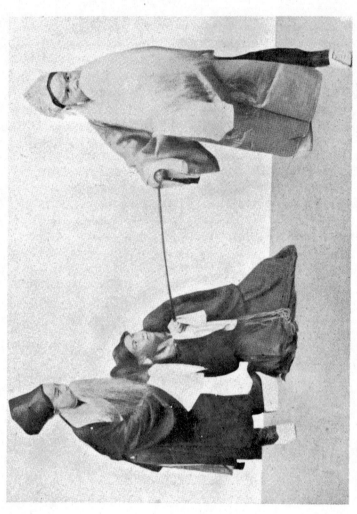

CH'ÊN PO-YÜ ABOUT TO BEAT HIS NEPHEW, THE FAMILY RETAINER INTERVENING

Chuang Yüan P'u

school and had you educated. How have I been remiss in my care for you ? But off you ran and mixed with vicious riff-raff, caused trouble in the home and demanded the division of our family property, making my life a burden beyond belief. I gave you the best and largest share, and instead of pursuing your studies and taking higher degrees, you spent the property in riotous living and are now a starveling. (*To wife*) How old is he ?

MRS. CH'ÊN. Twenty-one this year, my lord.

CH'ÊN. At twenty-one he can no longer be considered a boy. Alas ! I know not which of our ancestors committed some crime against the people in his official career, that our family should be blighted with such a despicable descendant as this Ta-kuan. Here, Ch'ên Chih ! Help me to rouse the slave and drive him out of the house. (*Ta-kuan has fallen senseless after the beating*).

MRS. CH'ÊN (*calling her husband, who is about to leave*). I am afraid Ta-kuan has ceased to live.

CH'ÊN (*returning, rubs his hands over him*). Rubbish ! Don't be idiotic ! I cannot allow such a vile cur to taint my threshold. (*To Ta-kuan*) Uncle and nephew are both as in a dream. Where did you spring from, and who am I ? Come here, Ch'ên Chih ! If this slave really be dead, help me to throw his carcass into the howling wilderness.   (*Exit Ch'ên Po-yü*).

MRS. CH'ÊN (*to servant*). Revive him !

CH'ÊN CHIH. He has come to.

TA-KUAN (*sings in hsi-p'i yao-pan*). As I open my weary eyes I suddenly see my aunt* before me standing. (*Speaks*) Alas, dear aunt !

MRS. CH'ÊN. This is due to your own perversity. Don't blame your uncle for that beating he gave you. You had better make up your mind to reform and acquire

---

*Shên Mu : wife of father's younger brother.

some culture and respectability. Let him have two packages of silver, Ch'ên Chih.

CH'ÊN CHIH. Do you mean two large or two small packages ? *

TA-KUAN. She means large packages, of course.

MRS. CH'ÊN. You had better wait a few days. I'll speak to your uncle and try to make him change his mind, and perhaps he will allow you to remain here.

TA-KUAN. I'll promptly obey your commands. (*Sings in yao-pan*) Now I shall take my leave, Mother.

CH'ÊN CHIH. Not so fast !   Come back !

TA-KUAN (*sings in yao-pan*). Why do you call me back ?

CH'ÊN CHIH. I have a few ounces of silver for you. Please take them to buy pens, ink and paper with.

TA-KUAN. How could I accept money from you !

CH'ÊN CHIH. When you have made a name for yourself you will view me with a favourable eye.

TA-KUAN. Dear brother, I feel too mortified to accept it ! (*Sings in yao-pan*) But O the heavy change ! The master now takes money from his servant. If fortune ever smiles upon my future, the first name that will rise to my lips will be that of my brother Ch'ên Chih.

Ch'ên Po-yü is heard coughing behind the stage.

CH'ÊN CHIH. Look out ! The Master's coming.

Exit Ta-kuan.

CHÊN PO-YÜ (*enters, singing in hsi-p'i yüan-pan*). A cruel fate to have no sons when life is nearly done !
     Tears trickle down my face the livelong day
     As mournfully I wander on my way.

MRS. CH'ÊN (*enters weeping and sings*). My little Min-shêng ! oh, my child, my son !

CH'ÊN PO-YÜ (*sings in hsi-p'i yüan-pan*). I hear my wife sobbing over Ta-kuan. The pity of it ! (*Speaks*) Where has Ta-kuan gone to, my dear ?

---

* Formerly a large package contained fifty ounces of silver, a small one ten ounces.

MRS. CH'ÊN. I only know he is gone—I know not whither.

CH'ÊN. Did you give him anything? (*Mrs. Ch'ên and the servant both deny their generosity. Ch'ên soliloquizes*) If I attain to a great age I may not be able to look after my affairs. Humph! Call him back!

CH'ÊN CHIH. But he has departed.

CH'ÊN. The beggar's rather lucky after all!

MRS. CH'ÊN. His departure was most unlucky in my opinion. Oh husband! To-day is the festival for worshipping at the graves,* and you went and flogged our poor Ta-kuan and drove him far away!

CH'ÊN. Had you not mentioned it, I would have clean forgotten. Here, Ch'ên Chih; prepare the sacrificial offerings and incense. We're going off to worship at the graves. (*Exit servant. To wife*) Please listen. (*Sings in hsi-p'i yüan-pan*) Ta-kuan has reached the age of twenty-one.

MRS. CH'ÊN (*sings in hsi-p'i yüan-pan*). True, he never should have squandered his inheritance like that.

CH'ÊN. We twain have now both passed the age of fifty, with nobody to lean on.

MRS. CH'ÊN. Who will worship at our tombs a century hence? (*Weeps*). Alas, Ta-kuan, my only child, my son! (*Exeunt*).

SCENE IV

TA-KUAN (*enters, singing in hsi-p'i yao-pan*). My broken shack lets in the cold, invites the bitter rain. My boat sails in the teeth of the wind, whithersoever I go. (*Speaks*) Woe is me! Misfortune dogs my steps. My aunt presents me with silver and I am robbed of it while sleeping in the Temple of the God of the Soil. To-day is the Festival of worshipping at the graves. I'll beg a few coppers to buy paper and incense, and repair to my

---

* Ch'ing Ming, early in April.

parents' graves to perform the ceremony due. The times are out of joint. All of my gold I exchanged for brass ; oh, what a fool am I! (*Arrives at graveyard and sings out to the custodian to open*).

CHU TS'ANG (*answering*). Well, well, if it isn't Ch'ên Ta-kuan ! Aye, so it is !

TA-KUAN. What ? A hireling such as you dares to address me thus ?

CHU TS'ANG. When you were in funds I properly called you "Young Master," but now the clothes on your back aren't half as good as mine. So if I call you by your name you should be more polite.

TA-KUAN. Alas ! When a gentleman fails in this world he is insulted by his inferiors.

CHU TS'ANG. What business brings you here ?

TA-KUAN. I have come to worship at the graves of my father and mother.

CHU TS'ANG. Very well then, you may come along with me.

TA-KUAN. Look here : there's a large hole in this mound. Bring me a spade so that I can repair it. (*To Chu Ts'ang, when it is brought*) You go outside and keep watch. If my uncle and his wife appear, let me know instantly. (*He kneels, burns incense, etc., weeps and sings in hsi-p'i yao-pan*) I kneel before your graves and my tears fall down like rain. Forgive your unfilial son! I beseech you to answer my prayers and render me assistance so that I may quickly rise to fame.

While he burns more offerings Chu Ts'ang comes to say that his uncle and aunt are approaching. Exeunt.

SCENE V

Ch'ên Po-yü and his wife appear with their servant and sing in hsi-p'i yüan-pan time throughout the ensuing dialogue.

CH'ÊN. It is now the third of the third moon of Pure Brightness.

MRS. CH'ÊN. Yes, everybody comes to worship at the graves.

CH'ÊN. Others have sons and daughters but we have none.

MRS. CH'ÊN. We have both reached the age of fifty without a single heir.

CH'ÊN. Behold I enter the burial pasture.

MRS. CH'ÊN. I see a goodly number of worshippers about.

CH'ÊN. I hope my ancestors in the glades below will fully answer my prayers.

MRS. CH'ÊN. Protect us in old age, and may we be hale and vigorous throughout the four seasons.

CH'ÊN. After kowtowing I try to stand up but feel that my strength is failing.

MRS. CH'ÊN. I put out a hand to steady my tired old man.

CH'ÊN (*to servant*). Give Chu Ts'ang the offerings . . .

MRS. CH'ÊN. Come, husband, let us take a stroll among the tombs.

CH'ÊN. We do this every year. What is the use of it?

MRS. CH'ÊN. I fear that in future there will only be you; for I shall have passed beyond.

CH'ÊN. It might as well be you! I return your compliment.

MRS. CH'ÊN. Yes, it amounts to the same.

They begin to argue about a tree. One says it is a pine, the other that it is a cypress, etc.

MRS. CH'ÊN. Look! Who has been worshipping at the graves of your brother and sister-in-law?

CH'ÊN. Who else should come here to worship apart from ourselves?

MRS. CHÊN. Look, there are still some ashes smouldering.

CH'ÊN. I'll call Chu Ts'ang and question him about it. (*To Chu Ts'ang*) Who has been worshipping at our family graves?

CHU TS'ANG. During the Spring Festival, Sir, a great many come here to worship: maybe someone was sacrificing at the wrong grave.

CH'ÊN. How could there be such a mistake? Come, let me hear the truth!

CHU TS'ANG. It was Ch'ên Ta-kuan, Sir.

CH'ÊN. What? How dare a menial like you refer to him thus! Tell him to come at once.

Enter Ta-kuan.

CHU TS'ANG. Young Master, your uncle has sent for you.

TA-KUAN. Tell him I have gone away.

CHU TS'ANG (*to Ch'ên Po-yü*) The young master has just told me to say that he has gone.

TA-KUAN. Pish, sirrah! What sort of talk is that?
          Chu Ts'ang pushes him on the ground.

CH'ÊN. What did you push him down for?

CHU TS'ANG. Well, since he tried soldier's tricks on me . . .

CH'ÊN. Be off with you! (*To Ta-kuan*) You miserable slave! I suppose you came here to steal timber from the cemetery.* It might bring in some ready money, eh?

TA-KUAN. Alas, Uncle, to-day being the Festival of Pure Brightness I begged a few coppers and bought some paper money to burn at my parents' graves.

CH'ÊN (*to his wife*). When we are dead, my dear, this wretch will never worship at our graves!

TA-KUAN. When you pass hence I'll worship at your graves just as I will at the graves of my parents. (*Sings in hsi-p'i yao-pan*) But this low thing grieves to utter such dismal words.

---

*A common practice in China.

MRS. CH'ÊN (*sings*). Your speech has filled my heart and soul with sorrow. (*Speaks*) Husband! Although Ta-kuan has sunk so low in life's estate, he still thinks of his parents and worships at their graves. I would like to adopt him as our son. How do you feel about it?

CH'ÊN. That all depends on you, my dear.

MRS. CH'ÊN (*to Ta-kuan*). My husband considers taking you back as our own son. How would you like that?

TA-KUAN. I am all willing. Please let me make my obeisance to you, oh Father and Mother. (*Sings in hsi-p'i yao-pan*) Father and Mother, I now make my bow. Henceforth I'll prove your own devoted son.

CH'ÊN (*to servant*). Fetch him a new cap and robe so that we may take him home looking respectable. (*Exit servant. To Ta-kuan*) I hope you will now reform, my son, and renounce your evil ways.

MRS. CH'ÊN. And never be a profligate again!

TA-KUAN. I am determined never to do anything that shall make men despise me.

CH'ÊN. Henceforth you must endeavour to distinguish yourself as a man above other men.

MRS. CH'ÊN. What are you waiting for, Ta-kuan-êrh? Why don't you come along?

TA-KUAN. I am afraid that Uncle will beat me as soon as he gets me home!

MRS. CH'ÊN (*sings*). Husband! (*Ch'ên has walked a few paces ahead*). Ta-kuan-êrh is afraid to go home with us for fear that you'll flog him.

CH'ÊN (*reassuringly*). Henceforth, my son, although I have a mouth, it will not curse you; my hand will never strike you; and I'll leave my fortune in your custody. Your success in this life entirely depends on you.

TA-KUAN. So be it! If one is inclined to be a wastrel, whether parents correct him or not, it is all to no purpose. It depends on the child himself whether he develops into a man of moral worth.

MR. AND MRS. CH'ÊN. Ta-kuan-êrh, return with your parents to your future home.

Finis

*   *   *

Needless to say Ta-kuan makes good, and wins the highest honours in the triennial examinations.

" When I consider how little of a rarity children are,—that every street and blind alley swarms with them,—that the poorest people commonly have them in most abundance,—that there are few marriages that are not blest with at least one of these bargains,—how often they turn out ill, and defeat the fond hopes of their parents, taking to vicious courses, which end in poverty, disgrace, the gallows, etc.—I cannot for my life tell what cause for pride there can possibly be in having them." Thus wrote Charles Lamb in an essay beloved of bachelors, which serves to illustrate one side of the gulf between the Confucian mentality and ours as this play illustrates the other. The agony of Ch'ên Po-yü and his wife because they are childless, the pathos of their conflict with the nephew they have adopted, who takes to vicious courses (which do not end in tragedy however), are very real to a Chinese audience. Hence the unqualified success of this moral melodrama, wherein the highest ambition of scholarship is realized by a belated burst of filial piety.

Of contemporary actors none excel T'an Fu-ying in the principal rôle of Ch'ên Po-yü.

CH'ÜN YING HUI 羣英會

The Meeting of the League of Heroes

Additionally called, from the successive episodes : *Ts'ao Ch'uan Chieh Chien*: " Grass boats borrowing arrows " ; *Ta Huang Kai*: " The Beating of Huang Kai " ; *Chiang Kan Tao Shu*: " Chiang Kan steals a Dispatch " ; *Chieh Tung Fêng*: " Borrowing an East Wind " ; *K'an Ts'ê Hsien Shu*: " K'an Ts'ê presents a Dispatch " ; *P'ang T'ung Hsien Lien Huan Chi*: " P'ang T'ung proposes the Chain-scheme " (i.e. chaining the ships together. For another chain-scheme see *Fêng I T'ing*, p. 353) ; *Huo Shao Chan Ch'uan*: " The destruction of the battle-fleet by fire-boats " ; and *Ch'ih Pi An Ping*: " Battle of the Red Cliff."

PERIOD : " Three Kingdoms." A *p'i-huang* play.

The drama is founded on some of the most stirring episodes of Chinese history. The Battle of the Red Cliff, where Chou Yü burnt Ts'ao Ts'ao's fleet and where a cliff is said to have been reddened by the flames, was fought in the present province of Hupeh in the year A.D. 208.

Chief Characters

Lu Su, Chou Yü's counsellor	*Lao-shêng*
K'ung-ming, or Chu-ko Liang, Liu Pei's counsellor and strategist...	*Lao-shêng*
Chou Yü, Commander-in-Chief of Wu	*Hsiao-shêng*
Huang Kai, veteran admiral of Wu	*Ching*
Ts'ao Ts'ao, Generalissimo of Wei	*Ching*
Chiang Kan, a secretary on Ts'ao's staff	*Wên-ch'ou*
K'an Ts'ê, an official of Wu	*Wu-shêng*
P'ang T'ung, a scholar protégé of Liu Pei's... ...	*Ching*
Ts'ai Mei, a captain	*Erh-hua-lien*
Chang Yün, a captain	*Erh-hua-lien*
Attendants, Soldiers, Sailors, etc.	

EPISODE I. TS'AO CH'UAN CHIEH CHIEN

"Grass Boats borrowing Arrows"

The beardless but nevertheless gorgeous young warrior Chou Yü appears with his temperamental adviser Lu Su, and they are joined by K'ung-ming, Liu Pei's superhuman strategist and counsellor, the darling hero of the Chinese people. Chou Yü is exceedingly jealous of K'ung-ming and wishes " to find a legitimate way of getting rid of him so that he shall go to his death without resentment." When all are seated Chou asks K'ung-ming whether it would be advisable to attack their common enemy Ts'ao Ts'ao by water or by land. K'ung-ming suggests attack by water, using arrows.* Chou Yü agrees with a proviso that K'ung-ming shall undertake to supply about a hundred thousand arrows, not only because he needs them but because he is convinced that such an undertaking is impossible. " I hope " he adds, " you will on no account decline or procrastinate."

K'UNG-MING. How dare I decline! Pray set a date for their delivery.

CHOU YÜ. Could you have them ready within fifteen days?

K'UNG-MING. Would not that delay matters?

CHOU YÜ. What about ten days?

K'UNG-MING. That would be too late.

CHOU YÜ. In how many days do you reckon that the arrows can be ready?

K'UNG-MING. Three days will suffice.

CHOU YÜ (*incredulous*). There is no joking, Sir, in military matters.

K'UNG-MING. Dare I trifle with the Commander-in-Chief? I shall write out a formal statement and sign it.

---

*These arrows are called *lang-ya-chien*, wolf-teeth, from their shape, and were in use from the earliest times until the introduction of modern arms in about 1850.

(Does so, hands it to Chou Yü and leaves the room.   Chou Yü is convinced that K'ung-ming has signed his own death warrant).

   Later Chou Yü tells Lu Su to visit K'ung-ming and see if he is making any preparations and how, since he suspects him of duplicity.   Lu Su finds him sitting quietly in his room as if he had not a care in the world : the one's suavity is an amusing foil to the other's impatience.

LU SU. What are you doing about those hundred thousand arrows you promised to provide ?

K'UNG-MING *(feigning alarm)*. Gracious, if you had not come along to remind me I would have forgotten all about it !

LU SU. Why, yesterday you gave your word to the Commander-in-Chief that you would have them ready within three days, and now you say you have forgotten all about it !

K'UNG-MING. Well, you'll have to cudgel your brains for a plan that will keep me out of disgrace.

LU SU. Count, count, count the days ! The time is getting short.

K'UNG-MING *(counting on his fingers)*. Yesterday, to-day, to-morrow . . .

LU SU. Hand over the arrows at once. This is no time for fooling.

K'UNG-MING. But you'll have to assist me.

LU SU. Better jump into the river and drown yourself.

K'UNG-MING. Death's no solution.

LU SU. Well then, get into a boat and abscond.

K'UNG-MING. That's no solution either.

LU SU. Well, if neither death nor flight are of any use, what alternative remains ?

K'UNG-MING. I beg you to oblige me with a loan.

LU SU. I have already prepared them for you.

K'UNG-MING. What have you prepared for me ?

LU SU. Your burial clothes and your cap and a capacious coffin.

K'UNG-MING. Don't laugh at me, Sir; I want you to lend me twenty boats, each manned by twenty sailors and provided with a hundred bundles of straw resembling men, also a number of gongs and drums and a table ready-laid with meat and wine.

LU SU. What is the feast for?

K'UNG-MING. For us to enjoy ourselves.

LU SU. I see you are still disposed to merriment.

K'UNG-MING. I only ask you to say nothing about this to Chou Yü, or my scheme will be ruined.

After further argument and persuasion from K'ung-ming, Lu Su consents and takes his leave. He reports to Chou Yü that as far as he can see K'ung-ming had taken no steps to procure the arrows : " He has only one day left. Of course he will have provided for his death as stipulated in his own handwriting. But I would not willingly witness his execution."

At twilight on the third day K'ung-ming sends a message inviting Lu Su to his boat. He finds K'ung-ming on board, sitting at a table ready laid.

LU SU. Why have you sent for me, Sir?

K'UNG-MING. Oh, just to share my repast and a bumper of wine, and then we'll go to fetch the arrows.

LU SU. Where are they?

K'UNG-MING. Please don't bother me with questions : you'll know that all in good time!

At the first watch of night, about 8 p.m., K'ung-ming orders the twenty boats to be taken down the river not far from Ts'ao Ts'ao's camp. As soon as they reach it orders are issued to form line lying prows west, whereupon the drums and gongs are to be struck so that the din shall reverberate for miles around. A thick fog descends; even at a distance of ten feet the boats are invisible. Lu Su jumps up in great alarm and begs K'ung-ming to let him disembark at once, but the latter assures him that this is out of the question ; he would surely be drowned. When Ts'ao Ts'ao hears that a battle-fleet is passing through his territory he orders fifty thousand marines to discharge their arrows at them and another thirty thousand archers and crossbowmen to line up on the river-bank and shoot their arrows in mass. K'ung-ming's little fleet drifts slowly through the fog until the fourth watch. When the starboard sides are gorged with arrows he orders them to turn round and present the port-sides until they bristle correspondingly. A red sun rises in the east ; the fog disperses as suddenly as it arose, while the boats sail down stream back to their stations. All the crews join in praising and thanking K'ung-ming for his wonderful strategy. " Thank Ts'ao Ts'ao for the loan," he retorts. He counts the arrows and finds that there are one hundred and thirty thousand all told—a surplus of thirty thousand over his stipulation.

LU SU. But how did you know that there would be a fog last night ?

K'UNG-MING. A general who is ignorant of astronomy and geography will never rise above mediocrity.

Lu Su reports K'ung-ming's success to Chou Yü, who exclaims in dismay : "With his great strategic skill I fear he is a dangerous rival. I must find a scheme to remove him or the outlook will be black for me."

EPISODE II. TA HUANG KAI

" The Beating of Huang Kai "

Chou Yü is sitting in his tent late at night when Huang Kai pays him a secret visit.

CHOU YÜ. You must have some communication of importance to bring you here at this late hour.

HUANG KAI. As Ts'ao Ts'ao's army is very numerous and powerful we must draw up our plans to defeat him without further delay. For three generations my family has received many favours from the House of Sun ; since I have never repaid them in the slightest degree I am willing to enter the enemy's camp and feign desertion to the other side. (*Here they whisper and work out the plan stated below*).

Next day when K'ung-ming and all his own staff are assembled in his tent, Chou Yü says : " Each of you generals is to prepare supplies for three months " . . . *Huang Kai interrupts him with blustering objections so that Chou Yü flares up in apparent anger and shouts : " Take him out and cut his head off." The other generals fall on their knees entreating his forgiveness, and the punishment is mitigated to " eighty strokes of the bamboo until the flesh breaks through the skin." Seeing that K'ung-ming sits silent and unconcerned at this exhibition of ferocity Lu Su asks why he did not plead for the veteran.*

K'UNG-MING. I am far too well acquainted with that ruse : the one pretends to inflict chastisement and the other is willing to receive it even it it kills him. It is only the old *K'u-jou-chi** ruse. Why should I interfere ?

LU SU. How did you guess it was the *K'u-jou-chi* ruse ?

K'UNG-MING. Because neither Chou Yü nor Huang Kai showed any sign of genuine anger.

Lu Su, doubtful of K'ung-ming's explanation, asks Chou Yü why he had so cruelly beaten a proved and trusty officer.

CHOU YÜ. What did K'ung-ming say ?

LU SU. He said you did it because you hate him.

CHOU YÜ (*laughs gleefully*). Aha, I have fooled him for once !

EPISODE III.　KIANG　KAN　TAO　SHU

" Chiang Kan steals a Dispatch "

Chou Yü is sitting in his tent when a guest is announced. This is the three-inch tongued Chiang Kan, one of the

---

*　**" Mortifying of the flesh ruse " ; which of course Chou Yü and Huang Kai had pre-arranged. The latter was to endure the utmost torture and thereby deceive his colleagues as well as Ts'ao Ts'ao, whose spies would substantiate the external facts, facilitating his feigned desertion.

YEH SHÊNG-LAN IN THE ROLE
OF CHOU YÜ

Ch'ün Ying Hui

Ma Fu-lu as Chiang Kan stealing the Letter

Ch'ün Ying Hui

secretary-staff in Ts'ao Ts'ao's camp, formerly a fellow student and intimate friend of Chou Yü's. Ts'ao Ts'ao had sent him over to persuade Chou Yü to surrender. He is admitted and a feast is prepared in his honour. Chou Yü removes the sword which he wears as Commander-in-Chief and hands it to one of his generals, saying : " This evening we meet only as friends; if any one so much as mentions politics, kill him at once." Chiang Kan is speechless and crestfallen while his host plies him with wine. All pretend to drink copiously ; the liquor is actually spilled. After the feast, Chou Yü takes him to visit his camp, filled with well-disciplined men and abundant provisions ; his purpose being to impress him so that his report will frighten Ts'ao Ts'ao. They return to the tent and fall to drinking again. Chou Yü, pointing to the others at the table, says : " These are all the best and bravest of the land of Wu; we may aptly be called ' The Meeting of Heroes' (hence the usual title of the play). Chou Yü proceeds to give a superb exhibition of swords-manship and invites his guest to spend the night with him, feigning complete intoxication. In the meantime he has told Lu Su to place a forged letter among his documents. As soon as Chiang Kan fancies he is fast asleep he tiptoes out of the tent, secretes the letter and, startled by Chou Yü's voice, creeps back to his couch. Chou Yü pretends to be talking in his sleep. " Within three days I shall have Ts'ao Ts'ao's head," he mutters and falls a-snoring again. At dawn Chiang Kan crawls furtively out ; bumping into Lu Su, who has come to see if the letter is still there, he explains that he has the colic, and makes his escape with Lu Su winking over the happy issue.

On opening the purloined letter Ts'ao Ts'ao is infuriated to find that two of his best admirals, Ts'ai Mao and Chang Yün, intend to assassinate him and join his enemies. He promptly summons them and asks if their fleet is ready and the men fully equipped for instant action. They reply in the negative. Ts'ao Ts'ao, striking the table with terrific force, bellows : " The men will be ready enough when you have dis-patched my head to Chou Yü, won't they? " The flabbergasted *admirals are sentenced to immediate execution. When he is in a calmer frame of mind he re-reads the letter and it suddenly dawns on him that he has been duped. He orders the admirals to be released. Too late! Their severed heads are submitted to his penitent inspection. Chiang Kan observes with some complacency that he deserves great credit for purloining the letter. All the reward he gets from Ts'ao Ts'ao is a face-full of spittle. Ts'ao appoints Mao Chieh and Yü Chin to the command of his naval camp in lieu of the decapitated admirals.*

EPISODE IV.   CHIEH TUNG FÊNG

" Borrowing an East Wind "

Chou Yü decides to destroy Ts'ao Ts'ao's fleet by fire. Wishing to consult K'ung-ming's opinion, he asks him to write it on the palm of his hand. Chou Yü does likewise. Then drawing close together each holds up his hand, palms out, and bursts out laughing, for each has written the character 火 *Huo, or Fire.*

It is now mid-winter, and while Chou Yü is watching for an east wind—indispensable if he is to attack Ts'ao Ts'ao's fleet without being destroyed himself—he is disgusted to see that the flags on his boats are fluttering towards the south. He has a stroke; staggers and falls unconscious with blood on his lips. He is borne to his tent, where he mutters on his couch incessantly. None of the physicians called for can diagnose his ailment. For two days he remains prostrate, refusing all nourishment. Lu Su suggests that K'ung-ming might be able to find a remedy. K'ung-ming is summoned, feels his pulse and asks how he happened to get into such a condition. Chou Yü remarks : " Joy and calamity may both occur on the selfsame day." "Yes," says K'ung-ming, " even Heaven cannot fathom the elements." Chou Yü groans and blanches at the thought that K'ung-ming can penetrate the innermost recesses of his mind, and that it is useless to try to conceal anything from him. He asks K'ung-ming if he has anything to prescribe. K'ung-ming dismisses the servants and

*writes four lines of verse as the prescription, to the effect that
" fire should be used to destroy Ts'ao's fleet ; after all is
prepared there is nothing further to do but wait for an
east wind."*

CHOU YÜ. But Ts'ao's army is massed in the north-
west, and mine in the south-east. If I attack him with
fire-boats and a northerly wind prevails, the fire will
only sweep back and destroy mine instead. Now that
it is mid-winter how can we possibly procure an east
wind? Anxiety on this account brought on my disease.
If you, Sir, have any treatment to recommend, pray
do so.

K'UNG-MING. Ease your mind, General. I'll have a
south-east wind ready for you within three days.

CHOU YÜ. How do you propose to do this ?

*K'ung-ming proposes to build an altar nine feet high, in three
tiers, on Nan P'ing Mountain : here he will work a spell to
procure a strong south-east gale for three days and three nights.
K'ung-ming successfully conjures the propitious wind and Ts'ao
Ts'ao's fleet is destroyed. Chou Yü is not grateful in the least :
he is now more determined than ever to remove the dangerous rival
whose help he had invoked. Even while the wind is blowing two
of Chou Yü's captains are hot on K'ung-ming's heels, having
received strict injunctions to seize and behead him. But K'ung-
ming is already in the stern of his boat on his way to Hsia K'ou,
where Liu Pei is awaiting him. When ordered to stop he shouts
back : " I had already foreseen this project of Chou Yü's and
told Chao Yün to have a boat ready for me. Go back to the
General and tell him that my fate is in the hands of Heaven,
not in his. Exhort him to go and kill Ts'ao Ts'ao instead."*

Finis

*   *   *

This is one of the best examples of a Chinese military play,
composed entirely of men : as on Mount Athos, not a woman is
to be seen. As may be inferred from the other military plays

included in this volume, the dialogue merely serves the action, which is highly elaborate in *Ch'ün Ying Hui* ; hence we have deemed a *résumé* sufficient.   The order of the incidents vary, with frequent modifications : the conglomerate mass will be found in Chapters XLV, XLVI, XLVII, pp. 476 onwards, in *The Three Kingdoms* Vol. I.   The *San Kuo* has been called a heroic period, an odd misnomer when we consider it as a whole, for treachery surpasses heroism throughout; subterfuge and deception prevail over valour. If we compare the protagonists of the San Kuo with those of, say, the *Morte D'Arthur*, we must fish for some other adjective. Machiavellian heroism ?   Nay, even the author of *del Principe* must look askance at his laurels after so rich a record of man's duplicity.

FA MÊN SSŬ 法門寺

BUDDHA'S TEMPLE

Consists of four episodes which are often performed separately :
I. *Shih Yü Cho*, " Picking up the Jade Bangle" ; II. *Fa Mên Ssŭ;*
III. *Ta Shên*, " The Great Trial " ; IV. *Shuang Chiao Ch'i Yüan*,
" The Wonderful Destiny of the Two Chiaos "—alluding to the
character *chiao* 姣 meaning " pretty," which occurs in the names
of Sung Ch'iao-chiao and Sun Yü-chiao. A *p'i-huang* play.

PERIOD : Ming

DRAMATIS PERSONÆ

EMPRESS DOWAGER	... ...	... *Lao-tan*
LIU CHIN, chief eunuch	... ...	... *Chia-tzŭ-hua-lien*
CHIA KUEI-ÊRH, sub-eunuch	... ...	... *Ch'ou*
SUNG CH'IAO-CHIAO, a good girl	... ...	... *Ch'ing-i*
SUN YÜ-CHIAO, a flirt	... ...	... *Hua-tan*
FU P'ÊNG, a young noble	... ...	... *Hsiao-shêng*
LIU MEI P'O, a go-between	... ...	... *Ch'ou-p'o*
LIU PIAO, her half-witted son	... ...	... *Erh-hua-lien*
LIU KUNG-TAO, the village beadle	...	... *Ch'ou*
SUNG KUO-SHIH, a villager	... ...	... *Mo*
HSING-ÊRH, his son	... ...	... *Hsiao-ch'ou*
CHAO LIEN, a magistrate ...	... ...	... *Lao-shêng*

The plot unfolds during the reign of the Ming Emperor Chêng
Tê, A.D. 1506-1521.

EPISODE I

SHIH YÜ CHO : " PICKING UP THE JADE BANGLE "

Fu P'êng, a young noble of hereditary rank and the
holder of a petty military office, happens to pass through
the Sun Family Village in the Mei Wu district of Shensi.
There he catches a glimpse of Yü-chiao, the Widow Sun's
attractive daughter, as she sits a-sunning and sewing by
her cottage door. Her fingers twirl a tiny embroidered
shoe, her eyes glitter with invitation. Fu P'êng is
tempted to approach her ; after a brief flirtation, he
slips a jade bangle off his wrist, which falls to the ground,

then wanders on his way. Yü-chiao picks it up and
tries it on, thrilled to see how it enhances the smooth
beauty of her arm. But an inquisitive beldam, old Liu
Mei P'o the go-between, has been prying.

"What was that you just picked up?" she asks.

"Nothing," the maiden falters.

Mrs. Liu grasps her arm and scrutinizes it.* "There's
nothing like this in your household. You needn't try
to hoodwink me : I know what you two turtle-doves
are up to ! What's more I can arrange this little affair
for you—just leave it to me."

The girl, all eagerness, entrusts the beldam with
her shoe, to be handed over to Fu P'êng as a love-token.

But Mrs. Liu is garrulous ; chuckling away she goes
and blabs to her half-wit son Liu Piao, the village butcher,
about this promising intrigue. Liu Piao makes off with
the shoe to blackmail the gallant. A struggle ensues ;
Liu Kung-tao, the village beadle, intervenes and accuses
Liu Piao of being the aggressor. In a violent rage, the
latter swears vengeance on both of them.

Unless the play is performed in its entirety this scene
is often omitted, since the action and dialogue are not
deemed conducive to good morals. "Rather too suggestive, my dear," as the euphemism goes, so suggestive,
in fact, that on one occasion many a female member
of the audience left visible traces of emotion behind her.

The action develops off the stage. A few nights
later Liu Piao steals by the Widow Sun's door with
the badge of his profession, a murderous knife. Hearing
voices, he imagines that Fu P'êng and Yü-chiao are
enjoying a *tête-à-tête*. The door is ajar. He pushes
it open and gropes his way through the darkness until
he finds the couple, then strikes out, stabbing them both
to death. Needless to say his victims are neither Fu

---

* In some versions Yü-chiao conceals the bangle, and Mrs Liu only unearths
it after a deal of by-play.

P'êng nor Yü-chiao. The woman's head he cuts off and throws over the wall into Liu Kung-tao's yard, hoping to implicate the beadle in the murder. Liu hears a thud and, discovering a human head, loses his nerve and decides to throw it down his well. A lad in his service called Hsing-êrh steps out and catches sight of him. The boy cries out in dismay ; the beadle, equally alarmed lest Hsing-êrh turn witness against him, tells him to look down the well, and while he is doing so gives him a fatal push. He then informs Hsing-êrh's father, Sung Kuo-shih, that the boy had run away with some of his belongings. The matter is reported to the magistrate Chao Lien, who promptly orders Sung to pay a fine of ten ounces of silver, without investigating the case. Sung cannot afford to pay, so his virtuous daughter Ch'iao-chiao surrenders herself to be imprisoned in his stead.

Fu P'êng and Yü-chiao, suspected as accomplices in the crime, are incarcerated in the same prison ; Yü-chiao finds herself sharing a cell with Ch'iao-chiao. They open their hearts to each other and confide all their woes : Yü-chiao persuades Fu P'êng to pay the fine and procure Ch'iao-chiao's release. Ch'iao-chiao invites the old go-between to dinner, and plies her with liquor till Mrs. Liu discloses that it was her own son who committed the murder, under the delusion that Fu P'êng and Yü-chiao were his victims : actually the victims were a couple called Chu. Satisfied that she has obtained a full account, Ch'iao-chiao tells her father, Sung Kuo-shih, who writes out a detailed plaint accordingly, adding (untruly) that his daughter was affianced to Fu P'êng.

EPISODE II

FA MÊN SSU : " BUDDHA'S TEMPLE "

Hearing that the Empress Dowager, accompanied by her favourite eunuch Liu Chin, is to worship at Fa Mên

SUNG CH'IAO-CHIAO (*kneeling, sings*). I kneel in Great Buddha's Palace and beg the Empress to give me hearing while I relate my family affairs. I have always dwelt in Mei Wu district.

Ssǔ, Ch'iao-chiao resolves to go and offer the plaint herself. The eunuch considers this gross *lèse-majesté* and is about to have the girl executed, but the Empress Dowager instructs him to admit her, observing that to consider her plaint was more salutary than merely to burn incense. After listening to it the Empress withdraws, and Liu Chin orders Chao Lien the magistrate, Ch'iao-chiao and Mrs. Liu to appear before him for investigation. He shows the plaint to the magistrate, and warns him to have the case cleared up within three days or his head will be the forfeit. All the suspects are rounded up and the magistrate proceeds to the Sun Family Village for the autopsy. Young Hsing-êrh's corpse is fished out of the well (whence the name *Chu Sha Ching*, " The Bloodstained Well," is often given to this section). His father breaks out into lamentations and roundly rates the grasping and inefficient magistrate. Liu Piao is beaten and tortured till he confesses ; Liu Kung-tao follows suit, and all are removed to Peking for further hearing before the eunuch.

EPISODES III AND IV

TA SHÊN : " THE GREAT TRIAL "

The great trial opens—the *pièce de résistance* of the entire drama. Liu Chin, the chief eunuch, sits in judgment with the magistrate Chao Lien as assessor. Liu Chin is practically ruled by Chia Kuei-êrh, his junior eunuch-factotum, who influences him in all his decisions. Since the magistrate has paid him a substantial bribe, Kuei-êrh sees that he is not only absolved from blame but also promoted to the post of prefect.

Fu P'êng is likewise promoted. Liu Piao is sentenced to execution ; Mrs. Liu exiled ; and the beadle strangled. The Empress issues an edict that the two girls Ch'iao-chiao and Yü-chiao are to marry Fu P'êng, and that both wives are to be granted equal status. As the play ends one is left wondering about the consequences of this authorized bigamy : was not the benevolent Empress too optimistic ?

Much of the action, i.e., Liu Piao's murder, the pushing of Hsing-êrh into the well, and Yü-chiao's imprisonment, takes place off the stage (what the Chinese term *an ch'ang*, or concealed). We include these necessary if trivial details in our summary for the benefit of Western theatre-goers not familiar with the plot.

* * *

To witness Hsiao Ts'ui-hua in the rôle of Yü-chiao in the first part, " Picking up the Jade Bangle," is a revelation of how super-realistic a personality may be under the most conventional mask. No other actor we have seen in the play compares with Hsiao's performance, despite his pronounced aquiline nose and harsh voice. His nimble fingers as he sews, pricking them in the process ; his combination of coyness and effrontery in flirting with the gallant ; his attempt to conceal the bangle from the inquisitive eyes of the old go-between, are Chinese comedy at its apogee. Ma Fu-lu excels as Liu Mei P'o. In the latter part it is the eunuch's factotum whose wit and antics keep the audience rocking, while he squeezes the magistrate for all he is worth. Liu Chin, the chief eunuch, is like some gorgeous bird of prey ; the rôle can be most impressive and not a little sinister. Here we have the quintessence of all those powerful eunuchs who, culminating with Li Lien-ying, distilled their subtle poison through the ruling dynasties of China.

T'an Fu-ying as Hsüeh Jên-kuei, and his son T'an Pai-sui as Ting-shan

Fên Ho Wan

FEN HO WAN 汾河灣

AT THE BEND OF FÊN RIVER

Also entitled : *Hsüeh Li Huan Chia,* "Hsüeh Li's Return Home."
PERIOD : T'ang.   A *hsi-p'i* play.

DRAMATIS PERSONÆ

HSÜEH JÊN-KUEI, soldier of fortune ...   *Lao-shêng*
LIU YING-CH'UN, his wife   ...   ...   *Chêng-tan,* or *Ch'ing-shan*
TING-SHAN, their only son   ...   ...   *Hsiao-shêng*

Hsüeh Li, or Hsüeh Jên-kuei, a historical figure of the T'ang
dynasty, was a native of the Lung-mên (Dragon Gate) district of
Shansi and began life as a poor tiller of the soil.   He first attracted
attention by various bold exploits against rebels and was soon
summoned to Court and given a military commission.   Later he
accompanied the T'ang Emperor Chêng Kuan (A.D. 627-649) on
his expeditions to Korea and was ennobled as Prince Pacificator
of Liaotung.   He subsequently fought against the Turfans, was
severely defeated and condemned to death, but the sentence was
commuted : he was only cashiered.   Later he was given a chance
to retrieve his reputation and won a decisive victory over the Turkic
tribes.

SCENE I.   TA YEN : "KILLING THE GEESE"

LIU YING-CH'UN (*to Ting-shan*). Your father is away soldiering, and I have never received a letter from him.

Hsüeh has been separated from his wife for eighteen years without writing her a single letter, and she has been true to him throughout this long period in spite of her extreme poverty. Riding homewards on his charger he sees a lad shooting geese and spearing fish.

HSÜEH (*greeting the lad asks*). How many geese could you bring down with one arrow?

BOY. With one arrow I can bring down one goose.

HSÜEH. Why, that's nothing extraordinary! I can bring down two with a single shot.

The boy is incredulous but says he would be delighted to learn how to do it.

HSÜEH. Give me your bow and arrow and you shall see.

BOY. Here come the geese!

HSÜEH. Thanks. (*Aside, singing*) Ah, he falls into the snare. His life is sped as swiftly as this arrow.

He shoots; the boy falls, and is borne off by a tiger.

HSÜEH. I might have spared the lad, but it would never do for a soldier like me to let another live when he was so superior a marksman with the weapons I excel in.

SCENE II. CHIN YAO: "ENTERING THE HUT"

Liu Ying-ch'un is sitting by the door of a ruined kiln, anxiously awaiting her son's return. Hsüeh Li arrives and dismounts.

HSÜEH. Madam, permit me to offer you my salutations.

LIU. Thank you! Excuse me from returning your courtesy. You are a soldier I presume, and have lost your way?

HSÜEH. No, I am a messenger, and I bear a letter to a certain person,—perhaps you know of her?

LIU. If it's any person of note I shall probably know of her.

HSÜEH. Well, I should say that this person *is* rather noted.

LIU. Who is it, then?

HSÜEH. Liu Yüan Wai's daughter and Hsüeh Jên-kuei's wife : her name is Liu Ying-ch'un.

LIU. Are you related to her?

HSÜEH. No, I'm no relation.

LIU. Perhaps you're old friends then?

HSÜEH. No, we're not even acquainted.

LIU. If you're neither a friend nor a relation, what's your business with her?

HSÜEH. Her husband and I were fellow-soldiers and fought under the same banner. I am now on my way home, and since the road goes past this village he charged me to deliver a letter for him.

LIU. What! do you mean to say you have a letter and wish to see her?

HSÜEH. Exactly.

LIU. Pray wait a moment, Sir.

HSÜEH. As you please, Madam.

LIU (*aside*). This is strange. My husband has been gone these eighteen years, and in all that time I have never received any news of him. To-day this man brings a letter : I must get hold of it. But my clothes are all in tatters. I fear he will mock my shabbiness. . . (*To Hsüeh*) Sir, Mrs. Liu is out. Leave the letter with me. I'll see that it reaches her safely.

HSÜEH. You are mistaken, Madam. The old saw has it, " The letter sent a thousand miles is in danger of never reaching its destination, but to deliver one into the wrong hands after travelling ten thousand miles is a sheer waste of time." I have the letter and must positively see the person it's addressed to.

LIU. And if you don't see her ?

HSÜEH. I shall have to take it back, that's all. (*He starts to lead his horse away*).

LIU. Stop, Sir, stop.

HSÜEH (*pausing*). Do you think she's at home ?

LIU (*aside*). What am I to do ? If I tell him the truth I fear he will despise me ; if I don't, he will take the letter back and then I may have to wait for my husband another eighteen years. Ah, Hsüeh-lang ! When you left me I had no respectable clothing, and shall I fear ridicule now ? I'll speak to him. . . (*To Hsüeh*) Sir, do you still insist on seeing Mrs. Liu in person ?

HSÜEH. To be sure I do.

LIU. Look yonder, then.

HSÜEH. I see nobody.

LIU. Look nearer.

HSÜEH. Then you must be the lady ?

LIU. Yes, Sir, I'm Jên-kuei's wife.

HSÜEH. Indeed ! Just now I failed to recognize you. Permit me to make my bow.

LIU. You have already done so.

HSÜEH. It's not unusual for a person to be polite, is it ?

LIU. Never mind politeness : give me the letter.

HSÜEH. Give you what ?

LIU. Give me my letter.

HSÜEH. Wait a moment, Madam, while I fetch it from the saddle. (*Aside*) Who could have imagined that I should return this very day and meet my wife face to face ? I must go a little nearer, then she'll recognize me. But stay ! Now I come to think of it I have been abroad for eighteen years, and I can't be certain whether she has remained faithful or not. As there's no one about, I'll embark on a little flirtation. (*To Liu*) Alack, alack!

LIU. What ails you?

HSÜEH. I have lost the letter.

LIU. You can't have lost it. What right have you to lose my husband's letter?

HSÜEH. Although I have lost it, Madam, I have another important matter for your ears.

LIU. What is it?

HSÜEH. There is an old and popular saying: "Announce joy but never sorrow."

LIU. What do you mean by that?

HSÜEH. Jên-kuei, my old comrade, caught cold and never recovered.

LIU. What do you say? Dead? Oh, Hsüeh-lang, my beloved! For eighteen years you've been away and never sent me word. And now that I have news, it is only that you are dead!

HSÜEH (*laughing*). You needn't cry. There's a proverb that "If the dead are dressed in red, there are others dressed in green." * I lent Hsüeh fifty taels; when he lay dying he called me to his side and said: "Elder brother! In this world I shall never be able to repay those fifty taels you lent me, but I have a wife at home called Liu. Take her in payment of the debt: she is yours." Now you're my wife, so come along with you. Off to my house!

LIU. What! Can this be true?

HSÜEH. I would never tell a lie.

LIU. Rebel! Robber! Knave!

HSÜEH. Aha, so you abuse me?

LIU (*sings*). Bold wretch, you had better look out

---

* i.e., There are as good fish in the sea as ever came out of it.

for yourself. Your tale is nothing but a pack of lies. The neighbours will soon come if I call them, and you won't find it easy to escape. Away with you, villain, impostor! Begone!

HSÜEH. Come, let us indoors. Dear wife, do hold your tongue. At last I'm home, dear, never more to roam.

LIU. I'm not your wife. I'm not Liu Ying-ch'un. She is in the cottage over there.

HSÜEH. What? Over there, is she?

LIU. Yes, yes, don't loiter here. Go in and look for yourself. (*He goes in and she bolts the door on him*).

HSÜEH. Why have you locked the door?

LIU. You came to capture a woman and she has captured you. Our positions are reversed.

HSÜEH. Open the door! I tell you I am your true husband back from the wars.

LIU. You talk a lot of nonsense. (*Sings*) You said you were a soldier bringing me a letter. Now you say you are my husband. That you'll have to prove before I open the door. Tell me something of our past. Where did we meet? When did you see me last? What did we say at parting? I must know every detail.

Hsüeh sings of their past life.

LIU (*aside*). While he has been talking I have been counting. Yes, he's my long-lost husband right enough. I'll open the door. (*Opens*). But my husband was quite a lad and you look like a brigand, with all that hair round your mouth.

HSÜEH. That's nice! When husband and wife meet after eighteen years, this beard must come between us and cause trouble.

LIU. What has been your occupation all this time?

HSÜEH (*aside*). How now! The very first question she asks me is about my occupation. Not a word about all the hardships I have suffered!... *. Wife, I am now a nobleman.

LIU. A noble! I can't believe it. What proof have you?

HSÜEH. I've my seal.

LIU. A seal? Let me see it.

HSÜEH (*producing seal*). There! What do you say to that?

LIU. Where did you get that old copper from?

HSÜEH. Copper indeed! It's solid gold. And it's the seal of a duke, my dear.

LIU. Then it must be valuable. But here we have been chattering away and you have not yet had a bite of food. Come in and sit down while I get something ready for you and make the place a bit more comfortable. (*She leaves the room*).

HSÜEH. These women are always worrying about household matters. Hello! What's this? (*Catches sight of a man's shoes under the bed*). This is odd: I did not leave my shoes here eighteen years ago. Besides, these have been worn just recently and they are far too small for me. (*Tries them on*) Curse my luck! She must have a lover! I'll look into this.

Re-enter Liu. Hsüeh seizes her and is about to kill her.

LIU. Mercy on me! What have I done that you should want to murder me?

HSÜEH. These shoes, where do they come from?

LIU. These shoes... these shoes...

HSÜEH. Aha! So you hesitate? Perhaps you are acquainted with their owner?

LIU. Oh, yes indeed, I know him well.

HSÜEH. Base and cruel woman! She does not even deny it. He is often here I suppose?

LIU. Yes, I am quite miserable when he is away. I've been wretched all day waiting for him.

---

* A deal of uninteresting verbiage follows which we omit.

HSUEH. You seem mighty anxious about him. I shouldn't be surprised if you told me that you slept with him.

LIU. Yes, many a night, with his head pillowed on my bosom.

HSÜEH (*walking about in a rage*). She'll drive me stark staring mad.

LIU (*aside*). Look how angry he is! I'll tantalize him till he's frantic. (*To Hsüeh*) During the eighteen years you spent abroad he has never been far from my side.

HSÜEH. I am dying of fury, blast her!

LIU. Do you really want to know who those shoes belong to? At the time you left I was with child, and you often said that if I had a boy he was to be called Ting-shan, if a girl, Chin-lien [Golden Lily]. These are Ting-shan's shoes.

HSÜEH. My son's? Where is he?

LIU. He went to the river to shoot wild geese.

HSÜEH. To the river to shoot. . . (*Aside*) Almighty God! Tell me, what clothes did he wear?

LIU. Why, how ghastly you're looking! He wore a blue gaberdine, a. . .

HSÜEH. Woe is me! He's utterly destroyed!

Hsüeh falls senseless. Liu revives him, but when he tells her of the tragedy she swoons. Hsüeh brings her to and both set out in search of their son's body.

Finis

* * *

In some performances Wang Ch'an, an old Taoist priest, appears, and introducing himself as Ting-shan's master, orders a tiger to rescue his pupil, whose life is in danger. In the sequel, entitled *Lu Hua Ho*, or *Nü Chan Tzŭ*, Liu Ying-ch'un threatens to kill her son for marrying without her permission. He is saved by the tiger.

The Penelope motive, as Dr. Lin Yutang has pointed out, is extremely popular with the Chinese. The same motive is exploited in many dramas, of which *Fên Ho Wan* and *Wu Chia P'o* (well known to English readers in Mr. S. I. Hsiung's translation as *Lady Precious Stream*) are by far the most famous. The names of the two chief male characters of these plays are almost identical (Hsüeh Jên-kuei and Hsüeh P'ing-kuei); both return to their respective spouess after an absence of eighteen years and set them fidelity tests. Both wives are fabulous models of conjugal devotion. Foreigners who have no penchant for high falsetto will not relish this play, but the dialogue is vivacious and amusing, and illustrates the fact that there is no intermediate between comedy and tragedy on the Chinese stage : comedy may turn to tragedy at any moment.

HU TIEH MÊNG 蝴蝶夢

The Butterfly's Dream

This play is also entitled *Chuang Tzŭ Shan Fên*, "Chuang Tzŭ Fanning the Grave," and *Ta P'i Kuan*, "Breaking Open the Coffin." As a satire on woman's inconsistency in general and on marriage in particular it might well be entitled "The Philosopher and his Wife." The story may be found among the six selected from the Late Ming collection called *Chin Ku Ch'i Kuan* and translated by E. B. Howell as "The Inconstancy of Madam Chuang" (Kelly and Walsh, Ltd.).

Period of the Warring States, 481-221 b.c. There are *k'un-ch'ü*, *pang-tzŭ* and *p'i-huang* versions.

Dramatis Personæ

Chuang Tzŭ	*Lao Tao*
A Merry Widow ... ... ⎫	
T'ien Shih, the philosopher's wife ... ... ⎬	*Hua-tan*
Wang Sun Kung Tzŭ, the philosopher's *alter ego* ...	*Hsiao-shêng*
Ts'ang T'ou, his servant	*Lao-shêng*

Rich are the anecdotes relating to Chuang Chou, more commonly known as Chuang Tzŭ (circa 330 b.c., see Giles' *Biographical Dictionary* No. 509); the richest and most familiar of these has been dramatized in this immortal play. The great philosopher has been handed down to posterity, perhaps by Confucian adversaries who wished to belittle him, in the ludicrous if pathetic character of a hen-pecked husband. Three wives were attributed to him, the third a veritable virago. He is said to have given vent to his joy at the latter's demise by beating an empty rice-bowl with his chopsticks. *Si non è vero è ben trovato :* the tradition that he was tied to a shrew would help to explain his cynical view of life and human nature.

In the play Chuang Tzŭ, having married "one to whom Heaven gave beauty, when it grafted roses on a briar," retires to lead the life of a philosopher in his

T'IEN SHIH, HER HUSBAND'S ALTER EGO AND HIS SERVANT

Hu Tieh Mêng

native province, now Shantung. One day while he is
wandering through the tomb-dotted countryside, he
comes upon a young woman breathlessly fanning a grave.
He asks her the reason for this strange exercise. She
replies, still busily fanning, that her husband had only
just expired ; with his last words he had begged her to
wait till the earth on his tomb was dry, if she wished to
marry again. Chuang Tzŭ offers to assist her, she seems
in such frantic haste. He waves her fan, mutters a
magic formula, and lo ! the mound is dry. The widow
thanks him profusely and trips away.

Chuang Tzu goes home in pensive mood and relates
this incident to his wife. " That woman's a monster," she
says, " a disgrace to humanity and the shame of her sex."
To soothe her, Chuang Tzŭ replies :

> " What is it to either of us,
> If she chooses to marry again ?
> Don't let this talk trouble you thus,
> Or cause you one moment of pain.
> What may happen there's no one can tell,
>> But I should quite satisfied be,
> Were *you* to do equally well—
>> If anything happened to me."

Vehemently his wife protests :

> " Oh fie, Sir ! I'd have you to know
>> That my family bears a good name :
> Do you think I could topple so low
>> As to slur it with falsehood and shame ?
> Should you, alas, from me be torn
>> Could I ever dissever my love ?
> Till death I'd your memory mourn,
>> If I lie—there's a Heaven above ! "

A few days later Chuang Tzŭ feigns serious illness.
He groans that his end is nigh and, to all appearances,
gives up the ghost.

While the widow is mourning, a young scholar arrives with the ostensible purpose of placing himself under the philosopher's instruction. Peeping between her tears she observes that he is handsome; her face lights up and she launches on a flirtation within half an hour. He is prevailed upon to stay in the house: meanwhile she asks his old servant if the young man is married. On hearing that he is still a bachelor, she urges the servant to propose a match between them. The youth demurs: *What would the neighbours say?* But all his scruples are swept away by the widow's gusty passion. She throws discretion and her widow's weeds to the winds and prepares for the wedding.

On the bridal eve the groom is suddenly seized with violent spasms. He gasps that the sole remedy for his complaint is the brain of a live man, or, if this be unobtainable, the brain of a man who has not been dead for more than three days. How providential that the remedy should be so close at hand! The woman fetches a kitchen chopper and, after some hesitation at sight of the coffin, tucks up her sleeves and summoning all her strength, begins to hack it open. Chuang Tzŭ wakes up with a start and pushing the lid aside, asks why she is so gaily clad.

" I wore this dress," she falters, " thinking you might be still alive."

" But why is there wine on your breath, wife ? "

" I drank a little in case you were dead after all, just as a precaution, to disinfect the air . . . "

Chuang Tzŭ retorts :

   " Your tale seems very plausible
   But I think you'd better stop.
   Don't tire yourself with telling lies,
   Pray let the matter drop.
   I merely died a bogus death
   To test your heart and head.

The youth you've newly wedded saith :
My widow I have wed ! "

Overwhelmed with mortification, she hangs herself
in an adjoining chamber, and Chuang Tzŭ bursts out
laughing.

*   *   *

There are several dramatizations of this tale ; the *k'un-ch'ü*
version has perhaps the liveliest tempo, for a terrible ghoul leaps
out of the coffin and chases the widow round and round the room.
Han Shih-ch'ang's interpretation of the widow is both subtle and
realistic, and he is well set off against Wei Ch'ing-lin as the caustic
philosopher.

As Dr. Lin Yutang has pointed out, this satire resembles
Petronius Arbiter's tale of another " chaste " widow—the one who
nailed her husband's corpse to the cross in lieu of the criminal's,
which had been snatched away while she was dallying with the
guard.

In China there has always been a prejudice against widows
remarrying. They were not forbidden by law to remarry, but
few dared defy the tyranny of social convention. Such a prejudice
dies hard. A widow's marriage usually takes place in the early
morning when few people are about. The bridal drums are lightly
tapped with one chopstick. Little noise is made and less ceremony.
A woman who remarries never mounts the sedan-chair inside the
premises but on the street. She descends and embraces the first
tree in view before entering her new home, to indicate a wish that
the tree will perish before her husband. There is a popular saying
that no grass will grow for three years wherever a widow's foot
has trod the ground.

HUANG HO LOU 黃 鶴 樓

THE YELLOW CRANE TOWER

PERIOD : Beginning of San Kuo, circa A.D. 210. A *hsi-p'i êrh-huang* play.

DRAMATIS PERSONÆ

LIU PEI, Emperor of Shu (present Szech'uan)...	*Shêng*
K'UNG-MING, his Prime Minister and Strategist (also known as Chu-ko Liang)	*Lao-shêng*
CHAO TZŬ-LUNG, OR CHAO YUN	*Wu-shêng*
CHANG FEI	*Chin-tzŭ-hua-lien*
WEI YEN ... ... ⎬ Generals	*Hua-lien*
HUANG CHUNG	*Mu*
KUAN P'ING	*Wu-shêng*
CHOU TS'ANG, Kuan Yü's horseman and armour-bearer	*Hua-lien*
CHOU YÜ, Admiral and Generalissimo of Sun Ch'üan, Emperor of Wu (present Kiangsu and Chêkiang)	*Hsiao-shêng*
LU SU, Counsellor	*Lao-shêng*
KAN NING, General	*Shêng*
SOLDIERS, ATTENDANTS, BOATMEN, ETC.	

ACT I. SCENE I

Interior of tent : raised seat in centre, table with writing materials, etc. Liu enters from back, preceded by eunuchs : these range themselves on either side of the table, Liu Pei stands in front of it.

LIU PEI. Thanks to the strategy of Chu-ko Liang and the valour of my troops, I have conquered my enemies and obtained the territory I coveted. However, I cannot consider my conquest firmly established until I come to a settlement with Sun Ch'üan regarding the actual possession of Ching-chou. He is constantly plaguing me about it, sending messengers demanding that I hand it over at once. Why should I concede to

his arrogant demands ?   If High Heaven is on my side, the Han dynasty will bloom again in all its former glory.
Enter a soldier with letter.

SOLDIER. A letter for Your Majesty.

LIU. Hand it to me. (*Reads on the cover*) " To Liu Pei, worthy son-in-law : to be opened by his own hand."   Aha ! A letter from the Dowager-Empress of Tung-wu. (*Opens letter and reads*) " Since you left us, my worthy son-in-law, I constantly think of you and my darling daughter. My tears never stop flowing, and I feel much depressed. Please come to me at once. I am sure that only your noble presence can console me. Besides, I have some important state affairs to discuss with you. I have prepared a banquet for you at the Yellow Crane Tower. As soon as you receive this letter, cross the river and come to me : I shall anxiously await you." Ha ! (*Folding the letter*) There is more in this letter than meets the eye : it may be some novel trickery. I must first consult K'ung-ming. (*Turns to a eunuch*) Invite K'ung-ming to come here.

K'UNG-MING (*enters smiling. Aside, to himself*). So Tung-wu has set another murderous snare, but I'll show him a thing or two this time. How can the wild cat hope to defeat the tiger ? (*Bows to Liu Pei*) Your Highness !

LIU. Please don't stand on ceremony : be seated.
Liu sits in centre.

K'UNG-MING. Your Highness sent for me : how can I make myself useful ?

LIU. The Empress-Dowager of Tung-wu has written to inform me that she is in poor health. Moreover she requests me to visit her at once, and has prepared a banquet at the Yellow Crane Tower. Here is the letter, read it yourself and tell me what you think of it.

K'UNG-MING. It is not necessary for me to see it : I am already familiar with its contents. As a matter of fact I have dispatched a messenger to say that you will go at once.

LIU. What? Has the messenger gone?

K'UNG-MING. He has.

LIU. Is the letter genuine, do you think? Or is this a plot against my life?

K'UNG-MING. Chou Yü is full of animal tricks, not always successful, and hardly worth the trouble as far as we are concerned.

LIU. Ha! Then there is a plot against me! I'll not cross the river. No, I'll certainly not cross the river! I should be a fool to do so.

K'UNG-MING. Keep calm, my Lord. Yours is a great destiny. High Heaven itself protects you: how can you be harmed by the machinations of mortals? You must go. If you don't, Tung-wu will say you are a mere poltroon. That would be shocking! No, Sire, you must go!

LIU. Well, if you say it is safe to go, I'll go. But see that a strong force accompanies me without delay. At least I can then set forth with an easy mind.

K'UNG-MING. It shall be done at once. (*Calls to those outside*) Ask Chao Tzŭ-lung to come hither.

Chao enters and kneels before Liu.

CHAO. My Lord is well?

LIU. Rise, sworn brother. (*Chao rises, salutes K'ung-ming, who returns it*). Be seated, please.

CHAO. Thank you. (*Sits*). You have summoned me. Pray, what are your commands?

K'UNG-MING. Our lord is invited to a banquet at the Yellow Crane Tower. You are to accompany him.

CHAO. How many men shall I take with me?

K'UNG-MING. None whatever. Only His Highness and you are to go.

LIU. What? The last time I crossed the river I nearly lost my life: if I cross it again, and without an escort, I shall lose it for sure. I will not go!

K'UNG-MING. Well, if Your Highness refuses to go, Ching-chou must be theirs.

LIU. It seems you wish to expose me to danger : I am running a mighty risk if I go.

K'UNG-MING. Your Highness may remember the ancient saying : " Heaven assists the fortunate." Why be alarmed ? Have you forgotten Ho-liang, and the banquet there ? Or the " Beautiful woman plot " afterwards, which was to entrap Your Highness ? All these schemes came to nought, you even benefited by them. In the latter case, instead of losing your life, you won a beautiful bride, and almost killed Chou Yü with rage and vexation. Now you are invited to a great banquet in the Yellow Crane Tower ; I have guarded against all dangers, so there is not the least cause for alarm, my Lord. Let our enemy [Chou Yü] have as many men as he likes : with our brother Chao Tzŭ-lung as your escort, you need be under no apprehension. I'll stake my life on that.

LIU. Your skill at divination is wonderful, I know. Chou Yü, of course, is very young, but he is subtle for his years. His confounded " Beautiful woman plot " would have cost me my life but for the intervention of the Empress, who arranged my marriage with her daughter. I am neither a strategist nor a hero : why expose me to unnecessary risk ? I don't think I'll go. No ! really I won't ! It's far too risky !

K'UNG-MING (aside). Hm ! His Highness is afraid to leave Ching-chou. But it is absolutely essential that he should. I have arranged everything quite satisfactorily, and am determined to fight Chou Yü with his own weapons. But how am I to induce my Lord to go ? That's the question. (Reflects for a few moments). I have it ! I'll egg on Chao Tzŭ-lung : he must help me to persuade Liu Pei, even against his will. At present I can see no other alternative. (To Chao) Prince and servant should share weal or woe together : yet there you stand looking on, with your hands up your sleeves, and never a word to say. Surely you are not afraid of Chou Yü too?

CHAO. Me, afraid! Ha! ha! That's good! Was I daunted when I charged through a host at Tang-yang to rescue my Lord, or when I cut my way through Ts'ao Ts'ao's camp? The word " fear " is unknown to me. I am famed throughout the empire as the " fearless general." All men admire the " Peach-Garden Heroes "; yet even they give me credit for bravery. (*Turning to Liu Pei*) My Lord, be under no apprehension. I will protect you with my life. Chou Yü dare not raise a finger against you while I am there to defend you.

LIU (*aside*). Hm! He is just as bad as K'ung-ming. They must have prearranged this between them : they hold exactly the same views. Mine don't seem to count! As for my will, I don't seem to have any. After all, one cannot be the arbiter of one's own fate. Whether one lives or dies is a matter of destiny, utterly beyond one's power to control. Well, I suppose I must go. Ultimately, it does not matter where one dies. One satisfaction is that a man can die anywhere ; there is no place without the few requisite feet of soil for that operation. If I should die at Tung-wu, they can at least call my spirit back and place it in the hall of my ancestors. (*To K'ung-ming*) I am ready to go, but you don't mean to say that I am to have no escort?

K'UNG-MING. Your Highness will require neither men nor horses. I have a scheme to counteract any plot that may be hatched against you.

CHAO. But if there's an ambuscade—if a large force attacks us—you don't mean to say that I shall have to fight the lot?

K'UNG-MING. 'Twill be easy to escape from any force that may be led against you. I'll see to that. Here is a bamboo tube : carry it with you, and even if tens of thousands attack you, you have only to break it open. Believe me ! You will be surprised by the result.

LIU. Well, break it open now, and let us see it.

K'UNG-MING. If I were to let you look at it now, it would lose its efficacy. Please don't wreck my plan.

LIU. If I look at it now, it loses its efficacy does it ? Well, if I lose my life at Chiang-tung, after it is broken, it will serve as a banner to guide my spirit home.

K'UNG-MING. Your Highness, this bamboo tube, as you see, is not three feet long, yet it contains a power which your enemies will not be able to withstand. (*To Chao*) General, I confide it to you, and I trust you will guard it carefully. (*Gives it*). That tube will render you greater service than if you take an army with you. If you encounter any danger or difficulty, break it : that is all you need do. Within is a plan which will easily subvert those of the cunning Chou Yü.

CHAO (*aside*). This seems an admirable device, and I must believe in its success, for Chu-ko Liang has never deceived me yet. (*To K'ung-ming*) When shall we be able to return to Ching-chou, Sir ?

K'UNG-MING. You will be able to return on the sixteenth of this moon. I shall send troops to await our Prince's arrival on shore.

LIU. I fear that you'll have to greet my spirit instead of my body. The latter will lie in the neighbourhood of the Yellow Crane Tower, with a dagger sticking through it.

K'UNG-MING. Why indulge in such gloomy forebodings, my Lord ? Let me escort you to your chariot.

LIU. To my chariot, say you ? Are you sure you are not escorting me to my grave ? All right, I'll go. It is plain that you want to get rid of me somehow !

Exeunt.

CHAO. My Prince, I will pledge my life that you return in safety. Leave everything to us.

K'UNG-MING (*laughing*). Yes, Mr. Chou Yü, your infamous schemes and subtle plots fail to bamboozle me! The life of our leader will never be shortened by you. If you hope to hoodwink K'ung-ming, you'll have to be born again, and learn better statesmanship. Aha! I've got you this time! (*Calls*) Kuan P'ing!* Chou Ts'ang!† Come hither! (*Enter the two from L.*).

BOTH. Your servants! What are your commands, Sir?

K'UNG-MING. Liu Pei has left for the Yellow Crane Tower. You will take three thousand men, place them in ambush on the bank of the river and await his arrival. He is due on the sixteenth, when you will escort him safely to his palace.

KUAN. But if that scoundrel Chou Yü has a large naval force with him, I fear we shall not be strong enough to cope with him; he is an expert in naval warfare.

K'UNG-MING. I have already provided against that contingency. You need not fear!

BOTH. Your orders shall be strictly obeyed, Sir.
Exeunt R.

K'UNG-MING (*calls*). Wei Yen! Come hither!

WEI (*enters*). What are your commands, Sir?

K'UNG-MING. His Highness has gone to the Yellow Crane Tower. You will lead your troops to T'u-kang, place them in ambush there, and on the sixteenth you must be ready for an engagement with Chou Yü. See that you do not fail.

WEI. Yes, Sir, your orders shall be obeyed. (*Exit R.*).

CHANG FEI (*enters L. Aside*). Chu-ko Liang must have been blind not to see through Chou Yü's reptile schemes. How is it that he didn't consult me first? If our Lord goes to that banquet, he'll lose his life. It's appalling! It's abominable! What had we better do?
(*Walks about in a rage*).

---

* The adopted son of Kuan Yü, the Chinese Mars.
† Kuan Yü's horseman and armour-bearer.

k'UNG-MING. What makes you so angry, General?

CHANG (*still in a rage, abruptly*). His Highness has gone to the banquet at the Yellow Crane Tower. Why did you not tell me about it?

k'UNG-MING. Had I done so, you would have wanted to go too, and of course my plans would be ruined.

CHANG. How many men has he taken along with him?

k'UNG-MING. He has only taken Chao Tzǔ-lung.

CHANG. What! Only Chao Tzǔ-lung?

k'UNG-MING. That's all!

CHANG. I'll follow them at once and fetch them back.

k'UNG-MING. Well, even if you do, His Highness will have to go.

CHANG. Why not let me accompany them?

k'UNG-MING. There is no need for you to do so.

CHANG. Sir, he is my brother. We have sworn to live and die together. He went to your hut three times to beg you to join him, hoping that you would champion his cause, and now you have sent him to his death. Is this your championship? It looks more like revenge!

k'UNG-MING (*laughing*). Watch and see, General.

CHANG. When we three * swore eternal friendship in the peach-garden, the black bull and the white horse were sacrificed to Heaven. Although we have not the same surname, it is as if we came from a single womb. If one lives, three live; and if one dies, three die. Our Prince's enemies have laid a snare for his life, and you are leading him into it! You have sent him to be murdered by his foes! Put your hand on your heart and reflect: have you not rather the heart of a beast than that of a man?

k'UNG-MING. Why needlessly upset yourself because our Lord is invited to a banquet? If Chou Yü's in-

---

* Liu Pei, Kuan Yü and Chang Fei.

tentions turn out to be treacherous, I have a plan to overreach them. Chao Tzu-lung is also to be reckoned with. Who would be so bold as to try and injure Liu Pei? He will return on the sixteenth of this moon: I have already sent troops to the river to await his arrival. You need not be alarmed about his safety; my calculations never fail!

CHANG. What if they do?

K'UNG-MING. My head will be forwarded to your camp as a gift.

CHANG. And if he fails to return by the sixteenth?

K'UNG-MING. In that event, my head shall still be yours.

CHANG. Good! I am satisfied. Forgive me, and please consider whatever I have said in vexation as due to anxiety for our leader's welfare. (*Turns to leave: as he goes, exclaims*) Ha! ha! If Chou Yü kills Liu Pei, I'll first have K'ung-ming's head: then I'll lead my troops against Tung-wu, annihilate the inhabitants, lay waste the entire land, and butcher Chou Yü as if he were a pig or a dog. (*Exit*).

K'UNG-MING. Chou Yü, if you harm our Lord, you will only destroy yourself. Sun Ch'üan, you have repeatedly demanded Ching-chou, and fancy you'll obtain it, but so long as I live, Han territory shall only be ruled by a member of the House of Han. All you can do is to scheme, and sigh, and gaze helplessly on. (*Exit*).

SCENE II

River with open country on both sides: a boat appears, propelled by boatmen, etc., Liu Pei and Chao Tzŭ-lung in the bow.

LIU. Confound K'ung-ming for compelling me to make this excursion. I would not mind it so much if he had provided me with a sufficient escort. I do not relish this visit to the Yellow Crane Tower with only one man to protect me. (*To Chao*) Of course I am quite aware that you are brave, but if there's treachery, what can you expect to do single-handed, I should like to know? The prospect is getting on my nerves : I shall probably lose my life for being so foolish as to come at all.

CHAO. Fear nothing, Sir : Ts'ao Ts'ao's myriads did not dismay me, and do you think I am intimidated by that stripling Chou Yü? Every one of your foes lives in terror of me, and has not the Son of Heaven hundreds of spirits to protect him? (*Sings*) My Lord is true Emperor ; and surely the land which he rules will flourish with blessings unnumbered. Of what avail the treachery of Ts'ao Ts'ao and Sun Ch'üan combined against the rightful sovereign of the empire? Out of the deepest misery, have not countless blessings descended upon him? Did not the foul treachery of his foes bring him a Tung-wu bride? Yea, let them come in hordes, I fear them not and will see my Lord in safety back to Ching-chou.

LIU. Your words have driven my doubts and fears away : my heart is lighter and I feel more bold. I have witnessed too much of your courage on my behalf to doubt it. Let us advance with a stiff breeze and a favouring tide. With a heart of oak Liu Pei proceeds to the place of assembly, nor fears the machinations of his foes. (*Boat proceeds and scene closes*).

SCENE III. CHOU'S PALACE

CHOU YÜ (*enters and sings*). My navy can subdue the great waves of the Long River [Yangtze]. My troops are the bravest of the brave, and perfectly disciplined. They have won many battles and honours, and have been rewarded by Tung-wu. Myriads respond to my call. All the civil and military officers rush forward, and all obey my slightest command. Liu Pei is in my power and his life is at stake : I shall soon seize Ching-chou. Ha ! ha ! we'll see who is master in this little game !

KAN NING (*enters from L. To Chou Yü*). General, Liu Pei has arrived.

CHOU (*affecting surprise*). What ? Liu Pei arrived ? What escort has he ?

KAN. Only Chao Tzŭ-lung.

CHOU. What ! Only Chao Tzŭ-lung ?

KAN. That's all, General.

CHOU. Get the boats ready, quick ! I'll go and meet him. (*Exit Kan, L.*) Liu Pei, you have certainly tumbled into the trap !

CHOU (*sings*). I have baited my hook and now await the fish. The bird, wounded by my arrow, enters the cage prepared for it. Liu Pei, you have fallen into my snare at last ! K'ung-ming, what do you know about divination, that you could not foresee this ? At the Yellow Crane Tower I have spread my net. My men are all ready for war, and all of a single heart to capture Liu Pei.   (*Exit L.*).

Boat with Liu Pei and Chao Tzŭ-lung seen passing at the back. Chou Yü enters with soldiers, crosses the stage and goes off again R.

SCENE IV

Deck of a boat, Chou and Liu seen saluting each other : Chao and Kan, each standing behind his respective chief.

CHOU. Emperor, I salute you !

LIU. General ! (*Both bow*).

CHOU. May I have the honour of escorting Your Majesty ?

LIU. Many thanks.

Both get into the boat. Chao is about to step in when Kan attempts to stop him.

KAN. Hm ! You need not come too !

CHAO (*pushing him aside*). Who dares hinder me : do you ? (*Enters boat and is followed by Kan. Scene closes*).

SCENE V

Landing place on R. of stage : entrance to the Yellow Crane Tower on L. Soldiers lined up at gateway. Boat goes alongside at landing stage.

KAN. Will Your Majesty deign to land ?
All disembark.

CHOU (*with his tongue in his cheek, of course*). I was not aware that Your Majesty had arrived, and therefore did not go to welcome you. I beg you to excuse my apparent carelessness.

LIU. Please don't mention it. It is only on account of the difficulty in crossing the river that I have not been able to visit you more often.

CHOU. Your Majesty is too gracious !

LIU (*looking round*). How is it that I do not see the Empress here ?

CHOU. The Empress is not feeling well. As the Prince is unable to leave her bedside, he commanded me to receive you.

LIU. I am really putting you to a lot of trouble.
Enter attendant.

ATTENDANT. The banquet is served, Your Honour.

CHOU. Ask the Minister Lu to be in attendance at the Yellow Crane Tower and promptly wait on His Majesty. (*Exit attendant. To Liu*) Please ascend !

LIU. Thanks.
Liu, Chou, and Chao climb the steps leading to the tower.

CHOU. Our meeting again is like adding flowers to embroidery : it confers an additional honour on myself.

LIU. Yes, we may now discuss in most friendly manner the topics of the day.
They disappear into the tower.

Act II. Scene I

Chamber in Yellow Crane Tower. Lu Su discovered therein.

LU SU. Aha! Liu Pei has fallen into the trap. Little does he dream how near he is to death. My curse goes with him! He has robbed us of Ching-chou, and has no intention of returning it. Now that Chou Yü has enticed him here he will force him to sign a document pledging to evacuate the place and hand it over to us. If he refuses, his fate is sealed. Men are in ambush to assassinate him if he does not comply. In either event, Ching-chou will be ours. Oh! Here they come already!

Enter Chou, Liu, Chao, and attendants.

CHOU (*to Liu*). Welcome to the Yellow Crane Tower, Your Majesty.

LIU. Thank you, General.

LU. Pardon me, Your Majesty, for any little shortcomings on my part to welcome you : I had no idea Your Majesty would arrive so soon.

LIU. Please don't mention it, General. I should be sorry to trouble you in any way.

LU. Please be seated, Your Majesty.

LIU. Thanks. (*Sits*).

CHOU. You may go, Lu Su, I shall not require your presence.

LU (*as he goes, aside*). Liu Pei! The banquet is laid for you all right : I hope you will enjoy it. Little do you imagine what's in store for you. I trust you'll have time to digest it!　　　　　　　　　　(*Exit R.*).

CHOU. May I offer Your Majesty a cup of wine?

LIU. Certainly, thanks! (*Takes it : both drink*).

CHOU (*now changing his manner altogether*). By the way, when we routed Ts'ao Ts'ao's army in the struggle for Ching-chou, you borrowed the place to quarter your troops. How is it, may I ask, that you have not yet restored it ? What sort of justice is that ?

CHOU YÜ, LIU PEI AND CHAO TZŬ-LUNG IN THE YELLOW CRANE TOWER

Huang Ho Lou

LIU (*stammering*). Oh, that is—is—

CHOU (*sharply*). I repeat : why have you not restored Ching-chou to my country ? I must have a definite answer now !

LIU (*apologetically, sings*). Since the time I was born I have had no place to rest in. East and west have I wandered, driven like straw in the wind, with no place to call my own. 'Tis true that I borrowed Ching-chou, and kept it over-long. I beg you will wait a few years before you demand its return. Let me keep it till I have recovered Hsi-chüan and settled there in safety. I shall then restore Ching-chou to you without delay.

CHOU. Mere subterfuge. A most transparent trick ! (*Sings*) Why does your heart not agree with your tongue when you utter ? You always use force or fraud to achieve your ends. At the battle of the Red Cliff it was I who gained the glory. Your country was helpless against Ts'ao Ts'ao's troops, so Tung-wu came to your aid and spilled both blood and treasure to assist you. All of us, military and civil, put forth our utmost strength in the struggle for Ching-chou. How were we rewarded ? You, YOU, I say, held on to the place, pretending you " merely borrowed " it. After keeping it all this time, instead of returning it, you seek frivolous excuses to cling to it still. You have only been able to do this through the bravery of your generals, and the knavery of K'ung-ming. Now, give us back Ching-chou without more ado, and we'll call it quits, or of a truth, I will utterly devastate the place and give it up to indiscriminate slaughter. Yield it, I say, and curb all further animosity. I'll tolerate no further subterfuge !

LIU. Alas ! Has it really come to this !

CHAO (*to Chou Yü*). Hold your tongue, you— !

LIU (*alarmed*). Why do you interrupt the General ?

CHAO (*sings*). Sire, I interrupt him because he is talking nonsense. There is neither reason nor justice in his speech. The old proverb has it that " reason should always be spoken." (*Turns to Chou Yü*) Did you invite us here to insult us ? Ts'ao Ts'ao's troops arrived in their tens of thousands, like a swarm of bees to overrun your land. What did you say to them, may I ask ? It was commonly said of you Tung-wu folks that you were a lot of old women, cowards afraid to fight for your kith and kin. Your women fled from their homes, and your men just followed the women. That stout warrior of yours, Lu Su, too fearful to attack them himself, begged our K'ung-ming to divine whether an attack would be successful. It was at Lu Su's entreaty that K'ung-ming invoked the east wind which burnt up Ts'ao Ts'ao's fleet.* In mortal terror, Ts'ao furled his banners, muffled his drums, and fled to far Hua-jung. You of Tung-wu were like a brood of old hens whose chicks had taken to the water, all startled out of your wits. 'Twas through K'ung-ming you gained the victory. But were you grateful for your own salvation ? Not in the least ! You spurned the hand that saved your wretched lives and crazily thought you were heroes ! The Empire of Han belongs to Liu Pei. What right has Tung-wu to it or any portion thereof ? What skill has he to govern it, even if he possessed it ? Be a little more reasonable in your demands if you would avoid the wrath of Chao Tzŭ-lung !

Chou Yü sinks back into his chair, speechless with rage.

LIU (*to Chou Yü*). Pray don't be angry, General.

CHOU. What ? I am choking with anger—like a mountain split by an earthquake. Chao Tzŭ-lung spurns my valiant deeds only to vaunt his own. When Ts'ao Ts'ao sent his myriads against Chiang-tung, and his fleet cleft the waters in their descent upon our

*Alluding to the occasion when K'ung-ming, at Chou Yü's request, offered up sacrifices to obtain an easterly wind, without which Chou-Yü's plan to destroy Ts'ao Ts'ao's fleet would have been impracticable. K'ung-ming was successful: the east wind came and Ts'ao's fleet was utterly destroyed. See p. 208.

shores, whose plan obstructed them? Who caused his
boats to be linked together and destroyed? As for the
east wind, why, that was bestowed by Heaven. If K'ung-
ming is able to establish the House of Han so firmly,
why must a member of that house borrow a place like
Ching-chou, as his only haven and refuge on this earth?
To-day I have received commands of my master to give
a banquet. This is but a stratagem; the site of our
feast is a mighty cage whence you will not find it easy to
escape.

CHAO. So! So!

LIU. General, I beg you to ignore what Chao Tzu-
lung has said through devotion to me. He may seem
proud and ignorant, but is not really so. I will show
you more consideration. Listen! My brother Liu
Chang's troops have carried all before them in their
recent campaign. A few days hence I shall be going to
my home and friends. Let me retain Ching-chou yet
a while and you will be granting me a signal favour:
I will definitely restore it as soon as I have Hsi-chüan.

CHAO. Sire! No more, I beg! (*Turning to Chou Yü*)
Who dares aspire to the empire of the House of Han?
Who dares contend for that which has belonged to that
family for four hundred years by Heaven's high decree?
Who dares—

CHOU. Enough! Beneath this very tower my
soldiers are in ambush: at the word of my command
they are ready to fall upon you. You are hemmed in on
every side. Be brisk! Make haste, I say! Either
restore Ching-chou or—

CHAO (*interrupting*). Do you fancy the tiger is scared
of a pack of dogs or wolves? If you want Ching-chou,
first return that east wind you borrowed; then Ching-
chou shall be yours, not otherwise.

CHOU. General, the less you say the better for all
of you! Your impudence only upsets my temper.

CHAO. If it does, you may vent it on me. Haply I shall be able to endure it.

CHOU. Oh! You brag excessively! Unless Ching-chou is promptly restored you will fall in my trap, nor will you escape with ease.

CHAO (*sneeringly*). If you want us to give back Ching-chou, you should turn to your old expedient and do it by means of a woman.

CHOU (*angrily*). What?

LIU. Take no notice of him, General, I beg you: he is talking at random. I must apologize for him.

CHOU (*aside*). This sort of thing only increases my fury and desire for vengeance. I'll go and give instructions to my men. (*Goes off R.*).

LIU (*moving about uneasily*). Where has the General gone to?

CHOU (*outside*). Ask Liu Pei quickly to draft the agreement restoring Ching-chou. If he doesn't, I shall know how to deal with him. But on no account let either of them leave unless they produce my warrant. See that my orders are strictly obeyed, or you lose your heads, the lot of you! *Enter soldiers from R.*

THE LEADER (*speaks*). Your Majesty, I am commanded to inform you that you are at once to write an order restoring Ching-chou to my royal master.

LIU (*staring stupidly*). K'ung-ming, K'ung-ming! You have cost me my life! You forced me to attend this banquet. But the worms will enjoy this banquet instead of me!* My curse on this Yellow Crane Tower: why was I ever so foolish as to come? Chou Yü is after my life, and I shall meet an untimely death with unclosed eyes.† Chao Tzŭ-lung, what am I to do in this predicament?

---

* "Instead of me enjoying a banquet, the worms will enjoy a banquet off me!"

† The Chinese believe that they cannot close their eyes in death while some worldly grievance remains unredressed.

CHAO. Make your mind easy, Prince, and leave it to me. Did I not cut my way seven times through the enemy at Ch'ang-pan P'o? And shall I now be daunted by Chou Yü—a stripling? Let him fetch in his soldiers, and you shall see how I—alone—am able to deal with them.

LIU. At Ch'ang-pan P'o we were in the open, with horse and sword and spear. Now we are pent up in a tower. How shall we wrestle with our foes in here?

CHAO. Prince, have you forgotten the tube K'ung-ming gave me before we started, and his counsel to open it in a quandary? K'ung-ming would never deceive us. You should trust to his skill.

LIU. Nonsense! That tube has lured me to my death, and probably you to yours! It was merely a ruse to induce me to go.

CHAO. No, Sire: it is to help us out of this dangerous hole. I am sure K'ung-ming foresaw it all, and gave us this tube to bear us into safety. I shall break it open, however, and see for myself. (*Breaks it, finds Chou Yü's warrant, and exclaims with joy*) This is worth more to us now than ten thousand soldiers. My Prince! This affords us infallible means of escape.

LIU. What is it?

CHAO. Chou Yü's warrant, which was hidden inside the tube.

LIU. Let's look at it! (*Looks*). "O-mi-t'o Fo!" Truly, this is the saviour of our lives. Living Universal Beneficence! Quick! Let us away from here!

CHAO. Follow me, Sire! If needs be this warrant will take us through fire and through flood. (*Going R.*).

1ST SOLDIER AT DOOR. You cannot pass.

CHAO. What? We have the General's warrant to give us free passage. Who gave you such orders?

1ST SOLDIER. Where is the warrant?

CHAO. Behold, it is here! (*Hands it to soldier*).

1ST SOLDIER. It is truly the General's pass. You may proceed.

CHAO. Though you obstructed us, this time I will spare your lives. (*Goes*).

LIU. Ha! The dragon speeds on to his home in the sea : the tiger returns to his lair on the mountain.

Exit R.

1ST SOLDIER (*after inspecting the tube*). I think we had better ask the General to come.

He is on the point of going out when Chou and Lu Su enter.

CHOU (*standing at door*). Has Liu Pei finished drafting the agreement?

1ST SOLDIER. I don't know, General.

CHOU. How's that? What do you mean?

1ST SOLDIER. He has just left.

CHOU. Left? Who let him go?

1ST SOLDIER. I allowed him to go on the strength of your warrant, which he showed me.

CHOU. I gave nobody a warrant.

1ST SOLDIER. Here it is, General. (*Produces it*).

CHOU (*examines it*). Ha! Duped! (*Sinks into a seat*). Yes, by Heaven, duped!

LU. General, pull yourself together. Don't get excited!

CHOU. Curse him, confound him! My precious time all wasted again! After my repeated demands for the restitution of Ching-chou, just as I feel sure I have him in my clutches, he slips away scot-free! K'ung-ming must have foreseen our plot and taken his precautions. Thwarted again!

LU. Since Liu Pei's gone, why foam with useless anger?

CHOU. He's gone, but it was not I who released him ; there's the rub!

LU. If you did not release him, how did he come by this warrant?

CHOU. This is the warrant I gave K'ung-ming when he went to raise the wind on Nan P'ing Shan; the scoundrel has stuck to it ever since. K'ung-ming! K'ung-ming! Either you or I must perish. I swear that both of us shall not inhabit this earth at the self-same time. You Taoist wizard, to steal my warrant, and dupe me with the instrument of my own authority! Liu Pei was lucky to escape as he did. Curses on K'ung-ming! I fear I shall die of rage! I hate myself for not getting a chance to murder him!

LU. Liu Pei has gone, and the warrant is returned. Ching-chou has been demanded and refused. Dying of rage is useless: better try some other means of revenge.

CHOU. You are right. Liu Pei is a hero, while I am a clown devoid of ability. (*Calls out*) You outside there! (*Generals enter R.*). Embark with your men at once and pursue Liu Pei: wherever you find him, slay him. (*Generals exit R.*). Now, Liu Pei, we shall see if you escape me on this occasion! (*Exit R.*).

LU (*looking after him as he goes, aside*). And mind you don't lose your warrant again. Ha! ha! Chou Yü has courage enough, but little skill. He has hatched scheme after scheme, but none to any advantage as far as I can see. To regain Ching-chou, he devised the factitious contract for an alliance with Liu Pei, whereby the latter gained a wife, and Chou Yü nearly lost all his men, and worst of all, his prestige. Then he inveigles Liu Pei to a banquet, but "the water is too shallow to hold the dragon." Chou Yü, with your incessant demands for the restitution of Ching-chou, you have only wasted precious time and trouble. Every one of your schemes has proved abortive: the subtlest of them could not deceive K'ung-ming. Well, we shall have to see what happens next.

Scene II

A camp in a wild landscape : Chang and Huang enter L.

CHANG. The more I think of my Prince, the more I'm alarmed for his safety.

HUANG. K'ung-ming declared he would return to-day.

CHANG. I shall only feel at ease when I see his face.

HUANG. Fear nothing. K'ung-ming never blunders in his calculations.

CHANG. I'll find out what he says, and let you know later. (*Goes off. K'ung-ming enters from R. and meets Chang, who exclaims*) Liu Pei has not yet returned : restore him to us at once !

K'UNG-MING. Don't be unreasonable ! Wait till he is due.

CHANG. I cannot so readily forget our sworn brother-hood as to be wholly reasonable.

HUANG. Sun Ch'üan bears us enmity because of our continued occupation of Ching-chou. Who knows to what dangers our Prince is exposed in the hands of such traitors ?

K'UNG-MING. The Tung-wu troops may number millions ; their plots may be incalculable ; but our Prince will be perfectly safe : depend upon that.

CHANG. Yes, but when will he return ? That's what I am anxious to know.

K'UNG-MING. On the sixteenth, as I have already told you. Consequently he is due to-day. The Empress of Wu has sent an escort to guide him safely back.

CHANG AND HUANG. How do you know that ?

K'UNG-MING. Look yonder, both of you. (*Pointing off R.*) Behold his coming ! Our Prince has safely returned. (*Enter Liu Pei, Chao Tzŭ-lung and followers R.*).

CHANG AND HUANG. Welcome back, Your Majesty !
(*Salutations, etc.*).

LIU. I thank you, kind friends, for your hearty welcome. But for the foresight of dear K'ung-ming I would not be here to receive it, for I was caught in our enemies' clutches and even despaired of my life. I did escape, however, as you see. K'ung-ming promised to meet me here to-day. He has kept his word, and I am once more surrounded by loyal friends.

CHANG. Good K'ung-ming! Most excellent K'ung-ming! I have always said that his breast was as full of schemes as an egg is full of meat. Your Majesty, he must be rewarded.

K'UNG-MING. I am sufficiently rewarded by seeing His Majesty safe. But go and order pigs and sheep and bullocks to be slain, for the troops must also share our happiness.

CHANG. And I should be punished for doubting your ability. In spite of all your skill, I can only believe our master safe when he is in the midst of his troops, with his sworn brothers at his side.

Finis

*　　*　　*

Although this episode is not to be found in the *San Kuo Chih*, or Romance of the Three Kingdoms, it might well form part of Chapter LVI. The playwright religiously adhered to the spirit of Lo Kuan-chung's great novel. Again the wit of K'ung-ming confounds Chou Yü; Chao Tzŭ-lung is as brave as usual, Liu Pei as timid and perplexed, and Chang Fei as tempestuous. The characters are as consistent as those of Dickens. It is worthy of note that the *sona*, or Chinese clarionet, is seldom heard to such advantage as in Act I, Scene IV, when Chou Yü is greeting Liu Pei. The actors talk in subtle syncopation with this strident instrument.

The Yellow Crane Tower used to stand 139 feet high on the bank of the Yangtze by Wu-ch'ang city wall, opposite Hankow. Lapped in legend, like the phœnix, it rose innumerable times from the flames before it was finally destroyed by fire in 1884. The hideous edifice which stands on the original foundation is known as the Ching Chung Lou, or Tower of the Alarm Bell, and was built by the Manchu Viceroy Tuan Fang in 1902.

HUNG I (or NI) KUAN 虹霓關

THE RAINBOW PASS

PERIOD : End of the Sui and beginning of the T'ang dynasty, *circa* A.D. 618, when several feudal lords were contending for mastery. A *p'i-huang* play in two parts : I. Military ; II. Civil.

DRAMATIS PERSONÆ

HSIN WÊN-LI, a general	...	...	...	*Ching*
TUNG FANG SHIH, Hsin's wife	...	...	...	*Hua-tan*
SLAVE-GIRL (Ya Huan)	...	...	...	*Ch'ing-i*
WANG PO-TANG, a general	...	...	...	*Hsiao-shêng*
CH'I P'AI KUAN, Hsin's ensign	...	...	...	*Ch'ou-êrh*
CH'IN CH'IUNG, Generalissimo	...	...	...	*Shêng*

In addition to the above there are four officers : two *Erh-hua-lien*, one *Ch'ou-êrh* and one *Wu-shêng*.

SCENE I

After many battles Hsin Wên-li and his wife hold the important Rainbow Pass against the rapacious Generalissimo Ch'in Ch'iung of Wa Kang. One night Hsin has a dream of ill omen which he describes to his wife.

TUNG FANG SHIH. As you are a great general, you should take no notice of nonsensical dreams.

HSIN. But there is nobody whom I can put in control of the Pass while I am away.

TUNG FANG SHIH. Leave it to me !

HSIN. That's all very well, but have you forgotten the old story of Hsi Shih ? *

Whereat Tung Fang Shih flushes with shame and falls on her knees, declaring that she would willingly die at the spear's point, if ever she forgot her plighted love.

SCENE II

General Hsin leads his troops out to attack the enemy, defeating four generals : these tell Wang Po-tang, Ch'in

---

* The famous beauty instrumental in the ruin of Wu, 5th century.

Ch'iung's second in command, that they could not withstand Hsin's unparalleled strategy and prowess; to save their army they had to beat a hasty retreat. Wang mounts his horse and waits near the pass until Hsin Wên-li is visible and shoots an arrow which proves fatal.

SCENE III

Hsin's standard-bearer brings Tung Fang Shih the news.

TUNG FANG SHIH (*weeps bitterly, calls out her husband's name and sings, the air changing from p'i-huang to hsi-p'i*). The news of my poor husband's cruel death is like a steel blade piercing through my vitals. Curses on that inhuman murderer Wang Po-tang! I'll raise an army and sweep the Wa Kang robbers' lair off the face of the earth. (*Her slave-girl asks if she intends to muster troops and avenge her husband*). Yes, tell the chief officers to announce that the whole army is to go into mourning.
Exit slave-girl.

Four of Hsin Wên-li's generals, clad in mourning, appear on an embankment, saying:

FIRST. Our general has lost his life in battle.

SECOND. His wife will lead the troops for his revenge.

THIRD. She is ready to capture Wang Po-tang alive.

FOURTH. Cut out his heart and offer it before our general's coffin.

Whereupon the widow appears in whitest mourning, accompanied by her standard-bearer. She weeps and performs the sacrificial rites, lamenting and singing (the air changes to hsi-p'i) that she will exterminate the rebels and avenge her husband. She then exhorts the troops, who declare that they will fight to the last man. Tung Fang Shih bows to express her thanks, and proceeds to exhort the generals in the same strain. Then mounting her horse she declares: "If I fail to avenge my dear lord's death I shall never return here again." *Exeunt.*

Scene IV

Tung Fang Shih fights several rounds with four generals of the enemy and defeats them. They report to Wang Po-tang that her tactics were incredible and they could not compete with her skill. Wang Po-tang calls for his charger and gallops to meet her.

TUNG. Are you Wang Po-tang ?

WANG. I am.

TUNG. Why did you slay my husband ?

WANG. Each mortal has his business to attend to : your husband was not the only one to lose his life.

During the contest they come in closer proximity. In a twinkling Tung Fang Shih tears the red silken rosette from Wang's breastplate and puts it into her corsage (as a sign that she has fallen in love with him). They cease fighting. Seeing this the slave-girl shouts : " Kill him, kill him ! " *Hurling the banner she has been holding on the ground she exclaims :* " They have given up the battle for love ! "

TUNG FANG SHIH (*aside, sings in hsi-p'i*). This Wang Po-tang is as handsome as P'an An and Wei T'o. He is a very Lü Pu for beauty *—so dazzling that I long to persuade him to join me : together we'll destroy Wa Kang and then we'll be united as husband and wife.

WANG PO-TANG (*sings, also in hsi-p'i*). I am a hero and a valiant son of Han. How could I yield to you, a vile and insignificant adulteress ?

Lifting his spear he advances to the fray. The widow is worsted, but she orders her men to stretch out a rope so that Wang's horse shall be entangled. Wang is consequently caught alive, taken to the Pass and shackled. Tung Fang Shih orders him to kneel.

---

* P'an An, of the Sung Dynasty, "the most beautiful youth known to Chinese history or legend. Whenever this Apollo appeared upon the streets in his carriage, the women gazed upon him with admiration, and threw pears, peaches and other fruits, so that his cart was filled with them."—Arthur H. Smith, *Chinese Proverbs and Common Sayings*, p. 114. Wei T'o was the Chinese version of Vihârapâla, the Deva protector of the Law of Buddha and Buddhist temples. For Lü Pu, see p. 354.

WANG (*refuses, exclaiming*).   How could I, an up-
right and conscientious man, kneel to a mere woman !
If you want to take my life, take it, but say no more for
I don't wish to listen.

*Whereupon the four generals clad in mourning and the
standard-bearer exclaim :* " Lady, since you have seized the
murderer of our general alive, cut off his head and
avenge your husband's death." *After some hesitation, the
widow says :* " Lead him away." *Again they entreat her to
kill him—without avail.   Tung Fang Shih appeases them by
saying :* " As to this, you fellows may not fathom my
intentions.   But never fear; I have a scheme of my
own."   *Exeunt omnes.*

SCENE V

CH'IN CH'IUNG (*enters and says*).   I hear that Wang
Po-tang has been captured alive.   I must send my soldiers
to attack the Pass.   (*Sings in hsi-p'i*) You have captured
my general Wang Po-tang alive.   If you injure him, I'll
attack the Pass and put you all to the sword.

ENSIGN (*sings hsi-p'i in êrh-liu, very slow*).   I'll slay Ch'in
Ch'iung in revenge for my master's death.   (*Taking up a
heavy wooden roller he says*)   I'll clear away this rabble: one
of you go and tell Tung Fang Shih what I intend to do.

*He begins to hurl rollers from the wall, knocking down
enemy horses and men.   Ch'in Ch'iung shouts :* " Beat a
retreat, or we'll be lost." *His general Ch'êng Yao-chin
shouts :* " Besiege the place and we'll starve them out."
Ch'in Ch'iung gives orders to this effect.   *Exeunt.*

SCENE VI

TUNG FANG SHIH (*enters, soliloquizing*).   Now that
I have Wang Po-tang in my power, how can I injure
him ?   He excels P'an An in beauty.   Alas, I am pining
to marry him but find the subject difficult to broach.
(*Sings in hsi-p'i*) My dear Wang Po-tang, my beautiful
Wang Po-tang, how deep is my love for you !   (*Taking
the red silk rosette from her bosom she twirls it tenderly.*

The slave-girl is quick to notice this as she is bringing in the tea. Tung Fang Shih hides the rosette under a chair-cushion, thinking she has not been observed).

SLAVE-GIRL (*looking round for the rosette*). You ought to kill Wang Po-tang and avenge our master.

TUNG FANG SHIH. Oh, if you had not reminded me, I would have forgotten all about him. Have him brought before me at once.   (*Wang is led in, shackled*).

SLAVE-GIRL. Get down on your knees. Why don't you kneel, you rebel, before my mistress?

WANG. You shameless hussy and worthless slave, don't put on any of your airs with me.

SLAVE-GIRL (*speaks*). My Lady, what are you waiting for? Why don't you dispatch him?

TUNG FANG SHIH (*vacillating*). This, this . . .

SLAVE-GIRL. Yes : avenge the slaughter of your lord.

TUNG FANG SHIH (*stammering*). He . . . he . . . he should be put to death, but . . .

SLAVE-GIRL. You don't mean to say he couldn't?

TUNG FANG SHIH. Alas! Wang Po-tang, I regard you as supreme above all men. If you join me I'll place you in command of this Pass and of all the others. I'll gladly take you for my husband, and . . .

SLAVE-GIRL. Husband? What, what, what?

TUNG FANG SHIH. The husband sings and the wife follows : would you be willing to sing? . . .

WANG. If you want me to submit to you, that's quite impossible.

SLAVE-GIRL. Are you not going to dispatch him, my Lady?

TUNG FANG SHIH. Fetch my sword, quickly! (*When the weapon is handed to her she holds it over her head, singing in hsi-p'i*) If you do not consent to marriage, this three-foot blade will end your life.

SLAVE-GIRL. Slay him, oh slay him! Or if you will not, let *me* destroy him!

TUNG FANG SHIH. Why such precipitation? Don't get so excited.

SLAVE-GIRL (*sings slowly in hsi-p'i êrh-liu*). This matter lies beyond the calculation of mortals. When I consider that my master lost his life in battle and that my mistress risked her life to capture Wang Po-tang, she should now be taking out his heart and offering it before my master's coffin. But no! she forgets her husband's death, forgets to avenge his wrongs. She can only think of marrying Wang Po-tang. Of old there was a saying that virtue has its own reward. Most bitterly I resent my Lady's callous heart. Her heart drifts with the tide.

My Lady, oh, my Lady! Deign to lend your ear to a word of counsel. His Honour lost his life in battle: and from death there can be no return.

My Lady, oh, my Lady! deign to lend your ear to a word of counsel. His Honour lost his life in battle: and from death there can be no return. Infatuated by the beauty of Wang Po-tang, your sole desire is to mate with the drake. To-night the flowery candle will light the bridal chamber, as if the Spinning Damsel had come to meet the Cowherd.*

TUNG FANG SHIH. Oh joy of joys! But who will persuade him to yield?

SLAVE-GIRL. I am at your service, my Lady.

TUNG FANG SHIH. If you can prevail upon him, I'll reward you handsomely.

SLAVE-GIRL (*to Wang*). You are the most illustrious man under heaven: if you marry my mistress, she'll place you in full control of the Pass and all its defences. But if you don't consent, you'll promptly be put to the sword.† Ponder this carefully and once for all, before it is too late.

TUNG FANG SHIH. Yes, think it over, think it over.

WANG (*after some hesitation, says*). I promise to marry you on three conditions. First you must hoist flags of surrender at each of the four gates of the Pass.

SLAVE-GIRL. It can't be done, it can't be done.

TUNG FANG SHIH. Yes it can, indeed it can.

SLAVE-GIRL. And what is your next condition?

WANG. Welcome all my comrades.

SLAVE-GIRL. It can't be done, my Lady, it can't be done.

TUNG FANG SHIH. Indeed it can, it can be done.

SLAVE-GIRL. And the next condition?

WANG. For three days worship Heaven and Earth and the Ancestors, and then I'll consent to the marriage.

SLAVE-GIRL. Utterly impossible!

TUNG FANG SHIH. I agree to every one of these conditions.

---

* See *T'ien Ho P'ei*, p. 360.
† Literally. " become the sword's devil."

TUNG FANG-SHIH AND WANG PO-TANG

from a photograph circa 1890

Hung I Kuan

SLAVE-GIRL. Then I'll loosen his bonds.

TUNG FANG SHIH. Let me help to unbind him.

Wang and Tung Fang Shih sit at a table drinking wine when the ensign in sackcloth comes to report the arrival of the Wa Kang comrades, who have challenged them to go out and fight. Enraged by this interruption the widow orders him to be taken out and executed.

WANG (*intercedes, saying*). This is a day of gladness : if you kill this man, I fear our marriage will turn out to be unlucky.

SLAVE-GIRL. Please, my Lady, respect your newly wedded husband's wishes. They are both reasonable and fair.

TUNG FANG SHIH. So be it, then.

WANG (*to ensign*). You are pardoned.

TUNG FANG SHIH (*having noted the ensign's joyful expression, breaks out with some heat*). You are pardoned from execution, yes, but not from a beating. (*She prescribes forty strokes and subsequent release*).

ENSIGN. Thank you, my Lady ; thank you, my new Lord !

TUNG FANG SHIH. Out of my sight, you beast ! (*To attendants, handing an arrow with flag attached*) Here is your authority to open the gates and welcome the comrades from Wa Kang.

WANG. Thank you, dear wife : now you will please retire.   (*Exeunt Tung Fang Shih and the slave-girl*).

The gates are opened forthwith and the Wa Kang comrades enter the Pass.

Finis

*   *   *

The finest female impersonators such as Mei Lan-fang, Ch'êng Yen-ch'iu, Hsün Hui-shêng and Shang Hsiao-yün generally enact the rôle of Tung Fang Shih in the military part and of the slave-girl in the civil part, which rôles alternatively require the best singers. Tung Fang Shih is the outstanding widow in Chinese history who fell in love with her husband's slaughterer : her lack of self-control

MEI LAN-FANG
(*Hartung photograph*)

is complete. The conflict between this infatuation and her duty is hardly given an innings, hence she gets little sympathy from the audience. The slave-girl who persists in urging her to avenge her husband is the real heroine of the play. She does her best to influence and restrain her, but after all she is but a slave-girl and must unwillingly give way when she realizes that the case is hopeless : her mistress is physically more of a slave than she is.

Here we may note that the *soubrette* is allotted as important a rôle in Chinese drama as it is in the French. In the thirteenth century even Molière's Dorine was forestalled by Hung Niang in the famous *Hsi Hsiang Chi* : "The Romance of the Western Chamber," translated by Mr. S. I. Hsiung. The *soubrettes* in fact are by far the most humorous and natural types in the Chinese drama. As Mr. Arthur Tilley wrote of Marivaux' Colombines and Lisettes, " all alike are alert in speech and action ; they advise and abet their mistresses with sympathetic intelligence," and with hardly an exception they are the confidential friends of the family, honest, outspoken and devoted to those they serve. That the equivalent to the devoted valet follows closely in their wake is proven by Ma I in *Chiu Kêng T'ien* (p. 118).

I P'ÊNG HSÜEH 一棒雪

A DOUBLE HANDFUL OF SNOW

Also known as *Shên T'oŭ:* "The Investigation of a Head"; *Tẕ'ŭ T'ang:* "The Murder of T'ang"; and *Hsüeh Pei Yüan:* "Affinity of the Snow Cup."

PERIOD : Ming, during the reign of the Emperor Chia Ching, A.D. 1522-1566.   A *p'i-huang* play.

SYNOPSIS

The plot is founded on a true story which, since it differs in certain respects from the play, we offer as *hors-d'œuvre*. It concerns Mo Huai-ku, a high official who seemed to have all that was necessary for happiness on earth. Besides a legal wife, *née* Fu (hence known as Fu Shih), he possessed a dazzling concubine, Hsüeh Yen, or "Beautiful Snow"; an only son named Wên-hao; and a devoted servant who, having been with the family since childhood, adopted his master's surname and was called Mo Ch'êng. This retainer was a living image of his master, and had a son named Wên-lu.

Last but not least, Mo Huai-ku had been bequeathed an extraordinary heirloom by his paternal grandfather. This was a goblet of white jade which behaved like a thermos flask : wine poured into it would retain its warmth indefinitely. Owing to the purity of its texture it was christened *I P'êng Hsüeh* : "A Double Handful of Snow."

A brilliant career lay before Mo Huai-ku. Appointed chief of the Civil Office in Peking, his entire household was transferred from its native south to take up residence in the southern quarter of the Capital.

One day Mo saw a youth lying outside his gate, who seemed to be dying of starvation. He ordered his servants to carry him indoors and provide him with food, clothing and restorative medicines. Upon his recovery it appeared that his name was T'ang Ch'in; that he was a native of Shao-hsing-fu in Chêkiang, and a mounter of paintings by profession. Impressed by his refinement, intelligence and ready eloquence, Mo commissioned him to mount his pictures, of which he had a choice collection. Hence T'ang Ch'in earned the nickname of T'ang *Piao Pei*, or

" Pasteboard " T'ang. He lived with the Mo family and was treated as if he belonged to it.

After a year or so, T'ang caught a glimpse of Mrs. Mo and Hsüeh Yen while they were enjoying a stroll in the garden (young women were jealously secluded in those days). The season was spring ; overcome by the graces of the lovely concubine, he stood feasting his eyes on her, not daring to make any advances or stir from where he was. Hsüeh Yen became a passionate obsession. He could not banish the vision from his mind. Day and night he pondered schemes to open an intrigue with her.

Not long afterwards his opportunity came ; he saw Hsüeh Yen alone in the garden, and braced himself to address her. But the lady affected to take no notice ; deeply shocked by his impudence, she swept out of the garden.

Fearing she would denounce him, T'ang hastily resigned ; a friend recommended his services to the notorious Yen Shih-fan, son of the still more notorious Yen Sung, doyen of the Six Wicked Ministers of the Ming Dynasty. T'ang soon ingratiated himself with his new patron, and played Mosca to Yen's Volpone ; the relation between these rôles recalls Ben Jonson's drama.

It was a dismal day for their enemies when this pair of schemers combined, since Yen Shih-fan had his powerful father to back him. Shih-fan would often carouse with his satellite, whose frustrated passion for Hsüeh Yen was like an open sore. Once when Yen was complaining that his wine cooled off too quickly, T'ang told him about his late master's remarkable heirloom, the " Double Handful of Snow." " Why doesn't Your Excellency demand it from him ? " he suggested. " Mo would never dare refuse such a request."

" The cup may be all you say it is," replied his patron. " But after all, it is an heirloom, and Mo and I were fellow-students ; we graduated in the same year. If I asked him for it, I fear I should lose his friendship."

" But Your Excellency's father is Prime Minister ; his power is supreme. Who would dare deny you anything ? That cup is a marvel. Your Excellency's fame and fortune will never be complete without it. At all costs you should try to acquire it : under heaven it has no peer."

After some hesitation, Yen decided to ask Mo Huai-ku to pay him a visit.

Mo duly arrived, and was greatly perturbed when Yen requested to examine the cup. Refusal would surely bring calamity ; assent would mean the loss of his precious heirloom.

" Indeed I have the goblet you describe, but it is now in my ancestral home at Ch'ien-t'ang [in Chêkiang]. If Your Excellency is really anxious to see it, please grant me a month's leave of absence to go home and fetch it."

" Granted," said Yen.

In this quandary Mo consulted his trusty retainer Mo Ch'êng, who suggested having an exact replica made and palming that off on Yen as the genuine article. A famous carver of jade was entrusted with this delicate task, and within twenty days he succeeded in producing a miraculous imitation. Yen was entirely deceived by it, and thanked Mo profusely for presenting him with such a priceless work of art. He showed it to his father, and asked him to promote Mo to the post of Chief Minister of the Court of Sacrificial Worship. The Prime Minister agreed, and Mo, thinking " all's well that ends well," celebrated the happy occasion with a banquet. Unfortunately he got so drunk that he bragged to his former protégé about the trick he had played on Yen Shih-fan. T'ang promptly told his new master, polishing the anecdote with little embellishments of his own. At first Yen could not believe his ears, but when the major-domo poured wine into the false cup and let it stand, the wine grew cold. " Besides," he said, " I saw the real cup at the banquet."

In a towering rage, Yen ordered a hundred runners to escort him to the Mo mansion, which was to be ransacked till the goblet was found. His intentions leaked out while he was on the way. Mo Ch'êng, happening to get wind of them, took a short cut home, and escaped with the cup through a dog's hole under the wall. Then, climbing a hillock near by, he watched events.

Yen posted his men at all the doors with orders not to let anyone else enter or leave the premises. He then told Mo to deliver the genuine cup. Mo assured him that he had already done so. " What about that cup you used at your feast the other day ? "

When Mo denied using it at the banquet and advised him not to be so credulous, Yen accused him of playing a low trick on him in return for his many favours, crying : " You have no conscience at all ! "

The house was turned topsy-turvy but no trace of the cup could be found. Finally Yen threatened to exterminate Mo's family unless it was delivered within three days, and withdrew in a terrific tantrum.

As soon as Yen was out of sight, Mo rushed to the room where his heirloom was preserved and unlocked its coffer, only to find it missing. Thinking it must have been stolen by one of Yen's runners, he asked Hsüeh Yen about it. But she could tell him nothing. He then summoned Mo Ch'êng, who was also missing. While he was making frantic inquiries, Mo Ch'êng appeared on the scene. Before the servant had a chance to open his mouth, he scolded him as a good-for-nothing loafer, cuffing and kicking him into the bargain. When his master's temper had cooled, the servant plaintively explained matters and produced the cup. Mo Huai-ku was too overjoyed to say much, though deeply touched by his servant's loyalty. So far he had not taken Yen's threat very seriously : he hardly believed him capable of murdering a whole family for the sake of a little cup. But Mo Ch'êng reminded him that the Yens were a vindictive and lawless crew and that T'ang Ch'in egged his patron on to acts of violence. He begged his master to take every precaution.

Thoroughly alarmed, Mo Huai-ku could only think of flight as a solution, but he vacillated at the prospect of abandoning his lucrative post. At last, persuaded by his servant, he decided to seek protection with a friend named Ch'i Chi-kuang, commander of the garrisons at Chi-chou. He escaped with Hsüeh Yen after nightfall, while the rest of his family scattered in other directions.

In the meantime Yen Shih-fan accused T'ang Ch'in of making false reports and ordered him to be bound hand and foot. The wily major-domo had just remarked that Mo would stick to his post if his conscience was clear, and abscond if it was not, when one of Yen's runners announced that Mo had fled with his concubine. Yen's first instinct was to pursue them, but T'ang argued that desertion of an official post was no trivial offence ; better send messengers with urgent despatches on his trail and have him arrested. Yen thought this measure excessive, but T'ang pressed him to write a dispatch to the effect that Mo, having stolen the State Seal and absconded with it, was to be arrested and sent back to the Capital for punishment. T'ang further prevailed upon him to add a clause that Mo should first be decapitated, and that his head should be sent to the Capital.

Captured at Chi-chou, Mo was confined for the night in the yamen of his friend Ch'i Chi-kuang. The latter contrived his escape, since Mo Ch'êng, who bore such a striking resemblance to his master, volunteered to suffer the supreme penalty in his stead. After which the loyal retainer's head was sent with Hsüeh Yen to the Capital. Subsequently Mo Huai-ku escaped to Shantung ; his son, with his teacher, to Ch'ien-t'ang in Chêkiang, where he took his *Chin Shih* (doctorate) degree ; Mrs. Mo, with the servant's son Wên-lu, to Shên-yang (Mukden) in Manchuria.

Hsüeh Yen and the head reached Peking and the judge Lu Ping was appointed to investigate the case. T'ang Ch'in, who was to watch the trial and report to his master, promptly declared that the head was not genuine, so Ch'i Chi-kuang was summoned to the Capital.

The judge suspected that T'ang was in love with the concubine ; and while he was called away to witness an execution, he had Hsüeh Yen confined in a special cell and asked T'ang Ch'in to question her in secret, at the same time telling a confidential servant to " listen in." The servant duly reported that T'ang had offered to marry her : if she accepted, the head was Mo's ; otherwise it was a fake.

After reopening the trial the judge announced his decision to give Hsüeh Yen in marriage to T'ang Ch'in ; it devolved upon the latter to identify the head. Unable to restrain his delight, T'ang blurted out that the head was Mo Huai-ku's. Turning to Hsüeh Yen, the judge pronounced : " I now join you in marriage to T'ang Ch'in." Then, having written the character *tz'ŭ* (kill) on one side of his fan, he proceeded to show it to Hsüeh Yen, who was kneeling on his right (hence T'ang, seated on his left, was unable to note this gesture), with advice to " *wait* upon His Honour faithfully "—a quibble on the word *tz'ŭ* (which by a change of tone can mean " wait upon "), to put T'ang off the scent. Whereupon the Court was dismissed. Subsequently the virtuous concubine stabbed the villain to death in the nuptial chamber and committed suicide.

In the 42nd year of the Ming Emperor Chia Ching (1563), the Prime Minister Yen Sung was impeached by the Censor Tsou Ying-lung, dismissed from his post and deprived of all his titles. His son Shih-fan was executed for his many crimes. Thus, after a lapse of fifteen years, Mo Huai-ku was restored to his former rank and titles. Going to worship at Mo Ch'êng's grave at Liu-lin (Willow Grove) he chanced to meet his wife and Wên-lu, Mo Ch'êng's son, who had also gone to worship there, under the impression that the grave was Mo Huai-ku's.

The family is reunited in the sequel *Hsüeh Pei Yüan*, " Affinity of the Snow Cup," which is seldom played together with *I P'êng Hsüeh*. Wên-hao, the son of Mo Huai-ku, after taking his degree, was appointed judge of circuit. During the course of his travels he arrived at Chi-chou, where Ch'i Chi-kuang invited him to a banquet, not knowing he was the son of his old friend. The jade cup was brought out and Wên-hao, recognizing it, asked how it had come into his host's possession. Ch'i then related the circumstances of his father's escape and Mo Ch'êng's decapitation, and invited his father, mother and Wên-lu to appear, as by magic, before his astonished eyes. Further to cement their friendship Ch'i betrothed his only daughter to Wên-hao, and the judge Lu Ping betrothed his only daughter to Wên-lu, who was now adopted as a son by Mo Huai-ku. Hence this act is called *I Chia T'uan Yüan*, "A Family Reunited." After the double nuptials were consummated, a memorial hall and arch were erected to commemorate the loyalty and devotion of Mo Ch'êng and Hsüeh Yen respectively.

DRAMATIS PERSONÆ

Mo HUAI-KU, owner of the jade cup ... ...
Mo CH'ÊNG, his loyal retainer ... ... } *Lao-shêng*
LU PING, Judge ... ...
CH'I CHI-KUANG, Commander of the Chi-chou garrison
YEN SHIH-FAN, a powerful official ... ... *Ching*
HSÜEH YEN, concubine of Mo Huai-ku ... ... *Ch'ing-i*
T'ANG CH'IN, creature of Yen Shih-fan ... ... *Ch'ou*
SOLDIERS, SERVANTS, YAMEN RUNNERS, ETC.

(*Fu Shih, Mo Huai-ku's wife, does not appear on the stage*)

NOTE : We give the correct character *Mo* 莫, as given in the *Po Chia Hsing* ("The Hundred Family Names"), instead of the usual 穆 *Mu*, used by the ignorant.

ACT I. SCENE I

Enter Yen Shih-fan and T'ang Ch'in.

T'ANG. Your Excellency has returned somewhat earlier than usual.

YEN. There was very little business to be transacted at Court to-day.

T'ANG. Was your quest for the jade cup successful ?

YEN. It was not. My old colleague Mo Huai-ku informed me that it is now in his ancestral home, at Ch'ien-t'ang.

T'ANG. He deceived you, Sir. At his banquet the other day I saw it with my own eyes. How can he pretend that it is at Ch'ien-t'ang ?

YEN. Compared to our friendship the cup is a bauble not worth fussing about.

T'ANG. It's obvious that Mo Huai-ku lacks a conscience.

YEN. What do you mean?

T'ANG. He seems to have forgotten how he rose to his present position.

YEN. True, I was responsible for his promotion.

T'ANG. That he should deny you such a trifling gift as a small jade cup only shows how ungrateful he is for all your kindness.

YEN. You make me realize how odious the creature is. (*To retainers*) Order my chair! (*Sings*) T'ang Ch'in's words are words of iron; the tip of his tongue is sharp enough to kill without letting blood. Make haste with that chair! I'll renew my search for the fabulous cup of jade.

Exeunt Yen and T'ang.

SCENE II

Enter Mo Huai-ku and Hsüeh Yen.

MO (*sings*). The restless rooks are cawing and flapping their wings. My eyes are twitching, my heart is thumping. I wonder what all this signifies! (*Servant rushes in to announce that Yen Shih-fan has arrived*). Invite him to come in. (*Exit Hsüeh and enter Yen*). Welcome, Your Excellency.

YEN. Dear colleague, didn't you tell me that that jade cup of yours was not in the Capital? Which cup did you use at the banquet the other day? Will you answer me that?

MO. So somebody told you I used my heirloom! Who was it, Sir?

YEN. T'ang Ch'in was my informer.

MO. You should not pay much heed to gossip, Sir.

YEN. What are you driving at?

MO. I mean you should not believe everything you hear.

YEN. Rubbish ! (*Sings*) It is maddening to listen to such feeble excuses. How I despise this Mo for his deceit ! I recommended him to the Throne for the post of Director of the Board of Sacrificial Worship, and this is the way he shows his gratitude. Here, my men ! (*Enter four runners*). Have you found the cup ?

CHIEF RUNNER. No, Your Excellency. We have searched every nook and cranny but the cup is missing.

YEN (*sings*). My failure fills me with mortification. My old friend and colleague has grossly insulted me ! Make haste, get my chair ready. Unless I receive the cup within three days, I'll utterly exterminate this household.   (*Exit Yen with runners*).

HSÜEH YEN (*entering*). So Yen has departed !

MO. I wonder where that slave Mo Ch'êng went off to.

MO CH'ÊNG (*arrives, saying*). Were you alarmed, Sir ?

MO. Where were you when His Excellency Yen came here for the cup ? I'll give you a beating, slave that you are ! (*Hsüeh Yen intercedes for the servant*). I'll brook no interference.

HSÜEH. Don't be vexed, Sir.

MO CH'ÊNG. Allow me to explain, Sir. As soon as your slave caught sight of His Excellency Yen swinging along in his official chair, I noticed he was in a rage and suspected he had come in search of the cup. Off I rushed to the room we keep it in, removed it from the chest, and hiding it in my clothes attempted to get away by the front gate. Some men were planted there, so I had to go to the back. When the sentries on guard there stopped me, I crept through the dog's hole under the wall, and climbing a hillock, watched and waited a while. As soon as the coast was clear I made my way back ; and then Your Honour began to curse and beat me . . .

HSÜEH. The master is anxious to know what happened to the cup. Where is it now ?

MO CH'ÊNG. Here, in the fold of my jacket. (*Producing the cup*). Am I right or wrong ?

MO (*sings*). My heart brims over with joy at the sight of it. Mo Ch'êng's a clever fellow after all ! (*Speaks*) Now that I have recovered my priceless heirloom I can retain my post. Why should I fear Yen Shih-fan now ?

MO CH'ÊNG. What did His Excellency Yen say when he took his departure, Sir ?

MO. Nothing in particular—just ordinary talk.

MO CH'ÊNG. What sort of ordinary talk, Sir ?

MO. Come to think of it, he said he would exterminate my whole family within three days.

MO CH'ÊNG. Surely Your Honour cannot mistake such talk for empty bluster !

MO (*suddenly alarmed, sings*). You fill me with dismay. I have no plan to prevent it. (*Speaks*) I had better abandon my post and get out of harm's way.

MO CH'ÊNG. Where do you propose to go, Sir ?

MO. I have a loyal friend called Ch'i Chi-kuang : he is now Defence Commissioner at Chi-chou. I had better seek his protection.

MO CH'ÊNG. Let us pack at once ; we have no time to lose.

MO. Go ahead. Alas, I am sorely reluctant to throw up my post like this. It will deprive me of all my honours.

MO CH'ÊNG. There is nothing else to be done in such a crisis. The life of your whole family is at stake.

MO. Alas, we will have to go !   (*Exeunt*).

SCENE III

Enter Yen Shih-fan, T'ang Ch'in and four runners.

T'ANG. Your Excellency has returned. Have you succeeded in tracing the cup, Your Excellency ?

YEN (*snarling*). No, I have not ! (*To runners*) Here ! Bind this fellow. Pinion him, shackle him, gag him !

T'ANG. Wait a minute. Easy there! Patience, Your Excellency; please allow me to explain. If the cup is not in Mo's mansion he will certainly stick to his post, but if it is, and he refuses to part with it, he is bound to escape with his family. (*Yen's runners arrive and report that Mo has escaped*). What shall we do now?

YEN (*to runners*). Send for my official chair at once.

T'ANG. Where are you going, Sir?

YEN. I intend to pursue him and urge him to return.

T'ANG. For him to abandon his post like this is no trivial offence.

YEN. What does your wit suggest?

T'ANG. Your Excellency should send despatches to every district, commanding his prompt arrest and punishment.

YEN. Not a bad suggestion. Fetch my writing materials.

T'ANG. I'll grind the ink for you, Sir.

YEN (*proceeds to write aloud as follows*). "Yen, Junior Guardian of the Heir Apparent and Vice-President of the Board of War, publishes this most urgent despatch. Be it known that a criminal official named Mo Huai-ku has abandoned his post and escaped with the State Seal. All the officials of the various prefectures and districts are hereby commanded to arrest him."

T'ANG. Better add: "Promptly decapitate and send his head to the Capital."

YEN. There is no such heavy punishment allowed.

T'ANG. If you fight a tiger and fail to kill him, he will only turn and rend you. In any case he has brought this on himself.

YEN. You are right. I'll put in that extra clause. (*Doing so, ends with the usual formula*) "An urgent despatch: let nobody disregard it!" (*To runners*) Here is a warrant for the arrest of Mo Huai-ku: you are to pursue and capture him with the utmost speed. (*Exeunt runners.*

To T'ang) Henceforth you are never to meddle in my official affairs, do you understand? You always make confusion worse confounded.

T'ANG. I'll bear that in mind, Your Excellency.

Exeunt.

SCENE IV

In some performances Fu Shih and Wên-lu are seen making for the frontier. Enter Mo Huai-ku, Hsüeh Yen and Mo Ch'êng. Hsüeh Yen sits weeping on the floor.

MO. Why don't you move on?

HSÜEH. My feet are so sore, I cannot walk another step.

MO (*to Mo Ch'êng*). Go and hire a small sedan-chair, but mind that nobody sees what you are about.

MO CH'ÊNG. Yes, I'll be very careful.

Exit servant. Two runners appear.

FIRST RUNNER. We've followed them so far. Where have they disappeared to?

SECOND RUNNER (*looking round*). There is a couple in that wood over there. I'll make believe I'm a friend. (*Shouting*) Mo Huai-ku!

HSÜEH YEN (*to Mo*). Some one is calling out your name.

MO. I'll see who it is. (*Sings out*) Who is calling my name there?

As soon as he approaches they grab and shackle him. Hsüeh Yen weeps. Exeunt omnes.

SCENE V

Runners arrive with Mo Huai-ku at Chi-chou city gate. When the latter is opened, they go in and beat the official drum to let the official know that he is wanted. Enter Ch'i Chi-kuang with four of his runners.

CH'I. Who beat the drum?

RUNNERS. We did. We have come with an official dispatch for your perusal, Sir.

CH'I. Hand it to me. (*Opens and reads it. To runners*) Where did you catch your prisoner?

RUNNERS. In the grove outside the eastern gate.

CH'I. Lead him in.

MO HUAI-KU (*entering*). Bless me if it isn't Ch'i in person!

CH'I (*dissembling*). Nonsense! I've already registered your name. How could my record be wrong?*

RUNNERS. The prisoner is named Mo Huai-ku, and the woman Hsüeh Yen.

CH'I (*to yamen runners*). Confine them in the yamen gaol till further orders.

MO (*soliloquizes*). Woe is me! Things have come to such an extremity that even my old colleague will not recognize me.

HSÜEH YEN. It looked to me as if His Honour Ch'i was only pretending not to know you.

Exeunt Mo and Hsüeh.

CH'I (*to runners*). This case appears to be of a very serious nature. It will have to be dealt with openly, so that all can witness the proceedings. There will have to be responsibility all round. (*The runners, being clowns, are apt to gag in this scene: we omit their crude ineptitudes*). Confine Mo Huai-ku in the main courtyard of the prison, and keep a sharp eye on him. See that he is bound and beheaded just after daylight. Put his head in a trunk, convey it to the Capital, deliver it to Yen Shih-fan, and return here.

Exeunt runners, wondering how much they will be paid.

CH'I (*soliloquizing*). How now! This Mo Huai-ku is an old friend of mine. What can he have done to offend Yen Shih-fan? He has a retainer by name of Mo Ch'êng, an extremely able fellow. I wonder where he

---

* Here he quibbles on the term *pu ch'i*, "not complete," to put the runners off the scent: if they discovered about their friendship, they would, of course, tell Yen Shih-fan.

is. (*Calling*) Here, fetch me a lamp. I'll go out secretly and look for him. *Exit*.

NIGHT-WATCHMAN (*entering*). I have to beat the watch for others : a very hard life is the life I lead ! In wind and rain I have to go out on my rounds. Unhappy me ! I am the night-watchman of Chi-chou. The latest bit of local news is that an absconding official called Mo Huai-ku has been arrested. On the very stroke of the fifth watch after daybreak he is to be executed, so I'll have to be on double guard to-night. (*Mo Ch'êng appears ; the watchman grabs him saying*) I've got you, I've got you !

MO CH'ÊNG. I'm just a man from the country. Let me go.

WATCHMAN. What are you doing here at this time of night ?

MO CH'ÊNG. I've come to pay my grain-tax.

WATCHMAN. You have to pay that in at the magistrate's. Why are you hovering round the yamen of the military official ? (*A hubbub is heard*).

MO CH'ÊNG. Hark ! What is all that noise about ?

WATCHMAN. Don't you know ? They have captured an absconding official named Mo Huai-ku. His head is to be chopped off at daybreak. (*Mo Ch'êng breaks down*). Hey, what are you blubbering about ?

MO CH'ÊNG. His Honour Mo Huai-ku is an honest and upright official. It is pity for him that moves me to tears.

WATCHMAN. You behave as if you had just seen some doleful play—" Bearing the burdens of the ancients," eh ? If you have nowhere to rest yourself, you are welcome to lie down in my watch-house yonder. (*Both arrive there*). I should like to snatch a little sleep myself. You beat the gong for me in the meantime. Whenever you hear a gong being struck elsewhere, all you have to do is to answer it by beating this one.

MO CH'ÊNG. All right.

Exit watchman. Mo bursts into tears. Enter Ch'i Chi-kuang.

CH'I (*sings*). Slowly I wander along . . . who is that I hear crying so bitterly?

MO CH'ÊNG. It is I, Mo Ch'êng.

CH'I. Hush, not so loud! Somebody might hear you. (*Takes hold of Mo, pulls him off the stage, then brings him on again and says*) Your master has been captured and imprisoned.

MO CH'ÊNG. Would Your Honour give me permission to speak with him?

CH'I. I came with that intention. (*To runner*) Go and ask His Honour Mo to come here, but see that you are not overheard. (*Exit runner and returns with Mo Huai-ku and Hsüeh Yen, the latter weeping*).

MO (*sings*). Don't weep so loud, my lady; you might alarm Yen's runners. We advance to the second hall in agony and shame, weighed down by heavy shackles.

CH'I. Be seated, brother Mo. Your servant Mo Ch'êng has also come.

MO. Where is he?

CH'I (*to servant within*). Come out, Mo Ch'êng, and meet your master.

MO CH'ÊNG (*to his master*). Oh, Master, you must have had a fearful shock!

MO. It's all your fault for mismanaging things.

MO CH'ENG. It is useless to blame me now, Sir.

CH'I (*to Mo Huai-ku*). What did you do to offend the Yens?

MO. It was on account of my jade cup, which Yen Shih-fan coveted.

CH'I. But that is insignificant. Why was a dispatch sent?

MO. Oh, was there a dispatch? Pray let me see it.

CH'I. Here it is! (*Hands it to him*).

MO CH'ÊNG, HSÜEH YEN, MO HUAI-KU AND CH'I CHI-KUANG AT CHI-CHOU

I P'êng Hsüeh

MO (*reading it aloud*). " Yen, Junior Guardian of the Heir-Apparent and Vice-President of the Board of War, publishes this most urgent dispatch. Be it known that a criminal official named Mo Huai-ku has abandoned his post and escaped with the State Seal. All the officials of the various prefectures and districts are hereby commanded to arrest him." (*Ch'i snatches it from him at this point*). Why don't you let me finish reading it ?

CH'I. I fear it will only increase your alarm.

MO CH'ÊNG. It is better to know the contents, and be fully prepared, Sir.

MO. Yes, it is best to be prepared. (*Ch'i hands him the document, and Mo continues to read it*) "After capture his head is to be severed from his body and sent to the Capital." (*Swoons away ; the others set about reviving him. Mo comes to and sings*) This dispatch has given me a terrible shock. I kneel to my worthy brother Chi-kuang to save my wretched life.

CH'I. The only way out is for us all to escape together.

MO. Yes, let us.

MO CH'ÊNG. Plausible, Sirs, but hardly feasible ! For my master to escape when he is about to be beheaded would be sensible enough, but it would be sheer madness for His Honour Ch'i to abandon his post and escape as well. Your Honour must not do it !

CH'I. Well, if we do not all escape together, why not muster men and horses, and rebel ?

MO CH'ÊNG. But that is out of the question.

CH'I. Why ?

MO CH'ÊNG. I ask you, Sir, how many men and horses have you in this city of Chi-chou ?

CH'I. I have a bodyguard of three hundred, besides five hundred troops to defend the city.

MO CH'ÊNG. What ? Only eight hundred to raise a rebellion ! What is the point of proposing to fight when you haven't enough horses to escape on ?   The thing's impossible !

CH'I (*sings*). Well, since you refuse to consider either plan, just wait here till daybreak and lose your head !   (*Mo Huai-ku and Hsüeh Yen break down*).

MO CH'ÊNG. Your Excellency, Your Honour, my Lady ! (*Sings*) I feel as if I were in a drunken stupor, seeing the whole family weeping bitter tears.   (*To Hsüeh Yen*) Weeping so much will only harm you, my Lady !   His Excellency Ch'i can do nothing to save my Lord.   (*Breaks down*) Oh Master !   Your servant's life is shattered. (*Speaks*) I am suddenly reminded of an incident when we first came to the Capital.   Her Ladyship [Fu Shih] poured me out a cup of wine and said : " Mo Ch'êng, since you have accompanied us to the Capital, I want you to take good care of Master ; you will earn the lasting gratitude of a mother and her son."   One day when I was out with His Honour, we passed the Hata Gate and had our fortunes told.   " You and your master look very much alike," said the fortune-teller.   " The pity of it is that you will never attain high rank and honours like him. But if ever he gets involved in serious trouble, it is you who will have to bear the brunt."   He added this almost inadvertently but I could never get it out of my mind. Hasn't his prediction come to pass to-day ?   Now that my master has met with this calamity, I must think of a plan to save him.   Alas, I am only a wretched slave without any future before me.   Since I resemble him in form and feature, why shouldn't I die for him ?   At least I'll leave a noble character behind me.   That is what I'll do ; yes, that is my resolve. (*Advances to Ch'i and kneels before him ; sings*) I come to tell you on my knees that my master has found an unlooked-for deliverer.

CH'I. What do you mean ?

MO CH'ÊNG. I am willing to die for my master.

MO. I am deeply touched and grateful for your words.

MO CH'ÊNG. But you did not ask me to die for you, Sir! I remember the tale of a Mr. Yang, who went off with his dog on an excursion into the hills and fell asleep on a hill-slope after drinking a drop too much. A foolish boy set fire to some grass below the slope and soon there was a mighty blaze. When the flames crept closer to Mr. Yang, his dog ran to a stream and wetting its coat rolled over and over his master until he woke up, and so his life was saved. There are horses that will not leave their master if he falls; a lamb has the grace to kneel while sucking; the crow disgorges its food to nourish its kin. Why should I differ from the birds and beasts of the field? If you will not allow me to die for you, Master, I shall kill myself here and now.

CH'I. You need not be so precipitate. Let master and servant exchange their raiment. (*They proceed to do so*).

MO CH'ÊNG (*sings*). I am to be executed in the yamen of Chi-chou instead of my master. Soon I shall join the spirits of the nether world. Towards Ch'ien-t'ang I gaze, and towards my son Wên-lu. Oh Son, I have left many words unspoken which I would fain speak to you before I die.

MO. Perhaps you now repent of your decision.

MO CH'ÊNG. Things having come to such a pass, why should I repent? I was only thinking of my little son. I hope Your Honour will treat him well for my sake.

MO. I'll treat him just like a son of my own. If I am not as good as my word, may heaven and earth combine to destroy me!

MO CH'ÊNG. Thank you, Sir. (*Sings*) Now that my lord has assured me that he will safeguard my son, I take the " Double Handful of Snow " from my bosom and entrust it to him.*

---

*Apparently he had taken it with him a second time on his flight, though there is no mention of the fact.

MO. The very sight of that cup enrages me. I have a good mind to throw it on the floor and dash it to pieces !

Mo is about to do so but Ch'i and Hsüeh Yen prevent him. The fourth watch of night—2 a.m.—is struck.

MO CH'ÊNG (*sings*). Now that my heart's desire is fulfilled I hear the drum in the tower sounding the fourth watch. (*Speaks*) Alas, my Master, the day will soon be breaking. Are two Mo's to suffer sentence in Chi-chou yamen ?

CH'I. Mo, my dear friend, you had better seize your chance to escape before dawn, for what will happen if you are seen, and word of your flight is passed from mouth to mouth ?

MO. I cannot think of a safe place to go to.

CH'I. I have an excellent friend at Chi-nan. I can give you a letter to him, and he will provide you with a safe retreat.

MO. Oh worthy brother, thanks.

MO CH'ÊNG. Make haste, Your Excellency, and write the letter now. Master, you had better dress yourself up as a scholar. (*He changes into a hsiu-ts'ai's black gown and cap. Ch'i hands the letter to Mo*).

MO. I entrust Hsüeh Yen to your care, my worthy brother. You may either give her in marriage or sell her at your own discretion.

MO CH'ÊNG. What about me, Sir ?

MO (*to Ch'i*). The fifth watch is near. After the execution, lay Mo Ch'êng's corpse in a decent coffin and bury him outside the eastern gate of Chi-chou at Liu-lin, erecting a headstone with this epitaph : "Tomb of Mr. Mo, Chief Minister of the Board of Sacrificial Worship." I desire that in years to come my sons and grandsons will all burn incense at the grave.

MO CH'ÊNG. Thank you, Sir.

MO (*to servant*). Fetch me a horse !

MO CH'ÊNG. After your escape, my Lord, be chary of wine and don't imbibe too much. In all your acts be cautious. Friends you will need, no doubt, but don't go befriending such treacherous curs as T'ang Ch'in. I fear you will never find another Mo Ch'êng to die for you again.

MO. Your counsel comes too late.

MO CH'ÊNG. Be that as it may, you had better mount your horse and gallop hence. (*Mo breaks down again*).

CH'I (*to servant*). The hour of execution is at hand. What is all this argument about? You have too much discourse. My duty as an official compels me to be hasty.

MO CH'ÊNG. I am all obedience, Sir. I crave that Your Honour will dispatch me quickly.

CH'I. Of course.

MO CH'ÊNG. Thank you, Sir. (*Exit Ch'i*). Father and son are yearning for each other, but never again shall we meet face to face. (*Weeps*) My son, oh my son! (*Exit*).

At daylight his head is cut off and packed in a wooden trunk. Yen Shih-fan's runners take it to the Capital. T'ang Ch'in, determined to get hold of Hsüeh Yen, tells Yen Shih-fan that the head is false and suggests that Ch'i Chi-kuang be brought to the Capital and arraigned for fraud before the Judge Lu Ping, Guardian of the City; Hsüeh Yen too.

ACT II. SCENE I.—SHÊN T'OU; TZ'Ŭ T'ANG

INVESTIGATION OF A HEAD; AND THE MURDER OF T'ANG CH'IN

Enter the Judge Lu Ping.

LU (*speaks*). I have received many Imperial favours, and a thousand pecks of grain is an emolument to be proud of. (*Recites four lines of verse*)

From childhood I was steeped in lore of classics new
and old;

I dwell in peace : the purple robe and belt of jade
     I hold.
But the Son of Heaven honours most his minister
     named Yen,*
Who's fawned upon by all who wield the sword and
     wield the pen.

I, Lu Ping, serve under His Imperial Majesty Chia Ching as Chief of the Imperial Bodyguard. Having offended the powerful House of Yen, my colleague and contemporary Mo absconded in terror from his post. The Yens caused him to be arrested and beheaded at Chi-chou and his head was sent to the Capital. To determine whether this be true or false, the case has been referred to me for investigation. (*Servant announces T'ang Ch'in*). Invite him to enter.

T'ANG (*on entering, speaks*). I have come in haste to witness the investigation of Mo's head. (*To Judge*) Your Excellency is above : I make my humble bow. (*Lu returns salutation and bids him be seated*).

LU. I suppose you have orders from the Yen palace to attend this trial and see if I make any blunders.

T'ANG. Fie, Your Excellency !

LU. Then why are you so excited ?

T'ANG. Why should Your Excellency assume that I have only come to pick faults ? I merely came to witness the proceedings.

LU. Let us examine the head together. Perhaps you will be able to offer me some advice.

T'ANG. How dare I presume, Sir ?

LU (*to runners*). Let the prisoners be summoned. (*Enter Ch'i and Hsüeh Yen. After their names are registered they retire. Lu to Court runners*) Ask Yen's runners to come in. (*They enter. Lu addresses them*) Where did you capture Mo Huai-ku ?

---

* Yen Sung, the father of Yen Shih-fan.

SERGEANTS. At Liu-lin, Your Excellency, outside the western gate of Chi-chou.

LU At what time ?

SERGEANTS. At dusk. The matter being urgent and the gates of the city closed, we beat the yamen drum. When His Excellency appeared we delivered our dispatch. His Excellency said : " This is an affair of the utmost importance : responsibility rests all round."

LU. What did he mean by that ?

SERGEANTS. His Excellency proceeded to say : " I'll post two sentries between the outer and inner gates of the yamen. They are to see the prisoner beheaded at daylight, whereupon the head is to be placed in a wooden trunk and sent to the Yen palace under escort."

LU. You two may leave the Court for the time being. (*Both retire. To Court runners*) Let Ch'i Chi-kuang be admitted. (*Enter Ch'i*).

CH'I. Your Excellency is above me !

LU (*to T'ang Ch'in*). Mr. T'ang, since Ch'i Chi-kuang holds a high military post, let us assume that he is not immediately concerned in this investigation. For the sake of appearances, therefore, we may offer him a seat.

T'ANG. As ·you please, Your Honour.

LU (*to Ch'i*). His Honour T'ang approves that you be granted a seat. I hope you will remember this in days to come.

CH'I. Thank you, Mr. T'ang.

Judge Lu questions Ch'i about Mo's capture, etc. After which he is asked to retire.

LU (*to T'ang*). Is this head genuine ?

T'ANG. What makes Your Honour fancy that it is ?

LU. The evidence of three distinct witnesses.

T'ANG. False evidence, Your Honour ! They have concocted it to deceive you.

LU. Then I shall have to resort to other means of clearing this up.

T'ANG. What means, Your Honour?

LU. Recently ten heads or so have been cut off, and they have just reached the Capital. I'll have them all brought here and ranged on the Court steps, with Mo's head mixed among them. Then I shall call upon Hsüeh Yen to identify it. If she succeeds, it must belong to Mo Huai-ku.

T'ANG. Your Honour's skill is most remarkable!

Lu orders runners to fetch the heads and arrange them accordingly. Hsüeh Yen is summoned, and salutes the Judge.

LU. Hsüeh Yen, your husband's head is now lying on the steps of this Court. Find it and bring it to me for inspection. (*Hsüeh Yen selects Mo Ch'êng's head and advances with it, weeping*). Put the head down and leave the Court. (*Exit Hsüeh Yen. Lu to T'ang*) I am convinced this head is genuine.

T'ANG. What makes Your Honour feel so sure?

LU. There was an abundance of heads to choose from; she went and chose her husband's without a moment's hesitation and burst into floods of tears. How can you dispute the fact that it is her husband's head?

T'ANG. Hsüeh Yen is like a cat weeping over a rat! She was merely simulating grief.

LU. See the two rows of yamen runners! All have tears in their eyes.

T'ANG. Pooh! theatrical tears—"Bearing the burdens of the ancients!"

LU. Well, Mr. T'ang, why don't you cry too?

T'ANG. Why should I? He was no relation of mine.

LU. How did Mo treat you?

T'ANG. Not so badly.

LU. If he treated you well, why do you persist in saying that the head is not his? (*Sings*) He that doth not reciprocate kindness is no gentleman. He returneth bitter resentment for good.

T'ANG. I'll be going.

LU. Whither?

T'ANG. I must return to the Yen palace.

LU. Bearing what message?

T'ANG. I shall have to say that Your Honour is bungling this case.

LU. Are the Yens wolves and tigers? Are you insinuating that they will devour me?

T'ANG. They may not be wolves and tigers, but at least two-thirds of the officials quake at the sound of their name.

LU. I still have other means of clearing up this case.

T'ANG. What is your next alternative?

LU. I can put Ch'i Chi-kuang to torture and extort a confession as to the head's identity. (*Enter yamen runners with an Imperial mandate. Lu kneeling opens it and reads*) " By Imperial command Lu Ping is to proceed at once to the execution-ground and superintend the beheading of thirteen criminals. He will subsequently report to the Throne. Respect this Mandate! " (*Turning to T'ang*) I have been instructed by Imperial mandate to superintend an execution. Hsüeh Yen will be confined in the western passageway; I enjoin you to examine her in secret.

T'ANG. Your Honour's orders will be obeyed.

LU (*to Ch'i*). You may follow my chair to the execution-ground to witness the beheading.

Exeunt Lu and Ch'i.

T'ANG. I'll go to Hsüeh Yen's cell.

Finding two soldiers on guard there he hands them a lump of silver and tells them to go and have a drink. Hsüeh Yen overhearing this smells a rat and prepares to fool him during the interview.

T'ANG. Well, well, my dear, at last we are able to meet alone!

HSÜEH YEN (*speaks*). You have been in my thoughts ever since we first met, Sir.

T'ANG. Why did you not tell me so before? It would have saved us a lot of trouble.

HSÜEH YEN. Mr. T'ang, since the head has been proven genuine, why do you persist in saying it is false?

T'ANG. If you submit to me in an affair of the heart, I shall submit to you and say that the head is real.

HSÜEH YEN. I shall yield to you in everything.

T'ANG (*laughing*). Ah, at last you are mine, my own little beauty! (*Is about to catch hold of her hand when Judge Lu Ping appears*).

LU. Your Honour T'ang!

T'ANG. Your Excellency has returned!

LU. Have you completed your private inquiry?

T'ANG. I have, Sir; and find that the head is genuine after all.

LU. Your words make plain that you have a conscience.

T'ANG. My conscience is clear, Sir.

LU (*to runners*). Call for the Yen retainers. (*On their appearance he tells them that they are dismissed, and that the head has been properly identified. Exeunt runners. Lu to T'ang*) What about Ch'i Chi-kuang?

T'ANG. Let him return to his post.

LU. As for Hsüeh Yen, since she has neither parents nor home, I had better keep her in my yamen.

T'ANG. But that won't do, Sir. Oh no! That would never do!

LU. What about keeping her in your yamen?

T'ANG (*hypocritically*). Oh, that wouldn't do either, Sir!

LU. Well, Mr. T'ang, you may take Hsüeh Yen as a concubine.

T'ANG (*falling on his knees, kotows and says*). Good, good, Your Excellency. Thank you kindly, Sir. You are like a second father to me!

Hsüeh Yen is released from her bonds and kneels to thank Lu for his clemency. Exeunt T'ang and Hsüeh.

LU (*to runners*). Bring Hsüeh Yen into Court again.

HSÜEH YEN (*on entering*). How has Your Honour settled this case?

LU. I have decided to consign you to T'ang Ch'in.

HSÜEH YEN. But my husband has not been revenged. What shall I do?

LU. I'll show you what to do. (*Writes on his fan the character* 刺 *which means to "kill" but which has the same sound and tone as* 伺 *to "wait upon"*).

HSÜEH YEN. I understand.

LU. I'll be sending you over shortly. In the meantime you may leave this Court.

HSÜEH YEN (*sings*). His Honour's scholarship is of the highest. He told me to conceal a knife and murder T'ang Ch'in. (*Exit Hsüeh. Enter Ch'i Chi-kuang*).

CH'I. Has Your Excellency settled my fate?

LU. You have been acquitted. You may return to your post.

CH'I. What is to become of Hsüeh Yen?

LU. I gave her to T'ang Ch'in.

CH'I. Who ever heard of giving a master's concubine to a servant?

LU. It is a ruse. (*Sings*) Hsüeh Yen may be compared to Sable Cicada, the singing girl,* while T'ang Ch'in may be likened to Tung Cho. I have laid that snare which Wang Yün called the chain-plan—a trap to kill a traitor.

CH'I (*sings*). My brother's great ability inspires me with the deepest respect : he has clearly distinguished the true head from the false one. Though I may still enjoy the fruits of office, I am distressed by the thought of Mo Ch'êng mouldering in his grave. I leave the Court and bid you farewell. Within three days I expect to hear significant news (*i.e., of T'ang Ch'in's death*).

---

* See *Tiao Ch'an* p. 353.

LU. T'ang Ch'in is vainly wallowing in the Yellow Millet Dream.* This marriage will never be consummated. (*Exeunt Lu and Ch'i*).

SCENE II

First watch of night, 8-9 p.m., is struck. Enter Hsüeh Yen.

HSÜEH YEN (*sings*). The first watch has just boomed from the tower, and my mind is so agitated that I cannot even sit down. I wonder if my lord has been able to recover a life of peace ; what rank he will attain ; what post he will be appointed to. How I regret that we ever took that traitor T'ang Ch'in into our service : to rear a tiger in a cage is a dangerous game. And all this misery has befallen us on account of a small jade cup ! Even His Excellency Ch'i Chi-kuang has been involved. With resolute steps I advance to the bridal chamber. Duty compels me to take that traitor's life and dispatch him to the Nether Regions.

Enter T'ang Ch'in with a few retainers.

T'ANG CH'IN (*sings*).
Ere the bliss of a tryst a man's spirits are lightest :
The moon of mid-autumn of all moons is brightest !
(*To servant*) Go and knock at the door.
(*Servant obeys*).

HSÜEH YEN. Who is there ?

SERVANT. His Honour T'ang has come.

HSÜEH YEN. Wait till I open. (*Opens*).

T'ANG (*to servants*). You may go.

SERVANTS. Being such a joyful occasion, Your Honour should tip us some silver.

T'ANG. You may come and fetch it at the yamen to-morrow.

SERVANTS. Who can tell if you'll be there to-morrow !
Exeunt.

---

*See p. 83.

T'ANG (*to Hsüeh Yen*). Lady, I salute you.

HSÜEH YEN. Pray be seated, Your Honour.

Four of T'ang's friends arrive.

FRIENDS (*severally*). Mr T'ang is about to be married to-day. Let us each subscribe three ounces of silver for this happy occasion and invite him to join us at the festive board. (*To T'ang*) Congratulations, friend T'ang. We come to bid you to a feast.

T'ANG. What do you mean?

FRIENDS. This being the death-day* of your bachelor-hood we have each subscribed three ounces of silver to stand you a death-banquet.

T'ANG. I cannot drink wine. Thanks, gentlemen, all the same.

FRIENDS. Even so, you must swallow a glass or two for the sake of good fellowship.

T'ANG. I tell you I will drink no wine.

FRIENDS. If you insist, you're not a good fellow; you insult us. Do you know anything about Hsüeh Yen's career? Do you realize that she was a harlot? If you can visit harlots, so can we.

T'ANG. Enough! You needn't comport yourselves like this. I'll drink your wine.

FRIENDS. Fine! Pour it out. Each of us will drink his health in three capacious goblets. He'll have to keep us company, willynilly. (*They ply him with liquor until he is drunk*).

T'ANG. Alas, I've had enough. I can't swallow another drop. Thank you, gentlemen. I beg you to retire. (*He totters off to bed and lies down*).

---

* The comedians are allowed much licence here. The pun is on the word *ssŭ* (death) which they pronounce for *hsi* (joy). It could be rendered more adequately in 17th century language: "dying" then had a more voluptuous sense: viz., Dryden's song from *Marriage à la Mode*:

Thus entranced they did lie
Till Alexis did try
To recover more breath that again he might die:
Then often they died; but the more they did so,
The nymph died more quick and the shepherd more slow.

ONE OF THE FRIENDS (*aloud*). Hsüeh Yen, His Honour T'ang is drunk as a lord. Whether you take your revenge is now up to you! (*Exeunt friends*).

HSÜEH YEN (*approaching T'ang's couch*). Are you asleep, Mr. T'ang?

T'ANG. I'm just taking a nap. (*Covers himself with a quilt and dozes off again*).

HSÜEH YEN. The traitor seems fast asleep. If I don't take my revenge now, when shall I have another chance? (*She draws a dagger and plunges it into the sleeper, singing*) I curse the traitor with all my soul: he brought great tribulation on our house. My blade has ended his earthly existence. The breath has left his body in a twinkling. (*Speaks*) Now that my husband is avenged I had better flee. But the hour is late and I am drenched in blood. Oh, whither can I flee? Alas! I shall return thanks to my lord by killing myself. (*Stabs herself to death. The four friends return*).

FRIENDS (*severally*). Let us call on our friends Hsüeh Yen and T'ang and see what sweet sport they are up to. (*They enter and find two corpses on the floor*). Hsüeh Yen must have killed T'ang Ch'in and then killed herself. We had better go off and report. (*Exeunt*).

Finis

HSÜEH PEI YÜAN 雪 盃 緣

AFFINITY OF THE SNOW CUP

(Sequel to *I P'êng Hsüeh*)

DRAMATIS PERSONÆ

Mo Huai-ku, Official in disgrace ... ...
Ch'i Chi-kuang, Commander of the Chi-chou garrison ... ... } *Lao-shêng*
Lu Ping, Judge ... ...
Wên-hao, son of Mo Huai-ku ... ... *Hsiao-shêng*
Wên-lu, son of Mo Ch'êng ... ... *Wa-wa-shêng*
Fu Shih, wife of Mo Huai-ku ... ... *Lao-tan*
Retainers, Soldiers, etc.

ACT I. SCENE I

MO HUAI-KU (*entering, sings*). Formerly I held an official post in the Capital . . . . . . How I abhor that traitor [T'ang Ch'in]! He has no conscience whatever! Mo Ch'êng sacrificed his life for my sake. Whenever I think of that loyal servant the tears stream down my face. (*Speaks*) I, Mo Huai-ku, am a native of Ch'ien-t'ang. When first I entered the Capital to seek official employment, I had the good fortune, through influence with the Yens, to obtain the post of Chief of the Board of Sacrificial Worship. But that foul T'ang Ch'in made trouble about the Jade Cup, and inflamed the Yens against me. I was forced to abandon my post and escape. The Yens sent petty officers in pursuit who captured me and took me to Chi-chou. Providentially, my old retainer Mo Ch'êng came forward and gave up his life for me. I made my way to Shantung where I lived in hiding. Yesterday I received a letter from my worthy friend Ch'i Chi-kuang, stating that the Emperor had been gracious enough to pardon me. Ch'i advised me to return without delay. Now within sight of Chi-chou, I urge on my horse full tilt. (*Sings*) Even a day's absence from kith and kin seems an eternity. I am like the lone wild goose asleep in a chilly forest. I can think of nought but my hatred of the vile T'ang Ch'in who caused my family to be broken up and dispersed. I grieve that poor Mo Ch'êng should have perished in my stead. At Chi-chou I'll inquire about his execution. Already my brother Ch'i has sent me a letter. Far in the distance I spy the city of Chi-chou. (*Exit*).

Scene II

FU SHIH (*enters and says*). I am lodging in an inn, far from my hearth and home. The year my lord went to seek an official post at the Capital ended in his cruel death at the hands of traitors. He is now in the Yellow Springs.* I fled to Manchuria and have now come back to Chi-chou. (*Speaks*) I am Fu Shih.† My husband was Chief of the Board of Sacrificial Worship. Suddenly disaster overtook him and he lost his life. He lies buried at Liu-lin outside the western gate of Chi-chou ; I am on my way thither with Mo Ch'êng's son Wên-lu to worship at his grave. The day is fine : I'll call Wên-lu to start upon our journey. (*Calls*).

WÊN-LU. Here I am, Mother. What is it ?

FU SHIH. Never mind ceremony ! As the weather is fine we'll pack our things and hurry on our way. (*Sings*) While we travel along, I think of all the trials I have endured since the year of our bereavement. My husband and our son were then so happy ! My lord was Chief of the Board of Sacrificial Worship, but he fell into trouble and lost his life. I was left all alone in the most deplorable plight. We have reached Liu-lin : I see a tombstone here. I had better examine it carefully. (*Speaks*) The epitaph runs : " The grave of Mr. Mo,

---

* The world beyond.
† "A woman of the Fu family."

Chief of the Board of Sacrificial Worship." (*Weeps*) Alas, alas, my husband! (*Sings*) Seeing his grave, I cannot check my tears. My lord, I charge you, hear the cause of our misfortune! As a Court official you nourished the highest hopes. Who could have foreseen that you would come to grief in the prime of life! After travelling thousands of miles, how pitiful that I should only find your grave! (*Weeps*) My lord, the heart within me feels as if it were pierced by ten thousand swords!

Enter Mo Huai-ku.

MO (*sings*). I flourish my whip to speed my horse: at last I reach Liu-lin. The wintry blast has chilled me to the bone. Dismounting I enter the Willow Grove to search for Mo Ch'êng's grave. (*Speaks*) Ah, there is a stone tablet: I'll read the inscription. (*Reads it*) Alas, my old retainer! Mo Chêng, my loyal servant! (*Sings*) I needs must weep to see this lonely grave. Ah, pitiful that you should die for me! Throughout the ages your fragrant name will stand as a symbol of loyalty.

Fu Shih draws nearer. Not having seen her husband for a decade and thinking him dead, she fails to recognize him.

FU SHIH (*speaks*). Who are you that come to mourn at my husband's grave?

MO. This grave belongs to my family. How can you say it is yours?

FU SHIH. I am quite sure that this is the grave of my husband, Mo Huai-ku. Why do you falsely claim it to be yours?

MO (*aside*). Stay! Her voice and features remind me of my wife. I'll go forward and address her. Are you not my wife, Fu Shih?

FU SHIH. Inasmuch as my name is Fu Shih you are right. But who are you?

MO. I am your husband, Mo Huai-ku.

FU SHIH (*hysterically*). Spirit, avaunt! Oh, drive this ghost away!

MO. Peace, dear wife! Don't alarm yourself. I am really Mo Huai-ku. I am alive; don't take me for a spirit.

FU SHIH. My husband was most noble in appearance. He also had three bony protuberances at the base of his brain. Have you such bumps as these?

MO. I have.

FU SHIH. Let me feel them. (*Does so*). My husband!

MO. My wife!   (*Both break down*).

FU SHIH. I weep tears of joy to see my mate again. My tongue can only repeat his name. I yearn to hear your news. Where is Hsüeh Yen?

MO. " The crow has occupied the phœnix nest." *

FU SHIH (*sings*). And Mo Ch'êng, where is he?

MO (*sings*). He has taken my place among the officials in the next world.

FU SHIH. Where do you intend to go now, my lord?

MO (*sings*). My worthy brother Ch'i has written inviting me to Chi-chou.

FU SHIH (*sings*). Then husband and wife may both proceed together.

MO (*sings a refrain to this effect, then indicating Wên-lu, speaks*). Who is this boy, wife?

FU SHIH. It is Wên-lu. Come here and greet your master.

WÊN-LU. Let me pay my respects, Your Honour!

MO. Never mind ceremony just now.

WÊN-LU. Where is my father, Sir?

MO. Your father? I came along first on horseback. He is following with the baggage.

WÊN-LU (*turning his head*). But I don't see him anywhere!

MO. Do you really wish to see your father, lad? He is in this grave. (*Wên-lu weeps;* " *tears in double streams,*" *etc ;—usual exclamations of grief*).

---

* i.e., T'ang Ch'in, of whose death he was ignorant, had appropriated his concubine.

FU SHIH. I would like to adopt Wên-lu as a son. What do you think of this idea, my lord ?

MO. Nothing could please me better. Ask the lad if he's willing.

Fu Shih proposes this to the child, who promptly accepts and kotows. The parents waive further ceremony for the present.

MO. My lady, can you see the city of Chi-chou, not far in the distance ? It is getting late. Let us proceed together.

FU SHIH. Yes, let us advance. Lead up the horse, my son.

Wên-lu does so. Mo mounts and leads the way ; the others follow.

ACT II. SCENE I

I CHIA T'UAN CHÜ : " The Family All United"

CH'I CHI-KUANG (*enters and prologizes*). Deeply versed in the art of war, I protect the Great Bright Dynasty [Ming], and wear the richly embroidered robes of high Imperial office. (*Recites*) For over ten years I have guarded the Capital : my awe-inspiring reputation reaches the very heavens and makes them tremble. All kinds of military tactics are locked within my breast ; 'tis I who command the brave garrisons of Chi-chou. (*Speaks*) I, Ch'i Chi-kuang, am Commander of the Eight Forts of Chi-chou. Mo Huai-ku and I have been close friends this many a long year, as if we were of the selfsame flesh and blood. T'ang Ch'in, devoid of all human decency, inflamed the powerful house of Yen against him and jeopardized his life. Fortunately his loyal retainer Mo Ch'êng immolated himself in his stead, so that Mo Huai-ku was able to flee to Shantung for safety. Since then more than a decade has elapsed. Only recently I sent him a letter inviting him hither. I wonder why he has not yet arrived !

Enter soldier announcing the arrival of Mo Huai-ku, Fu Shih and Wên-lu. Ch'i requests them to be admitted; the party arrives and after the usual ceremonies, Fu Shih and Wên-lu retire to the reception room, leaving Mo and Ch'i on the stage.

MO. I hope my worthy brother Ch'i is enjoying the best of health.

CH'I. You too, I hope. Pray take a seat. You must have had a hard time of it in all this wind and frost. Please forgive me for failing to meet and welcome you at some distance from the city.

MO. I am unworthy of such an honour. I owe you the deepest gratitude for saving my life. I have not yet expressed my heartfelt thanks. Let me do so now that we are face to face.

CH'I. How dare I accept such a compliment!

MO. May I inquire, Sir, what happened after the year of my escape? How was the matter settled eventually?

CH'I. Just after your flight, at daybreak, I ordered Mo Ch'êng's decapitation. His head was packed in a wooden trunk; Yen's runners took it to the Capital and delivered it to their master. T'ang Ch'in again made trouble during the subsequent investigation by declaring that the head was a fraud. This angered Yen Shih-fan, who caused me to be summoned to Peking, where I was given over to the constabulary. By a stroke of luck the case was tried by our colleague Lu Ping, who either knew or suspected that T'ang was desperately in love with the beautiful Hsüeh Yen and therefore wished to embroil me in the case. In order to acquit me Lu purposely muddled the investigation. But he did not show conspicuous ability in one respect.

MO. What was that?

CH'I. He gave Hsüeh Yen in marriage to T'ang Ch'in.

MO. Oh, there Lu Ping committed a monstrous error!

CH'I. We should not judge in haste. The facts were these: so long as T'ang Ch'in swore the head was false

the case could never be settled.   My own rank even was
endangered.   Thus it would not be quite fair to say that
Lu Ping betrayed incompetence by conferring Hsüeh
Yen on T'ang Ch'in.   Perhaps it was rather subtle !

MO. I don't follow your argument, Sir.

CH'I. T'ang Ch'in got drunk, and when he reeled
into the nuptial chamber, Hsüeh Yen stabbed him to
death, then slew herself.

MO (*in great alarm*). What do you mean ?

CH'I. She cut her throat and died.

MO (*breaks down*). Alas ! My poor dear wife !* (*Sings*)
Your words have given me a dreadful shock.   Griefs
wring my soul ; I cannot check my tears.   To the end
of my days I shall execrate T'ang Ch'in.   He was too
base, too vile !   He trampled the five human relation-
ships under foot.   He requited injury for kindness.
But his scheme against my life was wrecked by Mo
Ch'êng's sacrifice.   His allegation that the head was
false proves that he wished to possess Hsüeh Yen.   Lu
countered his plot by sanctioning a marriage ; and
T'ang was put to death in the chamber that was to serve
for his nuptials.   Hsüeh Yen was a woman of consummate loyalty and virtue.   How sad that she should
lose her life on my account !   Divine principles revolve
in a circle, and bring their just reward.   The good shall
be distinguished from the wicked.   I mourn my beloved
wife who soared to Heaven.   Hsüeh Yeh, your name
will shine throughout the ages !

CH'I (*sings*). I beg you not to weep so bitterly.
Worthy brother, listen to my words !   Hsüeh Yen has
killed the traitor.   Vengeance is wrought, and all are
gratified.   Mo Ch'êng was a true son of Han, a staunch
and loyal servant ; Hsüeh Yen a chaste and noble
heroine.

---

*Although Hsüeh Yen was a concubine, Mo had treated her as a *p'ing-ch'i*—
equal to a wife.

Soldiers come in and report that H.H. the Provincial Judge has arrived.

CH'I. Wait, brother Mo, while I go out to meet him.

MO. What is the best manner for me to receive him, I wonder.

CH'I. Just stand a while at the soldiers' rear : I don't suppose you have any objection to that ?

MO. Yes, that would be best.

CH'I (*to soldiers*). Form ranks and advance to welcome His Honour.

Exeunt soldiers. Wên-hao, Mo's son, arrives with a large retinue.

WÊN-HAO (*sings in hsi-p'i tao-pan*). I have received an Imperial Mandate to leave the Capital. (*Changes to hsi-p'i yüan-pan*) How can the nation and people subsist unless there be peace in the land ? I am out to seize all traitors and destroy them root and branch : no mercy will be shown to corrupt officials and their evil syco-phants. I nourish a deep, perpetual hatred of my father's murderer. I am determined to avenge him. Galloping switch and spur, we reach our destination. (*Four bodyguards, followed by runners, enter the city. Ch'i Chi-kuang receives them at the city gate*).

CH'I (*kneels*). Ch'i Chi-kuang, the commander of Chi-chou, welcomes Your Honour.

WÊN-HAO. Go first to the yamen, await me there, and I shall come directly.

All proceed to the judge's yamen : Wên-hao takes the central seat of honour.

CH'I. Respectful greetings to Your Honour !

WÊN-HAO. You may retire to divest yourself of your armour ; and then return to confer with me.

Exit Ch'i, and returns in official garb, blue robe and black gauze headgear, carrying archives of office.

CH'I (*speaks*). I submit the records of my office to your inspection.

wên-hao. First I desire to know about the state of your finances.

ch'i. My treasury is full: there is no deficiency.

wên-hao. What about your officers and men: are they fit?

ch'i. The officers have been fully trained in military tactics, and the troops are both well drilled and able-bodied.

wên-hao. And are the weapons kept in good condition?

ch'i. Spears and swords never flashed more brilliantly; helmets and coats of mail are spick and span.

wên-hao. What about the thoroughfares?

ch'i. All the roads within and without the city are in perfect repair.

wên-hao (*soliloquizing*). Ai ya! Here am I trying to pick faults instead of inquiring into my father's murder and avenging it. What shall I do? This man is certainly upright as an official and controls his affairs with caution.* (*Wên-hao is suddenly overcome with a headache and vomits blood*).

ch'i (*to major-domo*). His Honour has had a fit of vomiting. What can be the matter with him?

major-domo. Perhaps he caught cold on the journey.

ch'i. I'll give him a cup of warm tea: that may help to restore him.

major-domo. Yes, the sooner he drinks it the better.

Ch'i pours the tea into the " Double Handful of Snow," which the steward offers to Wên-hao.

wên-hao (*sings in hsi-p'i tao-pan*) Ah! I had a sudden headache and fainting spell. (*Examines the cup in dismay, and after significant exclamations, changes song to hsi-p'i yao-pan*) This jade cup greatly resembles our family heirloom.

---

* Wên-hao having heard that his father was killed by Ch'i, and not knowing that the servant had been killed in his stead came bent upon revenge.

(*To soldiers*)   Here! Seize General Ch'i Chi-kuang and bind him fast.   (*They do so*).

CH'I. Your Honour! Why are you having me bound?

WÊN-HAO. How did this cup, our family heirloom, come into your possession?   Answer me quickly!

CH'I. The jade cup, Your Honour?   There is one here, but it is not mine.

WÊN-HAO. Whose is it then?

CH'I. It belongs to Mo Huai-ku of Ch'ien-t'ang.

WÊN-HAO. Is he still alive?

CH'I. Assuredly!

WÊN-HAO. Where is he now?

CH'I. Inside my yamen.

WÊN-HAO. Please ask him to come here at once.

CH'I. How can I, Your Honour, when you tie me up like this?

WÊN-HAO (*to major-domo*). Unbind him.

CH'I (*released, sings out*). Brother Mo, make haste and come in here!

MO. You called while I was sipping wine.   Will you not join me over a cup?

CH'I. Leave that till later on; come quickly.   His Honour has sent me for you.

MO. What can he wish to see me about?

CH'I. An unforeseen circumstance, dear Sir!   Just now His Honour was ailing and I happened to use that heirloom of yours, the cup of jade, in offering him some tea.   As soon as he set eyes on it he demanded how it came into my possession; and when he heard that you were here, he requested your immediate presence.

Mo advances and takes a lower seat before the Judge without uttering a word.

WÊN-HAO. Is this gentleman Mo Huai-ku?

CH'I. Yes, Your Honour.

wên-hao. Ah me! My Father! Father! (*Leaves the Bench and kneels before him*).

mo. Who are you, Sir?

wên-hao. I am your son, Wên-hao.

mo. What? You are my son, Wên-hao?

wên-hao. Yes, Father! (*Both burst into tears*).

ch'i. So His Honour the Judge turns out to be my nephew! (*Laughs*) Ha, ha! The first occasion we meet you tie me up!

mo. Having offended your worthy uncle Ch'i, you ought to apologize.

wên-hao. Not knowing that he was my uncle, I did not wilfully offend. I beg your pardon, Sir.

ch'i. That's quite unnecessary since you did not know me.

wên-hao. Be seated, Sir.

mo. How did you come to get this high appointment, my son? *

wên-hao. Father, hear my petition!

Here what is called " Chi-san-ch'iang p'ai-tzŭ" takes place, a purposeful pandemonium of gongs and drums, to drown the speaker's voice and spare the audience a long and tedious narrative.

mo. My son, since you are now the Judge of Circuit for Eight Prefectures, you should memorialize the Throne, impeaching both Yen Sung and his son Yen Shih-fan.

wên-hao. Before leaving the Capital, a fellow-graduate and I sent in a memorial, as well as a lengthy statement of all the wrongs you suffered. I have not yet received the Imperial decree as to the result.

ch'i. I have prepared a banquet, and invite both father and son to enjoy some wine.

---

* This is the weakest and most improbable part of the plot, since Yen Shih-fan would be bound to detect his origin and visit his vengeance on any scion of Mo Huai-ku's.

MO. I thank you in advance, but I am anxious for my son to come along with me to the inner hall to meet his mother and Wên-lu.

WÊN-HAO. I'll obey your orders, Sir.

MO. The Yens were far too arrogant and overbearing.

CH'I. But blood relations are difficult to sever.

WÊN-HAO. This is a day of glad reunion.

CH'I. Reunion in Chi-chou !

Exeunt, laughing happily.

SCENE II

Enter Lu Ping, accompanied by four lung-t'ao, four petty officers or clerks and two retainers.

LU PING. I am to convey the Imperial Mandate to Chi-chou. (*Repeats*) I, Lu Ping, am the instrument of the Imperial Will to confer promotions and high honours on the house of Mo.   (*Exeunt*).

SCENE III

Enter Mo Huai-ku, Wên-hao and Ch'i Chi-kuang saying in syncopation : Flesh and bones have come together again after long separation. (*Enter servant to report that an Imperial Edict has arrived. Mo, Wên-hao and Ch'i exclaim in unison*) Prepare the altar to receive the Edict. (*Enter Lu Ping with the Edict in his hands*).

LU PING (*speaks*). Kneel before the Imperial Will ! *All kneel and repeat,* "Wan Sui, Wan Sui, Wan Wan Sui ! " [*Ten thousand years ! May His Majesty live for ever !*] Attention while I read the Imperial Edict ! Mo Wên-hao, who recently passed his examination for Chuang Yüan,* whose acts of filial piety are deserving of the highest praise, supported by all his fellow-graduates of the same year, has submitted a detailed memorial stating the total sum of wrongs and indignities put upon his father. Mo Huai-ku shall therefore be restored to his former rank

---

* i.e., took first place in the triennial Palace Examination.

and ennobled as Grand Preceptor and Sustainer of the Aged. Fu Shih is worthy of high merit for having trained her son in such an estimable manner, wherefore she shall be elevated as a Lady of the First Rank. Hsüeh Yen, who died upon revenging her husband, is worthy of approbation, and shall be canonized with the post-humous title of Lady Chaste and Loyal. Wên-lu, for supporting his mother beyond the frontiers, is also deserving of merit, and shall be appointed Director of the Imperial Banqueting Court. Ch'i Chi-kuang shall be promoted three grades in rank. Yen Sung and his son [Shih-fan] for obstructing State affairs, deceiving their Sovereign and committing grave and cruel outrages upon loyal officials, have roused our mighty anger. All officials impeached by them shall instantly be reinstated in their original ranks and posts. Yen Sung and his son shall be stripped of all official rank and abased to a footing with commoners ; they shall be driven from their palaces. Yen Sung shall be presented with a silver alms-bowl, with which to go from street to street a-begging. Merchants and others are forbidden to supply him with food. Whosoever offends against this command shall be severely punished. All are to kneel and knock their heads before the Imperial Mandate. Respect to this !

Mo, Wên-hao and Ch'i kneel down accordingly, shouting "Wan Sui," *etc. This done, Mo and Ch'i invite Lu Ping to be seated and ask if he had had a hard time travelling through wind and snow.*

LU. It is but meet that I should exert myself for the State weal. Brother Mo, now that you and your family have been reunited and have all received patents of nobility, let me offer you my congratulations !

MO. All due to your assistance, Sir.

LU. Pray come nearer, brother Ch'i ; I have a favour to beg of you.

CH'I. What are your commands, Sir ?

LU. I have an unmarried daughter, and would like you to act as go-between in arranging a marriage between her and Mo Wên-hao. Could you oblige me in this respect?

CH'I. Most gladly! I guarantee it will be settled as soon as the word is spoken.

LU. In that case, let it be spoken without delay.

CH'I. A word with you, brother Mo. (*Mo approaches*). Judge Lu has just told me that he has a daughter he would like to marry to Wên-hao. What are your views on the subject?

MO. Deeply grateful as I am for brother Lu's kindness, how dare I disdain such an offer? (*Calls Wên-hao*) Go over and greet your father-in-law.

WÊN-HAO (*kotows to Lu, saying*). Your Excellency my father-in-law is above: your son-in-law wishes to make obeisance to you.

LU. That's not necessary.

CH'I. Brother Lu, please come a little nearer. I have a request to make.

LU. Concerning what?

CH'I. I too have a little daughter who has not yet been betrothed. I should like to arrange a match between her and Wên-lu, and beg you to act as go-between.

LU. If the responsibility rests with me, a word will suffice. Come nearer, brother Mo! Brother Ch'i has just informed me that he has a daughter he would like to give Wên-lu in marriage. I don't suppose you have any objections, Sir?

MO. I fear such a match would be most irregular, Sir.

LU. How so?

MO. Because Wên-lu is the son of my old retainer: there is the respective status of master and servant to be considered. How could I give my consent?

LU. Surely there is a way of adjusting this matter.

MO. No, Sir, there is nothing to be done about it.

LU (*to Ch'i*). I regret that this affair cannot be arranged as you desire.

CH'I. Why not ?

LU. Brother Mo says that there is an impediment of social status. Wên-lu being the son of a servant, he cannot give his consent.

CH'I. Let me discuss it with him. (*Approaches Mo Huai-ku*) Do you remember the time when your servant Mo Ch'êng sacrificed his life for you ? You assured him that whatever happened you would treat his son Wên-lu as if he were a son of your own : if you failed to fulfil this pledge, you called upon Heaven and Earth to destroy you. Your family is now united ; you have been promoted and ennobled besides. You should not treat Wên-lu as a servant, but as if he were your own son. I can see that you are a man who has forgotten favours and turned on his benefactor—a man who is blind to all sense of justice !

MO. Oh ! (*Sings in êrh-huang yao-pan*) Your words amaze me ! Am I to prove ungrateful for past kindness ? His son is then my son : how dare I make any distinction between them ? I only fear that the daughter of a Brigade-Commander may deem herself of too exalted a station to marry a servant's offspring. I kneel in haste to express my accord, and cement our relationship in marriage. (*To Wên-lu*) Go forward and salute your father-in-law.

WÊN-LU (*to Ch'i*). Pray be seated to receive your son-in-law's obeisance.

CH'I. That is not necessary.

LU. After choosing an auspicious hour and day for the happy event, I'll send the little girl to the Ancestral Hall for the nuptial ceremony. What do you say to this, Sir ?

MO. I'll leave the arrangements to you, Sir.

CH'I (*to servants*).   See that the banquet is spread in
the hall at the rear.   We'll all drink wine together.

LU AND MO. Thank you.   (*Exeunt*).

Finis

*   *   *

There is more dialogue and less song in this popular trilogy
than in most Chinese dramas, and it is noteworthy that the dialogue
is almost as conventional as the gestures.

The plot offered opportunities for witty characterization,
(T'ang Ch'in's Mosca versus Yen Shih-fan's Volpone), even for a
lively comedy of errors (Mo Huai-ku and his domestic double ;
the jade cup and its replica ;   the investigation of the head) ;   it is
interesting to imagine how the situations might have been exploited
by one of our Jacobean dramatists, and with what relish a Webster
might have written the Court scene and the subsequent murder of
T'ang Ch'in.   But that neither novelty nor surprise are required
of the Chinese dramatist is clearly demonstrated by *I P'êng Hsüeh ;*
every situation is treated according to formula ;   the phrasing is as
stylized as the diction.   The symmetry of the plot is emphasized ;
the reunion scene reminds us of the courtyard matting, earthenware
fish-jar and pomegranate-tree in the Peking proverb ;   and the
marriage engagements of Wên-hao and Wên-lu are balanced like
a pair of complementary scrolls.   We are also reminded of reunions
in *Ch'i Shuang Hui, Chu Sha Chih* and a dozen other plays ;   whether
the paterfamilias be Li Ch'i or Mo Huai-ku, the sentiments expressed
are almost identical.   Yet *I P'êng Hsüeh* makes a great impression
on the stage—Yen Shih-fan ransacking Mo's household for the
coveted heirloom ;   the servant offering to impersonate his master ;
the virtuous concubine's revenge and suicide :   these are all famous
and thrilling scenes which tempt the ambition of first-rate actors
and never fail to move a Chinese audience.

Just as the old retainer Ma I is the hero of *Chiu Kêng T'ien*, Mo
Ch'êng is the hero of *I P'êng Hsüeh ;*   whenever there is a crisis it
is the servant who comes to the fore ;   his intelligence and resource-
fulness are such that one is apt to lose patience with his flabby,
indiscreet and distrustful master.   Indeed such a dummy as Mo Huai-
ku seems hardly worth the sacrifice.   And when the dummy breaks
out in objections to Wên-lu's marriage, we feel that this is the last
straw.   For one bewildering moment we wonder if this sudden spurt
of conservatism will break the symmetry.   Is poor Wên-lu to be
turned out of the Temple of Hymen ?   But we are soon left smiling
over the dramatist's ruse.   After all, it was only a false alarm !

MU YANG CHÜAN 牧羊圈

THE SHEPHERD'S PEN

Also called *Chu Hên Chi :* "The Red Scar."

A fan êrh-huang and *hsi-p'i* play.

PERIOD : Five Minor Dynasties (A.D. 907-960)

DRAMATIS PERSONÆ

CHU CH'UN-TÊNG, hero of the play	*Lao-shêng*
CHAO CHIN-T'ANG, his devoted wife...	*Chêng-tan*
CHU MU, his mother	*Lao-tan*
SUNG SHIH	*Ch'ou or Ts'ai-tan*
CHU CH'UN-K'O, her son	*Hsiao-shêng*
CHUNG CHÜN, Adjutant	*Ching*
SUNG CH'ÊNG, Sung Shih's nephew	*Ch'ou*
YAMEN RUNNERS, etc.	*Ch'ou*

SYNOPSIS

A wealthy native of Shuang-huai Ts'un (Twin Sophora Village) in the district of Shih Ho, Shantung, was summoned to join the campaign against the rebellious Ch'iang tribe in Western Szech'uan. Being ill and *hors de combat*, his nephew Chu Ch'un-têng was allowed to go in his stead. Chu Ch'un-têng set forth, leaving his mother and wife in the care of his uncle's sister-in-law, Sung Shih.

Ten years after his departure, his uncle dies while he is still on active service, leaving his possessions to be divided among the family. Sung Shih, capable, grasping, and dishonest, gets control of the property and tyrannizes over the two unfortunate women left to her charge. Telling Ch'un-têng's wife that her husband had been killed in battle, she tries to force her to marry her own nephew, the boorish Sung Ch'êng. When she flatly refuses, Sung Shih turns her out with her old mother-in-law to herd sheep and live in a pen with them. Unable to endure the hardships of such a life they abscond to beg for a living. Sung Shih then writes a letter to Chu Ch'un-têng informing him that both his mother and wife had died and been buried in the ancestral graves. In the meantime her own son Ch'un-k'o had gone to the Capital to compete in the civil service examinations, and knew nothing of all this.

The war over, Chu Ch'un-têng was rewarded with the title of Marquis Pacificator of the West for distinguished service. Ch'un-k'o meets him on the way home, having taken his degree. Hearing of their imminent arrival Sung Shih sends her nephew Sung Ch'êng to set up two grave-stones in the family cemetery to represent the departed mother and wife. When she confirms the news of their death, Ch'un-têng and Ch'un-k'o both proceed to the burial ground.

Here begins the most interesting part of the play : the first section *Mu Yang Shan* : " Herding Sheep on the Hill " is excessively lachrymose. The pitiable cast-out ladies are caught in a snow-storm—realistically conjured against a blasted heath in Ch'êng Yen-ch'iu's performances at the Chung Ho Theatre, and except for the entrance and exit of ludicrous toy-sheep this scene is one of monotonous moaning and groaning. The daughter-in-law's unselfish attentions to the snivelling and tottering old lady are laid on with a trowel. Most performances begin with Scene IV.

Scene IV

SUNG CH'ÊNG (*appears in a blue funk, saying*). We must erect a couple of fake tombstones, now that Ch'un-têng has returned as a high official.*

Two yamen runners appear.

ONE RUNNER. It is a hard thing to be in official employment : rain or shine a man has to be on the job. The Marquis has ordered us to sweep the graves.

The Adjutant comes in to see if they have made a good job of it, then tells them to wait outside. Enter Sung Shih with her son and Ch'un-têng.

SUNG SHIH (*weeping crocodile tears*). Oh my son, my son Ch'un-k'o !

CH'UN-TÊNG (*sings in êrh-huang tao-pan*). At sight of this grave I cannot help feeling as if my very vitals were rent asunder. (*In san-chiao-t'ou*) Oh Mother ! My dear departed Mother ! Hearken to the voice of your son.

---

*The action varies here : sometimes the wicked aunt is present and sometimes he mimes the making of the graves.

(*Changes to fan êrh-huang man-pan*) It was all on account of the rebellious Yellow Dragon of the Western tribes that your son had to take his uncle's place in the wars. With the favour of the gods we exterminated them, for which I have been created Marquis Pacificator of the West, a rank that is hereditary for ever. His Majesty has graciously allowed me to return and worship at my ancestors' graves. My fondest hope was that mother and son would meet again. But who would have thought that my dear mother had departed for the Yellow Springs! I grieve until my whole frame is shattered. (*Weeps*) Oh Mother, what is the use of my high rank and honours now that you are gone? My wife, my virtuous wife, whither have you drifted? We who lived so happily together can never meet again, unless perchance in our dreams!

SUNG SHIH (*speaks*). What is the use of tears? Once dead, we can never return.

CH'UN-TÊNG (*to Adjutant*). Bring me my official cap and robe and title of honour. (*After receiving them he holds them in front of his mother's spirit-tablet and says*) Mother! having been rewarded for pacifying the West, your son presents you with the official cap and robe and Imperial Patent. Why don't you come to accept them? (*Ch'un-têng performs this ceremony exactly as if his mother were alive. He then turns to Sung Shih and says*) Shên-niang!* These are for you to wear, and here is the title of honour for your keeping.

SUNG SHIH (*hypocritically*). These ought to be kept either by your mother or your wife; how could I presume to accept them?

CH'UN-TÊNG. Alas, my mother and wife can never hope to enjoy such happiness.

CH'UN-K'O (*to Sung Shih*). Take them, Mother.

She puts them on and leaves the room.

---

*Wife of father's younger brother.

CH'UN-TÊNG (*to Ch'un-k'o*). Now that your aunt has breathed her last, I think I shall resign from official life and retire to the mountains to cultivate the Way.*

CH'UN-K'O. As you please, elder brother.

CH'UN-TÊNG (*to Adjutant*). Here you shall construct a mat-shed and prepare a sufficiency of food for seven days' free distribution. Let none of the poor who come be molested or maltreated. Whoever does so shall have his dog's legs cracked. Bear this in mind.

Exit, after further exclamations of grief.

SCENE V

RUNNERS (*appear saying*). Well, there's soon going to be a bit of excitement with beggars and so on collecting around the neighbourhood.

Ch'un-têng's mother and wife appear.

CHU MU. Oh bitterness! (*Sings in êrh-huang tao-pan*) The crescent moon gleams over the land.

CHAO CHIN-T'ANG (*sings in êrh-huang yao-pan*). Mother and daughter-in-law are but beggars turned adrift.

CHU MU (*in êrh-huang yao-pan*). When will all this misery come to an end! (*Weeping*) Alas, daughter-in-law, I am gnawed with hunger! What can we do?

CHAO CHIN-T'ANG. I can see a mat-shed yonder. Some one is distributing rice free. I'll go over and beg for some. Sit on this mound while I'm away.

CHU MU. Oh hurry and bring me some food; I am faint unto death.

CHAO CHIN-T'ANG (*to yamen runners*). Gentlemen, pity a poor woman . . . My mother-in-law, who is eighty years old, has had nothing to eat for three days. Please grant her half a bowl of rice and a little weak tea to stay the pangs of hunger.

RUNNERS. The morning's rice is already finished. It is not noon yet. Why don't you look at your wrist-

---

*Tao, i.e. the " Wordless Doctrine " of Lao Tzŭ and the Quietists.

watch? Come along this afternoon and we'll add an extra portion to make up for it.

CHU MU (*is heard crying in the distance*). Oh, I'm dying of starvation!

CHAO CHIN-T'ANG (*sings in érh-huang yao-pan*). Soldiers, I beseech you. Be merciful. My poor old mother-in-law is eighty years old and has had nothing to eat for days. I implore you to grant me a little rice, just half a bowl will do ... (*She kneels and cries out in great sorrow*).

FIRST RUNNER (*melted, says to his assistant*). Look at this poor beggar-woman's plight: it is really too pitiful. Let's call the Adjutant.

RUNNERS (*to Adjutant*). A couple of poor women have come begging for food.

ADJUTANT. Tell them the time for serving food is past.

RUNNERS. We have. But they wailed so piteously that we thought we'd apply to you.

ADJUTANT. Stuff! Take me to the kitchen ... Here, cook, is there any rice left over?

COOK. Yes, just a bittock: the Marquis was so upset about his mother's death that he could not finish his breakfast. It'll be enough to stave off hunger. But mind that the Marquis's rice-bowl doesn't get smashed. (*Adjutant hands bowl to runner with the warning*) And take this too, the leavings of his broth. But be careful of the basin.

FIRST RUNNER (*examining contents*). Why there are some meat-dumplings left. I think I'll swallow these.

SECOND RUNNER. Then give me a taste of the broth.

FIRST RUNNER. No. I'll not eat the dumplings, so you'll not get the broth. I'll give all to the beggars. (*To women*) Here is some food for you. But whatever you do, don't break the bowl.

CHAO CHIN-T'ANG. Put it on the ground.

FIRST RUNNER. See how decorous this woman is ! *
(*Wife lifts bowl and urges her mother-in-law to eat*).

CHU MU. You must eat a little too.

CHAO CHIN-T'ANG. No. I am not feeling hungry.
(*Glancing about*) Stay ! This looks like our ancestral graveyard. Who can be dispensing free meals here ?

CHU MU. How can you be sure ?

CHAO CHIN-T'ANG. I remember the day after my
marriage when I came here to worship at the ancestral
tombs, I saw those two sophora trees standing in exactly
the same place.

CHU MU (*tottering half-blindly forward*).   Let me see.

RUNNER. Instead of eating, they've come to look at
the graves !

CHU MU (*sings in êrh-huang yao-pan*). At sight of the
graves I cannot check my tears. Oh, that we two
should ever come to this ! Dear ancestors, why have
you never defended or protected us ?

> She stumbles and the bowl is shattered.

RUNNERS (*in unison*). Since you've smashed the master's
bowl you'll have to pay for it ! (*Both women show great
alarm. The Adjutant comes and asks what the fuss is about*).
It is on account of their negligence. The old woman
dropped the bowl and broke it.

ADJUTANT. I'll go and tell the Marquis.

CHU CH'UN-TÊNG. What's that clamour outside ?
(*Adjutant tells him*). Away with you. Didn't I tell
you not to interfere with the beggars ? (*Pulls him
along to give him a beating*).

ADJUTANT. Please, Sir, call one of them in and ask
her if I have molested her in any way.   If so, it will not
be too late to punish me.

CHU CH'UN-TÊNG (*to Adjutant*). Kneel down there.

RUNNER (*to Adjutant*). Here is a nice clean spot, Sir.

---

*On the ground that a man and woman's hands must not touch.

CHU CH'UN-TÊNG (*to Runner*). Bring one of the women in. I'll ask her myself and see what she has to say. Instead of punishing, I'll help her. They need not be afraid of me. But whatever you do, don't alarm them. (*Exit runner*).

RUNNER (*to women*). The Marquis says that one of you is to come and explain how you broke the bowl. Afterwards he will do something for you. Now which of you will come?

CHAO CHIN-T'ANG (*to Chu Mu, who appears in a daze*). You go, Mother.

CHU MU. I am half-blind, dear daughter, and would not know what to say. You had better go and explain things, as I might not be able to express myself clearly.

CHAO CHIN-T'ANG. Since you wish it, I'll go. (*As she starts forward four soldiers (lung t'ao), who form the official's bodyguard, shout harshly to lead her in. She recoils in terror*). Oh, there is such an uproar that I am afraid to enter.

CHU MU. Be brave. If they maltreat you, I'll venture this old carcass of mine for your sake.

RUNNER. Now that they've filled their bellies they intend to risk their lives by kicking up a shindy! (*In a loud voice*) The beggar-woman's waiting to be admitted.

The soldiers set up the usual howl of ostentation.

CHAO CHIN-T'ANG (*goes into the mat-shed, kneels to Chu Ch'un-têng and says*). I have come, Sir.

CHU CH'UN-TÊNG. Who are you? Why don't you hold your head up?

CHAO CHIN-T'ANG. Being guilty I dare not.

CHU CH'UN-TÊNG. I forgive you.

CHAO CHIN-T'ANG. Thank you, Sir.

She looks up at him.

CHU CH'UN-TÊNG (*looking closely at her*). Strange! She bears a striking resemblance to my wife. But Shên-niang told me she was dead. How could she possibly still be alive?

CHAO CHIN-T'ANG. Ah me! This gentleman looks very like my husband. Sung Shih told us that he had been killed in the wars. How could he be living still!

CHU CH'UN-TÊNG. If she be truly my wife I ought to recognize her, but it would be terrible if I mistook another man's wife for my own! I've an idea . . .

CHAO CHIN-T'ANG. If this man is really my husband, I ought to recognize him. But I had better be cautious. If I were to mistake a high official for my husband, I should never recover from the shock. But I've an idea.

CHU CH'UN-TÊNG. Tell me, which of you two women was maltreated by my subordinates?

She loses her head and points at the Adjutant.

ADJUTANT. What! Which of our men molested you? Speak distinctly in the presence of the Marquis here and don't try on any subterfuge: although you're a beggar you ought to possess a conscience.

CHAO CHIN-T'ANG. He is a worthy man, Your Honour.

CHU CH'UN-TÊNG (*to Adjutant*). Stand aside, will you. (*To his wife*) Where do you live? What is your name and surname? Come, tell me everything; don't be afraid! I'll assist you in every way I can.

CHAO CHIN-T'ANG. I'll tell you all. (*Sings in hsi-p'i tao-pan*) I, Chao Chin-t'ang, kneeling in this mat-shed, with the tears streaming down my cheeks . . .

Here the soldiers set up a howling and Chu orders them out.

CHU CH'UN-TÊNG (*to his wife, whose back is turned*). Turn round and face me.

CHAO CHIN-T'ANG (*does so and sings in hsi-p'i man-pan*). Listen, kind Sir, and I'll tell you the story of my life.

CHU CH'UN-TÊNG (*interrupting*). Where is your home?

CHAO CHING-TANG, CHU CH'UN-TÊNG AND THE ADJUTANT

Mu Yang Chüan

CHAO CHIN-T'ANG (*in hsi-p'i man-pan*). My home is in Shantung, in the district of Shih-ho and the village of the Twin Sophora.

CHU. Who is your father?

CHAO CHIN-T'ANG. My father's name is Chao Tu-t'ang : he was an official of high degree.

CHU. So you are the daughter of Chao Tu-t'ang! Who is your husband?

CHAO CHIN-T'ANG (*sings*). My husband's name is Chu Ch'un-têng. (*Adjutant and Runners hearing her address their master by his ordinary name, a gross violation of etiquette, draw their swords with intent to kill her*).

CHU. Get out of here, you fools. I am conducting an investigation. Who ordered you to meddle in this case? (*Exeunt*). Continue your narrative, woman, and don't be dismayed.

CHAO CHIN-T'ANG (*sings*). My husband is Chu Ch'un-têng ; we were equally and happily matched.

CHU. Stay! From this woman's account she really must be my wife. And my aunt told me she was dead! How came she to be here? What sort of mystery is this? I'll have to ask her. Here, woman. Where did your husband go to?

CHAO CHIN-T'ANG (*sings in hsi-p'i yüan-pan*). It was all because of the revolt of the Western tribes under the Yellow Dragon that . . .

CHU (*interrupting*). What had the revolt of the Yellow Dragon to do with your husband?

CHAO CHIN-T'ANG (*sings*). My husband went to the wars instead of his uncle, who was too ill to go.

CHU. Did your husband ever write to you?

CHAO CHIN-T'ANG. Yes, there were letters, but Sung Shih intercepted them and told me that my husband perished in battle.

CHU. Oh cruel Shên-niang! This is all your fault. Why did you put this curse upon me? . . .

CHAO CHIN-T'ANG (*sings*). She tried to force me to marry her nephew, Sung Ch'êng.

CHU. To think that such a vulgar lout should aspire to marry the daughter of Tu-t'ang and the wife of a Marquis! It is simply outrageous. Did you hold out any promises? Make a clean breast of it!

CHAO CHIN-T'ANG. It was because I refused to have anything to do with him that I was shut up in the mill and beaten.

CHU. Very creditable of you. You had some determination, I see. Let me hear more.

CHAO CHIN-T'ANG (*sings in hsi-p'i êrh-liu-pan*). Afterwards I was driven out with my mother-in-law to herd sheep. The sheep subsist on grass, and so did we. When night came on we had to sleep in the pen with the animals. Every day we had to go out on the streets and beg for food. To-day we happened to meet you, Sir. Please have mercy on us and let your slave go free.   (*Weeps*).

CHU. To hear my wife talk thus cuts into my flesh like a sharp knife, and arrows seem to pierce my very heart. My aunt told me that both my mother and wife had passed away. How could they still be in the land of the living? Maybe their souls never became detached from their bodies on account of their cruel death. Maybe demons have come to torment me. I go out and look at the sky, but the sun has not yet set in the west. Chao Chin-t'ang had a red scar on her left hand. I'll see for myself. (*Speaks*) Here, woman. Are you in truth the daughter of Chao Tu-t'ang? Have you a red scar on the back of your left hand? (*His wife says:* "Yes"). Hold it out for me to see. (*She does so*). Ah me! my own wife! (*Weeps bitterly, then says*) My beloved virtuous wife. Don't be dismayed: I am your true husband Chu Ch'un-têng, who has returned as an official.

CHAO CHIN-T'ANG. Can this be true?

CHU. Incontestably true ! (*His wife catches him by the sleeve and both give way to their emotion*).

CHAO CHIN-T'ANG. Oh, my husband ! (*Sings in hsi-p'i yao-pan*) I had given up hope that we would ever meet again. Who could have dreamt that this day we would be re-united !

CHU (*also in hsi-p'i yao-pan*). Where is my poor old mother ? Is she at peace ?

CHAO CHIN-T'ANG (*sings*). She is just outside.

CHU. Lead me to her and let me explain. (*When they meet, he kneels and both weep*). Oh, my dear mother !

CHU MU. Who are you ?

CHU. I am your son Chu Ch'un-têng who has returned as an official.

Chu Mu absent-mindedly repeats the statement, merely observing that she is famished.

CHU (*to Adjutant*). Bring in the official robes and cap. (*The old lady is invested with them accordingly, and they all bow to each other*). Be seated, Mother, and let me make my obeisance as an unfilial son.

CHU MU. What unfilial conduct are you referring to ? My son, you will have to look into our family affairs.

CHU. Mother, I'll entirely obey your commands. (*To Adjutant*) Ask Chun-k'o to come here. (*To Chun-k'o, on his appearance*) Is it true that the wife of your father's elder brother is dead ?

CHUN-K'O. My mother told me so.

CHU. Well, just go forward and see for yourself.

CHUN-K'O (*does so and exclaims*). Alas, dear aunt !
(*Breaks down*).

CHU. It is so long since we have both been away from home on official duty that we could not attend to family affairs. This matter concerning your mother must be inquired into.

CHUN-K'O. I know nothing whatever about it. Ask her to come and explain. (*Sung Shih duly appears*). Is it true that my aunt and her daughter-in-law are dead?

SUNG SHIH. There cannot be the slightest doubt about it.

CH'UN-K'O. Well, look around you. Who are these?

SUNG SHIH. Ghosts!

CH'UN-K'O. How could you have done such a terrible thing? And how can I, your son, consider myself a human being? It would be best for me to dash my brains out!

SUNG SHIH. You need not do that. If I be guilty of that which I am accused, I hope that a dragon will bear me away in its claws.

Straightway an actor representing a dragon drags her off. Ch'un-k'o weeps.

CH'UN-TÊNG. Don't cry, brother. It was her fate to be dealt with in this manner.

ADJUTANT. We'll return to the palace and give a banquet in honour of the re-united couple.

CHU MU. Well, well, unjust as man may be, High Heaven is always just.

CH'UN-TÊNG. Good and evil, each has his due reward.

CHAO CHIN-T'ANG. If you don't believe it, lift your head and see. Who is it that Heaven protects? the righteous man!

Finis

*　　*　　*

Once the Westerner is acclimatized to the ranges of Chinese falsetto he is bound to appreciate Ch'êng Yen-ch'iu's superb singing in the rôle of Chao Chin-t'ang. The smooth liquid flowing modulations of his voice (*yu-yang* as the Chinese express it) have possibly been influenced, as well as his ideas concerning the orchestra and scenery, by his European tour: he is rarely shrill. One's only charge against him is a lack of versatility. He is always so correct and demure and romantic in the early Victorian sense that he is ill at ease amid scenes of gaiety, but these are the very qualities, or limitations, that make him a perfect *ch'ing-i*. His preponderant strains are sweetly melancholy: his expression, his gait and his sober apparel enhance this wistful 1840 atmosphere. At moments he is almost a parody of himself : when, for instance, trembling from top to toe, he sways downwards to the ground, to pick up the bowl of rice (which he refused to take from the orderly's male fingers), covered with a Confucian confusion that is truly exquisite. Moments, we said—he expends a quarter of an hour at least on this incident, while the mother-in-law is starving in the background, but the ultra-refined result is warmly applauded.

While others may be said to trip through their rôles with crisp, hard, clear-cut notes like their winking " golden lilies," Ch'êng Yen-ch'iu may be said to glide : were he given the chance he would waltz quite admirably. Let not the spectator be deceived, however, by this apparent languor, for it veils considerable strength. When occasion demands, he can brandish his whip and sword with the best of warriors. But he excels in *Mu Yang Chüan* : insipid as the play may seem to us, it is worth seeing for the sake of his performance ; Dumas' and Sardou's insipidities were worth seeing for Sarah Bernhardt.

It is on account of their musical value that a Chinese audience revels in repetitions that we may find irritating. The scene between Chu Ch'un-têng, his wife and mother, where each pretends not to recognize the other, may seem ridiculous to the Westerner. But the Chinese would consider it equally ridiculous if a man who had been away from home for many years rushed forward to embrace his long-lost mother or wife without any preliminary ceremony. Sung Shih may appear excessively malignant, but she is not overdrawn: unscrupulous females of that type abound in China as elsewhere. French fiction is full of them, rural products mostly, without any conscience or complexes, thrifty, astute, hard-as-nails, disposing of their obstacles with gradual doses of weed-killer. Coarse vixen though she may be, Sung Shih is an angel compared with, say, some of Julian Green's characters. She is merely out to promote the interests of her own peasant-clan. Ma Fu-lu is highly amusing in this heartless rôle. T'an Fu-ying, Ma Lien-liang and Wang Shao-lou have all scored successes as Chu Ch'un-têng.

Of old the monk Mu Lien as I've heard tell
Went down to save his mother out of Hell.
Were you to ask: How far the Holy Hills?
I'd answer you: From hence a myriad miles—
Nay, myriads of miles. O-mi-t'o Fo.

NI KU SSŬ FAN 尼 姑 思 凡

A NUN CRAVES WORLDLY VANITIES

PERIOD : Probably Ming.   A *k'un-ch'ü* monologue and *pas seul.*

SOLE CHARACTER

MISS CHAO   ...   . *Ni-ku*

(In some versions she is seen off on leaving the convent by an aged monk and the Eighteen Lohans*).

This play, of which there are many versions, was probably adapted from the Yüan story *Nieh Hai Chi* : " The Record of an Evil Sea "—a Buddhist term indicating a life of sorrow. The sole protagonist, a delicate girl whose surname is Chao, was committed by heartless parents to the Fairy Peach Convent (*Hsien T'ao An*) on the score of constant ill-health, and assumed the religious name of *Sê K'ung* : ' All is Void.' Being eminently human she longs for freedom—or what is nowadays termed self-expression. Her soliloquy is illustrated by dancing and vivid gestures throughout.

Enter a young nun (her vocation indicated by headgear and horsehair duster) she sings :

Of old the monk Mu Lien† as I've heard tell
Went down to save his mother out of Hell.
Were you to ask : How far the Holy Hills ? ‡
I'd answer you : From hence a myriad miles—
Nay, myriads of miles.   O-mi-t'o Fo.§

She speaks :

To be a nun with tresses shorn, how pitiful my
     plight,
The altar lamp my sole companion burning through
     the night !
The days and months speed swiftly by : too soon I
     shall be old,

---

* Buddha's disciples who have not yet attained Nirvana.
† See L.C. Arlington. *op. cit.* for synopsis of the play concerning this episode.
‡ Where Mu Lien became Buddha's " Disciple of the Left."
§ Amida Buddha ! (Amen).

My beauty gone, the glow of youth, shrivelled, pale
and cold.

My family name is Chao, my name in religion, Sê
K'ung. Since childhood I have dwelt sequestered in the
Convent of Mystical Peaches. During the day I do
naught but burn incense and repeat the name of Buddha.
At night I sleep alone without a mate. How chill and
dismally forlorn for me!

She sings :

I am now sixteen, the springtime of my life,
Yet daily since the abbess cut my hair
Must carry water, light the sticks of incense
Before the Buddha's altar. I have seen
The lads outside a-romping on the green
And one of them looked up and smiled at me
And I returned his smile. O sharp suspense,
If we may love each other with true love!
Can our affinity be plighted ever?
For him I'd face disfigurement and death
And all the tortures of the King of Hell :
Fry me in oil, right gladly would I bear it!
Yea, let him do his worst : I have no fear.
For I have seen the anguish of the living,
And who has seen a cangue upon a corpse?
And if mine eyebrows flickered into flame
Mine eyes would be my sole consideration. *

She speaks :

That I am here is all my parents' fault.

Sings :

Because I was a sickly child my parents
(Devout believers in the Buddha's lore)
Dispatched me to this dismal nunnery
To languish out my days. My locks are shorn
And I must pray to Buddha and light incense.

---

*i.e. The sweet little pagan has no belief in the terrors of the Buddhist
Inferno. She would only think of the present, not of the future.

In my heart of hearts I hate the go-between, for why did she not find me a mother-in-law?

Speaks : The more I ponder, the wilder I grow. I shall saunter out in the open gallery to drive away my sorrow.

Sings : Yes, I'll wander along and peep around while nobody's in sight (*bis*).

She trips to the Hall of the Five Hundred Lohans, exclaiming :
Oh, look at the rows of mud-made images! How grave, how pompous all of them appear!

Sings and mimes : One of them looks like a silly clown; and one is hugging his knees as if he were wanting to talk to me. And one is even holding his chin as if he were thinking of me. One of them leers with half-shut eyes as if he were dreaming of me. There's only that one of the Linen Bag* who seems to be laughing at me. For the spring of my youth is wasting away, and who will marry a shrivelled crone? The Lohan vanquishing the Dragon glares at me wrathfully. The Lohan subduing the Tiger shows his antipathy. And the long-browed one closes his eyes and takes no notice of me. When I am old, of what use will I be?

She sings : A convent is incompatible with a nuptial chamber, nor are these altar-candles befitted for bridal use. I am a pretty maiden, not a boy. Why should I wear these monastic robes and suffer my waist to be bound with a silken sash? All the young women I have seen are clad in embroidered gauze of red or green. Alas, Almighty Heaven! I cannot quench the flame that laps my heart (*bis*).

She speaks : To-day the Abbess has left the convent with her novices. Why should I not escape during their absence? I'll go and seek a husband to my liking: if

---

* Sobriquet of a famous Buddhist monk always represented with such a bag, which contained his religious paraphernalia.

there's a mutual affinity, I'll seize the chance. Yes, this is only reasonable and right.

She sings while disrobing: These robes I'll doff and tear to tatters. I'll burn my Buddhist prayers to ashes. I'll throw the wooden fish† away and fling the cymbals after. In the deep silence of the night I have to sleep alone; alone I sit in silence when I waken. Where can another be found so sad and forlorn as I? Why should I linger on here as a nun? Where are so many Buddhas to be found? Henceforth I'll keep myself aloof from nunneries and temples. I'll quit the cloister and seek a goodly mate. Let him beat me and curse me, scold me and mock me, oh to his heart's content! His whims I'll suffer with the best of grace. But I'll not become a Buddha! I'll not remain here mumbling Buddha's name. I would rather marry a proper man, and bear him chubby children, and lead a worldly life!

Finis

*   *   *

This is but the paltry skeleton of a vivacious lyrical poem, and we venture to include it because even as such it is unique in the entire repertoire of Chinese drama. Generally, to an ear that appreciates Mozart, the music of Chinese drama cannot be said, at best, to have independent existence as music. In *Ssŭ Fan* it is otherwise: these airs have life apart from their accompaniment of the text. The flute by itself can create a virginal atmosphere, and when the virgin takes shape before our enchanted eyes— no cold, calm, chaste, etiolate nymph, but a creature warm-limbed, in all her innocency, flushed with freshly awakened desire—it is almost too good to be true. When this little nun sings and dances her moods through the medium of Mei Lan-fang, poetry, music and movement fuse in the subtlest way imaginable. The mono-drama is so full of delicate shades that one must hear it again and again: every phrase is illustrated by some ravishing gesture. It

---

† *Note:* The *mu-yü*, or wooden fish, is made of a block of wood hollowed out and shaped somewhat like a skull. It is used by Buddhists to mark time in the recitation of prayers.

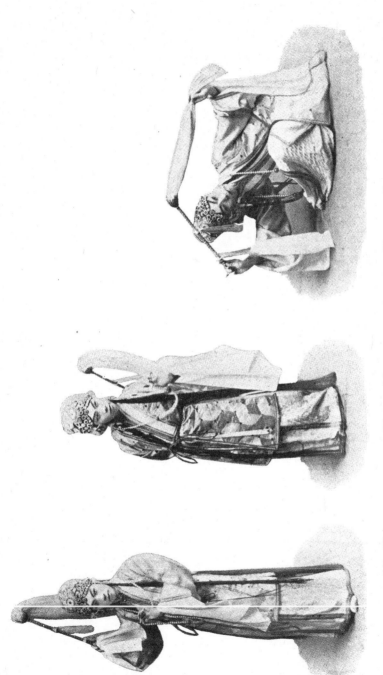

MA HSIANG-LIN AS THE YOUNG NUN WHO LONGS FOR WORLDLY PLEASURES

Ni Ku Ssŭ Fan

is a pity that no enterprising person has yet stepped forward to take a talking film of the entire performance : it would be the finest possible record and revelation of ancient Chinese choreography at its apogee—the greater the pity now that Mei Lan-fang and Han Shih-ch'ang are getting superannuated. As always in the Chinese theatre, the choreographer is *ignotus*, but whoever composed this series of solo dances was a master of his craft ; they are obviously the outcome of deep artistic experience. Loneliness, wistfulness, gaiety, *malaise*, nostalgia—the longing for motherhood even—are conveyed with a degree of sensibility and mimetic power that would amaze our *ballerinas* and *balletomanes*. It need hardly be said that *Ssŭ Fan* is highly conventionalized, but it is this that so strangely increases its poignancy. The costume is merely suggestive of a nun, with pearls doing duty as a " rosary " and a white horse-hair duster as a spiritual emblem and fairy's wand combined.

Dr. Lin Yutang has translated an extract from this play in *My Country and my People*, pp. 129-131, with an amusing commentary. There is a sequel called *Hsia Shan :* " Descending the Hill," where Miss Chao meets a young monk in a similar predicament : they flirt, arrange for a rendezvous after sunset, and elope. But the sequel is somewhat marred by the fact that the monk is enacted by a *ch'ou-êrh*, or comedian.

PAO LIEN TÊNG 寶蓮燈

PRECIOUS LOTUS-LANTERN

So called because when Liu Yen-ch'ang in his youth was attacked and swallowed by a python, an immortal of the fair sex came to his rescue. By placing a lotus-lantern in front of the serpent's fangs she caused it to disembogue the intended victim, *mens sana in corpore sano*. He subsequently married his redemptress. After giving birth to a son the immortal spouse retired to her mountain-cave and Liu married Wang Kuei-ying.   A *p'i-huang* play.

PERIOD : Southern Sung

DRAMATIS PERSONÆ

LIU YEN-CH'ANG	...	*Lao-shêng*
WANG KUEI-YING, Liu's second wife	... ...	*Ch'ing-i*
CH'ÊN-HSIANG, Liu's eldest son ⎫ CH'IU-ÊRH, Liu's younger son ⎭	... ...	*Wa-wa-shêng*
CH'IN TS'AN, a high official	... ...	*Ta-hua-lien*
CH'IN KUAN-PAO, his only son ⎫ TEACHER ⎭	... ...	*San-hua-lien*

SCENE I.—NAO HSÜEH : " THE BRAWL IN THE SCHOOLROOM "

Having distinguished himself as " Senior Wrangler " in the Imperial examination, Liu Yen-ch'ang was appointed Department Magistrate of Lo-chou, Chekiang. He begat two sons : Ch'ên-hsiang, born of his first wife, an immortal, and Ch'iu-êrh, born of his mortal second spouse, Wang Kuei-ying. These half-brothers attended the same school as Ch'in Kuan-pao, the son of the Minister Ch'in Ts'an [a descendant of the generally execrated statesman Ch'in Kuei, (Died 1155), who caused the heroic general Yo Fei to be put to death]. This Kuan-pao was a chip of the old block and the terror of the schoolroom. One day he disguised himself in eccentric garb with a hat and false beard and pretended that he was a stranger come from afar to pay the teacher his respects. As the latter failed to recognize his identity he returned the compliment and begged him to be seated. Kuan-pao then proceeded to plague the pedagogue with inane questions, such as : " How many stars are there in the sky? How many fish in the sea?" etc. When the teacher discovered he had been the victim of a practical joke he summoned the recalcitrant pupil and told him to kneel over a bench in preparation for a flogging. But Kuan-pao was not to be caught so easily. " I don't know how to kneel," he said ; " will you please show me ? " The teacher demonstrates ; and Kuan-pao seizes the ruler and inflicts some lusty blows on the elder's back. Ch'ên-hsiang and Ch'iu-êrh, being good boys, rush to their master's defence. The former picks up a heavy ink-slab and throws it with so sure an aim that Kuan-pao is killed instantaneously. Terrified, the two brothers run home, kneel before their father, and burst into tears.

The play continues under the general name of Pao Lien Têng.

Scene II

Liu Yen-ch'ang questions both his sons, and each stubbornly maintains that only himself was guilty of manslaughter. " As one of you will have to pay the penalty," says the father, "you had better declare who it is to be." Each persists in taking all the blame, so the distracted father threatens to arrogate the blame to himself. Before going to this extremity he gives each of them a drubbing which only proves a waste of time and energy. " Well," he says, " it is manifest that neither of you will betray the other." He then tells them the story of Po I and Shu Ch'i (12th cent. B.C.) who fled the State rather than accept the Throne. The Prince of Ku-chu (in Hopei) wished to appoint Shu Ch'i his heir, but the latter refused to deprive his elder brother Po I of his birthright and left the country on his father's death. Po I declared that he could not countermand his father's orders and followed Shu Ch'i into exile, leaving the Throne to a third brother. And until now, Liu concludes,

*their names radiate immortal glory. They are universally
respected.*

*With the appearance of Wang Kuei-ying the same pattern
is repeated and expanded. The boys remain obstinate. Father
and mother cross-examine them separately : in vain. The
last drop is squeezed out of the situation—in appearance, but
not in reality. For a fracas follows between the parents. The
husband accuses his wife of favouring her own child and vice
versa : and each parent blames the other for laying on the rod
too lightly. Liu tells Kuei-ying that she is obtuse and that her
heart is like paste. She retorts it's a fine specimen of official
who cannot settle a trifling case like this. " I'm far too clean-
handed to cope with family-affairs," says Liu (i.e. private
affairs are much more difficult to decide than public ones). And
so the heated discussion continues until Liu exclaims : " Why
should we allow our sons to interfere with our happiness? I
have an idea." " What is it ? " asks Kuei-ying. " Simply
this : you pump Ch'iu-êrh and I'll pump Ch'ên-hsiang." And
the last drop is still not squeezed from the situation ! Both
boys maintain that they are willing to die for the murder.
Asked if they are willing to leave their parents they reply :
"It is hard to part." " What about your own lives : how can
you be so indifferent ? " " We deserve death," say the boys in
unison. " What a shameless pair ! " says Liu. " It is
obvious that neither of you care whether you involve your parents
or not." And the cross-examination monotonously proceeds.*

*The plot now takes a Pirandellian turn. Liu says : " If
neither of you killed Kuan-pao it must have been myself.
Secretly, unknown to anyone, I must have killed him."
Whereupon he orders his official chair.*

KUEI-YING. Where are you off to ?

LIU. I'm going to the Ch'in Mansion to offer my
life for my two sons.

KUEI-YING. Alas ! As it was neither my husband
nor his children that killed Kuan-pao, it must have been
me. (*To the maid*) Order my chair !

LIU (*seeing that his wife is determined to sacrifice herself, cries*). Alas, if it was Ch'ên-hsiang who killed Kuan-pao, let him give life for life.

KUEI-YING (*interposing*). And if it was Ch'iu-êrh, what then?

LIU. The same applies to Ch'iu-êrh.

KUEI-YING. What do you mean?

LIU. My dear wife, after causing trouble in school, Ch'iu-êrh has brought much misery into our household, and all he can utter is " Father." (*Hearing this Ch'iu-êrh cries out:* "Mother"). My dear wife, will you bear the burden of responsibility? Supposing it was Ch'ên-hsiang, for instance, who killed Kuan-pao and brought all this trouble on us, and that he, like Ch'iu-êrh, then knelt before me and cried " Father "; supposing that I just gazed at him helplessly without giving him a word of advice and that he had cried out: " Mother! " . . . You know the particulars of his birth, that he is a motherless child. And yet I must send him to pay the penalty. (*Weeps*) Oh Ch'ên-hsiang, my son! my poor son!

KUEI-YING (*weeping*). Alas for *my* poor son!

LIU. Where has your son gone to? (*Kuei-ying weeps without answering*). (*Sings*) Judging from appearances it is mine who will have to pay the penalty. The motherless child whom I have reared, who has only me to cherish him.

Leading Ch'ên-hsiang by the hand Liu makes for the door. His wife asks where he is going.

LIU. To the Palace, to offer a life for a life.

KUEI-YING. Alas, dear husband, have you forgotten the affair of San Shêng Mu and the Red Lantern? (*i.e. the Immortal first wife and her magical emetic*).

LIU. Please don't remind me: I want to forget it. When I hear it mentioned I grow angrier than ever. I hate it, I hate it!

KUEI-YING. Surely you don't mean to imply that you hate me?

LIU. Why should I hate you? But if the San Shêng Mu had not saved me from the python there would be no Ch'ên-hsiang, nor this terrible sorrow that has befallen our house.

KUEI-YING. But that was great good fortune, my lord! (*i.e. to have a son by an immortal*).

LIU. Since you regard it as " good fortune," you should open your heart more.

KUEI-YING. Ah, now I begin to understand your gist.

LIU. What is it you understand?

KUEI-YING. I take your remarks to mean that if my son Ch'iu-êrh killed Kuan-pao, he is to give up his life.

LIU. And if it was Ch'ên-shiang?

KUEI-YING. Ch'ên-hsiang would also let Ch'iu-êrh sacrifice himself.

LIU. You must awaken from your dreams, dear.

KUEI-YING. I have not gone to sleep yet.

LIU. Every sentence you utter is like a dream.

KUEI-YING. Every word I utter is the truth!

LIU. I don't believe a word of it!

KUEI-YING. I can swear before . . .

LIU. I'll kneel and . . . (*to his son*) Ch'ên-hsiang, your mother has absolved and forgiven you. Kneel and kowtow to her.

KUEI-YING (*sings*). Alas! a slip of the tongue has condemned my poor boy to death.

> She drags off Ch'iu-êrh to her own apartment.

LIU. My dear wife, I am still kneeling before you.

KUEI-YING (*sings*). More than ever I fear that our love is blighted! (*She advances and kneels, saying*) I swear before all the gods in heaven that if I surrender my son it is not of my own free will.

LIU. What do you mean?

KUEI-YING (*sings*). I'll hang a rope high up on the beam (*i.e., hang myself*).

LIU. Thank you, my dear, for showing so much mercy! (*i.e. he is grateful to her for sacrificing her own son instead of Ch'ên-hsiang*).

In the meantime the Ch'in family surround Liu's house, growling and snarling for a prompt decision: there is the same nervous tension as in the last act of D'Annunzio's "FIGLIA DI IORIO."

KUEI-YING. What has become of Ch'ên-hsiang?

LIU. He is hiding in the garden, awaiting my decision.

KUEI-YING. Tell him to come here to me.

LIU. He has run away, far away.

KUEI-YING (*desperately*). I have something to tell him.

LIU (*in a loud voice*). Ch'ên-hsiang, come back! Your mother has something to say to you.

CH'ÊN-HSIANG. What instructions have you for me, Mother?

KUEI-YING. When you have escaped to your own mother, don't forget to remind her that to-day I have sacrificed my son for hers. And when your father and I are dead don't forget to buy a string of silver paper shoes * and burn them over our graves. We have only you to depend on for this.

Seizing Ch'iu-êrh by the arm she leaves the room.

LIU (*to maid*). Your mistress has gone to her chamber; be quick and prepare some tea for her. (*To Ch'ên-hsiang*) Father and son mingle their tears: how can such anguish ever be assuaged! (*Sings*) Come and listen to me, son. Wang Kuei-ying is not your real mother.

CH'ÊN-HSIANG. Softly, Father!

LIU (*to maid*). Still there! Be quick and serve your mistress's tea as I told you to. What are you standing about listening for?

---

*Silver bullion was melted into the form of shoes, hence shoes of silver paper are burnt at funerals as offerings to the dead.

The boy doesn't understand ; his father explains that San Shêng Mu is his mother.

CH'ÊN-HSIANG. I can't believe it !

LIU (*sings*). What ! You don't believe your own father ? Here I have a letter written in blood to prove it. (*Shows it*).

CH'ÊN-HSIANG. Now that I have seen the letter, I believe it. (*Both weep*). We'll ask Mother to come at once.

KUEI-YING (*enters with Ch'iu-êrh and sings*). How is it that you have not fled, dear child ?

CH'ÊN-HSIANG (*sings*). It breaks my heart to leave my dear mother and home. How shall I ever escape from Lo-chou city ?

LIU (*sings*). In Lo-chou you were born and reared.

KUEI-YING (*sings*). Who does not know Ch'ên-hsiang in Lo-chou city ?

LIU (*sings*). My son, rub some dirt on your face and you'll not be recognized.

KUEI-YING. My lord, at last you have awakened !

LIU (*sings*). My own eyes have witnessed my child's escape.

KUEI-YING. What ! Has Ch'ên-hsiang truly fled ?

LIU. Alas, he has. It is but a moment since we parted for ever. (*Kuei-ying and Ch'iu-êrh weep bitterly : Liu sings*) Mother and son weep as if they had just arisen from some delirious dream. Those whom we rear are those we love the best. I'll put a rope round Ch'iu-êrh's neck and take him to the Ch'in Mansion.

KUEI-YING. Where are you going ?

LIU. To the Ch'in Palace, to give a life for a life.

KUEI-YING. To let your own son escape and sacrifice mine is grossly unfair. I will not allow it on any account.

LIU. Have you already forgotten your oath ?

KUEI-YING. You are talking nonsense.

LIU. Let go of him ! (*She clings to her son's arm*).

KUEI-YING. I'll not let go.

LIU. If you don't let go of him, I'll . . .

KUEI-YING. You'll what?

There is a desperate tug of war between husband and wife with the wretched child in the middle; the rhythmical and symmetrical movements almost dovetail into conventional ballet. Finally Liu dashes his wife to the ground with his foot,— effectively managed, this gesture may meet with great applause— then, in a frenzy, he drags the child to his doom. This is the dramatic high-light of the whole performance.

SCENE III.—TA T'ANG : "THE STRUGGLE IN COURT"

CH'IN TS'AN (*enters and says*). Liu Yen-ch'ang's behaviour is outrageous. His son kills mine, yet he shows no sign of exchanging a life for a life.

LIU (*comes in with Ch'iu-êrh, exhorting the frightened child*). What are you afraid of? Step up boldly and show your mettle.

They are announced.

CH'IN TS'AN. So Liu Yen-ch'ang has come at last. Bid him enter. (*Liu enters*). How is it that you do not kneel?

LIU. You may be a Cabinet Minister but I, too, hold official rank. Why should I kneel to you?

CH'IN TS'AN. You allow your son to behave monstrously and murder my son Kuan-pao, yet you dare maintain a contemptuous attitude towards me.

LIU. It is true : your son was killed, but I am giving you another in return, a life for a life. What more do you require?

CH'IN. Where is he? Bring him in.

LIU. He is here, awaiting your summons.

CH'IN (*to servants*). Bring him forward . . . But it was Ch'en-hsiang who killed my son and you have brought Ch'iu-êrh in his stead.

LIU. So long as a life is given for a life, what does it matter to you whether it be Ch'ên-hsiang or Ch'iu-êrh ?

CH'IN (*to himself*). Well, I'll dispatch his son, and so carry out the right principles of all time. (*To underlings*) Beat him to death !

LIU. When my son killed yours you were not a witness of the act. Now you want to kill my son before my eyes and shame me in the sight of man. How can I endure that ?

CH'IN. If I were to beat your son it would wound your sensitive feelings, wouldn't it ? But look at me. At my age, nearly half a century, your son has cut off my posterity. Why shouldn't I grieve ? (*To underlings*) Take the boy out and beat him to death I tell you !

LIU (*leaves, moaning*). Alas, my son Ch'iu-êrh has been killed.

Ch'iu-êrh's corpse is then cast into the wilderness, where it is restored to life by an immortal. He is removed to a cave in the mountains and taught the art of war. Ch'in Ts'an has the entire Liu family cast into prison and prepares a memorial denouncing them to the Emperor.

*   *   *

Despite its supernatural trappings—Liu Yen-ch'ang's adventure with a fair immortal—this is a page out of many a Chinese family's log-book.

The physical or external action is of the slightest yet the play remains dramatic, and it is much appreciated by the Chinese as a realistic portrayal of the difficulties which tend to crop up in their domestic life wherever there are stepmothers and stepsons.

The rash European would censure its wearisome repetitions, but it is on account of these very repetitions that the dramatist's picture is so faithful.

PI YÜ TSAN 碧玉簪

The Green Jade Hairpin

A *p'i-huang* play, mostly in *êrh-liu* and *nan pang-tzŭ*.

Dramatis Personæ

Chao Ch'i-hsien, a jealous husband...	*Hsiao-shêng*
Chang Yü-chên, his injured wife	*Chêng-tan*
Chang Jui-hua, her father	*Lao-shêng*
Lu Fu Jên, her mother	*Ch'ing-i*
Chao An-Jên, Ch'i-hsien's mother	*Lao-tan*
Lu Shao-chuang, Yü-chen's cousin, a rake ...	*Ch'ou*
Ku Mei P'o, a go-between	*Ch'ou-p'o*
Hsiao Huei, Yü-chên's maid	*Hua-tan*
Ma Ju Fei, a messenger	*Wu-ching*

This is a specimen of that new wine in old bottles purveyed by the excellent female impersonator Ch'êng Yen-ch'iu. As such it is worth tasting once, to compare with the mellow ancient vintages. The play is not to be found in book-form: we give it as depicted on the stage; and beg the indulgence of those who may see it if some of the details are not registered in full.

Chang Jui-hua, a native of Huai-yang in Honan, is a retired official (ex-President of the Board of Civil Office). His wife, *née* Lu, has borne him an only daughter named Yü-chên, who is a beautiful and accomplished girl of eighteen when the play begins. Lu Shao-chuang, a nephew of Mrs. Chang's, and a professed libertine without a redeeming feature, harbours a secret passion for her. With his conspiracy to ruin her marriage the action of the play, such as it is, begins. The plot is of the slightest—unlike the majority—and the audience need not be taken aside every now and then between the acts for private explanations. The dialogue is self-sufficient.

Scene I

Chao Ch'i-hsien comes on the stage, takes a seat and orders a servant to invite his mother in. When she appears he informs her: To-day is Mr. Chang Jui-hua's birthday: I propose going over to congratulate him as he was a bosom friend of my deceased father's. *Exeunt both.*

Scene II

CHANG JUI-HUA (*enters soliloquizing*). To-day is my birthday : I am getting on in life. I have no sons and only one daughter. Though pretty and accomplished she is not yet engaged to be married. I'll ask my wife and daughter to come in and cheer themselves with wine and meat.

He sends for them : each arrives accompanied by her maid. They take their accustomed places at the table and are eating when a servant reports a knock at the door. In accordance with etiquette, wife and daughter retire. Servant admits Ch'i-hsien, who bows and congratulates the master of the house ; after some desultory talk on family affairs Chang Jui-hua, noting that his guest is an eminently eligible young man, proposes a match with his daughter.

CH'I-HSIEN (*accepts, saying*). I must go home and obtain my mother's approval. *Exeunt both.*

Scene III

LU SHAO-CHUANG (*enters soliloquizing*). I am an orphan. My father left me a large fortune which I don't know how to spend. I indulge in every kind of dissipation. Gambling and wenching are my principal objects in life, to say nought of wine and carousing. My aim is to capture that bewitching little cousin of mine, Yü-chên, but my aunt refuses to listen to my proposal. Now I discover that she is engaged to Chao Ch'i-hsien. What's to be done about it ? Aha, I'll enlist the services of Mrs. Ku the go-between, and get her to think of some effective ruse.

He sends for her. She appears and asks what is wanted of her.

LU. You're well acquainted with the Chang family aren't you ? I want you to contrive some way of stopping their daughter's marriage.

MRS. KU. How will you reward me if I succeed ?

LU. I'll give you a dress to hide your villainy.

MRS. KU. In that case it's quite easy to arrange. (*She whispers into his ear*).

LU (*laughing*). Go ahead, and you'll be handsomely remunerated, I promise you.

SCENE IV

Mrs. Ku proceeds to the Chang mansion and visits Yü-chên while her hair is being dressed by her maid Hsiao Huei. She makes a flattering speech about her beauty. Catching sight of a green jade hairpin on the table, she picks it up and after an admiring scrutiny asks : May I borrow this ? I should like to have it copied for a friend of mine.

YÜ-CHÊN. No ! my mother lent me this hairpin : I can hardly lend it to somebody else.

HSIAO HUEI. Dear mistress, we know Mrs. Ku well enough to let her keep it for a while : she'll surely return it to you.

YÜ-CHÊN. In that case you may take it.

SCENE V

Mrs. Ku goes straight off to Lu's house with the hairpin.

MRS. KU. I've managed to get hold of a valuable green jade hairpin : it belongs to Yü-chên.

LU. Whatever's the use of that ?

MRS. KU. What's the use of it ? Let me tell you. Write a love-letter purporting to come from Yü-chên to yourself and enclose the hairpin in an envelope, then hand it to me. On Yü-chên's wedding-day I'll take it to the Chao house and drop it on the floor of the nuptial chamber. Ch'i-hsien will find it and then the trouble will start : maybe you'll get the bride instead of the other fellow. Isn't this a fine scheme ? But are you capable of writing a love-letter ?

LU. Capable? What next? The very reason I was expelled from college was for writing amorous letters. (*He proceeds to write*) " My dear cousin, let us meet in secret on my wedding-day. Yü-chên."

This singularly unimaginative billet-doux is entrusted to Mrs. Ku.

SCENE VI

Mrs. Ku and the maid accompany the bride to the bridegroom's home. As they enter the nuptial chamber Mrs. Ku finds a pretext for getting rid of the maid and, watching her chance, throws the incriminating note on the floor and departs. The bride sits on the bed, her face covered with a veil. Ch'i-hsien, trembling with happy anticipation, lifts the lamp from the table and sees the letter gaping at his feet. He picks it up and goes into the garden. Putting the lamp on the ground he tears the envelope open. Overwhelmed by its contents, he dashes off to the library where he eventually falls asleep on a couch.

SCENE VII

After daybreak Hsiao Huei steps in and seeing the door ajar and the lamp still alight in the garden, wonders what could have happened. She finds Yü-chên still sitting on the bed with her face veiled as if hypnotized, a position she had maintained all night. Much dismayed she asks her the reason but Yü-chên can only profess her startled ignorance : she had not seen Ch'i-hsien since he picked something off the floor and left the room. The maid then goes in search of the bridegroom, whom she finds sound asleep in the study. She returns to suggest that Yü-chên's mother-in-law should be informed.

YÜ-CHÊN. No, don't do anything of the kind ! We must not worry the old lady. He is not worth it. I really believe he must be out of his wits.   *Exeunt.*

SCENE VIII

Ch'i-hsien goes to visit his mother, who is sitting in her room.

CH'I-HSIEN. Good morning, Mother. I hope you passed a pleasant night.

MRS. CHAO. You have a beautiful and talented wife, my son. How very fortunate you are !

CH'I-HSIEN (*ironically*). Oh yes, a very nice wife indeed !

Enter Yü-chên with maid.

YÜ-CHÊN. Good morning, Mother. Did you sleep well last night ?

Ch'i-hsien looks daggers at her and turns to leave the room.

MRS. CHAO. What is your hurry for, son ? Why leave as soon as your wife comes in ?

CH'I-HSIEN. I have a great deal to do and simply cannot waste my time like this. (*Goes off in a huff*).

MRS. CHAO (*soliloquizing*). I wonder what's the matter with him ! With such a lovely wife he ought to be blissfully happy, but apparently he isn't.

HSIAO HUEI. Last night he took no notice at all of his bride,—just vanished in a tantrum, leaving the door ajar and the lamp burning in the garden. He slept in his study instead of the bedroom and never went near my mistress. We cannot imagine what is the matter with him.

MRS. CHAO. I'll tell you what we'll do. To-night we'll lock them in the bedroom, so that neither can escape. (*Exeunt*).

SCENE IX

Yü-chên enters followed by her mother-in-law and the maid pushing Ch'i-hsien along.

MRS. CHAO (*to maid*). Lock the door. (*She stands outside, listening*). It's all right, I hear no disturbance. The neighbours to the east of us will cry : How lucky is

Mrs. Chao ! And the neighbours to the west of us will cry: How happy is Mrs. Chao! Next year she'll be coddling a chubby baby grandson. (*Sings out*) Oh dear, I have wrenched my poor old back again !

The maid escorts her out and Mrs. Chao tells her to keep an eye on the couple during her absence.

Scene X

Yü-chên is seen sitting on the bed and Ch'i-hsien on a chair leaning over the table, both asleep.

YÜ-CHÊN (*wakes up shivering with cold and sings in nan-pang-tzŭ*). Somebody must have been telling lies about me, or else he thinks I am not fair to look upon. But what can I say or do ? (*Seeing her husband shivering she takes her cloak with an impulse to cover him but withdraws, still singing*) If anyone saw me do this I'd be disgraced : no, I will not cover him ! (*She starts to cover him again and withdraws*). No, I cannot do it, I cannot do it! (*Still singing*) As the old lady treats me so kindly I'll cover him. (*Does so*).

CH'I-HSIEN (*waking up*). I don't want a slut like you to come near me. You are a deceitful trollop. (*Throws off the cloak*).

YÜ-CHÊN. What do you mean by treating me like this ? Who do you think I am ?

CH'I-HSIEN. Such a vile creature is not worth wasting breath on. (*He gives her a lusty kick and she falls down sobbing. Hsiao Huei, who has been listening at the door rushes in and Ch'i-hsien rushes out*).

HSIAO HUEI. This sort of thing won't do. I'll go and tell his mother. (*Does so, and both return together*).

MRS. CHAO. What is the trouble about ? (*Yü-chên tells her the whole story*). I am terribly sorry that this should have occurred : I'll apologize for him. (*To maid*) You look after your mistress while I go and remonstrate with the brute. I'll punish him even at the risk of my life.

Photo by Vargassoff

CH'ÊNG YEN-CH'IU AS CHANG YÜ-CHÊN, YÜ CHÊN-FEI AS
CHAO CH'I-HSIEN

(Above) the wife is about to cover her sleeping husband.
(Below) Chao tries to make it up with his wife.

Pi Yü Tsan

Scene XI

LU FU JÊN (*Yü-chên's mother comes on the stage soliloquizing*). To-day is my birthday. I'll send a servant to invite my daughter and her husband to come over for a cup of wine. (*Calls servant and gives him the message*).

Exeunt.

Scene XII

Enter Mrs. Chao, Yü-chên and her maid. A servant announces that Mrs. Chang's cart has arrived to take Yü-chên and her husband to her birthday celebration. Ch'i-hsien arrives and brusquely declines the invitation.

CH'I-HSIEN. I won't go, neither will my wife.

MRS. CHAO (*showing signs of anger*). What? Even if you have no desire to go, your wife should : she can't refuse to attend her mother's birthday celebration. (*Ch'i-hsien leaves the room in a rage*). (*To Yü-chên*) You may go to your mother's and enjoy yourself for a few days. But don't tell her about my son's vile temper; it would only upset her.

Yü-chên bows to her mother-in-law before taking her leave. Exeunt Yü-chên, maid, servant and mother-in-law. Ch'i-hsien rushes out and tells the servant that his wife is to return immediately ; it has suddenly struck him that she may have gone to meet Lu Shao-chuang.

Scene XIII

Mrs. Chang is sitting in her room. Enter Yü-chên, maid and servant.

YÜ-CHÊN. I've come to pay my respects on your birthday, Mother. I hope you are well?

MRS. CHANG. Sit down, my dear, and let us have a chat. Why didn't your husband come too?

YÜ-CHÊN. He was so busy that he had no time to accompany me.

MRS. CHANG (*rather doubtfully*). Well, never mind! Your father is not at home either, so you can stay with me a few days and keep me company. (*Turning to maid*) Your mistress looks changed: what is the matter with her? She seems terribly thin. Haven't you noticed it?

YÜ-CHÊN. There's nothing amiss, Mother. I am quite content as I am.

Ch'i-hsien's servant arrives to say that his master wishes his wife to return without delay.

MRS. CHANG. What is the meaning of this? You have no sooner arrived than he wants you to go back at once!

SERVANT. It is a custom of the Chao family: no member of the household can spend the night out.

YÜ-CHÊN (*sings in êrh-liu*). Please don't detain me, Mother: it would only be useless. It is my fate to be dealt with thus. I cannot blame anyone. Mother, I must leave you. (*Weeping she climbs into the cart and leaves the house. The maid, however, slips away and returns to tell Mrs. Chang about her daughter's unhappy condition, and that if she does not take steps to recall her, she may die of grief within a few days. She then returns to her mistress, who is unaware of this interview*).

SCENE XIV

Mrs. Chang sends an express courier who can travel 500 li a day to urge her husband to return.

SCENE XV

Chang Jui-hua bows before a table covered with yellow silk, behind which is a curtain to veil the Imperial Presence, begging His Majesty for two months' leave of absence. The absence granted, Chang retires backwards until he reaches the door. He travels home and a servant announces his arrival. Mrs.

Chang receives him very solemnly and rails at him for giving his daughter to Ch'i-hsien. He then proceeds to his son-in-law's to demand an explanation. When they meet, Ch'i-hsien addresses him as "uncle." "What do you mean by addressing me as uncle," *he asks;* "why have you treated my daughter so cruelly?" *Ch'i-hsien invites Chang Jui-hua into another room and privately shows him the forged billet-doux. In the meantime Mrs. Chao tells Yü-chên that her father has arrived and Yü-chên expresses her delight and longing to see him. But when she greets him he first reviles her for a slut and tells her that she has ruined the family reputation, then kicks her down, shouting:* "Why did you give your mother's green jade hairpin to your sweetheart?"

HSIAO HUEI. Oh, the green jade hairpin! Wait while I escort my mistress to her room and I'll come back and tell you. (*After helping Yü-chên out, she returns to say*) You happened to mention the green jade hairpin, Sir. I can tell you all about it. My mistress lent it to Mrs. Ku the go-between, who begged it as a sample. Since then we have been so busy with the marriage arrangements that we forgot all about it.

Chang tells a servant to fetch Ku Mei P'o instantly. She is dragged in, cursing the servant for handling her so roughly.

MRS. KU (*to Chang*). Oh, so Your Excellency has returned! I am glad to see you looking so well.

CHANG. Kneel down there! Tell me the story of the green jade hairpin. What did you do with it?

MRS. KU. It has nothing to do with me. Lu Shao-chuang asked me to procure it for him. Being enamoured of your daughter he wanted it for some scheme of his: he wrote a love-letter and put the hairpin in an envelope, then asked me to drop it on the floor of the bridal chamber. That's all I know about it, Sir ...

CHANG (*to servant*). Take her to the yamen and shackle her. (*She is dragged off by the servant, cursing like a fish-wife*).

CHANG (*to Ch'i-hsien*). Well, did you hear what she said?

CH'I-HSIEN. Yes, but that's no proof. Before I'll believe it I must compare their handwriting.

Chang sends Hsiao Hui to ask Yü-chên to write something on a sheet of paper and return with it. When she has done so Chang examines it and passes it to Ch'i-hsien, saying: " Here is the proof, if you want one." He throws the letter on the floor. Ch'i-hsien picks it up and scrutinizes it from every angle. Satisfied that there is no similarity in script he addresses his father-in-law : " I regret that I have made such a terrible blunder. I offer my sincerest apologies to you and your daughter and hope you will forgive me."

CHANG. Your apologies are worth nothing to me. (*To mother-in-law*) I leave my daughter in your care : see that you look after her well ! If anything happens to her I shall hold you responsible.

Exeunt Chang and his servant.

SCENE XVI

As soon as Chang reaches home he abuses his wife and tells her that her profligate nephew should be drawn and quartered—as if it was all her fault !

Mrs. Chang goes off to extract an explanation from the villain in question. Exeunt.

SCENE XVII

LU SHAO-CHUANG (*appears, accompanied by his servant*). I am thinking of my beloved.

SERVANT. You ought to be nursing your illness ; why think of love?

LU. I see my love approaching. She's over there !

SERVANT. That's not your sweetheart, it is a dragonfly.

Mrs. Chang enters.

LU (*leaning over the table, starts at the sight of her*). What ! are you not my dear cousin ? (*He continues to indulge*

*in an indecent soliloquy, then throws a fit, jumping about the
room until he falls exhausted on the floor, spits blood and
gives up the ghost. Mrs. Chang buys him a coffin and goes
home).*

Scene XVIII

Enter Mrs. Chao and Ch'i-hsien.

MRS. CHAO. What do you intend to do about your
wife now?

CH'I-HSIEN. I intend to go up for my examinations.
If I fail I shall never return. If I am successful, of course
I'll come back. *Exeunt.*

Scene XIX

*Yü-chên is now an invalid confined in her room; a maid-
servant announces that Mrs. Chao is coming to visit her.*

MRS. CHAO. I hope you are now feeling better, my
dear.

YÜ-CHÊN. Pray be seated, Mother. Yes, I am feeling
a little better.

MRS. CHAO (*to maid*). Look after your mistress well!
Exeunt omnes

Scene XX

*While Mrs. Chao is sitting in her room, four pages enter
with official robes and headgear, followed by Ch'i-hsien, who
comes and salutes his mother. Mrs. Chao sends for Yü-chên;
on whose appearance she tells her to don her official robes and
head-dress and make her obeisance to the Emperor in gratitude
for her husband's promotion, for Ch'i-hsien is now a Chuang
Yüan: a scholar of the first degree.*

YÜ-CHÊN. I do not want them. I am unworthy of
such things. (*Ch'i-hsien kneels and kowtows to his wife
while Mrs. Chao makes profuse apologies*).

YÜ-CHÊN (*to Mrs. Chao*). Well, if you insist upon it,
I'll wear one of these. But I shall never live with your
son again. I'll give him my maid, Hsiao Hui, as a

concubine. While she attends to him I'll serve you as long as you live. When you pass away, I'll cut off my hair and enter a convent. (*She dons the robe and head-dress and bows towards the north as a sign of thanking the Emperor*).

MRS. CHAO (*before leaving the room*). A son is a fearful debt to be saddled with.

YÜ-CHÊN. He may change as the years roll by.

Ch'i-hsien pulls his wife by the sleeve, but she says : "You have humiliated me : I want nothing more to do with you ! " *He then clutches the maid by the sleeve and she says archly :* "A nice creature you are, a rascal and a good-for-nothing ! " *Nevertheless she follows him out with a fluttering heart. Exeunt omnes.*

Finis

* * *

We include this play because it is frequently performed by Ch'êng Yen-ch'iu, who contrives to instil some life into it. As drama there is little to be said in its favour. It is highly improbable that Chao Ch'i-hsien or Chang Yü-chên would have left matters unexplained so long under the circumstances. The characters, like the incidents, are taken from a common conventional stock. The profligate and the go-between are too crude to be comical : we have heard better dialogue of that kind at T'ien Ch'iao. Since the acts may be followed without much cerebration, we can recommend it as an experiment to the student of Chinese theatrical technique.

TA CH'ÊNG HUANG 打城隍

BEATING THE TUTELAR DEITY

Every Chinese city has a *Ch'êng Huang Miao*, wherein the tutelar guardian of the place is installed. This farce is a lively satire on the god himself. We include it as such rather than for its theatrical value, although it contains a moral that could well be pointed at other gods throughout the universe in so far as the saving of mankind is concerned.   A burlesque in *hsi-p'i shu-pan*.

DRAMATIS PERSONÆ

KA CH'I	...	...	...	...	...	...	
MA PA	...	...	...	...	...	...	*Ch'ou-êrh*
LIU CHIN	...	...	...	...	...	...	
TWO YAMEN RUNNERS	...	...	...	...	...		

(*Ka Ch'i Ma Pa* is a colloquial expression for any rubbish).

KA CH'I (*soliloquizing*). Ever since I was first able to crawl I've been a restive person. I never cared for study : I'm just a good-for-nothing vagabond. I've travelled all over Eastern Asia and Western Europe and America to boot, to say nothing of Japan, the land of pretty wenches. I can utter precisely two words of foreign speech and understand still less, so don't talk to me about foreign learning, of which I know less still. However, in the course of my ramblings I have picked up something about eating, drinking and the wearing of clothes. The collar on a foreign shirt is stiff as a poker and throttles one to death. Their shoes are all mates : there's no way of interchanging them.* American hats conform to the four seasons ; their spectacles grind one's eyelids. To taste their food one must go to the barbarian

---

*Until recently there used to be no difference between the right and left shoe, and the Chinese cobbler's was an easy profession. But the foreign fashion of " mating " footgear now holds sway, with the gradual *crescendo* of comfort and diminuendo of picturesqueness.

restaurant.*   I've drunk their brandy and danced in their
cabarets.   I'm quite fond of mah-jong but give me poker
as a game that can be played by sheer bluff.   I've lost
and won tens of thousands at both these games.   As
for earning a living, well—I think I'll either become an
official or a merchant.   But so far as I can see, I'm nothing but a factory for producing manure !   (*Speaks*) Well,
here I am, Ka Ch'i, in very person !   Ch'in Shih Huang
is forcing all the loafers to help him build the Great Wall.
So unreasonable of him ! I have a stupendous family to
support : what is to happen to them all if I'm torn away
from their bosoms ?   Ah, I've a bright idea !   The
tutelar deity of this place is noted for his kindness and
intelligence.   I'll go in and see him, and beg him not to
allow me to be taken away.   (*Enters the temple and falls
down on his knees*).   Your Honour is above, I am below.
Ch'in Shih Huang is dragooning all the lounge-lizards
to work at the Great Wall.   Please protect me.   Don't
allow him to take me !   (*Stands up and gazes at the god*).
Hello !   His Honour must have gone away for the week-
end : he has left his hat and coat behind.   Well, I'll
represent him during his absence : I'll grab all the lazy-
bones, excluding immortals, of course.   (*He puts on the
god's hat and robe and takes his seat in the god's niche*).   Hello !
Somebody's coming !

MA PA (*enters and says*).   Last night I had a dream.   I
dreamt that the God of Longevity was riding on a fly.
With his left hand he was holding the fly's wings and
with his right the fly's whiskers.   *Wêng, wêng, wêng*, he
flew half-way to heaven :   I looked up and saw the sky
was full of stars.   I looked down and saw the earth was
full of pits.   The pits were full of ice ; on top of the ice
a pine-tree grew, on top of the pine was an eagle.   Into
a room I peered and saw a lamp.   I glanced at the walls

---

*The term *fan-ts'ai*, " barbarian food," is generally applied to foreign victuals,
in conversation as on sign-boards and bills of fare.

and when I glanced again, I saw that they were riddled through with nails. On one of the nails a bow was hanging. From the north-west a furious wind arose; it blew all the clouds away and the stars came out. Everything out of the pits it blew, and melted all the ice on the ground. It blew the pines down into the slush. It blew the eagle off the pine. It blew the lamp out in the room. It bent the nails all upside down. With scattered stars and levelled pits and melted ice and pine capsized, the eagle flown, the lamp put out, nail head over heels, the bow turned round—the whole arena's empty. (*To the god*) Here I am, Your Honour! I am Ma Pa. (*He proceeds to repeat the same rigmarole that Ka Chi has just gabbled through. Ka Ch'i suddenly stirs*). Ha! The god moves. How's that?

KA CH'I. What brings you in here?

MA PA. So it is only you! What are you up to in there?

KA CH'I. The god has gone out for an excursion, so I put on his clothes. I'll grab men but no gods. What do you think of my plan?

MA PA. Excellent! Ponder a scheme for me too.

KA CH'I. Let's arrange it this way. You be my henchman.

MA PA. Ah, that would be the very thing for me!

KA CH'I. The henchman (P'an Kuan) holds the Book of Life and Death in his left hand, and an ink-brush in his right.

Ma Pa togs himself out accordingly and takes up his station.

MA PA. That's right, but if anyone comes, don't budge! Ah, somebody's coming already!

LIU CHIN (*enters and says*). Aha! We're plumb in the middle of the dog-days now. We three brothers got cut adrift. We had gone off to the fields to plough when a spotted pig came up from the south. Elder brother said it was a wolf; younger brother said it was a tiger;

while I maintained it was a spotted deer. Then that meddling Uncle Tung appeared from the north and fetched us each a slap on the neck. You fools, quoth he, it isn't a wolf, or a tiger, or even a spotted deer. It's just a camel's cub, you see, its hair isn't long—that will sprout nicely later. (*He then addresses the god in the same rigmarole as his predecessors*). Oho ! you are actually stirring !

MA PA. So you have come too ?

KA CH'I. What's your business ?

LIU CHIN. Bless me if it isn't you two fellows ! What are you both up to ?

KA CH'I. We're fleeing from adversity.

MA PA. Ka Ch'i's rigged out in the tutelar deity's clothes and I in his assistant's : we came here to avoid trouble with the Emperor's press-gang. What do you think of our plan ?

LIU CHIN. Capital ! What do you say to finding me a position too ?

KA CH'I. Let's do it this way. You impersonate the little demon. (*Liu Chin agrees*) . . . Open your mouth and show your tusks and, if anybody comes along, don't budge ! (*Liu Chin does so*). Sh ! somebody's coming.

Two runners appear.

FIRST RUNNER. I've received my commission as an official.

SECOND RUNNER. We have to do as we're bid.

FIRST RUNNER. Ch'in Shih Huang has ordered us to collar all the slackers in the place to help him build the Great Wall. So unreasonable of him ! Here we've been on the look-out for many a day and haven't caught a single slacker yet. This city-god here is mighty clever, we had better apply to him for assistance. (*Both enter the temple and fall on their knees*). Your Honour, you are above, and we two are below. Please help us to catch a few sluggards and we'll offer you three pig's-heads, as well as a motor-car to tour the whole town in :—

jogging along as you do in a dilapidated cart simply isn't done nowadays : it's not modern !

They knock heads and withdraw to continue their chase.

KA CH'I (*laughing*). I say, did you see that ? They not only failed to discover us, but also left three pig's-heads and a motor-car. These are all mine !

MA PA. They must be divided among the three of us.

KA CH'I. Not at all ! They were placed right here in front of me.

LIU CHIN. No, no ! Each of us must have a proper share. (*In the midst of their dispute they see the two runners returning. Much alarmed, the trio hurry back to their posts*).

FIRST RUNNER. Well, we haven't caught a soul yet.

SECOND RUNNER. We'll ask the Ch'êng Huang about it.

FIRST RUNNER (*addressing the god*). Hie, you ! Not a single soul have we caught yet—and after all those lavish offerings. What do you intend to do about it ?

SECOND RUNNER. No use arguing with him ; we'd better give him a spanking. (*The first runner agrees ; they both catch hold of the pseudo-deity, who hits back*).

FIRST RUNNER (*surprised and frightened*). If we don't catch anyone this time, we'll come back and thrash you for sure.

SECOND RUNNER. Come on, let's get out of this !

FIRST RUNNER. Don't be in such a fluster ! The Ch'êng Huang has ordered his assistant to attend to such matters. If he hasn't entered it on the register, we won't be able to grab anyone. Let's ask him. (*Both kneel*). The assistant is above, us twain at your big toes. If you help us to catch any loafers we'll present you with a brand new waterproof, and a hundred dollars besides. (*Exeunt*).

KA CH'I (*to Ma Pa*). Here ! Will you share this ? I got a flogging ; you heard it, didn't you ? If they don't grab anyone this time they've threatened to pitch into me again ! What's to be done about it ? We'll exchange : you be the Ch'êng Huang and I'll be your henchman.

MA PA. No thanks. I'd rather not.

KA CH'I. I'll give you everything they gave me, pig's heads, motor-car and all. (*Ma Pa agrees. As soon as they have exchanged the runners return*).

FIRST RUNNER. We have'nt caught anyone yet. Let's beat up the Ch'êng Huang !

SECOND RUNNER. No, not the god : we'll attack his assistant, since you wasted your last offerings on him.

They pull Ka Ch'i off his pedestal, give him a second buffeting and put him back again, saying : " If we don't catch any loafers this time, we'll come back presently and give you another thrashing."

SECOND RUNNER. The small demon takes his orders from the assistant god, we had better make him an offering.

FIRST RUNNER. All right ! (*Addressing the small demon*) You, elder brother, are above ; I am below. If you help me to catch any lounge-lizards, I'll give you one thousand dollars. (*Exeunt*).

KA CH'I. This is rough on me ! If they don't succeed, it means I'm in for it again. (*To Liu Chin, personifying the small demon*) Here ! we'll exchange places !

LIU CHIN. I'm hanged if we will !

KA CH'I. If you will, I'll give you all they gave me.

LIU CHIN. Agreed then. (*Proceeds to do so. The runners return*).

FIRST RUNNER. Still failure dogs our footsteps ! We'll batter the assistant.

SECOND RUNNER. Not so fast ! The small demon takes his orders from the assistant ; he has evidently been disobedient. Let's wallop him. (*Ka Ch'i gets a third thwacking*).

FIRST RUNNER. His ears are bunged up : clean them out ! (*They begin to bore into Ka Ch'i's ears : he puts on a dreadful stare and wriggles about as if in agony*).

SECOND RUNNER. Here ! bore into his nostrils too !
(*They do so, despite grotesque contortions. Exeunt*).

FIRST RUNNER (*sotto voce*). Say, look at them ! It seems to me they've been swopping places. I think they must be fakes. Let's go out and spy on them.
(*Both stand in attitude of listening*).

KA CH'I (*to his companions*). How is it that they only seem to recognize me, and always concentrate on my poor body for chastisement ? It must be because the two of you moved.

MA AND LIU. We never budged !

KA CH'I. Well, how is it that I was the only one to suffer ? We had better change back again as we were in the first place. (*They see the runners approaching*).

MA AND LIU. Look out ! They're returning. Too late to change now.

RUNNERS (*while the trio are busily resuming their pedestals*). What ho ! Where are you off to ? We'll nab the three of you.

They capture them and the game is up.

* * *

As the incident from which the action springs is Ch'in Shih Huang's building of the Great Wall, the theme, at any rate, is of considerable antiquity, but as the dialogue is more or less extemporaneous it has probably always been full of topical interpolations. References such as those to poker, motor-cars and foreign restaurants are all the more fantastic, set in so ancient a frame.

It is a play to be seen and heard : no description could render justice to the fantasy of the actors, the variety of antics and grimaces with which the dialogue is lavishly besprinkled. The libretto lends itself ill to translation, as the dialogue loses much on the printed page, depending as it does for effect on swift transitions of tone, vivacious gesture and facial expression. It comes very near to our conception of what the *Commedia dell' Arte* must have been in the early years of Louis XIV's reign : but there is nothing on Western boards to compare with it to-day, unless, were they more meaty and sustained, some of the buffoonery of Nikita Balieff's " Bats." " Comedies are written solely to be acted," wrote Molière, " I should advise only those who can visualize all the dumb show which is necessary on the stage to read this play" (*L'Amour médecin*). No easy condition, now that the productions of Hollywood are stultifying our visual capacities. Molière's words apply to the generality of Chinese farces. Hence it is for the imaginative reader that we venture to give a rendering of *Ta Ch'êng Huang*. To students of Chinese it may be recommended as a little thesaurus of racy Pekingese expressions.

TIAO CH'AN 貂 嬋

SABLE CICADA

Also known as *Fêng I T'ing :* "Phœnix Ceremonial Pavilion," and *Lü Pu Hsi Tiao Ch'an :* "Lü Pu's Dalliance with Sable Cicada."

PERIOD: End of Han, circa A.D. 192.   A *p'i-huang* play.

DRAMATIS PERSONÆ

WANG YÜN, Minister of Education	*Lao-shêng*
TUNG CHO, General and Minister wielding supremepower	*Ta-hua-lien*
LÜ PU	*Hsiao-wu-shêng*
LI JU, Tung Cho's son-in-law	*San-hua-lien*
TIAO CH'AN, a singing-girl	*Hua-tan*
ATTENDANTS, MAIDS, SOLDIERS, ETC.	

HISTORICAL SETTING

The plot will be found in the *Romance of the Three Kingdoms*, Vol. I, Chapters VIII and IX, but the drama varies considerably, and our version is that which is generally performed. For those unfamiliar with the foremost of popular Chinese historical novels which, as Mr. Brewitt-Taylor the translator wrote, is "perhaps better known through stage-performances than by actual reading," we give a brief history of the protagonists in this drama.

Wang Yün (died A.D. 193) was a high official at the Court of Han Ling Ti, who having incurred the hostility of the infamous eunuch Chang Jang was forced to flee for his life. Upon the accession of the Emperor Hsien Ti in A.D. 190 he returned and was restored to high office but he was so disgusted by Tung Cho's atrocities that he contrived his assassination at the hands of Lü Pu. How this was compassed is the theme of the play.

Tung Cho (died A.D. 192) had risen to distinction as a military commander during the turbulent times before the close of the Han dynasty. With Yüan Shao's co-operation he recovered the young Emperor, who had been abducted by the faction of eunuchs during a revolution, and restored him to the Throne, only to depose him as soon as mutual jealousies left him in supreme control. He then set up a still younger child, the Prince of Ch'ên-liu, under the style of Hsien Ti. His tyranny and cruelty have made him one of the monsters of Chinese history.

Lü Pu (died A.D. 198), albeit the hero of the play, had little to recommend him but personal beauty and military prowess. He was an opportunist, utterly unscrupulous and devoid of loyalty. He first entered the service of Ting Yüan, who treated him like a son and was assassinated by him for his pains at Tung Cho's instigation. History repeated itself with his assassination of Tung Cho, for which service he was created a marquis. After a brief interval of power, he was ousted, captured and put to death by the formidable Ts'ao Ts'ao.

Tiao Ch'an, the Chinese type of *femme fatale*, was a singing-girl in Wang Yün's establishment, and the delicate but none the less effective instrument in his plot to destroy Tung Cho.

The Play

Deeply dejected and consumed with loathing for Tung Cho, Wang Yün saunters in his moonlit garden, meditating means to exterminate his enemy. He hears a voice not far away. Stealthily approaching he sees his singing-girl, Tiao Ch'an, and asks her what she is doing. She replies : " Your handmaid is praying Heaven to protect the people from pending calamity and destruction." Wang Yün exclaims in amazement : " How can a frivolous little thing like you know anything of State concerns ? You must have some private motive for your prayers." Tiao Ch'an replies : " Although your slave may be poor and uneducated, she is aware that there are troubles in store for our land. She could not help noticing her lord's countenance and that his anxiety was on account of certain treacherous ministers usurping Imperial power. Could she render any service, she would die without regret."

A sudden idea flashes through Wang's mind : he summons her to a secluded spot and tells her of his scheme. This is the Lien Huan Chi, or " Chain-plan," so-called because the objective is to be obtained by various stages, leading to each another. He writes a letter to Lü Pu, inviting him to a feast. Tiao Ch'an appears while the banquet is in progress, exquisitely apparelled, a figure so dazzling that Lü Pu is visibly enthralled. Observing this his host says : " As you are almost one of the family and not to be reckoned as an outsider, I bade my little daughter come in and serve wine to us."

Lü Pu promptly falls in love with her and she is swift to practise the arts of her coquetry upon him. Wang Yün slips out of the room to give them a better chance to flirt and to see if Lü Pu will take full advantage of it. Tiao Ch'an ogles him and sighs with all the eloquence of simulated passion. Somewhat brazenly, she leads matters to a crisis. "Ah, would that I could serve you, General," she lisps," for I am no longer mistress of my heart : I love you too deeply and tenderly to tell." "And I long to have you for wife," says Lü Pu, enraptured. Wang Yün returns, dissembling blissful ignorance of these developments. Lü Pu pronounces boldly : "Your daughter is wondrously beautiful. Have you any objection to bestowing her on me as a wife ? " " She has not yet been engaged to any one," says Wang Yün, "and if you, General, do not despise her common appearance, I am more than willing to let you take her." Lü Pu is overjoyed and in token of thanks salutes his host as father-in-law. " I shall at once make all arrangements for the dowry, ornaments and nuptial apparel," says Wang Yün. "Let the General himself select the propitious day and time for the ceremony." The guest drinks his health and departs with profuse expressions of gratitude.

A few days later, Wang Yün invites Tung Cho to a banquet even more lavish. Tiao Ch'an on this occasion appears with four auxiliary singing-girls, each with the musical instrument she excels in : they play, dance and warble for the corpulent usurper's delectation. Tiao Ch'an exploits her ravishing charms to the limit : she only has eyes for Tung Cho, who is of course captivated. While he is applauding her with a carnal gleam in his eye, Wang Yün seizes his opportunity. "If the Grand Secretary would care to take her, she is his for the asking," says he. Tung Cho, whose fondness of women and wine is his only natural trait, eagerly exclaims : " How could I be grateful enough for such generosity ! "

Without more ado he orders a covered chair to convey Tiao Ch'an to his palace.

Lü Pu soon hears that his patron has installed a new concubine and becomes suspicious. Strolling through Tung Cho's pleasure-grounds he catches sight of his enchantress at a window : she is sitting beside Tung Cho, drinking wine. In spite of the rage that surges in him he dares not enter the room. Tiao Ch'an is quick to recognize him and at once pretends to weep behind the Grand Secretary's back. Tung Cho discerns him also. " What brings you here ? " he asks, " You have no business to sneak around like this. If you have nothing of importance to communicate, make yourself scarce ; don't let me catch you loitering in my premises again ! " Lü Pu can only withdraw in high dudgeon. One day, hearing that Tung Cho has left his palace, Lü Pu renews his " quest of the golden girl." While he is reconnoitring in the park, Tung Cho's bodyguard warn him of the master's approach : again he has to scamper off ignominiously. He waits until Tung Cho has gone to Court and is likely to stay there for some duration. Then, halberd in hand, he enters his chief's residence a third time and discovers his beloved sitting in her bower. She motions him towards the garden, where she joins him, and together they retire to the Phœnix Pavilion (which has given its name to the play). He places his halberd outside and follows her in. With tears streaming down her cheeks she tells him her version of the tale : how Wang Yün entrusted her to his " adopted " father Tung Cho ; and how the latter came to her chamber by night and took her by force. So artful is her narrative that Lü Pu is goaded to the verge of insanity. He swears eternal vengeance on the robber of his sweetheart. And again she sobs and moans : " I am compelled to remain in this place where every day seems like a dismal year. Oh, think of some way to save me, or I shall surely destroy myself ! "

Thus Lü Pu is ensnared in Wang Yün's " chain-plan." Tung Cho suddenly arrives on the scene, and at sight of the lovers in the pavilion he loses all self-control. But Lü Pu is too nimble for him and takes to his heels in a trice. Tung Cho seizes the halberd he left behind in his flight, hurls it and misses. Then picking it up he follows in hot pursuit but Lü Pu has already effected his escape. As he runs out of the garden-gate he collides full tilt with his son-in-law Li Ju. Tung Cho is sent sprawling. Li, who had not tumbled in spite of the shock, helps him to his feet, and handing him the halberd asks who he has been chasing. " It was that un-mannerly wretch Lü Pu. I caught him dallying with my favourite concubine."

" Why don't you make him a present of her?" *suggests Li Ju,* " that would win him over. Otherwise there's danger that he may bear you a grudge and rebel against you."

Remembering that Lü Pu had already put one of his patrons out of the way (Ting Yüan), Tung Cho is somewhat sobered. He says he will think it over. He then goes to see Tiao Ch'an, whom he finds in tears, and asks her whether Lü Pu made any advances to her.

TIAO CH'AN. Had Your Excellency not returned in the nick of time, he would have forced me to yield to his vicious desires.

TUNG CHO. Li Ju has just advised me to hand you over to him : are you willing to go?

TIAO CH'AN (*feigning terror*). My lord is cruelly wrong. Everybody knows that Lü Pu's relations with you are the same as those between father and son. Besides I have been your handmaid for some time ; my destiny is fixed. Were you now to hand me over to Lü Pu I should become a laughing-stock : it would be like com-mitting incest. I would rather perish than submit to such ignominy. (*She falls on Tung Cho's breast, weeping as if her heart would break*).

TUNG CHO. You need not cry ; I had not the slightest in-tention to let you go. I was merely testing your devotion.

When shortly after Li Ju goes to ask Tung Cho why he has not yet sent her to Lü Pu, he exclaims, bristling with indignation : " Would you be willing to give your wife to Lü Pu ? " Li Ju retires in confusion and never refers to the subject again.

Tung Cho decides to take Tiao Ch'an to Mei Wu, the new pleasure-city he had laid out beyond the Capital. They are seen off by all the high military and civil officials. Lü Pu climbs a hill to watch the cavalcade with his beloved disappear in the distance. Suddenly someone taps him on the shoulder ; he turns and sees Wang Yün.

WANG YÜN. What are you doing here all by yourself, General ?

LÜ PU. I was feeling depressed and came to dispel my sorrow.

WANG YÜN. Just now I saw Tiao Ch'an in a carriage accompanying Tung Cho to Mei Wu. How is it that after all this time you have made no arrangements with the Grand Secretary for your wedding ?

LÜ PU (*flushing with anger*). Are you not aware that the old rebel has taken her into his own palace and installed her as a concubine ?

WANG YÜN (*feigning surprise*). How can this be, General ! Can it be true ?

LÜ PU. Aye, so it is : only too true, and the whole palace knows about it. (*Naïvely he proceeds to relate the whole story*).

WANG YÜN. If this be so, General, you have been grossly insulted and put to shame. This time the old reprobate has certainly gone too far !

LÜ PU. Were it not for our relationship I would have killed him long ago.

WANG YÜN. When the Grand Secretary hurled your own halberd at you in the Phœnix Pavilion, where was the relationship you refer to, I would like to know ?

LÜ PU. Had you not reminded me of that incident, I might have overlooked it. I am now fully determined to kill the villain and have done with it.

*Seeing the effect of his words, Wang Yün takes him to his palace and broaches his scheme for Tung Cho's assassination. This is to bide his time till Tung Cho is summoned to Court; lay an ambush just inside the palace-gates and kill him as he enters. And so it happens. Tung Cho arrives for an audience and is attacked from both sides. As he sinks he sings: " Where is my son and protector? Where is Fêng-hsien? * Lü Pu roars out savagely: " Behold, he is here," and thrusts his halberd through his " father's " throat.*

---

*Lü Pu's *hao*, or distinguishing name.

T'IEN HO P'EI 天 河 配

The Mating at Heaven's Bridge

PERIOD : The fable probably dates from the T'ang dynasty, the play from the Ming. A *hsi-p'i êrh-huang* play.

DRAMATIS PERSONÆ

HSI WANG MU, " Western Royal Mother "	...	*Lao-tan*
YÜ HUANG, the Jade Emperor	...	*Lao-shêng*
CHIH NÜ, the Spinning Damsel	...	*Hua-shan*
CHIN NIU HSING, the Golden Ox Star ...	...	*Hua-lien*
NIU LANG, the Oxherd	...	*Hsiao-shêng*
HIS ELDER BROTHER	...	*Lao-shêng*
HIS SISTER-IN-LAW	...	*Ch'ou-p'o-tzŭ*

NIU LANG'S TWO CHILDREN ; SEVEN FAIRY MAIDENS

This picturesque play, which is always performed throughout the seventh moon in the Lunar Calendar, bears a close relation to our Christmas pantomimes.   In recent years all sorts of diversions and novelties have been introduced, especially into the Fu Lien Ch'êng productions ; and a regrettable, though comical, European influence reminiscent of ' Dick Whittington ' has been manifest in the costumes and dances of the fairy maidens.   The ancient fable, however, still holds its own in the heart of the people and continues to inspire innumerable painters.   As usual, there are copious variations on the theme.

THE PROLOGUE

The Sovereign Queen of the Western Air, Hsi Wang Mu (*lit.*, Western Royal Mother) is disporting herself in the Jasper Pool with Yü Huang,* the Jade Emperor and superintendent of the world, while seven fairy maidens dance attendance on them. They are kept waiting by Chih Nü, the Spinning Damsel, who arrives late. To punish this unpunctuality, Hsi Wang Mu

---

* The latter is sometimes left out of modern performances, as his presence might shock the new puritans.

NIU LANG AND CHIH NU ON THE MAGPIE BRIDGE

The T'ang Emperor Ming Huang and Yang Kuei-fei in the foreground

T'ien Ho P'ei

banishes her to earth for a period of seven days, which implies seven years, as a single day in Heaven is equal to a year on earth. Hsi Wang Mu also sends for Chin Niu Hsing, the Golden Ox Star, and informs him that he is to descend to earth to protect Niu Lang, the Ox-herd, who later becomes the Spinning Damsel's husband. This is to represent the engagement between Lyra (Chih Nü) and Aquila (Niu Lang) separated by the Milky Way which is the T'ien Ho, or Celestial River, in Chinese popular astronomy.

Synopsis

Niu Lang appears with his elder brother and the latter's wife. The elder brother is about to set forth on a long journey to collect debts, so he instructs his wife to keep an eye on the boy and see that he diligently pursues his studies. As soon as he is gone the wife, who has little affection for Niu Lang, tells him plainly that he must either do the household work or clear out to chop firewood and herd cattle. When he refuses she gives him such a thrashing that he decides to run away, taking their solitary ox to graze in the hills. While he is bewailing his fate, the ox suddenly turns to him and says: "If your sister-in-law offers you anything to eat, don't accept it. She intends to poison you." Extremely startled, Niu Lang inquires how the ox came to know what was in his sister-in-law's mind. "Don't trouble your head about that"; replies the ox, which is really the spirit of the Golden Ox Star, "just do as I say, and if she insists, tell her you will quit the family. Then ask her to give you myself as well as an old cart and a couple of boxes to carry your clothes in."

Niu Lang wends his way home. His sister-in-law meets him with a face wreathed in smiles and offers him some fresh cakes which she says she has baked especially for him. Niu Lang refuses them, convinced by now that his ox had told him the truth. He is on the point of leaving when his brother, just back from his journey, comes in and implores him to stay. The woman is finally compelled to sign a document granting Niu Lang's wishes, after which he takes himself off with his bovine companion.

When they have travelled a considerable distance, the boy asks the ox where they are to procure food and money. The ox replies that he need only brandish his knife and his wishes will promptly be fulfilled. Niu Lang waves his weapon accordingly and money arrives ; he waves it again and food is provided. Whereupon he confides to the ox that he is yearning for a lovely bride. " I'll conduct you to the river," says the ox, " where you will discover a girl both beautiful and charming." They come to the Celestial River, and Niu Lang catches sight of seven bathing beauties ; their garments lie scattered on the bank. The ox points to the seventh, who is none other than the Spinning Damsel. " Seize her clothes ! " says he. As soon as the fairies espy a mortal in their midst, each makes a dash for her apparel and decamps. But the Spinning Damsel has no chance of escape because her garments are in the possession of a mortal. Being in a state of nature she is forced to compromise by becoming his handmaid. They live together happily for several years, during which they are blessed with twins, a boy and a girl.

One day the ox, forboding that his days are numbered, says to Niu Lang : " Master, I am getting old and will soon have to leave you. After my death, I advise you to cut off my head and keep my stomach. The robes your wife was wearing on the day you captured her had best be hidden in the stomach and hung up on the house-beam. If she tries to escape to Heaven, rap on my head with a stick, then strap your children to a carrying-pole and pursue her wherever she goes."

When the ox expires Chih Nü is suddenly aware that her seven years of banishment are over. She recovers her robes from the dead ox's alimentary sac, embraces her children and slips out of the house, heavenwards bound. Niu Lang wakes up to find her gone. He follows the ox's instructions and with his children hurries in pursuit. At the River of Heaven he sees her standing on the opposite bank, chaperoned by Hsi Wang Mu, who waves him back.* Niu Lang, his children and the Spinning Damsel, all burst out weeping and wailing. Hsi Wang Mu herself is moved to tears by their distress and promises to allow them a rendezvous on *every seventh day*, which they mistake, however, for the 7th day of the Seventh Moon.

On the latter date in the Lunar Calendar friendly magpies are supposed to build a bridge for the couple to cross over and embrace each other. It is said that no birds are to be seen in the sky on the dawn of that day, as they are busily engaged in constructing the feathery viaduct. Children often put a pan full of water under a grape-vine arbour and gaze into the liquid reflection. If any birds are visible they imagine themselves in good luck. They also believe that the lovers' lamentations can clearly be heard in the upper heavens ; and the children start weeping in sympathy. It is a matter of fact that it generally rains on this day every year.

---

* Hsi Wang Mu throws a strip of white cloth across the stage to represent the Celestial River. Sometimes a boat with the Spinning Damsel seated therein, revolves like a gramophone-disk, which indicates the swirling of the current.

TS'UI P'ING SHAN 翠屏山

JADE SCREEN MOUNTAIN

(*from its colour and fancied resemblance to a screen*)

Also called *Shih Hsiu Sha Sao:* "Shih Hsiu murders his Elder Brother's Wife." An *êrh-huang*, *pang-tzŭ* and *nan pang-tzŭ* play.

PERIOD: Northern Sung, A.D. 420-478

DRAMATIS PERSONÆ

YANG HSIUNG, head gaoler of Chi-chou	*Hu-tzŭ-shêng*
SHIH HSIU, his sworn brother	*Wu-shêng*
YING-ÊRH, a maidservant	*Hua-tan*
P'AN CH'IAO-YÜN, Yang Hsiung's wife	*Hua-tan*
P'AN LAO-CHANG, her father	*Ch'ou-êrh*
HAI HO SHÊNG, a Buddhist monk	*Ch'ou-êrh*
INNKEEPER	*Ch'ou-êrh*

SYNOPSIS

Yang Hsiung, the head gaoler of Chi-chou, Hopei (not far from Tung Ling), was an expert swordsman of handsome appearance and, like many an athlete, less interested in the fair sex than in cultivating his own physique. His spouse, the sensual P'an Ch'iao-yün, sought consolation with a monk named Hai, whose temperament was more akin to her own. Shih Hsiu, Yang's sworn brother, had also been trained in the noble art of self-defence and prided himself on his muscular prowess, to such an extent that whenever he saw anybody being bullied he would defend him against the aggressor. Yang Hsiung had set him up as a pork-butcher and allowed him to open a stall in front of his house out of gratitude for assistance rendered; and he ate and slept in his lodging like a member of the family.

P'an Ch'iao-yün kept secret assignations with her lover. Whenever her husband had to sleep at the gaol, a beat on the "wooden fish" drum was the signal for their rendezvous; if the coast was clear, the maid Ying-êrh admitted him through the back-door. One morning Shih Hsiu rose early and caught sight of the monk's retreating figure while the little maid was closing the back-door. This convinced him that Yang Hsiung's wife and the monk had

KAO WEI-LIEN (left), AND KAO CH'ING-K'UEI (right), IN THE ROLE OF SHIH HSIU

Ts'ui P'ing Shan

made a cuckold of his crony, so he went and told him the whole story. Despite his friend's injunctions to hold his tongue, Yang Hsiung returned to his wife besotted and let the cat out of the bag. The wily woman indignantly denied his drunken accusations, asserting that Shih Hsiu had tried to take liberties with her and concocted the slander out of spite because she had disdained him. The too-credulous Yang gave her the benefit of the doubt and rebuked Shih Hsiu for conduct unworthy of a sworn brother. The latter, realizing that the wife had turned the tables on him, departed resolved upon a swift revenge. After waiting in ambush for the monk, he murdered and stripped him of certain tell-tale garments to show Yang Hsiung as proofs of the woman's adultery. He then proposed that Yang Hsiung inveigle his wife and her maid to a distant temple on Ts'ui P'ing Shan, where they put them to death. Having burned their boats they went to join the robbers' lair at Liang Shan P'o.

The story will be found in *Shui Hu Chuan*, translated by Pearl S. Buck as " All Men are Brothers," Vol. II, Chapters XLIV and XLV, pp. 813-830, but the play differs from the novel in many respects ; the dialogue is cruder, and the details are less sadistic.

Scene I

P'AN CH'IAO-YÜN (*appears and prologizes*). I am feeling much worried and distressed in mind, yet I cannot for the life of me explain why.

> *Sits and recites a few lines of verse.*
> In spring the peach-buds ope their petals cool ;
> In summer lotus fills each dazzling pool ;
> ' Neath autumn's moon we sip chrysanthemum-wine ;
> Mid winter snow the *lamei** smells divine.

(*Speaks*) I, P'an Ch'iao-yün, was wedded to Wang the Scribe, but unfortunately he took ill and expired. So I married Yang Hsiung. I did not realize that he was more attached to boxing than to women. So now I have voluptuous intercourse with my spiritual adviser, the Monk Hai of the Buddhist " Monastery for Favours Received." He often comes to partake of blissful communion with me. But recently Shih Hsiu has found this out and I fear that he will alarm my husband. There

---

* Prunus, or Chimonanthus Fragrans, Lindl.

will be a fine catastrophe in store for him if he does !
(*Sings in nan pang-tzŭ*) As I sit in the front parlour I
cherish secret longings and a hope that my monk's
ardour will never decrease in length or strength. If
only Yang Hsiung would quickly shuffle off this mortal
coil, then day by day I wouldn't have to be forever on
my guard !

YANG HSIUNG (*enters singing*). I have just been practis-
ing with my fists at the yamen and am as full of wine as
I can be. Merrily I roll my way homewards. (*Speaks*)
That was a first-rate exhibition of boxing I gave them
to-day ; His Honour was so pleased that he presented me
with a big jar of wine and a lavish supply of meat.
That's why I am so drunk. Shih Hsiu told me that my
wife had sly intercourse with Hai, her spiritual adviser.
I am now on my way home to investigate this affair.
If it doesn't happen to be true, well and good ! But if
it does, there is going to be havoc between me and that
accursed hussy. (*Sings*) My head is swimming and my
eyes so blurred that I can hardly see the road. Still
staggering I come to my own threshold. (*Speaks*) Open
the door ; open the door !

P'AN CH'IAO-YÜN. That sounds like my old man.
I'll open the door and take a look. (*She opens and Yang
enters*). Ah ! so you have returned !

YANG. A pretty creature you are !

Wife shows alarm ; Yang takes a seat.

P'AN CH'IAO-YÜN. You have come back late to-day.

YANG. You beastly trollop ! (*Twirls his whiskers
with rage. His wife hastily summons the maid. Ying-êrh
appears and asks what she is wanted for*).

P'AN CH'IAO-YÜN. Your master has returned. He
wants some tea. Make haste and fetch it.

YANG. Come back here. I don't want any tea.

P'AN CH'IAO-YÜN. You have not had your rice yet.
Better have some straight away.

YANG. I don't want any rice either!

P'AN CH'IAO-YÜN. What's the matter with you to-day? You don't want either tea or food. What's on your mind?

YANG (*to maid*). Ying-êrh, light the lamp and put it in my bedroom.

YING-ÊRH. Oh, Master, are you already wanting to sleep? (*She takes the lantern, followed by Yang and his wife. Then all return to the stage and go to bed. A swallow is heard twittering*).

YANG. Ying-êrh, what is that noise?

YING-ÊRH. It's the swallows that built their nests in the beams overhead.

YANG. The swallows going to their nests, eh? What a din! How I loathe it!

P'AN CH'IAO-YÜN. Why are you grumbling about the swallows, husband? Why should you say you loathe them?

YANG. When the wild goose dies, the female does not mate again. But these swallows meet every night and mate promiscuously. Why shouldn't I loathe them?

P'AN CH'IAO-YÜN. If that's the case you have good reason to detest them.

YANG. When I rise early to go to the yamen my mind is as muddled as tangled hemp. Even so, when a fierce tiger snatches the tender bone in his mouth, beware of his fangs. (*After this veiled threat he proceeds to vomit. P'an Ch'iao-yün whispers to Ying-êrh and the latter leaves. It is now the first watch—8 p.m.*).

P'AN CH'IAO-YÜN (*sings in nan pang-tzŭ*). I hear the first watch striking in the tower. I cannot sit at ease nor sleep in peace. I ponder to myself. (*Sings*) But stay! Usually my husband is as happy as he can be when he comes home, but to-day he seems in a terrible temper. I wonder why. Aha, I know! (*The second watch is struck*). It must be because that Shih Hsiu went and told him about our disagreement. (*Speaks*) Ah me! He must have been boozing with my husband and blabbed about my affair with Hai the monk. Yes, that's at the bottom of it. Hm! If it isn't that, Shih Hsiu, all well and good. But if it is, you and I are going to have a settlement! (*At the third watch a young monk is seen striking a watchman's rattle, a signal for P'an Ch'iao-yün, who sings*) I hear the sound of a rattle close by.

Monk loudly claps his hands. Ying-êrh appears, opens the door and tells him that the master is at home. Exit monk. Yang Hsiung asks who made that sound outside.

YING-ÊRH. It was only a cat scampering after a mouse. (*Exit Ying-êrh. It is now the fourth watch*).

P'AN CH'IAO-YÜN (*sings*). It must be Hai the monk who has come to meet me, but now that my husband is at home, the love-birds must be parted. I wish my husband would die, so that I could always enjoy the favours of my spiritual adviser. I'll lay me down on my ivory couch till daylight and then delude my mate. I shall convince him that I am a chaste domestic spouse.

YING-ÊRH (*comes in at the fifth watch*). Master and Mistress, it is daylight now and time to bestir yourselves.

YANG. Ying-êrh, bring me some water to wash my face. (*Both rise and perform their ablutions. Yang to his wife*) What did I say when I came back drunk last night?

P'AN CH'IAO-YÜN. You didn't say anything in particular—it was only tipsy twaddle.

YANG. I had had a few drinks with a friend of mine and must have talked a lot of gibberish. Henceforth I'll go on the water-wagon.

P'AN CH'IAO-YÜN. Oh, you needn't go so far as that! Only drink a little now and then.

YANG. My wife, I have noticed quite a change come over you lately. What's weighing on your mind?

P'AN CH'IAO-YÜN. We have plenty to eat and drink, what should be weighing on my mind?

YANG. I can see by your face that something is amiss.

P'AN CH'IAO-YÜN. Well, even so, you couldn't tell what it was in any case.

YANG. Quite apart from your thoughts, I could not even read my master's : you are both enigmas to me.

P'AN CH'IAO-YÜN. Well, you may guess.

YANG. I can guess at least eight or nine tenths of it.

P'AN CH'IAO-YÜN. As you have nothing much to do to-day, you might make an attempt.

YANG. And the very first time I'll prove right. Isn't it because one of the neighbours provoked you?

P'AN CH'IAO-YÜN. Your first guess is wrong.

YANG. Wait : let me guess again. Isn't it because old P'an offended you?

P'AN CH'IAO-YÜN. Wrong again ! Don't you believe that that old fellow is my father? * (*Yang nods assent*). Even if he were to beat or insult me, what could I do about it?

YANG. Then it must have been the wench Ying-êrh. I'll give her a thrashing to pacify you.

P'AN CH'IAO-YÜN. Not at all. Do you think that because we bought her, she is free to do as she likes ; that if I tell her to go east she'll go west, and if I tell her to beat a dog she'll beat a chicken? She would never dare to disobey my orders.

YANG. So that isn't it. Oh my, it's a tough job to guess what's on another's mind ! (*Rubs his head in frenzied cerebration*). Oh, I have it ! This time I'll guess right.

P'AN CH'IAO-YÜN. Go ahead.

YANG. Wasn't it because I said something that upset you when I came home drunk last night?

---

* i.e., a father could not offend a filial daughter.

P'AN CH'IAO-YÜN. Gramercy, man! There's a lot of truth in the old saying that a husband and wife bear no grudges o'nights. They should enjoy each other's company. By midnight all squabbles are settled, all runs smooth again! You're hopelessly wrong!

YANG. What! Another failure? I am sure I shall hit the nail on the head this time. Was it because Shih Hsiu offended you?

P'AN CH'IAO-YÜN (*showing signs of anger*). Who did you say?

YANG. I said Shih Hsiu.

P'AN CH'IAO-YÜN (*rising in wrath*). You had better not mention him. You will only annoy me if you do.

YANG. Why do you get so vexed at the sound of his name? What did he do to displease you?

P'AN CH'IAO-YÜN. I cannot tell you.

YANG. Why not?

P'AN CH'IAO-YÜN. If I did you would not believe me. You would only say that since we have enough to eat and drink there's no need to worry about anything else. So I won't tell you.

YANG. I promise not to get angry. I'll hearken to my good wife's words of counsel.

P'AN CH'IAO-YÜN. If you take my advice, you'll be a wealthy man.

YANG. Oh! so it's because I have never taken your advice that I am a poor man! But tell me, how did Shih Hsiu offend you?

P'AN CH'IAO-YÜN. Well, one day while I was busy with domestic duties Shih Hsiu stood in the doorway, gazing at me as if he had something very special to say, so I invited him to come in and sit down.

YANG. Did he do so?

P'AN CH'IAO-YÜN. Without a moment's hesitation. There was a chair and a stool in the room. Instead of sitting on either of these, he went deliberately and sat on my bed.

YANG. What! He sat on your bed?

P'AN CH'IAO-YÜN. Do you think it was proper to sit on the bed I sleep in?

YANG. As he's a sworn brother of mine, I can see no harm in that.

P'AN CH'IAO-YÜN. I dare say not; but for him to make certain gestures to me—that's quite another thing.

YANG. What did he do?

P'AN CH'IAO-YÜN. Well, he clutched my hand and murmured, "Sister-in-law, my own beloved sister-in-law!"

YANG. I cannot believe that Shih Hsiu would try on anything of that sort in this house.

P'AN CH'IAO-YÜN. " Sister-in-law," he coaxed, " we two have an inclination for each other."

YANG. What did he mean by that?

P'AN CH'IAO-YÜN. Don't you understand what he meant by " we two have an inclination for each other " ?

YANG. No, I don't.

P'AN CH'IAO-YÜN. He wanted to kindle my emotions.

YANG. Mercy, what a scoundrel! You ought to have mentioned my name.

P'AN CH'IAO-YÜN. It's lucky that I didn't. He would have only got worse.

YANG. What do you mean by " got worse " ?

P'AN CH'IAO-YÜN. He might have forced me down on the bed and, and . . . you know.

YANG. This is monstrous! Did you yield to him?

P'AN CH'IAO-YÜN. Now don't get excited! With both my legs I gave him a lusty kick and sent him sprawling.

YANG. I don't believe a word of it. My sworn brother Shih Hsiu is not that kind of man.

P'AN CH'IAO-YÜN. If you don't believe me, ask Ying-êrh. She fell into his snare.

YANG. Here, Ying-êrh. How did Shih Hsiu ensnare you?

YING-ÊRH. I dare not tell you—Uncle Shih would beat me.

YANG. You needn't be afraid while I am here. Speak out and tell me quickly.

YING-ÊRH. Let me see. Oh yes! The other day when I was in my room doing up my hair, Uncle Shih was just outside killing a pig. When I had finished with my hair, he had finished with the pig. So he came and stood by my door, then he walked in and tugging me by the hand, said, " Ying-êrh, my darling, how old are you? " I told him I was sixteen. He said, " Sixteen is not too young. Have you a mother-in-law yet? If not, will you be mine, and I'll give you some jewellery and a nice new dress."

YANG. Ai ya! Shih Hsiu, I thought you were a gentleman! But now I discover you are a man with the heart of a beast. Good wife, do you know that he slandered you behind your back?

P'AN CH'IAO-YÜN. What did he say about me?

YANG. It's not necessary to repeat it.

P'AN CH'IAO-YÜN. But you must.

YANG. He told me something about you only yesterday, but . . .

P'AN CH'IAO-YÜN. Be quick and tell me. I want to know.

YANG. I had better not.

P'AN CH'IAO-YÜN. Never mind that. I insist on your telling me.

YANG (*after prolonged hesitation*). He said that you had illicit intercourse with a monk.

P'AN CH'IAO-YÜN (*showing alarm*). Ah me! Shih Hsiu actually said that!

YANG. If he didn't, do you think that I would invent such a thing?

P'AN CH'IAO-YÜN. Shih Hsiu, you scoundrelly spawn of a turtle, you !* I bore you no ill-will, nor had I any quarrel with you. It's enough to make me spit blood. Here, Ying-êrh, bring me the scissors. I'll cut off my hair and become a nun. Then you will be able to say that I have a monk for a lover. (*Weeps*). I don't want to live any more ! *Ying-êrh also bursts into tears.*

YANG. You needn't cry like this. I'll tell Shih Hsiu to settle his accounts with me and leave the house at once.

P'AN CH'IAO-YÜN. The sooner he goes the better.

YANG. Ying-êrh ! Call your mistress's father.

P'AN LAO-CHANG (*enters, reciting a nonsense-rhyme*).
Seventy-seven years are mine.
I have a son of eighty-one,
A grandson hale at ninety-nine,
And a grandson-great of a hundred and one.
(*In answer to greetings*) Son-in-law, high official, be seated—be seated !

P'AN CH'IAO-YÜN. Father, I salute you.
Ying-êrh does the same.

P'AN LAO-CHANG. Why all this scurrying out of bed so early in the morning ?

YANG. Our butchery business is a fiasco.

P'AN LAO-CHANG. What ! How can a thriving trade like that be called a fiasco ?

YANG. Men's hearts have changed.

P'AN LAO-CHANG. I don't understand you. Mercy on me ! Ying-êrh's a clever wench : I'll ask her. Come here, Ying-êrh.

YING-ÊRH. What is it, Your Honour ?

P'AN LAO-CHANG. What does he mean by saying men's hearts are changed ?

---

* Being a woman, she actually pronounced a milder-sounding form of invective with the same significance : *hsiao t'u-tsai-tzŭ*, "mean offspring of a rabbit." But this hardly has the same connotations in English as in Chinese, and the classical expression " turtle-spawn " is just a soupçon more effective.

YING-ÊRH. With your snow-white beard don't you know what he means by that?

P'AN LAO-CHANG. In truth I don't.

YING-ÊRH. By saying that men's hearts are changed he means that a change has come over their minds.

P'AN LAO-CHANG. Your talk muddles me more than ever. Who is it that has changed his mind?

YANG AND P'AN CH'IAO-YÜN. Shih Hsiu, Shih Hsiu!

P'AN LAO-CHANG. But he is our worthy partner!

YANG. Never mind that. Fetch my hat and coat: I am off to the yamen. (*Puts on a grave, dignified air*).

P'AN CH'IAO-YÜN. Still being tipsy, don't go making a fool of yourself with a lot of nonsensical gabble.

YANG. My good intentions have come to naught.*

P'AN CH'IAO-YÜN. Yes, and when you strike up friendships with people, look out that they are gentlemen.

YANG. All right. A fine friend and gentleman have I been harbouring in my home!

SHIH HSIU (*is heard behind the stage*). Ha, ha! (*On entering, to Yang*) So you have risen betimes, Brother Yang!

YANG. Out of my sight, you scurvy beggar!

SHIH. He lends an ear to his wife's chatter and then goes for me!

YANG. You have the face of a gentleman, but the heart of a vile blackguard.

SHIH. You don't recognize a great man when you see one.

YANG. Where is the personage you are referring to?

SHIH. I am he.

YANG. Come here: great man indeed! (*Hits him*). Faugh! You spawn of a base degenerate! (*Exit*).

SHIH. We have been excellent friends, Yang Hsiung and I; and now he treats me like this! Well, let that pass. I'll settle the accounts and leave his house.

---

* Referring to his sworn brotherhood with Shih Hsiu, whom he thinks has betrayed him.

If I stay any longer I'll only incur more hatred. The poor do not lack near or distant relations. Even if I were to linger our friendship wouldn't be the same as it was in the beginning.

P'AN LAO-CHANG. Glad to see you, partner. Take a seat.

P'AN CH'IAO-YÜN. Here, this isn't a hostel or a nunnery, for you to come and go as you please. Mind you scold him, Ying-êrh, and drive him out.

YING-ÊRH (obediently). Shih Hsiu : you are the spawn of a turtle, a true turtle's egg !

SHIH. Sister-in-law, is it because I owe you a few dollars that you are cursing me ?

P'AN CH'IAO-YÜN. Repay me, then. Bring me the money.

SHIH. Fetch my luggage.

P'AN CH'IAO-YÜN. Ying-êrh, fetch the luggage he brought with him when he first walked into this house.

YING-ÊRH (returning with a bundle of cloth). Here you are.

SHIH. I want my own things, not your dirty rags.

P'AN CH'IAO-YÜN. I told you to fetch his belongings. Who told you to fetch my " riding-horse-cloth " ?

YING-ÊRH. Goodness gracious, I have brought the wrong article !

P'AN CH'IAO-YÜN. Make haste and do as you're bid. (Ying-êrh obeys. Then to Shih) Here are your worldly goods. Be off with you now ! Out of the house, and get you gone !

P'AN LAO-CHANG. That's what I call a mighty change in people's hearts !

SHIH (sings in hsi-p'i yüan-pan). Ying-êrh insults me as soon as I step into the room. I blush with shame to think that such as she should abuse a young hero like myself. I cannot endure it : my heart is aflame with fury and indignation. I'll have it out with her.

SHIH (*sings in hsi-p'i yüan-pan*). Ying-êrh insults me as soon as I step into the room. I blush with shame to think that such as she should abuse a young

P'AN LAO-CHANG. Partner Shih Hsiu, there is an apt and worthy saying that a gentleman does not fight with a woman, nor a chicken with a dog. If you have anything to say, ponder well before you say it. Show some consideration for my feelings!

SHIH (*sings in yüan-pan*). I still feel friendship and respect for Brother Yang Hsiung. But when I leave this house you will never set eyes on me again.

P'AN LAO-CHANG. Partner Shih, have you enough for travelling expenses?

SHIH. I feel ashamed to . . .

P'AN LAO-CHANG. Young folks always fancy themselves superior to others, and don't like to ask their elders for money. I'll give you some for the journey. Ying-êrh, come here! (*She obeys*). Open the treasury.

YING-ÊRH. Where do commoners keep a treasury? Are you wanting to rebel against the State?

P'AN LAO-CHANG. Official families have their own treasury: mine is in my wadded cotton pants, where you will find a solid lump of silver. Go and fetch it: it is for Shih Hsiu.

YING-ÊRH. You don't want to give it to him, do you?

P'AN LAO-CHANG. Never you mind. Be brisk.

YING-ÊRH (*soon returning with the money*). Here it is.

P'AN LAO-CHANG. Here is what?

YING-ÊRH. The silver, of course. Grandfather, you should not part with so much. It is the money to buy your coffin with.

P'AN LAO-CHANG. For a servant-girl you have far too much gab. Here, Shih Hsiu! Here's some money for your travelling expenses. It will come in handy for wine and victuals.

SHIH. How much is it?

---

hero like myself: my heart is aflame with fury and indignation. I'll have it out with her.

NOTE.—臉 *lien,* 爭 *chêng* : stage practice requires to be read *chien* and *chên* respectively. See ARLINGTON, *op. cit.,* p. 68, for these *shang k'ou tzŭ* 上 口 字.

P'AN LAO-CHANG (*remembering that he is a comedian*). It is only eight-tenths short of a thousandth, in twenty-four pieces, plus two extra pieces of alloyed silver.

SHIH (*taking the money, says*). I accept it with great reluctance. (*Sings in yüan-pan*) Thank you very much, Mr. P'an, for all your abundant favours and kindness. But as for your daughter, she treats me like trampled grass. As soon as I catch sight of her, I flare up.

P'AN LAO-CHANG (*to his daughter*). Shih Hsiu is leaving us. Say a few kind words to him, for the sake of his friendship with your husband.

P'AN CH'IAO-YÜN. Much as I would like to, the very sight of him provokes me, so where are my kind words to come from?

P'AN LAO-CHANG. At least you could pretend that you are sorry he is going; a few obliging words will preserve the friendship between him and your husband in the future as in the past.

P'AN CH'IAO-YÜN. Uncle Shih. Ha, ha! Excuse me if I have taken a drop too much wine to-day and given you offence. You needn't be vexed with me. Stay another two or three days if you like, or even half a day! As my husband isn't at home that's not for me to decide. If you wish to go, then go! I'm not the one to detain you.

SHIH HSIU (*speaks*). How could I remain under your roof another minute? (*Sings*) Mistress P'an makes false pretence of inviting me to stay. Well, I'll go forward and call her sister-in-law, and give her a polite bow.

P'AN CH'IAO-YÜN. You call me sister-in-law quite rightly. But of what use have I ever been to you?

SHIH. You have done some good.

P'AN CH'IAO-YÜN. How so?

SHIH (*sings*). I have put you to a lot of trouble these few days.

P'AN CH'IAO-YÜN. This must be the first time you have said anything decent about me. Every morning I have had to rise at the peep of day, my hair uncombed and my feet unbound, running to and fro almost worried to death, and all for whom?

SHIH. For whom indeed?

P'AN CH'IAO-YÜN. Entirely for you!

SHIH. No, not for me.

P'AN CH'IAO-YÜN. True as my heart, it was for you.

SHIH. Certainly not for me.

P'AN CH'IAO-YÜN. For whom then?

SHIH. It was for that Hai . . .

P'AN CH'IAO-YÜN. What Hai?

P'AN LAO-CHANG (*whispers*). Hai the monk.

(*His daughter pretends not to hear*).

SHIH (*sings*). When Brother Yang returns, tell him the truth; and after I have gone, don't malign me.

P'AN CH'IAO-YÜN. Never in my life have I slandered anyone behind his back.

SHIH. What! You never slander anyone?

P'AN CH'IAO-YÜN. Never.

P'AN LAO-CHANG. How can you say such a thing! Why nobody is spared your vituperation!

SHIH (*speaks*). Just fancy that! (*Sings*) You have a mouth like granulated sugar and a tongue that cuts like a knife.

P'AN CH'IAO-YÜN. We women abide by three principles. First, walk on the straight path; second, always conform to moral conduct; and third, keep to the middle of the road. There is nothing lewd or low about me!

SHIH. What about that second principle of yours—moral conduct?

P'AN CH'IAO-YÜN. It's none of your business.

SHIH. I was only asking. Well, well! If you won't tell me I'll tell you. There's a common saying that women should not be false, they should not have paramours, or indulge in unlawful intercourse.

P'AN LAO-CHANG. What is that you're saying?

SHIH. Your daughter says she isn't false : that's the first point.

P'AN LAO-CHANG. What about the second ?

SHIH. She said it was none of my business.

P'AN LAO-CHANG. Here, Ch'iao-yün, what is the meaning of that first principle ?

P'AN CH'IAO-YÜN. It means that a woman should not be false.

P'AN LAO-CHANG. And what about the second ?

P'AN CH'IAO-YÜN. Father, you should not ask me that.

P'AN LAO-CHANG. Then it's on account of the second principle that you ruined your reputation.

SHIH (*sings*). You have the heart of a ravenous crop-haired tigress. Some day you'll run against my blade without a soul to protect you.

P'AN CH'IAO-YÜN. I am sure you would never dare.

SHIH. I maintain it will happen. (*Sings*) To-day we part. Only your death can settle this matter between us ! (*Laughs sardonically*) I'll not come here again.
Exit.

P'AN CH'IAO-YÜN AND YING-ÊRH. Good riddance ! At last he is going. Let him go !

P'AN LAO-CHANG. You seem delighted because Shih Hsiu has left us. But I am not.

P'AN CH'IAO-YÜN. Why not ?

P'AN LAO-CHANG. When Shih Hsiu was running the butchery business here, he always gave me titbits to munch with my wine. Now that he is gone I'll have no relish with my liquor. That's why I don't feel glad.

P'AN CH'IAO-YÜN. Never mind. Ying-êrh and I will let you have our titbits.

P'AN LAO-CHANG. I don't want either's : your titbits are tainted. If you should be brought to bed of a son, Ch'iao-yün, what name would you give him ?

P'AN CH'IAO-YÜN. Yang Hsiung's son would of course be named by his father.

P'AN LAO-CHANG. If you had a son his name would be Hai. *Exit*.

P'AN CH'IAO-YÜN (*sings*). Papa is just amusing himself at my expense. Feeling abashed, I could not answer him back. Close the door, Ying-êrh, and see that it is safely bolted. My spiritual adviser will soon be coming to see me.

HAI (*enters singing*). Just as I was reciting my prayers in the temple Ch'iao-yün's image floated into my mind. So I told my acolyte to come along with me and sound the watchman's rattle.* When the door is opened, I'll meet my pretty lass.

The rattle sounds. Ying-êrh opens the back-door, peeps out, and runs back to announce the visitor.

P'AN CH'IAO-YÜN (*sings*). I hear the watchman's rattle : my spiritual adviser must have arrived. I'll bid Ying-êrh open the door and admit him. We'll then retire behind the red silk curtains, to bill and coo like love-birds.

The monk enters and taking her by the arm—the height of demonstrative affection on the stage—withdraws to the bower of dalliance.

SCENE II

SHIH HSIU (*enters singing*). Since my brawl with that disgraceful strumpet I cannot contain my fury. My face is burning with mortification. Now that I have come to the market-place my bowels are yearning for something to quench my fever. Otherwise my hatred will never be appeased.

INNKEEPER (*entering*). May I venture to ask if you are not Shih Hsiu the shop-assistant ?

SHIH. That's me.

INNKEEPER. You seem to be much flustered this morning. Where are you off to ?

---

* The prearranged signal for the lovers' rendezvous.

SHIH. I have a particular engagement.

INNKEEPER. But your looks belie your actions.

SHIH. Brother Yang asked me to keep watch for him at night, but I have no weapon in case there's trouble.

INNKEEPER. I could lend you a knife of mine.

SHIH. Capital! Do lend it to me. (*He seizes it and goes off saying good-bye*).

INNKEEPER (*stopping him*). Mr. Shih Hsiu, I have some excellent wine here. Swallow a couple of bumpers before you leave : they will give courage. What do you say ?

SHIH. Good, fetch me some. (*Innkeeper pours out the wine. Shih is about to leave again; the innkeeper urges him to drink a couple more. Shih excuses himself and tells him to put it down to his account*) I'll pay you later on. Now I really must be going. (*Sings*) I've got me a good stout blade from the wine-shop. (*Brandishes it as he makes his exit*).

SCENE III

P'AN CH'IAO-YÜN (*sings in tao-pan behind the stage*). To-night reminds me of the seventh day of the seventh moon, when lovers meet at last.*

Enter Hai and P'an Ch'iao-yün.

HAI. Yes, I am the Oxherd and you are the Spinning Damsel. (*Sighs*).

P'AN CH'IAO-YÜN. Why do you sigh like that ?

HAI. I had two very bad dreams last night.

P'AN CH'IAO-YÜN. What was the first dream like ?

HAI. I saw a horn grow out of my head.

P'AN CH'IAO-YÜN. Wasn't there a vision of some kind connected with it, showing a head or a face?

HAI. No, nothing at all : I really can't explain it.

YING-ÊRH. I can. The character for horn 角 is made up of 刀 " knife " and 用 " use."

---

* Referring to the legend of the Spinning Damsel and the Oxherd: see *T'ien Ho P'ei* (p. 360).

HAI AND P'AN CH'IAO-YÜN (*cry out in unison*). Don't prattle so much.

P'AN CH'IAO-YÜN. And what was the second dream about ?

HAI. I saw a coffin floating on the sea.

P'AN CH'IAO-YÜN. That is a sign of good promise for you.

YING-ÊRH. Indeed it's not ! His name being Hai, if there is a coffin in the *hai* [*sea*], it means that there will be no place on land for his burial when he dies, but that he'll be buried in the water.

HAI. Ying-êrh, you are too inconsiderate in your chatter. Your words upset me more than I can say. Open the door, I'll be going. (*Makes a few rounds of the stage, which denote his departure. Exit P'an Ch'iao-yün and Ying-êrh*).

SHIH HSIU (*entering with a knife, accosts Hai*). Who are you ?

HAI. I am Hai . . Hai the monk.

SHIH. How do you happen to be sneaking out of my brother Yang's house at midnight ?

HAI. I came to beg alms.

SHIH. Why don't you come in the day time ? What are you begging alms for at this time of night ?

HAI (*stammering*). I . . . I have no time during the day, so have to beg by night.

SHIH (*threatening with his knife*). You had better tell the truth, otherwise I'll kill you.

HAI (*stuttering and trembling all over*). P'an . . . P'an . . . Ch'iao-yün, she . . . she . . . she invited me to come.

SHIH. Take off your monkish robe and cap and hand them to me.

HAI. No ! I won't do that !

SHIH. Will you take them off or not ?

HAI. I won't.

SHIH (*brandishing knife*). Then I'll have to kill you.

HAI (*terrified*). Very well, I'll remove them. (*Undresses and discovers a woman's embroidered jacket which he wears inside his robe*).

SHIH. What are you, a monk, doing with a woman's jacket on you?

HAI. P'an Ch'iao-yün gave it to me.

SHIH. Off with it!

HAI. No, I won't take it off—not even if you butcher me.

SHIH. Will you take it off, I ask you?

HAI. No.

SHIH (*again brandishing his knife*). Well then, I'll simply have to kill you.

HAI (*pulling off the jacket, hands it to Shih*). Now let me go.

SHIH. Will you come here again?

HAI. Never again!

SHIH. I don't believe you.

HAI. I'm willing to swear to it.

SHIH. All right. Give me your oath.

HAI (*sings*). I, the spiritual adviser Hai,
　　　　　Before the gods up in the sky,
　　　　　Now nimbly kneel to swear that I
　　　　　Will nevermore come here or nigh.
　　　　　If I do, when I die,
　　　　　May I be reincarnated as a fly!

SHIH (*sings*). Since you left home to become a monk, you have never had the slightest respect for the religion of Buddha. To-day you will perish by my blade. Your miserable existence has drawn to its limit. (*Slaughters him, then speaks*) Having slain the monk I'll strip him of his crimson jacket and throw it with his carcass outside Yang Hsiung's back-door.

YANG HSIUNG (*enters; seeing Shih Hsiu, exclaims*). Who are you?

SHIH. It is I, Shih Hsiu.

YANG. What ! Still here !

SHIH. Some one has been murdered on your premises.

YANG. Who is it ?

SHIH. Hai the monk. And I am his murderer.

YANG. Where is the corpse ?

SHIH. Lying at your own back-door.

Yang goes out to inspect it.

YANG (*returning*). You were right. My contemptible wife has committed adultery with Hai the monk. I must go and kill the strumpet.

SHIH. Wait ! Don't be in such a hurry. If you kill her here we may never be able to get outside the gates of Chi-chou.

YANG. What do you suggest ?

SHIH. Persuade her to accompany us to Ts'ui P'ing Shan, to burn incense at the old temple. There you can choose a quiet spot and dispose of her. You and I can then escape to another district. Won't that be safer ?

YANG. I quite agree. A capital solution !

SHIH. But don't let anything of this leak out. (*Exeunt*).

YING-ÊRH (*appears and seeing the monk's corpse, screams out*). Oh, my Lady ! A terrible thing has happened.

P'AN CH'IAO-YÜN (*entering*). Why, what is the matter ?

YING-ÊRH. Someone has murdered the monk Hai.

P'AN CH'IAO-YÜN. Where is the corpse ?

YING-ÊRH. It is just outside the back-door.

P'AN CH'IAO-YÜN. Wait here while I go and look at it. (*Bursts into loud lamentation*) Ah me ! My teacher Hai !

YANG (*enters saying*). The vile creature ! (*Seeing his wife in tears*). What are you doing here ?

P'AN CH'IAO-YÜN. I was only playing with Ying-êrh.

YANG. Then why are tears streaming from your eyes.

P'AN CH'IAO-YÜN. Ying-êrh's handkerchief flicked me in the eye.

YANG. You are clever at dissembling. (*To Ying-êrh*) Bring me my incense-bag and knife.

P'AN CH'IAO-YÜN. What do you need them for ?

YANG. I must go to Ts'ui P'ing Shan to burn incense and redeem a vow.

P'AN CH'IAO-YÜN. May I accompany you ?

YANG. I was just about to ask you to come along.

YING-ÊRH. I want to go too, Sir.

YANG. All right. You may join us. (*Exit Yang*).

P'AN CH'IAO-YÜN (*weeping*). Alas, sweet monk ! I wonder who it was that murdered you, leaving me to bewail you in secrecy and solitude. Ying-êrh, go hire some men to bury the corpse, and then engage a chair to take me up the Jade Screen Mountain. (*Exeunt*).

SCENE IV

SHIH (*enters, singing*). I killed the monk and kept his cap and robe. Now Mistress P'an has been inveigled into burning incense on the mountain. Gazing towards its summit I can descry a temple. When Yang Hsiung arrives I'll make him a sign. (*He hides, so as to be invisible to P'an Ch'iao-yün*).

YANG (*enters and says*). My wife is utterly without a conscience. She should never have committed adultery with Hai the monk. I'll slowly climb the mountain, and when that despicable strumpet arrives, I'll inquire more closely into the details.

Enter P'an Ch'iao-yün and Ying-êrh.

P'AN CH'IAO-YÜN (*sings*). The tears stream down my face as I travel along. In the twinkling of an eye I have reached the summit of Jade Screen Mountain. Suddenly I see Shih Hsiu, stationed on yonder slope. How does he happen to be here, I should like to know !

SHIH. Oh, sister-in-law, so you decided to come ?

P'AN CH'IAO-YÜN (*showing great alarm*). Yes, I came too.

SHIH. It is as well.

P'AN CH'IAO-YÜN (*to Ying-êrh*). We'll go back at once.
YANG (*appearing suddenly*). Where are you off to?
Do you already think of going home?

P'AN CH'IAO-YÜN. The month is taking its toll. So
I really must return. Ying-êrh, we'll go back.

YANG. Do you still think of returning?

P'AN CH'IAO-YÜN. It is not a fine day to-day.

YANG. But it is an auspicious day. There is no
need for you to go back. Here, Shih Hsiu, you told
me that your sister-in-law committed adultery with Hai
the monk. Where is your proof?

P'AN CH'IAO-YÜN. Shih Hsiu : from of old it has been
said that both must be caught in the act of adultery, not
one alone. If you catch a thief you must produce the
stolen goods. Where is the proof of your accusations?

SHIH. I have incontestable proofs, but it is hardly
necessary for you to see them.

P'AN CH'IAO-YÜN. I *must* see them!

SHIH. I'll quickly open the bundle and show the
monk's cap and robe. I have already killed the fornicator,
so don't begin any of your deceitful hysterics.

YANG. Let me see your proofs.

SHIH. Here they are. (*Shows them to Yang, then
sings*) And here is my sister-in-law's embroidered silk
jacket. (*Speaks*) Is this not her very own?

YANG (*examining them*). Quite so : that is her jacket.
Have you any more of her things?

SHIH (*sings*). Yes, here are the monk's robe and
cap. (*Speaks*) Examine them carefully! (*Sings*) Your
wife does not mind her own affairs ; instead she plays the
injured innocent, trying to spoil a staunch friend's
reputation.

YANG (*seizing his knife in fury*). Ying-êrh is utterly
worthless ; I'll dispose of her first. (*Kills her*).

P'AN CH'IAO-YÜN (*in a panic, sings*). To see Ying-êrh
murdered like this has frightened my soul away.

SHIH. Yang Hsiung, help me to kill this lewd woman. Sister-in-law, since you are to die by our hands, don't bear us any hatred. The wrong was of your doing; the fault is all your own.

P'AN CH'IAO-YÜN (*sings*). His words frighten me to death. I'll beg my husband's forgiveness. (*Speaks*) Oh husband, my husband! (*Sings*) Please spare my life and do not let me come to this untimely end. Think of our love in the days gone by!

Yang's knife is raised, arrested in hesitation.

SHIH. Why don't you slay her, brother?

YANG. The affection between man and wife cannot be so lightly dismissed.

SHIH. If you don't kill her, I shall kill you.

YANG. Truly I cannot bring myself to do the deed. You do it for me!

SHIH. Do you mean that you wish me to be implicated in the murder?

YANG. No: I'll vow to Heaven that that is not my intention. (*Sings*) I, Yang Hsiung, kneel and swear before all the gods in Heaven that I shall be true to my oath. If I break it, may I meet with an untimely death!

Hearing this oath Shih Hsiu seizes his knife and stabs P'an Ch'iao-yün to death.

YANG. Now that this couple of traitresses are dead and done with, whither shall we go?

SHIH. Let us escape to Liang Shan P'o, and join Sung Chiang and his band of jolly rovers.

YANG. Yes, that's the best course. Let us be going. (*Yang turns towards the carcasses and heaves a deep sigh*).

SHIH. Surely, my brother, you cannot have any regrets?

YANG. How can a gallant man indulge in regrets!

Exeunt.

Finis

This is scarcely a refined play, but it has the accent of veracity and a certain psychological interest, showing how notions of bravery may differ. P'an Ch'iao-yün's technique in questioning her husband (see pp. 364-6) is strikingly modern : it might almost be that of a professional psychologist, probing the secrets of a patient's soul! The means adopted by Yang Hsiung and Shih Hsiu to gain their ends are not such as to recommend them to our eyes, nor does their self-congratulation as they preen themselves on the slaughter of the miserable women ring pleasantly in our ears. Nevertheless they are taken at their own moral evaluation and regarded as fine fellows by the audience in general. Shih Hsiu is the hero of many a play. " I wish I had such a pal as that," exclaimed a Chinese acquaintance of ours, who had suffered from domestic troubles and consequently identified himself with Yang Hsiung. Hsün Hui-sheng and Hsiao Ts'ui-hua are both admirable as P'an Ch'iao-yün. Monks are generally the butt of Chinese playwrights : see Dr. Lin Yutang's *My Country and My People*, p. 128.

T'UNG WANG CHÊN 銅網陣

THE BRASS NET PLAN

Also called *Ch'ung Hsiao Lou*: "The Tower that Pierces the Clouds"

PERIOD : Sung. A semi-military *êrh-huang fan-tiao* play.

DRAMATIS PERSONÆ

PAI YÜ-T'ANG, the hero	*Wu-shêng*
YEN CH'A-SAN, an official on circuit	*Hsiao-shêng*
CHAO CHIO, Prince of Hsiang-yang	*Ta-hua-lien*
TÊNG CH'Ê, robber of the seal	*Erh-hua-lien*
SHÊN HU, his assistant...	*P'ei-chüeh*
LU FANG, eldest of the sworn brethren	*Ta-hua-lien*
CHIANG P'ING ⎫	⎧ *Wu Ch'ou*
HSÜ CH'ING ⎬ Sworn brethren	⎨
HAN CHANG ⎭	⎩ *Erh-hua-lien*
KUNG SUN-TS'Ê, Yen's secretary	*Lao-sheng*
SHÊN CHUNG-YÜAN, a brigand in the Prince's employ	*Wên-ch'ou*
LU PIN, a woodcutter	*Wu-shêng*
LU SHIH, his wife	*Ch'ing-i*
MA KAKA-ÊRH, a guard in the Prince's service ...	*Ch'ou-êrh*
THE PRINCE'S RETAINERS, ETC.	

Chao Chio, Prince of Hsiang-yang (a prefecture in Hupeh), has plotted to overthrow the Emperor and set himself up in his stead ; he enrolls a band of brigands to further his designs and has them secretly trained in his palace. Each swears fealty to the Prince and signs with his own blood a corresponding document which is deposited in the *Ch'ung Hsiao Lou*, or "Tower that Pierces the Clouds," especially erected for that purpose. The tower is compassed with mechanical traps that discharge arrows so set that any trespasser shall be transfixed.

The Emperor, having got wind of the Prince's designs, dispatches one of his personal favourites, Yen

MA FU-LU AS CHIANG P'ING

T'ung Wang Chên

YEH SHÊNG-CHANG

as Chiang P'ing
recovering the seal

THE PRINCE OF HSIANG-YANG

T'ung Wang Chên

Ch'a-san, as a special envoy for investigation. The judge on circuit, as Yen's actual status is, takes five heroes along with him, sworn brothers all, and commonly known as the Five Loyal Rats, with appropriate rodent pseudonyms. The fifth and junior member of the brotherhood, Pai Yü-t'ang, was also sworn brother to Yen ; his sobriquet being *Chin Mao Shu,* " Flowery Haired Rat." On account of this affinity Yen appoints him chief of his bodyguard. The Prince of Hsiang-yang discovers the purpose of Yen's visit and accordingly sends two of his brigands, Têng Ch'ê and Shên Hu, to assassinate him at his yamen by night, and purloin his seal of office. But he is too well guarded ; and as they are unable to approach him Shên Hu sets fire to the yamen and Têng Ch'ê makes off with the precious seal. Deeply chagrined at his master's loss, Pai Yü-t'ang pursues the robbers and captures Shên Hu, whom he leads back to the yamen. But when Shên Hu's " attaché-case " is opened it is found to contain a mere lump of lead. Têng Ch'ê had filched the genuine seal without Shên Hu's knowledge, tricking his partner to ingratiate himself with the Prince. Shên Hu's cousin, Shên Chung-yüan, vows that one day he will avenge this double-crossing.

In his rage and disappointment at catching the wrong man and the false seal Pai Yü-t'ang swears to retaliate by entering the Cloud-Piercing Tower and seizing the incriminating document. He goes there by night but another of Yen's men warns him of danger ahead, so he withdraws with a determination to renew his attempt later on. Fearing that Yen Ch'a-san will not allow him to run such a risk if he makes his intentions known, he writes a letter and entrusts it to his servant with orders to deliver it to his master if he fails to reappear within three days. He then returns to the tower after dusk, climbs to the top and falling into the trap, is transfixed

with arrows. The same night Lu Fang, eldest of the
sworn brothers, is told in a vision of Pai Yü-t'ang's
death, and sings a lament in *êrh-huang fan-tiao* style.
The brethren make a compact to avenge him.*

The Prince of Hsiang-yang goes with a number of
attendants to inspect the tower and finds Pai Yü-t'ang's
corpse. One of the cold hands still clasps a dagger;
not far away a dead sentry lies in a pool of blood: his
many gashes indicate that Pai had struggled with him
until his last breath. The hero's fame had already
reached the Prince, who now considers a ruse to wipe
out the rest of the brotherhood. He has the remains
cremated; the ashes put in a jar and buried in a
wilderness with a headstone over them. Deep pits are
dug all round to entrap any of the brethren who should
attempt to remove their comrade's relics, and two
woodcutters are detailed to keep watch.

Chiang P'ing, the fourth of the brethren (said to
possess the faculty of living under water for three days
with his eyes open), is sceptical about Pai's death. He
goes to the yamen and questions Yen's secretary, Kung
Sun-ts'ê. Convinced of the melancholy truth he
is about to leave when he is told that Yen Ch'a-san is so
overcome with grief that he has threatened to starve
himself to death. He persuades him to swallow some
food after which he regains a little strength. During the
meal his three brothers Lu Fang, Han Chang and Hsü
Ch'ing arrive with another henchman of Yen's named
Chan Hsiung-fei. They confer together and decide
that Lu Fang, Chiang P'ing and Han Chang shall go in
search of Pai's body and try to recover the seal, while
Hsü Ch'ing and Chan Hsiung-fei will remain to protect
Yen Ch'a-san. The first three separate.

Lu Fang, wandering by himself, intercepts a man
whom he sees chasing a woman, and asks him who he is

*Often the play ends at this point.

and what he is doing. He answers that the woman is his adopted sister-in-law and that he was just having a bit of fun with her. The woman declares that he is an utter stranger who tried to rape her in her husband's absence. "You go home and I'll deal with him," says Lu Fang. He then threatens the man with a knife, who confesses that his name is Ma Kaka-êrh, and that the Prince of Hsiang-yang had ordered him to guard Pai Yü-t'ang's grave. Lu Fang swoons away at the sound of his sworn brother's name and when he recovers he decides to commit suicide.

In the meantime the woman had told her husband Lu Pin about her gallant rescuer, and he arrives on the scene in the nick of time to seize Lu Fang's arm and prevent him from cutting his throat.* In the course of conversation they tell him that they are woodcutters and that only the day before they had seen a man throw something into a pool called Ni-shui-han-t'an : "Muddy Water Cold Pool." They suspect that this was the stolen seal, in which case it is beyond salvage, for the pool is so constituted that the slightest weight, a chicken's feather even, will sink for ever in its oozy depths.

Lu Fang joins Chiang P'ing and Han Chang, and all proceed to the mysterious pool. Here Chiang P'ing puts his subaqueous faculties to the test. After copious draughts of wine to keep up his circulation he takes the plunge. The water-sprites are all utterly confounded, and he recovers the seal. Generally the performance ends here.

The Prince of Hsiang-yang then sends Yen Ch'a-san a dispatch to elicit whether Yen's seal is a fake. When the reply comes he is amazed to find that it is genuine. He appoints Têng Ch'ê and Shên Chung-yüan to make a second attempt on Yen's life and recapture the evasive

---

*In the text he hangs himself to a tree, and Lu Pin cuts him down ; in *Fu Lien Ch'êng* performances he tries to cut his throat.

guarantee but they are observed and chased for a considerable distance. Têng Ch'ê hides under a bridge but Shên, who still bears him a grudge for cheating his cousin, sings in so loud a voice that those on his track can hear : " It's useless hiding under the bridge : you'll be easily seen and caught." His cousin is thus avenged, for both are captured and taken to the yamen where they reveal the Prince's treasonable machinations. And so concludes this somewhat unwieldy play.

* * *

The plot was adapted from a long and complicated novel entitled *San Hsia Wu I*, which bears a family resemblance to the *Shui Hu Chuan*, translated by Pearl Buck as " All Men Are Brothers." Though not pre-eminently suitable for the theatre, it offers such a large company as the Fu Lien Ch'êng some splendid opportunities for improvisation and the display of acrobatic finesse. It is indeed little more than an outline to be filled in by clever and exceptional actors like Yeh Shêng-chang. One high-light is in the scene where Pai Yü-t'ang falls into the trap, another where Chiang P'ing dives into the pool, and swims with every velleity of watery motion until the seal is found : both require a Nijinski-ish nimbleness and grace. Formerly both trap and pool were invisible to the naked eye, but recently there has been a regrettable tendency to depict them on back-cloths in the " realistic " foreign manner : in one instance the pool might have been a seascape by one of our most popular and formal Royal Academicians.

Psychologically the play illustrates the robust loyalty of sworn brothers : no risk is too great to avenge a comrade's death.

WANG HUA MAI FU 王 華 買 父

WANG HUA BUYS A FATHER

PERIOD : Sung. A *p'i-huang* and also *pang-tzŭ* play.

DRAMATIS PERSONÆ

WANG HUA, son of the Prince	...	*Ch'ou-êrh*
YANG HSIU-YING, wife of Wang Hua ...	...	*Ch'ing-i*
YANG CHI-FÊNG, her father, an official ...	...	*Hu-tzŭ*
HIS WIFE	...	*Ch'ing-i*
PRINCE (Pa Ch'ien Sui)	...	*Hu-tzŭ*
OLD FISHERMAN	...	*Ch'ou-êrh*
HIS WIFE	...	*Ch'ou-p'o*
JUDGE PAO	...⎫	*Ta Hua-lien*
LIU WÊN-CHIN, a Minister	...⎭	
LIANG-ÊRH ⎫ children of Wang Hua ... CHU-ÊRH ⎭	...	*Wa-wa-shêng*
WANG LAO-HAO, a neighbour of the Wangs		
SERVANTS, GAOLERS, SOLDIERS, ETC.		

Evidently the author of this play shared Hamlet's belief that
> "There's a divinity that shapes our ends
> Rough-hew them how we will."

It is a piquant historical fantasia, with Fate as *leit-motiv*, and the story depends much on supernatural intervention. The author also reveals recondite knowledge of mythological obstetrics *en passant*. Maybe, like Mr. Somerset Maugham, he deserted medicine for the drama.

The son of Chao K'uang-yin, first Emperor of the Sung dynasty, was known as Pa Ch'ien Sui (the Emperor being styled *Wan Sui*, " Ten Thousand Years," the Prince's appellation was " Eight Thousand," only two thousand years less). Appropriately he begets a son in a manner which differentiates him from other mortals. The goddess Hsi Wang Mu (" Royal Western Mother ") dispatches the K'un-lung (" Ill-fated Dragon ") to fertilize the Prince's bride, who is brought to bed of a water-melon in consequence.

According to a tradition of the Chinese the occurrence of *hsi-kua t'ai* (water-melon wombs) is not unusual among their fruitful womenfolk. In such cases the fœtus is shaped like the succulent gourd, and this is considered lucky. But we anticipate : in the days of Pa Ch'ien Sui it had not attained its auspicious repute. When the delivery is reported to the Prince, instead of rejoicing, he gives orders that the " water-melon " be committed to the swirling river forthwith.

By a happy coincidence—and where would many a Chinese drama be without such coincidences ?—an old fisherman and his spouse, who are casting their nets, rescue the placenta intact from a watery grave. On discovering a live male child within, they take the infant home and name it Wang Hua.

Some seven years elapse during which the boy never once addresses his foster-parents as " Papa " or " Mamma." Sorely perplexed, one day his foster-mother asks him :

" How is it that you never address either of us as father or mother ? We took the trouble to rear you ; one would think that at least you could show a little more filial piety."

In reply the boy sings out, " Papa "; promptly the old fisherman drops dead. He then calls " Mamma," with equally dire effect. Whereupon his loud lamentations attract the village headman, who naturally is sceptical when the child explains how these calamities occurred.

" Well," says the headman, " you call me ' Uncle,' and we'll see what happens next."

Rash proposition ! At the word uncle, the headman throws up his hands and collapses, another corpse. (The idea conveyed is that Wang Hua, albeit ignorant of the fact, is of Imperial descent and therefore not at liberty to address any commoner as a parent or kinsman).

The lad proceeds to pawn the meagre relics of his foster-parents. The money spent, being almost a half-wit, he turns to begging for a livelihood.

The scene changes. Although not circumscribed as such, Act II begins with a banquet.

Yang Chi-fêng, who has just obtained his doctoral degree (*chin shih*) at the Capital, is feasting his friends and boasting that he had to thank his own genius for his recent success ; fate had nothing to do with it. His daughter, however, thinks otherwise.

" Nonsense," she says to her maid while walking in the garden, " of course it's all due to fate; poor Father has hardly any genius worth mention."

Yang hears of this and sends for her.

" What do you mean by saying such a thing about your father ? " he asks.

Miss Yang Hsiu-ying adheres to her opinion and, exasperatingly feminine, repeats it again and again.

So Yang decides to teach her a lesson. He bids a servant go out and fetch the very first man he sees.

" I'll show you whether this is a matter of fate," says he to the obstinate daughter.

The core of tragedy and comedy, as has been justly observed, is situation. At this juncture Wang Hua is passing by with his alms-bowl. The servant invites him in and Yang offers to bestow his daughter upon him. At first Wang Hua is astonished, then suspicious, but he is persuaded to accept this strange and sudden proposal when Yang explains his motives. The young lady is quite ready to have her fate put to the test, and accompanies the beggar to his hovel, where they live contentedly for several years. Twins are born to them, both male : one is called Liang-êrh, "Beam of the House," the other Chu-êrh, " Pillar of the House."

Eventually funds run low. Mrs. Wang, having all but exhausted her dowry, hands her half-wit husband ten

silver taels and commissions him to buy a few cheap
sundries. These he is to dispose of at a profit and procure some food withal. On the way Wang's attention
is drawn to a group of people laughing uproariously.
The butt of their mirth, an elderly man, sits holding a
staff, and attached thereto is a placard with the words :
" A Father for Sale, Cheap at Taels Ten." This strikes
Wang Hua as such an excellent bargain that he offers to
buy him and take him home on the spot. There is
some method in such apparent madness when we remember Confucius, the circumstances of his birth (the Sage
did not know his father in the flesh) and his consequent
emphasis on filial piety. A father is the Confucian
summum bonum.

The dramatist digresses and we are shown that this
was due to heavenly interference. Hsi Wang Mu had
sent a star, in the guise of a fortune-teller, to inform Pa
Ch'ien Sui that he has a son in the land of the living.
Meeting the Prince, the immortal fortune-teller calls
out : " Fortunes told, cheap. I have something of
great importance to tell you."

The Prince's fortune is told as follows : " A son of
yours is living in a certain quarter of the city. Take
this card and study it with care."

True to type, the celestial fortune-teller vanishes.
The Prince goes home with the card, changes into
beggar's rags and sets forth with his advertisement
about a father for sale until Wang Hua discovers him.

Mrs. Wang is convinced that her husband is demented
when he returns to introduce a supernumerary member
to their indigent household. In this amusing scene the
Prince, who realizes that Wang Hua is his long-lost son,
is exquisitely polite until chopsticks-time. Then, confronted by bean-curd and sour cabbage, his gorge rises.
He indignantly refuses to touch this unpalatable diet
and dashes it to the ground. Forgetting his rôle, he

insists upon being served such delicacies as shark's-fins, birds'-nest and the most *recherché* rice.   Poor long-suffering Mrs. Wang is obliged to pawn her last jewels to gratify her new father-in-law's fastidious appetite. The old man dotes on his grandsons, however, and grandiosely renames them Chin Liang, " Golden Beam," and Yü Chu, " Jade Pillar."   But soon the Wangs have nothing left to pawn ; they decide to dispose of their beloved twins.

The scene changes.   Mrs. Yang Chi-fêng has not seen or heard of her daughter since her sudden exit with the beggar.   She never lets her husband hear the end of it, and nags at him until he promises to adopt a boy or girl to pacify her.   The servant he sends to reconnoitre runs straight into Wang Hua and the twins.   When he learns who is to be their adoptive father Wang Hua is more inclined to part with them.

The old Prince is much mortified to hear that the Wangs have sold their only children to keep him nourished.   He realizes what a filial and kind-hearted couple they are and decides, somewhat tardily one cannot help thinking, to make amends.   He gives Wang Hua a letter, and says :

" Take this to the Minister Liu Wên-chin and he will hand you fifty thousand taels.   But before you hand it to him, order him to kneel to you."

Accordingly Wang Hua proceeds to the yamen. The Minister Liu Wên-chin, suspecting that Wang may be a prince or even the Emperor in disguise, obeys his instructions.   After the ceremony he demands the letter. Wang searches his wallet ; to his consternation it is no longer there.   He must have lost it on the way.   So the Minister orders him to be beaten with the heavy bamboo and drives him out of the yamen.   The god of the district having found the letter in the meantime, entrusts it to Judge Pao, that upright and disinterested

statesman who, because of the inflexibility of his countenance, gained the sobriquet of " Iron Face," which
since became a synonym for unselfishness.

Wang Hua tells his father about the lost letter and
the beating. So the Prince writes another and tells Mrs.
Wang to sew it in her husband's coat for safety.

Judge Pao gives the original letter to Liu Wên-chin,
who is so appalled to discover that Wang Hua was a
genuine prince that he makes up his mind to murder
him if ever he returns. Return he does, with the second
epistle. Liu denies having received it and hands him over
to the chief gaoler with instructions to dispose of him.
As the gaoler guesses his identity, he conceals him in
his own house and substitutes a thief in his stead.

Mrs. Wang is in desperate straits. Penniless, childless, husbandless, she turns to her adopted father-in-law
for advice.

" Never mind," he says. " Here is a priceless pearl;
you may pawn it for what it will fetch."

Unable to go herself, she sends her neighbour Wang
Lao-hao to transact the business for her. The pawn-
broker is amazed at the sum demanded for the pearl—
twenty thousand taels—and tells him he must be out of
his wits. Two " detectives," on the trail of certain
articles said to have been stolen from the palace, are
drinking tea at the back of the shop. Overhearing the
argument, they suspect that the pearl is one of the articles
in question. They ask Wang how he came by it. He
takes them to Mrs. Wang Hua, who refers them to her
adopted father-in-law. The latter declares that it is
his and that he possesses many others like it. They
are prevented from putting him in irons by the shadow
of the local god, who waves his brush and, by supernatural legerdemain, one of the detectives is manacled.
Assuming that he must be a magician, they entice him to
the magistrate's yamen with gentle words.

The magistrate is infuriated when the old man refuses to kneel to him. "Why don't you get down on all fours?" he asks.

The Prince incognito replies: "I would not bow or kneel to the highest in the land, let alone an insignificant magistrate." So he is shuffled off to prison pending investigations. As in the beggar's hovel, he remains very fastidious: he demands the highest quality of food or threatens to go on a hunger-strike. The turnkeys, as in Wang Hua's case, suspect his high rank and treat him with deference accordingly: evidently prisons were good schools of psychology. They supply him with the choicest viands and promise to protect him. The Prince adopts them both as sons in return for their kindness.

Mrs. Wang makes inquiries at the magistracy and is admitted to the gaol, where again she tells him that her husband has not yet returned, that she is destitute and does not know what to do. And again the old man advises her not to worry. "Here," he says, "is an Imperial decree (*shêng chih*). Take it to Yang Chi-fêng [her own father] and he'll assist you."

At once Mrs. Wang falls on her knees, thinking he must be the Emperor.

When she arrives at her parents' home, her mother tells her that she has had two sons in her absence. As soon as the children are brought in Mrs. Wang recognizes them as her own and acquaints her mother with the facts. She visits her father, who happens to be indisposed, but when he hears of the Imperial decree he prostrates himself before it, as if it were the Emperor in person. Reverently opening it, he reads that his presence is immediately required at the magistracy gaol. He dons his official cap and robes and hurries off to the magistrate, who is very much alarmed. The Prince is to be escorted to his palace without delay.

Soon Judge Pao arrives with Wang Hua to report that Liu Wên-chin had fled on hearing of the Prince's release. They all proceed to the Emperor's throne-hall, where the Prince bids Wang Hua be seated, himself sitting on the left. He discloses Wang Hua's identity and distributes high honours among those who had assisted him, including the adopted turnkeys, henceforth Grand Guardians of the Imperial Domain.

Wang Hua's wife and children are ennobled ; Yang Chi-fêng is ordered to capture the runaway Minister, who is duly executed for his attempt on the Prince's life.

Finis

*   *   *

Chao K'uang-yin, who reigned as first Emperor of the Sung dynasty (960-976) is said to have been foully dealt with by his brother, Chao K'uang-i, or Chao Huang, in order to gain the throne. It is recorded that when the Emperor fell fatally ill, he sent for his brother and was closeted with him for a considerable time. The guards outside heard a heavy thud and Chao K'uang-i came out and reported the Emperor's sudden decease. That Sung T'ai-tsung appointed himself Emperor before his brother's body was cold, lends some credence to the story. That he was anxious to forestall Pa Ch'ien Sui, the heir apparent and first Emperor's favourite, gives further cause for suspicion. It is also recorded that Chao K'uang-yin was much attached to Chao Huang, but it is possible that the latter allowed personal ties to be overridden by ambition.

Chinese dramatists have made the most of these rumours and have not been altogether kind to Chao Huang. In this play he is made to give up his throne to the heir apparent's son, Wang Hua the simpleton, born in a water-melon womb. In *Ho Hou Ma Tien* he is openly reviled by his sister-in-law the Empress Ho, and made to acknowledge that he was not justified in ascending the Throne.

Six Famous Female Impersonators in the role of P'an Chin-lien, and Six Wu Ta Langs
in the foreground

Wu Hua Tung

WU HUA TUNG 五花洞

THE FIVE FLOWER GROTTO

So-called because each flower is supposed to contain a spirit or demon. A *p'i-huang* burlesque.

PERIOD : Sung

DRAMATIS PERSONÆ

T'IEN SHIH, the Taoist Pope	...	...	...	...	*Taoist*
PAO KUNG	... ...	...	...	...	*Ta-hua-lien*
WU TA LANG, the dwarf	...	...	...	...	*Ch'ou-êrh*
PSEUDO WU TA LANG	...	...	...	...	
P'AN CHIN-LIEN, the dwarf's wife	...	...	...	*Tan*
PSEUDO P'AN CHIN-LIEN	...	...	...	
WU TA-P'AO, a magistrate	...	...	...	...	*Ch'ou-êrh*
FIVE DEMONS, DONKEY BOY, ETC.					

The dwarf Wu Ta Lang is the Chinese " national by-word and laughing stock "* and his pretty wife P'an Chin-lien is scarcely less notorious. Both figure in the *Shui Hu Chuan* (translated by Pearl S. Buck : " All Men are Brothers," Vol. I, Chapters XXIII-XXVI, pp. 391 onwards) and *Chin P'ing Mei*, of which there is a German translation by Franz Kuhn and a French adaptation by M. Georges Soulié de Morant entitled *Lotus-d'or*. Wu Ta Lang, as the Rev. Arthur H. Smith pointed out, " is now the Chinese Man-of-ill-fame, as his name has come to suggest all varieties of unfavourable predicates ; in short he has become the ideal Mean Man. Even a tiger, it is said, would not eat him, for he did not seem to be a man at all." He was poisoned by P'an Chin-lien and her paramour, but his heroic younger brother, Wu Sung the Tiger-killer, avenged the murder by cutting off both their heads and disembowelling the adulteress, whose heart, liver and entrails he offered to the dwarf's manes. After which he joined the robbers' lair and became a general under Sung Chiang. (*See* L. C. Arlington, *op. cit.*, p. 166).

This burlesque opens with a tableau of the Taoist Pope, T'ien Shih, dressed in Taoist cloak and cap and a gold

---

* *See* Arthur H. Smith : *Proverbs and Common Sayings from the Chinese*, pp. 125-127, etc.

symbol 壽 *for Longevity painted on his forehead. He is attended by a band of acolytes, represented as sitting and punting a boat—the Ark of Heaven—warbling songs of glee as they airily float along. As soon as these spiritual people vanish Wu Ta Lang, vivid personification of the grotesque, toddles in front of an uproarious audience.*

WU TA LANG (*sings*). Times are bad indeed and this year's harvest could not be worse : it is hard to keep one's head above water. I think I'll go and visit my brother Wu Sung at Yang-ku Hsien [in Shantung]. Here, Missus !

P'AN CHIN-LIEN (*appears singing*). I come of a very poor family and am married to a three-inch manikin who can do nothing but sell cakes. Woe is me! Alack-a-day !

WU. We'll both go and see my brother Wu Sung. I'll hire a donkey for you.* In the meantime you get things ready for the journey.

A donkey-boy appears : after a rattling argument about the animal's hire, P'an Chin-lien mounts it with a bright red bundle of clothing strapped to her shoulders.   (Exeunt).

SCENE II

The five demon-tenants of the Five Flowers Grotto arrive in their natural forms in the following order : snake, toad, lizard, scorpion and centipede. They comment on their present plight.

THE DEMONS. It is many years since we have been living in a grotto, trying to cultivate immortality, and we have not yet attained to human shape : to be an angel is decidedly preferable to being a demon.

Just then they espy Wu Ta Lang and P'an Chin-lien ; and the spectacle of the dwarf trudging after the woman on the jackass provokes their loud hilarity. Two of them decide to

---

* She has tiny bound feet.

change their shapes to impersonate this ill-assorted couple and indulge in a practical joke at their expense.

Scene III

The couple arrive at a hamlet on the verge of a desert. P'an Chin-lien complains of hunger and Wu Ta Lang says he will go and fetch her something to eat.

WU. Mind you don't move while I'm away.

The demon who precisely impersonates the dwarf chooses this moment to approach her, a fan in one hand and some fritters in the other.

PAN (*thinking it is her real husband*). How can we breakfast out here in the wilderness?

DEMON. Let's go into that temple yonder. (*Off they go*).

With the usual Chinese symmetry Wu Ta Lang appears armed with fan and fritters, differing nowise from his " double." His wife's " double " repeats P'an Chin-lien's remark and they likewise wend their way to the temple. Whereupon the original couple are astounded to find themselves confronted by their exact replicas in feature, speech and intonation. The demons ape their every word, their every gesture. After an interminable argument as to who is who, they decide to have the matter settled by the magistrate.

Scene IV

This magistrate, Wu Ta-p'ao (Wu the Big Gun), happens also to be a dwarf. Accompanied by two of his scribes and four lictors he orders the plaintiffs to be brought before him. He is surprised when two men crawl up in what he mistakes for a half-kneeling attitude.* "Don't be alarmed," *he reassures them* : "I am an honest upright official." *Then, to his clerk* : "Just look at these people crawling along on their bended knees. What can it signify?" *The clerk's*

---

* All the actors impersonating dwarfs shuffle along in a squatting posture.

reply is that that is their normal size. " I don't believe it,"
*replies the dwarf-judge ; jumping down from his chair, he goes
up to them and turning himself about and about, compares his
height with theirs.* " That's very funny indeed," *he concludes,* " we are all of the same size ! " *Returning to the
Bench, he inquires :* " Who is the defendant and who is
the plaintiff? Speak the truth, and avoid evil consequences." *Both dwarfs claim to be the original Wu Ta Lang
and, in turn, both P'an Chin-liens claim similar authenticity.
The magistrate confesses his inability to adjudicate and orders
them to take their case to a higher court. At this juncture
the advent of the famous Judge Pao is announced. While the
magistrate is explaining the muddle that has arisen, the T'ien
Shih and his Heavenly Soldiers arrive and participate in the
inquiry.*

*Judge Pao produces his magic mirror whereby he can detect
the true from the false. Wu Ta Lang and P'an Chin-lien
are ordered to retire, and as the two demons refuse to abide by
the Court's decision, the T'ien Shih commands his Heavenly
Soldiers to attack them. A fast and furious battle ensues,
and with the demons routed and captured the comic opera
closes.*

*   *   *

Recently this extravaganza has been expanded by the addition
of three more Wu Ta Langs and P'an Chin-liens. Thus there are
four of each, genuine and fake—a total of sixteen—converting
the performance into a fantastic ballet which the actors enjoy as
riotously as the audience. The amplified version is entitled *Pa
Wu Hua Tung :* " The Eight Five-Flower Grotto." It is one huge
frolic, and one is liable to forget that its success depends on a technique built up by years of training.

Mêng Yüeh-hua in the Pavilion of the Imperial
Tablet; Liu Shêng-ch'un
Outside in the Rain

Yü Pei T'ing

YÜ PEI T'ING 御碑亭

PAVILION OF THE IMPERIAL TABLET

Also called *Wang Yu-tao Hsiu Ch'i*: "Wang Yū-tao puts his Wife
away"; and *Chin Pang Lo Ta T'uan Yüan*: "The Happy Reunion
of a Successful Graduate." A *hsi-p'i* play.

PERIOD: Ming

DRAMATIS PERSONÆ

WANG YU-TAO, a young scholar	*Hu-tzŭ*	
MÊNG YÜEH-HUA, his virtuous wife	*Ch'ing-i*	
WANG SHU-YING, his playful sister	*Hua-tan*	
SHÊN SUNG, the Literary Examiner	*Lao-shêng*	
TÊ LU, a servant of the Mêng household	*Ch'ou-êrh*	
LIU SHÊNG-CH'UN, a very proper graduate ...	*Hsiao-shêng*	
MÊNG YUAN WAI, Yüeh-hua's father...	*Wai*	
MÊNG FU JÊN, ,, ,, mother	*Lao-tan*	

How gently a Chinese playwright tackles that perennial pet
theme of all our Western playwrights—conjugal jealousy. Herein
lies the main interest of this extremely popular play from our point
of view.

SCENE I

Wang Yu-tao is about to leave for Peking to compete
in the Triennial Examinations: it is a critical moment:
does not his entire career depend on the issue? He
exhorts his young wife Yüeh-hua and eighteen-year-old
sister Shu-ying to be heedful of the family reputation
during his absence, and the women pour out wine with
wishes for his success.

When the Spring Festival (*Ch'ing Ming*) approaches,
Yüeh-hua's parents send a page-boy called Tê Lu to
invite her to join them in worshipping at the ancestral
tombs. Yüeh-hua's first instinct is to refuse as she does
not care to leave her young sister-in-law alone, but the
latter and the servant persuade her to go.

SCENE II

After the ceremony her mother prevails on `her to stay, but Yüeh-hua is eager to return to her sister-in-law. As the old lady is obstinate she goes out into the garden with the excuse that she is " feeling indisposed," thence she sets forth by stealth and unaccompanied.

SCENE III

On the way she is caught in a downpour of rain. Panting and dripping she takes refuge in a small memorial pavilion, whence the play derives its name. Shortly afterwards a young man appears. What is to be done ? He is soaked to the skin and no other shelter in sight. Nor is there any prospect of the downpour ceasing. The shades of night are gathering moreover. But rather than embarrass a lady the young man modestly withdraws, and makes the best of what exiguous shelter the outer eaves afford him. All night long he remains there, while the rain relentlessly pelts on and Yüeh-hua's fears for her chastity and reputation keep her awake and trembling. Truly a terrible night for this couple of virtuous individuals. What untold misery and discomfort must be debited to virtue's account ! How Don Juan would chuckle ! It seems as if day will never come. Eventually dawn flushes the horizon, the rain stops, and the young man continues on his way. At last the coast is clear : Yüeh-hua is free to go home without further interruption.

SCENE IV

Safe and sound across her threshold, she tells her sister-in-law about her shattering experience, warmly praising the young man's chivalry and virtue. Her sister-in-law is somewhat sceptical and malicious about the incident : one feels sure that the warm-blooded Shu-ying would not have been so staid under the circumstances. Perhaps

she is irritated by Yüeh-hua's excessively moral tone.
When the young matron composes three gushing
stanzas to commemorate the stranger's conduct, the
little tease adds a fourth with a different twist to it,
hinting that Yüeh-hua had been far more susceptible
than she cared to admit.

Scene V

As a result of her drenching Yüeh-hua catches a
chill. When Wang Yu-tao returns from the Examination to find that his wife is laid up in bed, he questions his
sister. Shu-ying is only too ready to gossip about the
night in the pavilion : she spares no details and he
promptly suspects the worst. Without more ado he
writes out a bill of divorcement, which he encloses in
an envelope addressed to his father-in-law. Anxious to
avoid a brawl and the consequent ridicule (pre-eminently
preoccupied with the preservation of his own " face "), he
tells his wife that her father is longing to see her, and as
he is seriously ill she must go home at once.

Scene VI

Much alarmed she takes leave of him to find both
parents flourishing. They open the letter, and are
horrified to read that her husband has put her away for
no specific reason. Her father, a retired official, is
highly incensed and threatens to interview Wang, but
his wife dissuades him : it would only make matters
worse. So Yüeh-hua remains with her parents in
deepest dejection but fortunately does not commit
suicide.

Scene VII

*According to etiquette Wang Yu-tao and the other success-
ful graduates pay a visit to Shên Sung, the Literary Examiner.*

SHÊN. A very curious thing happened during this examination. No less than three times I rejected one paper as worthless, and in each instance it reappeared on my desk. Thinking to myself it must belong to one who had performed some meritorious deed, I looked for the signature, and found Liu Shêng-ch'un's, so I placed his name at the bottom of the list.

As Liu is among the graduates assembled, Shên Sung inquires what righteous action he has to his credit.

LIU. I really can't remember that I ever did anything particularly laudable.

SHÊN. Ponder carefully : how else could your paper return to me thrice after rejection ? What have you been doing recently ?

LIU (*modestly*). I can only recollect one trivial incident. One night not long ago I was overtaken by a rain-storm and was about to seek shelter in the Pavilion of the Imperial Tablet when I saw it was already occupied by a young lady, so I withdrew and stayed all night outside under the eaves. Would Your Excellency consider this a deed of any merit ?

Wang Yu-tao puts two and two together and asks Liu if he discovered the lady's name.

LIU. How could I know her name when neither of us exchanged a word?

WANG (*convinced of his wife's innocence and overcome by remorse, sings out*). The woman who spent all night in the pavilion was Mêng Yüeh-hua, the wife I put away !

SHÊN How very strange ! I had placed Wang Yu-tao first on the list of successful graduates, and now he is second. There must be some supernatural agency in this, or how could a *primus* drop to *secundus*, unless it was because of his foolish action in putting his wife away without any proof of her guilt ! *

---

* The Examiner, of course, was the " supernatural agency " that turned the trick.

He then proposes that Wang should induce his wife to return and ask her forgiveness, and that the worthy Liu be rewarded by the gift of his sister in marriage.

SCENE VIII

At first Yüeh-hua, still smarting from her injuries, will not listen to Wang's pleading : he is even on the point of kneeling to her, when she raises him up, deeply touched by such an evident sign of contrition. One cannot but feel that Liu's betrothal to the tittle-tattle is a doubtful blessing, but the nuptial music brings the play to an end with a lively flourish.

Wang Yu-tao is less blamed for jumping to unkind conclusions than Yüeh-hua's parents, who should have known better than to invite her during her husband's absence. Nor was it discreet of Yüeh-hua to leave her old home clandestinely without a suitable escort : much worse might have befallen such an attractive young matron under the circumstances.

* * *

The terror of cuckoldom is universal : from Othello downwards how much torrential dialogue has it not inspired ? The Chinese dramatist spares us emotional excesses : hence this play, so circumspect, so suave and punctilious throughout, would satisfy even the Victorian's canon of not bringing a blush to the maiden's cheek. And for this very reason, we doubt if it could ever achieve success in the average Western theatre, or whether a Western actress, since we have no actors of Mei Lan-fang's calibre, would choose to illuminate it by her genius. Nevertheless we warmly recommend it to the Western playgoer, for whom it should provide a pleasant change of diet.

YÜ T'ANG-CH'UN 玉 堂 春

THE HAPPY HALL OF JADE

As it is not always performed in its entirety, this play has various names derived from its constituent acts, such as *Wang Kung-tzŭ P'iao Yüan*: "Young Gentleman Wang visits a Brothel"; *Kuan Ti Miao*: "God of War's Temple"; *Nü Ch'i Chieh*: "A Maiden starts on a Journey under Arrest"; *Hung-t'ung Hsien*: from the place where she suffered imprisonment; *San T'ang Hui Shên*: "Three Officials hold Court"; *Chien Hui*: "The Meeting in Gaol," and the sequel *T'uan Yüan*: "Reunited."

PERIOD: Early Ming. A *p'i-huang* play, but *pang-tzŭ* airs are introduced into the God of War's Temple scene and whenever Shên Yen-lin, the Shansi merchant, appears: *pang-tzŭ* being indigenous to Shansi.

DRAMATIS PERSONÆ

WANG CHIN-LUNG, a high official's son	... ...	*Hsiao-shêng*
SU-SAN, OR YÜ T'ANG-CH'UN		*Ch'ing-i*
A PROCURESS		*Hua-tan*
HER HUSBAND	...⎫	*Ch'ou-êrh*
CHIN KO, a flower-seller	...⎬	
SHÊN YEN-LIN, a wealthy Shansi merchant		*San-hua-lien*
HIS SERVANT		*Ch'ou-êrh*
P'I SHIH, Shên Yen-lin's wife	...⎫	*Hua-tan*
HER MAID	...⎬	
CHAO CHIEN-SHÊNG, her paramour ...	...⎫	*Ch'ou-êrh*
WANG, a corrupt magistrate	...⎬	
LIU PING-I, Judge, in blue robe ...	...	*Lao-shêng*
CHOU LIANG-CHIEH, Judge, in red robe ...	...	*Li-tzŭ*
CH'UNG KUNG-TAO, a kindly turnkey ...	...	*San-hua-lien*
ROBBERS, WARDENS, ETC., ETC.		

WANG KUNG-TZŬ P'IAO YÜAN: "WANG VISITS A BROTHEL"

The plot was taken from real life. Wang Chin-lung, the third son of a high official, is induced by two rascally acquaintances to visit a high-class brothel. Eventually an exquisite girl is brought in called Su-san, and they fall in love with each other at first sight. Wang is so dazzled that he almost falls off his chair : after a single cup of tea which he spills under the spell of her gaze, he orders his servant to hand her three hundred ounces of silver and takes his departure. A few days later he returns with thirty-six thousand ounces of silver, which are duly pounced upon by the mistress of the establishment.

Su-san is only sixteen and still a virgin : she surrenders herself wholly to her first true love and they live blissfully together. Wang, the complete prodigal, builds a pavilion worthy of their raptures in the adjacent garden : he calls it the *Yü T'ang-ch'un :* "Happy Hall of Jade" (which name is also conferred on Su-san), and fills it with works of art.

> *Sans dépenser, c'est en vain qu'on espère*
> *De s'avancer au pays de Cythère.*

He is "all for love," or the world well lost, but the world, fittingly characterized by the brothel-keeper, reminds him that he cannot live for ever in an artificial paradise. "One sucks the orange, throws away the peel," is her motto. Winter comes and Wang is squeezed dry. She tells him in no uncertain terms to quit the premises.

KUAN TI MIAO : "AT THE TEMPLE OF KUAN TI"

The pampered prodigal, shooed out into the cold, eventually takes refuge in the Temple of Kuan Ti, the God of War. Wang has the fragile physique which used to be the hall-mark of Chinese scholars, and is utterly unfitted for manual labour : it is noteworthy that a muscular, deep-throated, broad-chested he-man has but little sex-appeal for a Chinese audience. A young scholar's face, for instance, should be "beautifully pale with study as if powdered" if he is to prove a successful lady-killer. Chin Ko, a flower-vendor he had lavishly patronized in his prosperity, happens to discover his retreat and tells Su-san about her lover's plight. Feigning illness, she begs leave of absence to offer incense at the temple. Setting forth with three hundred ounces of silver, she finds him half-starved and emaciated, numb with cold. Su-san removes her satin cloak and wraps it round her shivering adorer. They weep and embrace. This tender and pathetic scene can be very moving when rendered by accomplished actors, and it is saved from sentimentality by delightful humorous touches : the lovers bill and coo in spite of chattering teeth and sombre surroundings. No Venus and Cupid but the frowning God of War looms in the background. Su-san advises Wang to compete in the Examinations at the Capital and gives him the three hundred ounces of silver to cover his expenses. Before parting they take an oath that neither will marry anyone else.

On his way to the Capital, Wang is robbed of the precious cloak and all his money. He becomes a beggar. " Kind ladies and gentlemen," he cries, " take pity on a poor unfortunate scholar ! " One day Su-san recognizes his voice, hurries out and smuggles him up to her room. On hearing his tale of woe she give him another three hundred ounces of silver to enable him to pursue his journey. Fearful of being seen by the procuress, he jumps out of the window and leaves the city. Eventually he takes his degree and is appointed a judge of circuit of the eight Shansi prefectures.

HUNG-T'UNG HSIEN

Su-san is very unhappy in the meantime. As she will have nothing to do with the clientele, the procuress maltreats her. Shên Yen-lin, a wealthy Shansi merchant, does his best to seduce her but she spurns his overtures and his money ; which only adds fuel to his ardour. After considerable argument Shên's servant arranges to buy her from the procuress for three hundred ounces of silver. She is told that Wang Chin-lung has received an official post in Shansi, and that he is yearning to see her again. She falls into the trap, and is taken to the inn where Shên is staying. Shên covers his face with his wide sleeves, and to further the deception, disguises himself as an official. Together they kneel and worship Heaven and Earth as a sign of marriage.* Shên's first wife, P'i Shih, had always made his home intolerable: when he arrives with Su-san she slaps the newcomer's face and puts her in an attic. Nor has P'i Shih the excuse of chastity for such behaviour. On Shên's return from a business trip he hears her playing "guess-fingers" with a stranger. He listens for a while outside the door before knocking. This gives her time to hide her lover under the table: she warns him not to come out until she raps it. Shên asks why the table is laid for two.

P'I SHIH. I was expecting you at any moment.

SHÊN (*striking the table full force*). How on earth could you know precisely when to expect me?

Her lover pops out. Shên catches him.

SHÊN. What are you doing here?

CHAO. Oh, I've just been acting as your substitute during your absence.

Shên's first impulse is to have a brawl but he is held in abeyance by the virago.

SHÊN (*meekly*). Well, you go your way, and I'll go mine. I'm off to enjoy myself with my new concubine.

Su-san has been pining and starving herself in the meantime. P'i Shih conspires with her lover and the maid to dispose of her. She offers her a bowl of poisoned

---

* In Mr. Wang Yao-ch'ing the actor-playwright's version, Shên is arrested on his way home for impersonating an official, and fined one thousand ounces of silver.

broth while Shên is clumsily trying to console her. As
she rejects it Shên says he will drink it himself but P'i
Shih tells him she will fetch him some more. Greed
gets the better of him and he ravenously gobbles the
fatal concoction. In a few minutes he shrieks that he
is poisoned and drops dead on the floor. Hearing
Su-san's screams, P'i Shih comes in and accuses her of
the crime.

Su-san is dragged off to the magistracy, which is
presided over by a rascal named Wang. " I believe
you are the criminal," he remarks to P'i Shih, " it is
written on your face." " Is it indeed ? " she retorts,
scenting bribery. But she had come prepared: she
presents him with a thousand ounces of silver and distributes eight hundred among the yamen underlings.
Su-san is shackled and flogged to extort a confession.
Unable to endure the pain, she confesses. A fellow-
prisoner, however, writes out her true statement ver-
batim, which she manages to conceal. The case is referred to the higher court of T'ai-yüan-fu in Shansi for
approval of the death-sentence.

NÜ CH'I CHIEH : " A MAIDEN JOURNEYS UNDER
ARREST "

Su-san kneels and prays the prison-god to support
her on the journey before she sets forth, her head in a
cangue, her hands manacled, escorted by a kindly old
warden who has taken pity on her. She asks him where
she can put her petition for safety, so that it will reach
her lover Wang Chin-lung. He tells her to hide it
inside the cangue, whence it will drop out as soon as
her head is released.

On the road to T'ai-yüan-fu she sings a hymn of
hate : " I hate my parents for selling me into a life
of shame. I hate Shên Yen-lin for redeeming me. I
hate the wicked P'i Shih for poisoning her husband. I

MEI LAN-FANG AS SU-SAN UNDER ARREST, HSIAO CH'ANG-HUA
AS CH'UNG KUNG-TAO, THE KINDLY OLD GAOLER

Yü T'ang Ch'un

hate her maid Ch'un Chin and her paramour Chao Chien-shêng for conniving against me. I hate the avaricious magistrate Wang and his satellites for taking bribes. I hate myself for being so foolish as to confess . . . The more I think of it the more I hate them all. There is not an honest man in the Hung-t'ung Yamen ! "

The song, which lasts for more than half an hour, gives some justification to the term " opera " so oft applied to Chinese drama. The scene is highly operatic : the old warden repeatedly interrupts either to exhort or take umbrage, especially after all his kindness, at her sweeping condemnation of his native Hung-t'ung Hsien.

SAN T'ANG HUI SHÊN : " THREE OFFICIALS HOLD COURT "

At the trial in T'ai-yüan-fu, Su-san kneels, her shackles and the cangue are removed, the secret petition drops out and is handed to Wang Chin-lung, the central figure, (supported by the Provincial Judge in blue and the Provincial Treasurer in red). Su-san has a gruelling time of it. For an hour or more on her bended knees she sings of her trials and tribulations in high falsetto. Unfortunately the Provincial Judge, who bears Wang Chin-lung a grudge for having ignored him on taking up his new post, is in charge of the cross-examination. He has more than an inkling of Wang's relations with the prisoner ; to embarrass him he questions Su-san about her private life. Her vivid autobiographical description and references to Wang San Kung Tzŭ, " Young Gentleman Wang, the third son," convulse the judges, the more so as Wang himself strenuously objects to matters of a personal nature being brought up, and keeps repeating : " Investigate the murder : her private life is not at issue." But his colleagues insist. She is asked who first possessed her and when, and how much was paid for the transaction. It does not require much wit to identify the seducer. The Provincial Treasurer is full of praise for the young man's generosity but the Provincial Judge inveighs against him as a worker of iniquity. Wang is so shocked and mortified that he collapses and has to leave Court.

The trial is adjourned for the time being : Wang and Su-san are left alone together. Decorum will not allow them more than a formal interview. Su-san recounts her tale from beginning to end, and Wang can only say that she must return to gaol (in the Provincial Judge's yamen), pending the final decision.

CHIEN HUI : "THE MEETING IN GAOL"

That night he visits her, in civilian clothes. The Provincial Judge had anticipated this move and instructed the jailors to demand heavy bribes, so that Wang is squeezed all round on his arrival. While the lovers confabulate, the Provincial Judge walks in, pretending to make an inspection. At first he fails to recognize Wang, who has rapidly disguised himself ; after careful scrutiny, which gives considerable scope for buffoonery, with Wang running round like a lunatic, he pulls off his false moustache and, in the ensuing scuffle, snatches the official seal from his belt. With this tangible proof he at first intends to impeach him and have him dismissed—it was disgraceful for a judge on circuit secretly to associate with a woman accused of murder. But the more tolerant Provincial Treasurer strongly dissuades him : such a passionate pair deserve to be married in peace. Unwillingly the Provincial Judge concurs.

T'UAN YÜAN : "REUNITED IN MARRIAGE"

The case continues. P'i Shih and her paramour are arrested, tried and condemned to death. Proven innocent, Yü T'ang-ch'un is released and, on her re-appearance in court, is presented with the robes and insignia of her lover. The judges act as go-betweens ; the wedding takes place immediately in presence of the whole Court.

* * *

The graves of Wang Chin-lung and Su-san are still pointed out at some 40 *li* north-west of Ch'ü-chou in Chêng-ting Prefecture, Hopei. Be that as it may, the dramatist must have had in mind the famous T'ang story of that Countess of Yen who had been a singing girl at Ch'ang-an—written by Po Hsing-chien, a brother of the poet Po Chü-i. The hero is an exact counterpart of Wang Chin-lung : he falls in love at first sight, ruins himself, is turned out of the house and becomes a beggar. One night when it was snowing his beloved heard him pitifully crying for food. " Quickly she went out but found him so dirty and emaciated that it was hard to realize he was a man. When she spoke to him, he was so choked with shame that he could not answer ; he only nodded his head and fell in a faint. She put her embroidered cloak around him and carried him to her room." The T'ang story is less complicated but the romantic theme, unorthodox and dangerous from the old Chinese point of view, is the same. In this case the prodigal's father, who had previously beaten him almost to death, was so touched by the story of the singing-girl's devotion, that he provided every-thing for their wedding and they were formally married.

Yü T'ang-ch'un is one of Ch'êng Yen-ch'iu's favourite rôles ; and as it requires sustained vocal powers through long acts the play is very popular with Peking audiences. But it should interest the foreign theatre-goer if only for its realism ; it comes far closer to " life-in-the-raw " than most Chinese plays. And Yü T'ang-ch'un herself is a figure that stirs the heart. In spite of the " odi-ousness of comparisons " we dare maintain that she has precisely the same hold on affections in Peking as Manon Lescaut in Paris : both heroines are exquisitely symptomatic of the sentimental-erotic ideals of their respective races and both fulfil the same demands. A student of relative psychology might do worse than take these as points of departure. Not only is the theme of this play—romantic love—exceptional, but the characterization is also less stilted and conventional : Chin Ko the flower-vendor and Ch'ung Kung-tao the gaoler are unusually human and sympathetic, and clever actors can make them live. We rate it highly, and above the strait-jacket Confucian morality-plays, though as usual the scenes act far better than they read.   In *Yü Tang-ch'un* the European's charge of monotony and repetition falls to the ground.

Performances vary : several scenes are often omitted owing to the length of the play.   Recently a garbled version entitled *Hsin* (New) *Yü T'ang-ch'un* has by no means improved upon the original, for the Shansi merchant Shên Yen-lin is resurrected during the trial of his wife and her paramour for poisoning him, as a result of which these charming people are freed and forgiven.   More preposterous still, Shên goes home with the happy bride and bridegroom.

CHINESE DYNASTIES

The Three Dynasties or San Tai 三 代

Hsia 夏 (legendary) . . . . 2205-1767 B.C.
Shang 商 (also known as Yin 殷) . . 1766-1122 B.C.
Chou 周 1122-255

Chinese archæologists now divide the Chou Period into: Chou Dynasty proper 1122-722 B.C., Period of the *Spring and Autumn Annals*, 722-481 B.C., Warring States Period or Lieh Kuo 列 國, 481-221 B.C.

From 255 to 249 B.C. the nominal ruler was the Chou emperor, but his authority was practically non existent.

Ch'in 秦 . . . . . . 249-206 B.C.
Han 漢 . . . . . . 206 B.C.—A.D. 220
The Three Kingdoms or San Kuo Period 三 國 . . 220-277

After the fall of Han, the empire was divided into the three kingdoms of Wei 魏, Wu 吳 and Shu 蜀. Wei comprised the central and northern provinces with its capital at Lo-yang. Wu consisted of the provinces south of the Yangtze; its capital was at Nanking. Shu included the western part, the present Szech'uan, with Ch'êng-tu as capital; it was ruled by the Minor Han.

The Six Dynasties or Liu Chao 六 朝 . . . 222-589

The Wu 吳 of the San Kuo Period, the Eastern Chin 東 晉 (317-419), the Northern Sung 北 宋 (420-478), the Ch'i 齊 (479-501), the Liang 梁 (502- 556), and the Ch'en 陳 (557-587).

The following dynasties also ruled parts of the empire: the Western Chin (317-316), the Northern Ch'i (557-581), the Northern Wei (386-535), the Western Wei (535-557), the Eastern Wei (535-550), and the Northern Chou (557-581).

Sui 隋 589-617
T'ang 唐 617-906
The Five Minor Dynasties or Wu Chao 五 朝 . 907-960
Northern Sung 北 宋 960-1127
Southern Sung 南 宋 1127-1280
Yüan or Mongol dynasty 元 1280-1368
Ming 明 1368-1643
Ch'ing 清 or Manchu dynasty . . . 1644-1911

INDEX

Important references are given in bold face. The figures between square brackets are for the illustrations.

O

O-mi-to Fo 阿彌陀佛, Buddhist invocation 247, 319
oar, to represent boat, xvi
oath in the Peach-orchard, 26, 163
Official Banquet (*Ch'ün Ch'ên Yen*), 39
official garb (blue robe, black gauze headgear), 296, 307
omens, unlucky, 267
orange bandeau, xxiv
orchestra, Chinese theatrical, xx-xxi
orchestra leader, *see* tan-p'i-ku;
Orphan of Chao, 100
Othello, 411
owl, medium of Spirit of Venus, 55, 57
Oxherd, *see* Niu Lang, 258, **360**, 382

P

Pa Ch'ien Sui 八千歲 (Prince of 'Eight Thousand Years'), 395
Pa Wu Hua Tung 八五花洞 (*The Eight Five Flower Grotto*) a burlesque, **406**
Pai Yü-t'ang 白玉堂, 390
Pai Yün-shêng 白雲生, actor, [65], 75
painted face rôle, *see* ta-hua-lien, xxiii
xxiv
P'an An 潘安, a Chinese Apollo, 254
P'an Ch'iao-yün 潘巧雲, 364
P'an Chin-lien 潘金蓮, 403, [403]
P'an Kuan 判官, 347
P'an Lao-chang 潘老丈, 364
P'ang T'ung 龐統, 201
P'ang T'ung Hsien Lien Huan Chi 龐統獻連環計 (*P'ang T'ung proposes the Chain-scheme*), 201
pang-tzǔ plays 梆子, xxii, 76, 93, 226, 364, 395, 412
Pao-ch'êng 襄城 (in Shensi), 62
Pao Kung 包公 (sobriquet ' Iron Face '), 395, 399, 407
Pao Lien Têng 寶蓮燈 (*Precious Lotus-Lantern*), a civil play, 131, **324**
passing from room to room, xxvii
'Pasteboard' Tang, *see* T'ang Ch'in
Pavilion of the Imperial Tablet (*Yü Pei T'ing*), 407, [407]
Peach-Garden, Three Brothers of 桃園三結義, 26, 163, 234, 237

Pearl, The Lucky, see *Ch'ing Ting Chu*, 101
Pearly Screen Castle (*Chu Lien Chai*), **152**
P'ei 沛 (birth-place of Ts'ao Ts'ao in Kiangsu), 2
Pei-hai 北海 (in Shantung), 山東, 39
pei-hu-ch'i 背護旗 (' back protecting flags '), xxvi, **xxix**
Peitaiho Beach 北戴河, 117
Pei Tou 北斗 (Ursa Major constellation), 132
Peking, xxv, 1, 130, 261, 265, 419
Pekingese colloquial expressions in *Ta Ch'êng Huang*, 352
Penelope motive, 94, 225
p'êng-chung 砰鐘 (clanging bells), xxii
perambulating the stage, xvii
petition, presenting a, 64 ff.
Petronius Arbiter, 229
Phœnix Ceremonial Pavilion, see *Fêng I T'ing*, 353, 356, 358
physiognomy, 183
p'i-huang 皮黃 (abbrev. for hsi-p'i êrh-huang), xxi, 25, 201, 211, 226, 252, 261, 324, 333, 353, 395, 403, 412
p'i-pa 琵琶 (balloon guitar), xxi
P'i Shih 皮氏, 412
Pi Yü Tsan 碧玉簪 (*The Green Jade Hairpin*), a civil play, **333**
p'ing ch'i 平妻 (family relationship), 295
P'ing-yüan district 平原縣 (Shansi), 39, 49
plays, *see* civil, military
Plopper, H. (quoted), 55
plumes, pheasant, xix
Po Chü-i 白居易, 419
Po Hsing-chien 白行簡, 419
Po I 伯夷, 325
poisoned broth, 94, 416
poisoned cakes in *T'ien Ho P'ei*, 361
Pole Star, 98, 159
popular sayings, Chinese, 377
Portia, 130
Precious Gifts, Sending (*Chieh Pao*), 152
Precious Lotus Lantern (*Pao Lien Têng*), **324**
prisoner's costume, xviii
procuress, a, 412
Prodrecca, Vittorio, xii
progeny, importance attached to, 185

中華民國廿六年三月初版

戲劇之精華

著作者　阿林敦
　　　　艾克敦

出版者　魏智

印刷者　上海字林報社

發行者　北平法文圖書館